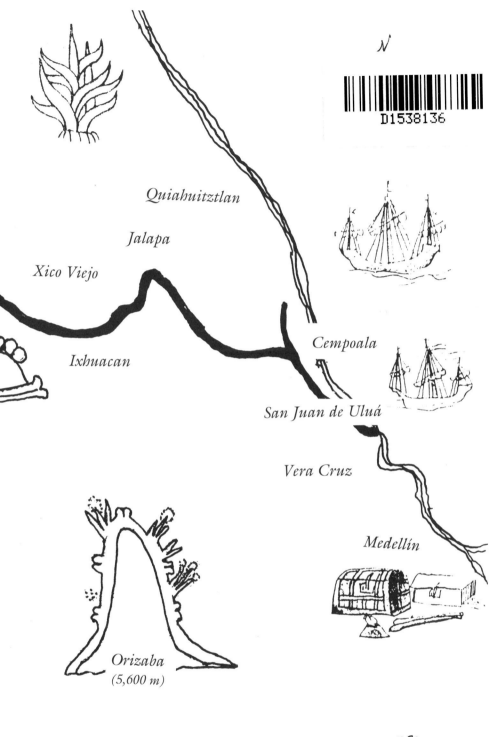

N

Quiahuitztlan

Jalapa

Xico Viejo

Ixhuacan

Cempoala

San Juan de Uluá

Vera Cruz

Medellín

Orizaba
(5,600 m)

They Are Coming ...

They Are Coming ...

THE CONQUEST OF MEXICO

text and drawings by

JOSÉ LÓPEZ PORTILLO y PACHECO

translated by
Beatrice Berler

University of North Texas Press

Originally published as *Ellos Vienen . . . La Conquista de México*
©1987 by José López Portillo y Pacheco. Fernández editores, s.a. de c.v.

© 1992 University of North Texas Press
All rights reserved. Published 1992
Printed in the United States of America

10 9 8 7 6 5 4 3 2 1

Requests for permission to reproduce material from this work should be sent to:
University of North Texas Press
P. O. Box 13856
Denton, Texas 76203-3856

Library of Congress Cataloging-in-Publication Data

López Portillo, José
    [Ellos vienen— . English]
    They are coming— : the conquest of Mexico / text and drawings by
José López Portillo y Pacheco : translated by Beatrice Berler.
        p.   cm.
    Translation of : Ellos vienen— .
    Includes bibliographical references and index.
    ISBN 0-929398-35-1 :
    1. Mexico—History—Conquest, 1519–1540—Fiction. 2. Aztecs—
Fiction.   I. Title.
PQ298.22.06E4513   1992
863—dc20   92-3142
                                        CIP

The paper used in this book meets the minimum requirements of the American
National Standard
for Permanence of Paper for Printed Library Materials, Z39.48.1984

Illustrations by José López Portillo y Pacheco
Book and Cover Design by Teel Sale

Dedication

 mis queridos amigos Federico Ruiz Fulcheri y Lala Sacristán de Ruiz en recuerdo del afecto amistad de todo la vida y de los inumerables atenciones de que he sido objeto.

Afectuosamente

Beatrice

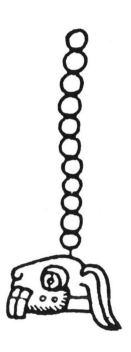

Contents

Acknowledgements

I am indeed grateful to those who gave their time and advice as I was translating this work. Their input made the translation as "true" as possible.

Carlos Freymann, Rubén Mungía, María Cossio-Amerduri, Olivia and Professor Guillermo Mendoza, Carla Somers and Rachel Weiner, all from San Antonio, were generous with their time and suggestions.

From Mexico City, Niní Ruiz de Cerezo and Juan Mariano Cerezo introduced me to Salvador Madariaga's *Hernán Cortés* and Lali Ruiz de Sordo and Ramón Sordo de Porrúa interpreted many of the ambiguous passages.

Gaylon Finklea typed the manuscript and Charles Neighbors was an adept editor with a sharp pencil.

Señor Licenciado Francisco Porrúa became my mentor for this translation, especially with those challenging "old-Spanish" words and phrases.

The confidence and support of Georgia Kemp Caraway, managing editor of the University of North Texas Press, encouraged me to polish and shape José López Portillo y Pacheco's work.

Astute editorial judgment guides a book through the labyrinth from the genesis to the folds of the dust jacket. Frances B. Vick, Director of the University of North Texas Press, filled the needs and then some. She is an editor's editor.

Any errors regarding the text are my own.

Beatrice Berler
¡Viva México!

To Set the Scene . . .

or the present history of the Spaniards and the *Conquest of Mexico*, modern readers will have to keep in mind the distinct moral standards of the sixteenth century, for the conquerors and Aztecs alike must be judged in the spirit of those faraway times.

Mythology in some form may be contemplated in religion. The Mexican religion, if we can call it that, had many deities and at the head of all stood Huitzilopotchtli, the god of war—the protective deity of the Aztecs.

A most interesting persona in their mythology was Quetzalcóatl. He instructed the natives how to plow, engage in the use of metals, and even the art of government.

We do not know the reason why, but one of the principal gods became angered at Quetzalcóatl and compelled him to leave the country. On the shores of Mexico as he was about to board his raft, he vowed that he would return. He was tall, had very light skin, and a long beard. His appearance probably prepared the way for the future success of the Spaniards. "White men with beards would come from where the Sun rises."

About 1510–19, there were signs that Quetzalcóatl would live up to his promise. Nature provided many catastrophes—a tempest, a fire that water could not extinguish, an earthquake, and many other disasters that reinforced the thinking of Moctezuma's wizards that "Quetzalcóatl will soon return." The rumors took root long before the Spaniards entered Mexico and the many acts visited by nature cast their shadows over the country and the heavy hearts of the people.

Several expeditions came close to the Mexican shores but returned to Cuba after many mishaps. The fact that the "sea houses" were seen filled Moctezuma with fear. He was devastated.

Although many accuse the Mexicans of cannibalism, they did not feed on human flesh to satisfy their appetite. They feasted on the victims, whose blood was poured out on the sacrificial altar. Their religion commanded this act. The blood gave strength to the Sun.

The Aztecs had no written alphabet and drew pictures of what they saw. Their picture writing is what we call the codices. These manuscripts were made of cotton cloths or skins but for the most part on a fine fabric from the leaves of the aloe, *agave Americana*, called by the natives *maguey*. Today very few of these precious documents remain; some were lost in the Conquest and others were destroyed.

The Aztecs' social customs and mores are numerous. The following is an overview of Aztec lifestyles for the reader who is unacquainted with their history. The Aztecs devised a system in their arithmetic to calculate the measurement of time. Their agriculture was as advanced as the other arts of social life. Public taxes were paid in agricultural produce. Both men and women cultivated the soil, and areas of land would lie fallow for a time when they appeared worn out. They irrigated by the use of canals. The great staple of the country was maize, Indian corn. Some stalks afforded a sweetener and supplied the natives with a sugar substance. Sugar was not introduced in the hemisphere until after the Conquest. They were very well acquainted with silver, lead, tin, and copper. Gold found on the surface was cast into bars; while the use of iron was unknown to them. Obsidian, a dark transparent mineral, was formed into knives, razors, and swords. They decapitated the head of a horse with one stroke of their serrated broadsword.

Most utensils were made of earthenware or wood. Lacquer or paint colored the wooden cups and vases. Commerce was carried on by barter and the merchants visited different provinces.

Discipline of children in public schools was severe. Polygamy was usual among the Mexicans, though chiefly confined to the wealthy classes. Fruits, vegetables, turkey, a small dog bred for meat, insects, fish, and game provided the food.

The houses of the wealthy Aztecs were made of stone with courtyards enhanced by fruit trees and beautiful flowers. The interior decorations included handsome draperies, and ceilings inlaid with cedar and other fragrant woods were held together without a nail. Cortés remarked that Moctezuma's palaces were superior to anything of the kind in Spain. Extensive gardens surrounded these buildings, filled with fragrant shrubs and flowers. Their medical botany was studied as a science.

Moctezuma bathed every day and changed his clothes three or four times daily. Aztec cooks provided luxurious meals. The emperor only drank *chocolatl*, a potion of chocolate flavored with vanilla and reduced to a froth which dissolved in the mouth. This was served in golden goblets. The emperor was very fond of it—many jars or pitchers were prepared for daily consumption.

At the time of the Conquest, Hernán Cortés was thirty-three or thirty-four years old. He was about middle size and his complexion pale. The slender figure set off his deep chest. He wore few ornaments, but very fine ones. His manner was frank and soldierlike, which concealed a cool, calculating spirit. Most of his men were drawn to him like a magnet and they felt a strong desire to obey the *Conquistador*. It was love tempered by authority.

At the time of the Conquest, Moctezuma was about forty years old, tall, thin, and well-built. His black, straight hair was not very long; his beard was thin and his complexion somewhat paler than his copper-colored race.

Cortés, the Spanish soldier, like his mythical countryman Don Quixote, possessed a "wise madness" but did not engage in a battle with "foolish sanity." Don Hernán was a man convinced that he knew who he was and what he was capable of achieving. He would have said with Quixote, "All things are possible—first the dream, then fulfillment."

Whatever may be thought of the Conquest in a moral view, regarded as a military achievement it fills us with astonishment. That a handful of adventurers, indifferently armed and equipped, landed on the shores of a powerful empire inhabited by a fierce and warlike race and forced their way into the interior is incredible. There were no roads, no charts or compasses to guide them. They did not speak any of the languages (later they had interpreters). Yet they succeeded in overturning Tenochtitlan—Mexico, Moctezuma's capital, where more than three hundred thousand people* lived in sixty thousand houses. That this hardy band of four hundred Spaniards, six thousand Indian allies, sixteen horses, and some dogs accomplished this is a fact little short of the miraculous—too startling for the probabilities demanded by fiction and with no parallel in the pages of history.

Yet this must not be understood too literally—it would be unjust to the Aztecs themselves. The Indian empire was in a manner conquered by the Indians. The Aztec monarchy fell by the hands of its own subjects under the direction of European sagacity and science. Had those Indian tribes been united it might have had a different outcome.

As we read the historical dramatic narrative, *They Are Coming... The Conquest of Mexico*, we are confronted, not with dry and distant facts, but instead with pensive interior monologues, dramatic dialogues, and shifting points of view. Author José López Portillo y Pacheco displays uncanny narrative skill when he imagines the conversations between Hernán Cortés and *Doña* Marina, the banter between Cortés and Moctezuma, or the dialogue between Cortés and his soldiers. What he creates is, in a sense, fiction—for no one who actually took part in the Conquest reported the exact words or minute actions as López Portillo has written. Yet *They Are Coming* is more than a fiction; it is a history enlivened by the imagination of an informed and educated author, and thus made more accessible to a modern audience.

Although this is a relatively new style of history, López Portillo is not the first to indulge in the writing of it. Recently, Harvard historian Simon Schama published his experiment in postmodern, non-analytical history, *Dead Certainties* (Knopf, 1991), which mingles fiction with historical fact. Schama, also author of highly-respected volumes of more traditional history, has come to believe that "to write history without the play of imagination is to dig in an intellectual graveyard," and that only by combining the two can an author "bring a world to life rather than entomb it in erudite discourse."

Lopéz Portillo's work is yet another classic example in support of Schama's thesis. We appreciate the aplomb with which this historian utilizes fiction to portray history, yet does not veer off course from the historical perspective of the work.

There is no public monument to Cortés in all Mexico (only the Sea of Cortés bears his name). "It's too soon," a Mexican National told me. The *caballero* from Spain has as many enemies as those who praise his prowess. The Spaniards brought a language, a religion, and a culture to the New World. These, when mixed with the indigenous population, give us the *mestizaje* that is now Mexico. Perhaps this work will serve as a written monument to Cortés' accomplishments.

Beatrice Berler

[I have selected excerpts from William Prescott's *History of the Conquest of Mexico* and an abridged and edited edition of the same work by C. Harvey Gardiner, University of Chicago Press, plus my own *The Conquest of Mexico, A Modern Rendering* of William H. Prescott's *History of the Conquest*, published by Corona Publishing Company, 1988.]

---

* Some historians claim it was close to six hundred thousand.

Introduction

Although it is seldom considered, the viewpoint of the Indians must be taken into account in any review of the Conquest of Mexico. Incorporating the Indian position emphasizes the magic and the truly supernatural factors underlying the Conquest. It also explains one of the most extraordinary feats of human history.

For the Mexican Indian, the Conquest was a cosmic tragedy that transformed his gods into demons, his kings into slaves, and his slaves into dust. It was a veritable calamity of religious faith.

For the West, it was an adventure without equal; the risk and subsequent good fortune of another altogether different faith. What occurred was the violent collision of two worlds, two markedly distinct conceptions of man himself, between two cultures mysteriously bound by one prophecy—the return of Quetzalcóatl—which underscored the Conquest, especially during its early repressive stages.

In order to understand better these events, it is well to remember the philosophical principles of the Indian theogony which, from the original Omeyocan, *Lugar Dos*,* propounds the struggle of two opposed principles that dialectically and fatally follow one another in a universe whose order and beauty are sustained by the pain and blood of men; by a responsibility that has no personal hope, other than to preserve the heavenly bodies and the Sun in their places, paths and movements.

From this philosophical background, the cosmic force of the prophecy can be understood: it presaged the fateful birth of yet another Sun.

What is astonishing is not merely that this theogony was conceived, but that during the Conquest the prophecy was fulfilled by real men who undertook their own roles in its drama.

Moctezuma. The dogmatic fatalist entrusted with and convinced of the secrets of his race, realizes that he is faced with one of the most dramatic problems ever confronted by any man: as a political leader to accept the fate of his faith with all of its consequences, even to tolerate the annihilation of his world. This author is unaware of any other historical figure who ever lived through such a drama.

Hernán Cortés. A man born in the medieval era but thrust by events into the Renaissance; a man who embodies adventure, *the uncertainty* for universal probability in the search for the unknown—with all its risks and satisfactions. A man also compelled by a dogmatic faith, convinced of its excellence and its universality, a catechistic and intolerant man who considers Christian salvation an expansionist imperative to justify the path toward immense fortune.

---

* Omeyocan, *Lugar Dos* is the original source of the Indian theogony. It is like a dialectic idea. It is not a temple or a religious site. It is the beginning of everything. (Letter from author to translator, December 3, 1987.)—Trans.

Doña Marina, la Malinche, a woman who links both worlds, first through the language and later through childbirth. She receives the love of some gods, who for her become men, and from whom others will be born; through whom the conflict among victors and vanquished will be transformed into conflicting blood lines, which we believe will become one.

Cuauhtémoc, the young rebel who struggles within his world against fate and adventurism into the nearly incredible limit of his strength. As a result, he becomes an exemplary hero.

These four, then, are the chief players, supported by many others, whose significance will be revealed as our story unfolds.

José López Portillo y Pacheco

They Are Coming ...

In the Beginning

yn! Ya! Omeyocan! And I will soar to the *Lugar Dos*. Where only Winds and Darkness prevail: the Yoalli Ehecatl, where the infinite calm whirls before the unifying will of the Word.

"Once there. Am I someone?" my spirit wonders.

"Once there. Am I this that I am?"

"Before time, in a point beyond space, in the navel where in a reciprocal dark vortex the infinitely great becomes the infinitely small. . . in the navel where the Diverse becomes Universe, where the Tloque Nahuaque is a nocturnal storm of infinite possibilities; where the Lord of Night, the Black Tezcatlipoca, denies himself, bursts into light and the Universe is born. The Universe longs to please Quetzalcóatl, the precious twin with feathered scales. He crawls and flies. He is eagle and serpent.

"The suns were created.

"The feathers were created.

"The tigers* were created.

"The chants were created.

"The pain began and the blood was throbbing.

"I am the one who is," said the Word.

"I know what I am," said the man.

Ever since then, man emerged from the hands of his Creator yet remained under his own care. Yoalli Ehecatl. Wind and Darkness!

---

* Many historians call it "tiger," an animal *unknown* in America. Some have compared the "ocelotl" [ocelot] with the jaguar. It is smaller, though quite as ferocious, and is as graceful and beautiful as the leopard, which it more nearly resembles.—Trans.

The Prophecy

he great gale blows on; the darkness pales until, lined in gray, a long shore appears beside the mouth of the Coatzacoalcos River. The sea battles the shore. An old man, whose white hair and beard mark the passage of a once vigorous person, faces the raging sea; from his left, the thrashing force of the North Wind flutters his hair, beard and cloak. Around him are four young Indian men, two dressed in green, two in russet. Further away is a wooden raft, its planks carved to resemble serpents.

The old man shouts:

"Ayn! Ya! Inya! Inye! Au!

I am this that I am!

Still, I am myself!"

The four young men roar in unison:

"Mighty is Quetzalcóatl, Lord of Tula, he brings the East Wind and splits the halves. He is Lord of the two halves!"

"Tula, City of Quetzalcóatl," the old man cries out. "Tula, my Tula, where for fifty-two years I lived, I reigned, I sinned, I redeemed myself!

"From the North came the spotted tiger, Tezcatlipoca, to devour my Tula. Tula is lost!"

"Ayn! Ya! Yu! Ya! Inye! Au!"

"I am returning to the edge. I am leaving. I refuse to be the cause of destruction. The infinite has turned in upon itself. Now is the time to leave. I hear my father calling me. I must go and see if the vessel is clean. I am returning to the edge!

"Land, once my land! During these final moments I place myself at your very edge, as before, as always! The land and the time!

"Everything, everything rebels and turns on itself, on the other one, on me! My world rebels, the cycle is complete and my time in the world is departing. All is being devoured. Everything! Time confronts earth! Earth confronts emptiness, plant vies with earth, beast with plant, man with beast, gods oppose man. And God? Where is God? Who is he who does not show himself? Who is he who is beyond the Omeyocan, beyond the *Lugar Dos*, beyond all possibilities? Who is the motionless One?

"God! God! Here I am before you. Now, while I am still myself, while I am a person, while I am the one who still is. And afterward? And tomorrow?"

After the wind subsided, there was a long silence; then Quetzalcóatl yelled to the four young men:

"Ce-Acatl Quetzalcóatl! The first day of the Plumed Serpent! That is I and still is I!

"Listen and remember that now I can see the future.

"I shall return! I shall return! I love this land, once mine, in which for fifty-two years I was what I am.

"I shall return! My white brothers with beards like mine will come.

"Listen! Listen!

"The gods will become demons!

"The kings, vassals!

"The slaves, nothing!

"Your gods will crumble and you will worship them without succor.

"I see! I see!

"People like me will come. That will be the tiding.

"In multitudes they will come as if in a torrent; they will create a whirlwind of dust. They will bear their steel cane, their shining spear, and their curved metal sword; like waves from the sea, like the sound of tambourines. They will come with their shirts of iron mesh and their iron helmets.

"They will come as the children of the rising Sun. All white, they will have yellow beards; they will come from the East. Upon their arrival they will become lords of this land. They are white men, from the beginning of time. . . . Be prepared! The white twin will come from the heavens; the white child, all white, will come; the white tree will descend from the sky. A shout, from far away, will be their omen.

"Alas! It will be dusk for you when they arrive! They are great gatherers of wood and stone, these white hawks of the earth. Fire will come from the tips of their fingers, yet they will disguise their venom and the ropes with which to hang your parents. You will bow down before these bearded guests who carry the sign of God. They come to ask for your offering! The earth will be scorched. On the day of their arrival will appear white circles, lights in the sky, and fire on the earth. This will mean that they are coming. Your words will become slaves, the trees will become slaves, the stones will become slaves, all men will become slaves when they appear. They are coming!

"You will see them. Your world will be filled with sorrow. On the day they arrive, this part of the land will tremble and the very center of the land will tremble the day that they come.

"Listen to me! Tell everyone! They will come from the East."

With that he fell to his knees and in desperation, he chewed the sand.

A low, dark cloud appeared between the sea and the earth. Once again, the wind howled and immense waves lashed the shore. Sand and foam became one in the swirling gusts.

When he arose from the ground, once again the mighty wind ruffled Quetzalcóatl's white beard. He said to the young men:

"Now all that is needed is to place the mast on my raft of serpents."

So the young men nailed the cross to the serpent raft and on it Quetzalcóatl placed his cloak, which flapped wildly against the wind. Left naked, his old flesh was splashed by the salt foam.

Then, he said:

"All the hours, all the years, all the days, all the winds, also come and go. Just as all blood arrives at a moment of calm, just as it reaches its power and throne. My year has come, my day has come. So I go into the wind. I am leaving. I shall depart into my own moment of calm, for I am already at the edge."

Solemn, the young men removed their own robes, which the wind blew away as if they were flower petals or butterflies.

They kissed Quetzalcóatl's feet and he placed his frail, trembling hands upon their heads.

Three times they pushed the raft into the sea. Three times the sea thrust it back.

The fourth time, Quetzalcóatl insisted they tie him to the cross. Once they did, on a huge wave, the raft of serpents departed. At last, Quetzalcóatl was bound for the Tree of the Universe.

Birth and Baptism of Cuauhtémoc

Tlilalcapan, wife of Ahuizotl, the Aztec king, was giving birth in one of the large rooms of the palace. She was attended by the old women, the midwives, the oldest of whom was in charge. They were beautifully dressed. Everything was in order: bathing tubs, clothes, potions.[1]

Ahuizotl waited in a nearby room in the company of the lords of Texcoco and Tacuba, who form the Culúa Alliance. At the first cry of the newborn, there was also a cry of war and a challenge (a quick tapping of the lips with the hand) that sprang as a chorus from the group of midwives. Afterwards they recited: "You are very welcome, my son, beloved son of Ahuizotl, the king, and of Tlilalcapan, his wife."

And once the oldest of the women cut the umbilical cord, she said:

"My son, loved and tender, listen to the doctrine that our gods left us. From your middle part, I cut your umbilical cord."

And she added:

"Oh, precious stone, oh rich feather, oh emerald, oh sapphire! You were formed in the *Lugar Dos*, the Omeyocan, where reside our great god and great goddess, our parents, Ometecutli and Omecihuatle. You have come to this world, a place of many difficulties and torments, where there is extreme heat, cold and winds; where there is hunger and thirst, fatigue and crying. Your function here is the crying and the tears, the sadness and the weariness. . . .

"We do not know if the child will grow up to live for a few days or years; or if he will become the image, pride and reputation of his ancestors. We do not know if he will be lucky enough to revive the good fortune, and to raise again his grandparents' pride."

After a while, the child was presented to his father, King Ahuizotl, and to the Council.

The old midwife, with the child in her arms, said to the king:

"I have come into your presence, Ahuizotl, king of the Aztecs, and I stand here in front of you. The gods have been merciful by giving you a son, his form, birth and arrival into this world are like a precious stone and a splendid feather, he is the body and soul of our lords, those kings who have passed on and left your generation with

---

[1] The birth probably occurred in 1496.

pieces of themselves in their hair and their nails, and he is of your blood and in your image. Renown and glory have sprung forth and flowered which will restore the reputation and glory of the ancestors."

And then she said to the child:

"Understand that this house where you were born is not your house because you are a soldier and a servant. You are a bird and a soldier who gives courage to all. The house where you were born is but a nest, an inn where you have arrived today: it is merely your entrance into this world. Here you spring forth, you bloom, and here you will be separated from your mother like a chip cut from the rock. This is your cradle and the place where you rest your head. This house is only your dwelling because your own land is in another place; you are promised in another place; where wars are fought and where battles rage. For that you have been sent. Your fate and your aptitude is war. Your duty is to give the Sun the blood of your enemies. Your own land, your inheritance, and your father make up the house of the Sun. This is the sign that you are offered and promised to the Sun and that you will learn the hard task of war. Your name is written in the battlefields so that neither it nor your person will ever be forgotten. This thorn of maguey, this smoke pipe, and this cluster of flowers are an offering. This offering confirms your virtue and your vow. Live long and work well, my beloved son!"

Ahuizotl, upon receiving the child in his arms, said:

"My Lords of Texcoco and Tlacopan, who with Tenochtitlan swore the Alliance, I present my son, my blood, my image. He will be my heritage and preserve my good name. And you, beloved nephew Moctezuma, the high priest who knows the secrets and the rites of our beliefs: this is your cousin who was born as a precious stone, like a glorious feather our gods have sent to our home. Take him, feel him and in keeping with the day and the hour of his birth, the signs of the books and the forecasts of the stars, foretell his destiny. Tell us the name the old midwife should give him."

Moctezuma made a gesture of intense concentration and addressing himself to the Council, said:

"He was born under a good sign; he will be an extremely courageous warrior; he will be distinguished among those who rule warfare; he will be a slayer and conqueror; he will lead his people. He will end old eras and bear witness to our future, he will be the eagle that ascends through the heroic deeds of his people and of his ancestry, and from there, he will descend to his own death throes. Consequently, his name will be Cuauhtémoc, the Eagle that Descends."

Ahuizotl, adorned with the symbols of his tradition, placed over the child a small round shield, a small bow with tiny arrows and an obsidian knife.

"Oh, eagle! Oh, tiger! Oh, courageous man!" said the oldest midwife who moistened the lips of the child with water and, lifting him four times toward the sky, shouted:

"Oh, Cuauhtémoc! Oh, Cuauhtémoc! Go to the battlefield, place yourself in its center, where wars are fought. Oh, Cuauhtémoc! Your duty is to please the Sun and the earth and give them food and drink. You are the good fortune of the soldiers who are eagles and tigers, who died in war and who now sing joyfully before the Sun."

Afterwards, leaving the premises, the old woman shouted to the soldiers who were there:

"Oh soldiers, oh men of war! Come here; come and taste Cuauhtémoc's umbilical cord."

Thus consecrated, Cuauhtémoc began his life, the difficult, austere existence of an Aztec soldier.

He lived his first years in Tlatelolco, close to his mother, enjoying her tender affections. An instructor helped him to perfect his learning of the language, reverential proceedings, and rites of initiation.

When he was six years old, his father, Ahuizotl, delivered him to the Calmecac school (a communal academy for the nobility) in a solemn ceremony graced not only by his mother, but by his uncles and cousins, among whom were Moctezuma and

Cuitláhuac, who later would precede him in the reign before his own. Cuauhtémoc was the last of the Aztec kings. Also present were other lords and trainees who were going to the *Guerra Florida* in the service of the chief lords, as an exercise in humility.

And Ahuizotl said to him:

"My son, who stands before me. Here we are, your father and mother who gave you life. And although we are your father and mother, even more so will be those who will rear you and teach you good manners; who will open your ears and eyes so that you will learn and discover. You will go to the Calmecac school, a dwelling of tears and sorrow. In that place are reared those who rule and command; those who are in charge of the towns; the professional soldiers who have the power to kill and shed blood. You are not going there to be honored, obeyed or loved. You will be humiliated, scorned and despised. Heed what you must do. Each day you will cut the thorns of the maguey for penance, and you will cluster and tie twigs; you will beat yourself and draw blood from your body with the thorns of the maguey. You will toughen your body with the cold. You must learn from your grandparents' old and sacred books. You must live a chaste life.

"Worthy teachers, I am delivering my son Cuauhtémoc to the house of Quetzalcóatl, a house of penance and tears."

[And they answered him:]

"It is to Quetzalcóatl that you speak. He knows what he has to do with your splendid feather and precious stone and with you, the boy's parents. Doubtfully, we unworthy servants wonder what this child may become. We do not know for certain what to tell you, if he will be or will not be your son. We shall wait for our gods to decide what to make of him."

Death of Ahuizotl; Moctezuma Becomes Emperor

Cuauhtémoc's life in the Calmecac school was no different from the other students' in its strictness and discipline.

Early one morning, everyone in the Calmecac was awakened by the pounding of the huge wooden drums and the gigantic one made of stretched serpents' skins that was atop the *teocalli* [great temple]. Its grave and mournful tones announced the death of Ahuizotl.

Cuauhtémoc sat up on his straw mat when the superior of the Calmecac approached him and said:

"Strengthen your spirit: may it be like the eagle. There is news: Ahuizotl, your father, has died, leaving the great Aztec nation in darkness, and the place and chair of time empty. I must lead you to his lifeless body before it is consumed by flames."

They arrived at Ahuizotl's palaces at dawn. The body of the dead king, adorned with ritualistic symbols, was being prepared for cremation in front of Huitzilopochtli's temple in the great Tenochtitlan plaza.

Moctezuma and Cuitláhuac, together with other relatives, were already there. Before long, the Lord of Tlacopan arrived and later the Lord of Texcoco.

Cuauhtémoc, stoic, restrained himself before his dead father. Solemnly, close to the pyre, he attended the ceremony. Not a muscle moved on his face when the closest servants to the King, adorned like the dead sovereign, were sacrificed in front of the cadaver. The blood flowed everywhere about the pyre as the ripped out hearts of the victims were placed around the dead king. His jewels, necklaces, precious stones and rich plumes were splattered by the servants' blood. As the rites continued, the priests painted the body, combed its hair and adorned the face with gold lip ornaments and gold ear caps. Finally, they lit the great pyre and eventually, all was consumed. Only Ahuizotl's ashes remained.

Throughout the ceremony, the doleful sound of the trumpet shells and the grave rumble of the drums resounded. At the great plaza, the Council and its allies attended the ceremony, together with the common people.

Cuauhtémoc returned to the Calmecac school while the Council, with the lords from Texcoco and Tlacopan, returned to the palace to begin the process of nominating a new king (*Uei Tlatoani*).[1] To consecrate Moctezuma, the Lords of Texcoco and Tlacopan on behalf of the Culúa Empire, sat him on the throne, a luxuriously crafted *icpalli* (chair); then they placed on him the blue mantle, the gold diadem, the gold ear caps and the gold lip ornaments.

Afterwards, while burning the aromatic copal incense in the big braziers, they perfumed him. Then his electors said to him:

"Dawn has arrived; once we were in darkness, but now the Empire glows as a mirror reflects light."

[1] "After the ritual and its auspicious ceremonies, the fourteen electors, among them the Lords of Texcoco and Tlacopan, nominated Moctezuma Xocoyotzin, the Rancorous Lord, distinguishing him among many candidates, as much for his military valor as for his piety, as supreme priest [. . .] The two kings Netzahualpilli and Totoquihuaztli [. . .] with twelve electors of the Empire said that Moctezuma should be chosen and named King. Moctezuma, son and heir of King Axayácatl who is not a boy but already a man [. . .], who is a courageous, brave and capable youth [. . .] and also pious. (Alvarado Tezozómoc, Fernando, *Crónica Mexicana*, México: Editorial Porrúa, 1975.)

Moctezuma, arrogant, but with gentle dignity, accepted their homage. Carried on his elaborate litter, he withdrew to his palace where he was joined only by his relatives, outstanding among them the young Cuitláhuac. From the beginning, Moctezuma dictated that as soon as his litter passed, the street must be cleaned and that anyone appearing before him wearing luxurious garments must cover them with rags.

A few days later, he met with the Council, and the Lords of Texcoco and Tlacopan, and announced his imperial plan:

"We must enforce, even more sternly than Ahuizotl, the power and strength of the Culúa Alliance to all of its borders so that the people of Huitzilopochtli can better serve their gods. First, we will wage war against the Achiotlán people; then we will march against Tlaxcala and the Mixteca. We shall carry our power into the great waters of the East, where we will subdue the Cempoala and Totonaca tribes as well as the people of the South and West."

"But, Lord Moctezuma," said a member of the Council, "we have the *Guerra Florida* pact with Tlaxcala; we fight them only to capture victims to sacrifice and appease our gods, and we have respected the other people. If we violate the pact, it will be difficult to subdue them, as they are strong and resolute."

"I hear you and I understand," Moctezuma replied vigorously, "but I have made up my mind and my orders will be followed to the letter. We shall overcome the Tlaxcala nation even though they may be stronger and have a larger army. Of course, Lord of Texcoco, you will cut off the road to the salt mines and permit no trade with them. Let them understand that we shall ignore the *Guerra Florida* pact. With Tenochtitlan as the vanguard, the Great Empire will be equal to the epochs of Tezcatlipoca and our Huitzilopochtli's desire to kill. I want their precious fluid, their very blood, to serve better the Sun which takes its strength from it in order to rise from the night of Mictlán; so that the Sun will be reborn with greater strength each day; so that through their blood and their death the stars will remain in their places; so that the beauty of Tehutlampa may be infinite. Blood! Follow your orders faithfully and we will honor our pact with the gods we serve. Indeed, are we anyone at all when we do not serve the gods? Without fearing them? Do we deserve something greater than to complete the sublime mission to preserve with blood the order of our world, with its flowers and crops, its human beings who breathe with the fervor of the gods, so that this beautiful world may remain as it is? This is the ultimate mission of our destiny. We have always accepted this mission, without asking the gods anything more than the opportunity to serve them."

Then he added:

"And we will do so to the limit of our strength, no matter who falls or who suffers. Everyone will have to pay more tribute. No one will stop us! We shall subdue everyone! They will have to yield unconditionally. We will fortify the Empire of Huitzilopochtli to provide blood and satisfaction for the gods.

"This I command."

Astounded, the Council listened. Then, enthusiastically, they shouted in unison as Moctezuma was leaving:

"Lord, my lord, great lord."

Thus began Moctezuma's reign, which was even more severe and unmerciful than Ahuizotl's. He expanded the Empire to its utmost, increasing taxes from the vanquished, from whom he demanded treasures and victims for sacrifice. The rancor and hate increased among those he subjugated.

All of this occurred in the year 10-Conejo, 1502 on the Christian calendar.

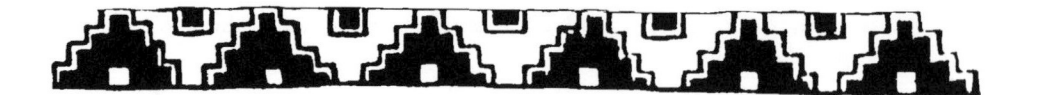

Hernán Cortés

That same year, in Medellín, Extremadura [Spain], a young man about eighteen was discovered in a lady's bed. Hernán Cortés threw his clothes on, snatched up his sword and shield and leaped through the window into the night. He dashed through the garden. Attempting to scale the wall, he knocked it down, which tumbled him to the ground bewildered and bruised. This mishap enabled the offended husband to reach Hernán and attempt to inflict knife slashes, which the youth barely managed to fend off with his sword. Just when the husband was beginning to gain the upper hand, he was yanked away by the unfaithful woman's mother.

"I beg you, son!" the woman cried. "Don't kill him. In the darkness we do not know who he is or what has happened. He looks so young. Oh, don't kill him! For God's sake! Protect my daughter's honor. She sleeps peacefully. You must avoid a scandal."

Considerably battered, Hernán took advantage of the woman's intervention and escaped into the darkness. Limping painfully, leaning on his sheathed sword, he arrived at the home of his parents—Martín Cortés and Catalina Pizarro. Urgently, he knocked on the door. When it was opened by a servant, he slipped quickly inside. Breathless, his clothes dirty and bloody and his leg injured, Hernán cried out and collapsed face down in the hallway. At his call, his parents hurried in and with the servant's aid they carried the young man to his bed. Once Hernán's mother and father were sure the gash in his leg wasn't fatal and none of his other wounds was serious, their anxiety turned quickly to anger.

Don Martín started: "Hernán! Hernán, son of my sins, unquestionably it is I who pays the price for your merrymaking and pranks. You and your affinity for weapons! Look how you come home, fleeing through the night, battered and bruised, your sword still in your hand. Just look at your mother's anguish. Do you not feel it? Or is this just one more of your so-called heroic deeds!"

"Son!" said his mother. "Why do you do this to us? Why do you bring us these troubles? We want you to be a gentleman, not a loud, rude lout. We have tried everything. But you did not want to become a man of the cloth, so we sent you to Salamanca to study and be educated."

"Educated," interrupted Martín Cortés. "You have knife gashes inflicted by some scoundrel in the night. After two years in Salamanca you have yet to give us the pride of earning a bachelor's degree. Bad Latin and average grammar with at best the false pretensions of being erudite. And such arrogance! You should be thrown out in shame. And look at you! There you lie . . . speechless."

Hernán shrugged. "Merely an unfortunate occurrence, father. The wall fell on me and then came that fool and his dagger . . . it wasn't my fault."

"Indeed, it is your fault and a serious one. That wall and the wounds seem to be the result of an offended brother or husband. Although you are only a novice, you insist on your escapades. Thank your saints that your 'unfortunate occurrence' had no more consequence than an injured leg. At least that will keep you immobilized for a while."

"Come on father. Is it that bad? What about my trip to the Indies with *Don* Nicolás de Ovando's fleet?"

"You will just have to give that up, Hernán. Ovando will be sailing well before your leg is healed. So you see, every sin has its price. Oh, my son! Once and for all, will you stop these restless and quarrelsome ways? I hope this experience teaches you a lesson. Because of your foolishness, a great opportunity is slipping away. Maybe this will be a good lesson!" Martín Cortés sighed.

"Well, don't expect me to return to Salamanca. I am more fit for soldiering than for the humanities, anyway. What I have already learned is more than enough and I don't need to be entangled in the quest for a degree, anyway. I prefer to be a notary."

"Enough of your insolence, Hernán! You never learn! Fortunately, that lame leg will keep you at home."

"But not for long," Hernán said, "because as soon as it heals I am off to Italy to pursue my fortune and glory with the Great Captain Gonzalo de Córdoba."

In fact, the fleet of the new governor of the Indies, Nicolás de Ovando, did set sail without the young Hernán among its crew. When he recovered, Hernán Cortés left to seek his fortune in Italy.

"Give me your blessing, mother and father. I am going to find the Great Captain and I will share his glory in Italy."

"Give it some thought," pleaded his mother. "You have the qualities to continue your education and we are prepared to send you to Salamanca, where you can complete your studies and honor us. Think about it, for your mother's sake."

"I have already thought about it, *Doña* Catalina. Soldiering and its glory attracts me more than the study of letters and its [fame]. So, to war I go, mother. Give me your blessing."

"I will not deny you my blessing, son, but we will give you no money for such a purpose, for such knavery," cried *Don* Martín.

"With your benediction, I have all I need, my parents. I shall overcome your displeasure with glory!"

Cortés set out on the road to Valencia, his sword on his shoulder, a small bundle with his clothes and his very fate dancing from its tip. But he never arrived in Italy. For about a year, he wandered, though not without work to meet his needs.

The Goddess of Fortune who favors the audacious carried him from adventure to adventure, to Seville, Cádiz, Palos and Sanlúcar. There, in a tavern, he became

Yo comeré al son de trompetas o moriré en la horca.

"I will eat at the sound of trumpets or I will die on the gallows."

acquainted with a certain Alonso Quintero, who, in early 1504 would command a ship sailing in a commercial convoy from Sanlúcar to Santo Domingo, twelve years after its discovery.

In Seville, young Hernán was dazzled by the personalities and the boastings of the explorers who ostentatiously showed off their gold, feathers, birds, jewels and precious stones. While strolling through the streets of that important city, between the offices of the Royal Chancellery and of Bishop Fonseca, who was responsible for affairs in the Indies, Cortés decided to cross the Atlantic. He discussed his place with Quintero and soon booked passage.

Hernán returned to Medellín to bid his parents farewell. They greeted his news with cautious joy.

"Welcome, son! Judging by the lamentable state of your velvet clothes, you are probably returning from Italy without much glory. Surely, the Great Captain misses you," said his father mockingly. "Nevertheless, my son, Hernán, I am so happy to see you."

His mother greeted him. "But look how thin and shabby you are, and with a beard that reminds me of my own father's. I hope you are back to stay. We have missed you so much."

"Alas, no, mother. I will be here only a short while."

14

"What? But why? It's been a year since you left and you want to leave again so soon?"

"Yes, mother. And it was a year of adventure, but I have learned more than if I had spent my whole life in Salamanca."

"Bah! I don't want to hear about what you have learned, Hernán, you ne'er do well," said *Don* Martín. "Not about your dealing with scoundrels from the taverns and bordellos. Nevertheless, something has happened, Hernán, something that has reminded you of your parents."

"Yes, father. I have come to ask for your blessing, again, and this will have to last for a long time. I have made up my mind to go to the Indies and to find my fame and fortune there."

"Oh, no, my son! So far? To the other side of the world? We will never see you again; you will never see us again."

"But I am young, mother, and Spain has become too small for me now. I need to see other lands and I believe that there I will accomplish great deeds that will honor you."

While his mother wailed her disappointment, *Don* Martín, pensive, looked straight at his son. "Now you are a man, Hernán. You left us a child and in one short year you have changed. And that is good. However, you are correct about your plans. If I could, I would also go to the Indies. I know that great events are going to take place in that world whose boundaries we scarcely know. So we will give you our benediction as well as some money so that you do not suffer hardships during the journey."

In early 1504, when he was nineteen, Hernán Cortés left Sanlúcar de Barrameda to meet his destiny in the New World. He sailed in Quintero's ship which was the last to arrive in Santo Domingo because of the captain's vagaries and slip-shod manner in the command of the vessel.

Medina, the secretary to the Governor of Santo Domingo, relieved of his concern of the ship's delay, went to the port to greet Cortés with a warm, friendly welcome. Medina found lodgings for Cortés in the hostelry and invited him to have a jug of wine in the tavern.

"How happy I am to see you, Hernán. How wonderful that you have decided to come to these islands. As you will see, they are full of promise and opportunity. And for a shrewd and able swordsman. . . ."

"Yes, Medina, here I am despite that scoundrel Quintero who, with Francisco Niño, by no means an asset to the Niño family, nearly lost us at sea. Toward the last, we had only rain water to drink and stale crackers to eat. We thought we were going to die, so we heard each other's confessions. Just when we thought all was lost, we saw a beautiful dove perched on the mast. When it flew away, we realized land was nearby, so we followed the flight of the bird and finally arrived at this island of promise, unfortunately for Quintero, and despite his avarice and ineptitude. But here we are, anyway, brother Medina, ready for everything. To fight with the sword or with our wits."

As they got to the tavern, Medina responded.

"Always the same old Hernán! What a pleasure! Listen, I'm going to give you your first advice. As soon as possible, become a citizen of Santo Domingo so you can enjoy all the privileges of the conquerors: land for a farm and a plot of ground in the city to build a house. Once you are established, some Indians will be placed under your command."

"What's the basis of all this generosity?"

"Your promise to stay on this island for five years, and not leaving without the governor's permission. After that, you may go wherever and whenever you please."

"My dear Medina, not on this island or on any other in the New World do I expect or wish to spend so long a time. Remember what I told you in Medellín: either I dine to the sound of trumpets or I die on the gallows."

Although that retort startled his good friend Medina, Cortés nevertheless registered the next day at the Santo Domingo census office.

Cortés, Public Notary* and Farmer

 et's get these matters settled, good friend Medina. If it's not too inconvenient, let's stroll over to the Registry and, according to your wishes, arrange an interview for me with Governor de Ovando, for whom I have certain letters of recommendation."

"Since the governor is away just now, let's just go to the Citizen's Registry. We can arrange your interview another time. He will have to come back soon, anyway, in order to answer those who criticize his lack of assistance to the Great Admiral Columbus. For the fourth time, he has tried to land on the shores of the Great Khan [China], but his ships are in such bad repair, he could hardly make it to Jamaica. Ovando would not even allow him to come ashore at La Hispañola. Today, even those who did not support Columbus before are demanding that the Discoverer be assisted."

"God help me! my friend Medina. *Gloria sic transit mundi* (and may your honor pardon my poor Latin) but how fleeting is glory in this world! The Discoverer himself mistreated in the very place he himself discovered! There is much to learn before one can understand such complicated matters."

They left the tavern and walked to the hostel.

"Here, public opinion is created and destroyed in the Sunday sermons. Soon you will become aware, my friend Cortés, of the rivalries and contradictions that prevail between the monks and the noblemen, to the extent that the latter, who asked them to come to bring spiritual order, now claim that the religious go to extremes to defend the rights of the Indians, thus compromising the work at the gold mines, the farms and in the trades."

"And in this case, who is right, Medina? According to my understanding of Roman Law, I remember there is a Law of Conquest."

"Which the monks severely denounce. There is one of them, a particular agitator, a Brother Bartolomé de Las Casas, who makes a lot of noise and insists that there is no legitimate cause for Christians to enter this land and kingdom other than to bring to the Indians the news and wisdom of the one and true God, and of his son, Jesus Christ, the Universal Redeemer."

---

* The occupation of a notary, or scribe, was more an art of editing contracts, wills, summons and judicial formalities, emphasizing grammar and Latin rhetoric, than a legal science. It was not until 1548 that the study of notorial proceedings was included in the school of law. (Castillo, Bernardo Pérez Fernández del, *Hernán Cortés como escribano*, *Revista de Derecho Notorial*, Abril-Junio, 1984.)—Trans.

"According to that theory, my good Medina, then we can only use the sword to raise up the cross. I heard something about this matter in Seville and now we shall find out first hand what is going on here."

"You may have your first opportunity next Sunday. There are many rumors that the Dominicans are plotting among themselves so that upon the Governor's return, a certain brother will preach a sermon on the topic before Governor de Ovando and the important people of the island."

"Well, we must hear it then. With your help, I shall take advantage of the occasion to kiss the hand of His Excellency, the Governor, and to present the letters I brought."

"We shall try to do it, friend Cortés."

At the hostel, they parted.

With great anticipation of all the people, Sunday arrived. A large crowd gathered, among them the principal noblemen, led by the Governor. Off to one side, but paying close attention, stood young Cortés. After the Mass, which was solemnly sung, Father Montesinos stood on the step of the altar, which was still under construction. With deep emotion, he directed his remarks to the angry noblemen, who were armed and surrounded him while he reproached them.

El sermón del Padre Montesinos

Padre Montesinos preaching the sermon.

"Tell me, by what right and what law do you hold these Indians in such horrible and cruel servitude? By what authority do you wage such detestible wars against the docile and peaceful people who live in this land?"

"And what kind of regard do you have for instructing them so that they may know their God and Creator, be baptized, attend Mass, and observe the holy days and Sabbaths?"

Raising his voice so he would be heard over the protests of the furious parishioners who began to reach for their swords, he concluded:

"Are these not men? Do they not have rational souls? Are you not obligated to love them as you love yourselves? Don't you understand this? Don't you have any feelings?"

The protests and angry voices drowned out the rest of the sermon. The noblemen, indignant, surrounded the priest and shoved him about. Governor de Ovando had to impose all of his authority to prevent them from injuring the courageous priest. Shielded by his Dominican companions, he eventually left the church safely. The parishioners stayed behind to discuss the priest's effrontery with the Governor. Then, they, too, left in groups. Outside the church, Medina took advantage of the confusion and managed to introduce the young Cortés to the Governor.

"Your Excellency," he said. "I don't know if this may be the proper time, but Your Honor, who holds friendship in high regard, might allow me to introduce a young man and dear friend, Hernán Cortés, a native of Extremadura and son of Martín Cortés and Catalina Pizarro. He brings certain letters of recommendation."

"You are being imprudent, Medina," the Governor said, stiffening. "Can't you see that this is not the proper. . . ."

Audaciously, Cortés came forward.

"I kiss the hand of Your Excellency. Please do not reproach my friend Medina. Out of friendship, what he is doing I am totally responsible for, as I was anxious to deliver these letters to you. Unfortunately, I am in need of assistance."

"You are too audacious, young Hernán. I remember your father, to whom I once spoke about you. If I remember, you caused him some trouble with those brawls you enjoyed so well. Regardless, allow me. . . ."

And he read the letters.

"I see here that you are practically a scholar, a learned man with some knowledge of Latin. So I welcome you. There are not many here who know how to write. You witnessed the rough kind of people who inhabit this island. Did you notice how they flared up at the inappropriate comments of Father Montesinos? Tell me, you, who went to the University of Salamanca, what is your opinion of what was said here?"

"Your Excellency, I lack the insight to discuss that question. I shall need some time to think carefully about these matters which so deeply affect fairness and feelings."

De Ovando interrupted: "How prudent you are, young nobleman. Quite prudent. Since you have some education, I seem to remember that I need a notary in Azúa. If you would consider the post. . . ."

"At once, Excellency, but do not think I am too forward if I remind you that I also have a sword and know how to use it."

"How convenient. Start your work immediately and soon we shall have a grant of land for you to farm and some Indians to work it."

"Indians! Why, what will Montesinos say! I am indeed much obliged to Your Excellency. From now on, you can count on my modest pen, but also upon my sword." Cortés bowed deeply.

Cortés, the public notary in Azúa

"Which you handle well, as is indicated in these letters. But remember this: use it to defend just causes, not in duels, where you may lose more honor than you gain. Take care, young nobleman!"

For six years, to everyone's satisfaction, Cortés fulfilled his duty as Azúa's notary. He also raised crops and cattle and became a prosperous farmer.

Young and strong as he was, despite several fights that resulted from amorous affairs, he came out well, thanks to his skill with the sword.

Bernal Díaz del Castillo relates:

I have heard it said that as a youth in the Española island he was prankish when it came to women and that he successfully fought dexterous and vigorous swordsmen. He had a dueling scar near his mouth, noticeable only when one looked close, because it was covered by his beard. It happened because he couldn't resist such affairs.

The Omens[1]: First Omen

Ten years before the Spaniards landed in Mexico, the first fateful omen appeared in the sky: like a blazing sprig of wheat, like a flame, like an aurora, as if emitting sparks of fire, piercing the sky. Wide at the base, narrow at the top, it reached midway in the sky, touching the heavens.

It came in view during the span of a single year, beginning in 12-Casa (1509–10). While it was visible, the world erupted in turmoil. People slapped their lips, became confused, and talked about it constantly.

Moctezuma, bewildered and isolated, went up on the roof of the *Casa de lo Negro* [House of Darkness], The House of Magic Studies, to consider the phenomenon.

"My wise seers," he said. "this great serpent of fire appearing in the sky seems an omen of mournful events. I wish to hear your opinion of it."

"Lord, my lord, great lord," said the oldest of the oracles, "terrified and frightened, we have seen the serpent of light in the sky and we believe with you that it is a grave omen, which, perhaps, is announcing a change of Sun, a new era."

"I agree," Moctezuma nodded, "a change of Sun. Within ten years, fifty-two years of our last cycle will be complete and I foresee, by that time, that the Sun will change. Long have I been meditating about it; I have studied our codices; I have consulted our elders. This serpent confirms that within ten years our era will end. The Sun will change. I am certain that Quetzalcóatl, with his people, will return to claim his throne, this seat of honor that we have only borrowed. . . . We must be vigilant. Collect the evidence of all occurrences, of all omens, and bring them to me here at the *Casa de lo Negro*. My heart grieves; times will change, I am sure."

Once again, preoccupied, he went up to the roof to look at the serpent of light that shone in the Tehutlampa.

From that time on, the wise men ordered that all omens be recorded and that Moctezuma be told about them at the *Casa de lo Negro*.

---

[1] From 1509, the Indian world suffered from the omens of its decline. Prophecy passed on to catastrophe. Moctezuma, in his mystical fanaticism, associated the omens with the arrival of the Spaniards as a fulfillment of the prophecy. Furthermore, the occasion allowed a close observance of the character differences between Moctezuma and Cuauhtémoc. This material is based on Sahagún's history. The omens were woven into the dates and events occurring in the Spanish world as Cortés arrived in Mexico.

The Conquest of Cuba

In July, 1509, when the omens began their eerie message in Tenochtitlan, *Don* Diego Columbus, son and heir of *Don* Cristóbal, arrived at the island of La Hispañola. He had regained his title as Viceroy and Governor-General of the Indies and had come to succeed de Ovando. The entourage he brought with him included chaperones and noble young girls, among whom was the Juárez family and Catalina, called the Marcaida, who would become Hernán Cortés' wife.

Among the crowd that awaited the gaudy fleet decorated with colorful pennants was Hernán Cortés and his friend Medina.

"What will the administration of *Don* Diego Columbus mean for you, friend Medina, now that—after so many battles and intrigues in the Spanish court to regain the hereditary title of Viceroy and Governor of La Española from his father—he is arriving to rule the island? The younger Columbus must be quite concerned about vindications and reprisals alike."

"I will have to leave with my good friend de Ovando. All things have a beginning and an end and I have nothing more to accomplish here. Gossip and persecutions will soon commence toward those who have served the former Governor. And you, Hernán, what will you do?"

"I, my good friend, shall stay on as a notary in Azúa. In these six years, I have built a prosperous business on the farm and have mined some gold. I am not wealthy yet, but I have made a good start and now I can see a bright future for myself. I am satisfied and so I wrote to my parents. I shall remain on this island, especially if I can marry one of the beautiful ladies that *Don* Diego has brought in his entourage. Just look at them."

"Indeed, they are beautiful. But none will be mine, Hernán, for soon I will depart for Spain."

When the Viceroy-General arrived, formal greeting began from the officials, among them Diego Velázquez, a rich man of the island, fat, red-haired and presumptuous. Behind him in the receiving line was Hernán Cortés.

"*Don* Diego Velázquez, old friend," said Columbus, "I see that you have prospered in size and the talk about your wealth has traveled the seas. It is a pleasure to see Your Honor. Soon, I shall need you. So be ready. I am thinking about enlarging the domain of the Indies and taking our army to the lands discovered by my father, *Don* Cristóbal. We will assert our authority over Borinquen [Puerto Rico], Cuba, in La Fernandina [Florida], and we shall reach the mainland, Darién and southward. We will need the fortunes and the bravery of noblemen such as Your Honor."

"I am at your service, as are young men such as Hernán Cortés here, whom I would like to introduce to Your Excellency. He is a competent notary and has a good education, as well as a good head and a strong sword. See if you are able to convince him; he is as fond of cultivating crops as he is love affairs."

"I kiss your hand, Your Excellency," said Cortés, "and I am at your command. Don't believe everything about me that *Don* Diego is telling you. I am well satisfied with my situation and with my farm. However, I must confess to Your Excellency that I am not enthusiastic about expeditions destined for failure, like those of Alonso de Ojeda, or even of Pedro Alonso Niño. Although they discovered some lands, they abandoned them, leaving no rewards for our Catholic Majesty, mainly because of rivalries, lack of organization and misguided ambition."

Columbus smiled, "You are young, yet already you are critical. Well, we shall take advantage of your ideas, Hernán. I can tell you now that I have already committed myself with Nicuesa and Ojeda. They will command an expedition from Darién [Panama] toward the south. And now that I find myself with this voluminous nobleman, *Don* Diego Velázquez, I would like to propose to him the conquest of Cuba."

"And that, of course, I accept, if Your Excellency will confirm it."

"Consider it confirmed, *Don* Diego."

"You heard that, Hernán. Now you are bound to assist me in the conquest of Cuba," *Don* Velázquez said.

Hernán smiled broadly. "Thank you, Your Honor. I would only leave my profession and farm under orders from a gentleman like yourself. As for Nicuesa and Ojeda, although they are courageous men, I expect nothing much from them. Even if they are strong, valiant and daring, they are not well organized. Which is what I said to a certain Francisco Pizarro, a relative of mine, who persists in joining them."

"Well, gentlemen," said *Don* Diego, "we have disrupted the welcome ceremony, but it has been my fault. We shall formalize these plans later. May God be with you."

23

Second Omen

And this is how the second doleful omen appeared in Mexico: All of a sudden, it burst into flames; it began to burn; perhaps no one set the fire, but by spontaneous combustion, the Huitzilopotchtli temple was ablaze. The divine place was named Tlacatecan (*Casa de Mando*), [The House of Command].

It appeared; then the columns burned. From inside the flames burst out in tongues of fire, in flashes of fire.

Quickly and completely the fire consumed the wooden framework of the temple. Immediately, there arose a thunderous outcry: "Mexicans, come quickly; help put out the fire. Bring your water jugs!"

But when they poured water on the flames, trying to extinguish the blaze, it intensified even more. They could not stem the fire; everything burned to ashes.

This happened when the serpent of light disappeared from the sky. Moctezuma watched this strange phenomenon from the roof of the *Casa de lo Negro*. When the fire had burned out, he assembled the wise men and said to them:

"My sages, my prophets, the serpent of light has just disappeared in the sky, and now there is a second mournful omen thrust upon us. What do you think about it?"

The oldest among them answered:

"We are certain that when the serpent left, it sent this second sign, now on earth and just as deadly as the first one. We believe it is announcing new eras with new manifestations.

"That must be it!" concluded Moctezuma. "The temple of Huitzilopochtli, herald of Tezcatlipoca, is lost by fire."

Conquest of Cuba

Late in 1511, Diego Velázquez set out from La Española to conquer Cuba. He was a man of good presence and, although fat, he was merry, extravagant, affable and arbitrary. According to Father Bartolomé de Las Casas, "He had much experience spilling, or helping to spill, the blood of the unfortunate people." Among his principal companions came Cortés as partner and advisor (both had pledged their fortunes to organize the expedition). Because of Velázquez's obesity, he depended on Cortés and Pánfilo de Narváez, who had come voluntarily from Jamaica to help with the conquest.

Third Omen

Lightning struck the Xiuhtecuhtli temple. There was no rain, so it was taken as an omen. This is how they described it: no more than a blow from the Sun.

No one heard any thunder.

Moctezuma received the news of this omen in the *Casa de lo Negro*.

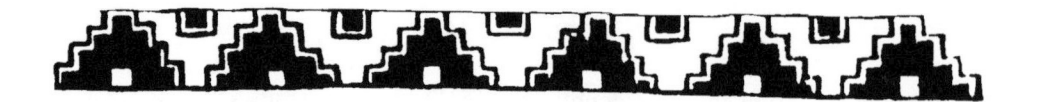

In Cuba: Prison and Marriage of Cortés

I n 1512, the conquest of Cuba completed, Diego Velázquez, Hernán Cortés and Pánfilo de Narváez met in Santiago at the Government House which was still under construction.

"Thanks to your ability and gift of command, *Don* Diego, it has taken longer to build this house than to conquer the island," remarked Cortés.

"Without your collaboration it would have been difficult. I am obliged to you gentlemen, especially to *Don* Pánfilo, who offered his services so willingly. To you, *Don* Hernando, I shall fulfill the promise I made when I asked you to join me. I am sure that by offering you the moon, I persuaded you to join the effort."

"This campaign was *easy*, my lords," said Cortés. "These were docile Indians frightened by our arms and force, who never gave us any trouble even when they surprised *Don* Pánfilo and his men asleep. In fact, the Indians were more attracted by our beautiful clothes than by blood. Without any noise they surprised our companions and without any harm they vanished."

"Don't make fun of my carelessness, *Don* Hernán. They may have found us asleep, but then we drove them off."

"Well, gentlemen, reminiscence is good, but reality is even better. It is time to organize ourselves to govern this island, much larger and richer than the others in the Indies governed by *Don* Diego Columbus."

"May his control of the lands he governs please him, but I believe, *Don* Diego, that the conqueror has the right to govern what he has conquered. Do not take offense that I seem critical. You have the right to govern Cuba independently of the Government of La Hispañola. You are the Conqueror and have better judgment and more experience than your namesake, *Don* Diego Columbus."

"Be still, Hernán. You know these matters are resolved only by His Majesty the King."

"Then go to him, so he will give justice to your achievement and merits."

"We shall see, *Don* Hernán, we shall see. Let us leave to each time its own effort. Now is the moment to organize the government. So with the authority delegated to me by *Don* Diego Columbus, I appoint you, *Don* Pánfilo de Narváez, Captain-General of this island of Cuba."

"I am honored and delighted to accept the position you have given me."

"I am glad, *Don* Pánfilo. And for you, *Don* Hernán Cortés, as of this moment I name you my Secretary as well as Treasurer of the King in this island of Cuba. As

I am acquainted with your devotion to farming, very soon I shall give you land enough to satisfy your ambition."

Cortés, farmer in Cuba

"You honor me greatly, *Don* Diego. I was already aware of your prudence and energy. Now I can also add graciousness and generosity. Without a doubt you will become very prosperous, for you know how to employ men. I am grateful and at your disposal."

"Well, let us get down to work," concluded Diego Velázquez. "By the way, *Don* Hernán, do you remember Juan Juárez from Granada, or more specifically, do you remember the Juárez sisters?"

"Of course, *Don* Diego, and especially *Doña* Catalina, a beautiful and great lady."

"Well then, I have asked Juan to bring them to this island, as we must populate and settle the land, which can only be done with children born here in the sacrament of marriage. We must get ready to welcome them, *Don* Hernán."

"Nothing will please me more, Your Honor."

A few months later, the Juárez sisters arrived. Velázquez courted María and Hernán, Catalina with even more success than he expected, for when the time came to fulfill the promise of matrimony, he had to fight his way out of the contract. María complained to the Governor that Cortés' disdain was an insult to her sister. Velázquez had heard rumors and libelous remarks about Cortés' political attitudes which, it was said, were drawing complaints against the government from those who were resentful and ambitious. In order to pressure his secretary to marry Catalina, as well as to curb his political activities, Velázquez reprimanded him and ordered him placed in jail.

"Cortés," he said abruptly when he received him in his office, already finished and decorated with the luxuries of the time. "I am truly surprised at your behavior. You have honored neither your name or my friendship and confidence. Why don't you respect the promise you made to marry *Doña* Catalina Juárez, after having intimate relations and, as I have been informed, even having made her pregnant. This is not the behavior of a gentleman, or of the person I want as a Secretary. You must honor your obligations."

"But, Your Excellency, you put me in such a difficult position! I am young, and matrimony is a serious obligation. It is not true that Catalina is pregnant; that is a ruse. . . ."

"Ah, *Don* Hernán, besides not being a gentleman, you are irresponsible. Do you refuse to marry *Doña* Catalina immediately?"

"Let me think about it, Excellency."

"You can think about it in prison, where your irresponsibility has led you. Also, I have received information that you listen to and defend those who dislike me and that you prepare information for those who, on behalf of the Court of Justice must investigate the unjust accusations made against me by rogues and non-conformists. Think in jail."

"Allow me, Your Excellency. I have been loyal and devoted to you. Catalina is plotting against me, just as are those who seek your favor and feel hindered by the control I maintain on your behalf. If I listen to the discontented and sly ones, it is only to keep you informed and to defend you. Don't believe these intrigues and slanders."

"Then you admit that you have listened to the mischief-makers and that you continue to be rebellious of your obligations to Catalina. Guards! To prison with this wicked-born Secretary. To prison!"

Don Hernán did not remain long in jail. The Mayor, a bit distrustful and a friend of Cortés, did not put him behind bars but in a room with a thick wooden door. Cortés broke the lock, opened the door and subdued the Mayor. With his sword and shield, he repelled the prison guards and sought sanctuary in the church, resorting to a sacred asylum.

Energetic and enterprising as he was, Cortés could remain secluded only for a short time. To straighten out his situation with Catalina, he asked her to meet him at the church. She came at night and waited for him outside. When Cortés appeared, Velázquez' men recaptured him, but only with great resistance. Once more he was locked up, this time placed in shackles on board a ship, as Velázquez planned to send him to Spain to be tried.

With great effort and boldness, his feet bleeding, Cortés broke loose from the chains and put on his servant's clothes. He went up to the main deck and walked around casually until he came upon a group of sailors sitting around a stove. Boldly he slipped down a rope and boarded a small skiff. Then he rowed over to the ship, the only one anchored in the bay, cutting the rope so no one could follow him. The current of the river prevented him from reaching the shore, but in a safe place where no one could see him, he undressed, placed his clothes as well as some compromising documents about Diego Velázquez on his head, and jumped into the shark-infested Barracoa Bay. With great difficulty, but still unnoticed, he reached the coast. After dressing, he went to the home of Juan Juárez, Catalina's brother, whom he surprised at dawn.

"*Don* Juan Juárez, contrite and ashamed, here is the person who wishes to be your brother-in-law. I ask your permission to take your sister, *Doña* Catalina, for my wife."

"I am amazed, *Don* Hernán. I thought you were a prisoner aboard a boat headed for Spain, to be brought to trial for I don't know what insolences to the Governor Diego Velázquez."

"Deceitful information from intriguers and flatterers! I am devoted and loyal to *Don* Diego, with whom I earnestly wish to reconcile. So, if it is not inconvenient, I request your good services to accomplish it."

"My role as your future brother-in-law, I shall gladly fulfill, as I am aware of the good feelings my sister Catalina has for you. I know that *Don* Diego is on an expedition in the interior of the island to castigate some rebellious Indians. Let us go look for him and place ourselves at his service as good friends."

"I welcome the idea. Let's go."

So it was, that night Cortés appeared unexpectedly with Juárez, armed with a lance and crossbow, ready to take part in the operations.

He surprised the Governor, who was in his office. From an open window, he said:

"Greetings, gentlemen, here comes Cortés to offer himself to his courageous Captain."

Startled, Velázquez stood up abruptly.

"You should be in chains, if not on the way to Spain. How is it possible? You have escaped twice. You are a demon, Hernán, and with daring audacity I shall seize you again. Guards!"

"I beg you, Your Excellency," said Juárez, "don't mistreat or harm him. Soon he will be my brother-in-law."

"What! The rebel comes to reason. Well, Hernán, this is a good beginning."

"It will be a good end, *Don* Diego. Your Grace can be certain that worthless people have plotted against me, envious of the confidence you have toward me and of which I have never become worthy. Please forgive outward appearances and never doubt my loyalty. Be the best man at my wedding and in good time give me the honor of being the godfather of my son."

"Hombre! Congratulations! Who would have told me that before this day is over, I would be a *compadre* of *Don* Hernán."

And he laughed heartily. The pardon was granted and Cortés fought with his usual bravery and success. The reconciliation was complete. Hernán married Catalina. Velázquez was the best man and stood for Martín Cortés at the ceremony. Later, he became godfather at the baptism of a little girl.[1]

---

[1] We are not certain if the mother of his child was Catalina or a Cuban Indian, *Doña* Fulana Pizarro. I attribute the child to Catalina in order to round out the scene. It is a fact that Velázquez and Cortés became *compadres*.

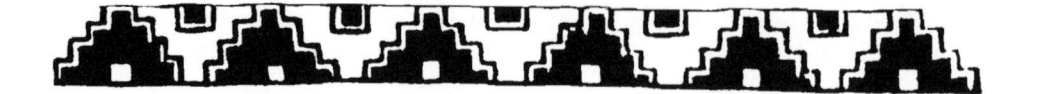

Fourth Omen

The sun was still shining when the fire fell. In three stages it appeared: rising where the Sun sets, soaring straight toward where the Sun rises, as if it were a live coal falling in a rain of sparks: its train extended in a broad sweep and its tail spanned a great distance. When it appeared there came forth a great outcry, as if mighty bells were resounding. (No doubt, it was a large meteorite.) Although tormented, Moctezuma accepted the omen.

Cortés, Alcalde de Santiago

Following his marriage, and with the land and Indians his benefactor had bestowed upon him, Cortés prospered and became wealthy. All of his contemporaries praised his enterprising spirit in mining, farming, raising and breeding sheep and cattle. He was the first in those parts to have a cattle ranch and to introduce a variety of cattle into the country. He was also the first to prospect for gold in Cuba. Later, he became *Alcalde* [Mayor] of Santiago, in honor of which, he ordered a pretentious emblem of authority.

Two Failed Expeditions

Many who wished to make their fortunes from expeditions and conquests visited *Alcalde* Hernán Cortés, a wealthy and famous man with good connections and winning manners.

Early in 1517, Bernal Díaz del Castillo, born in 1492, in Medina del Campo [Spain], was one of those visitors. Returning from a journey with Balboa to the south, where they had discovered Darién, Díaz del Castillo requested Cortés' support for the expedition of Hernández de Córdoba and 110 men to continue exploring Darién.

"Pardon my boldness, *Don* Hernán Cortés, *Alcalde* de Santiago. Your Grace does not know me. I am Bernal Díaz del Castillo, a native of Medina del Campo."

"I have heard about you, Bernal, a young soldier, brave, frank, serious and upright. Your fame exceeds your modesty."

"I do not deserve your praise, *Don* Hernán. I aspire, as my forefathers did, simply to serve the Royal Crown loyally. To serve it better, may I venture a proposal to Your Grace?"

"Tell me about it."

"I represent 110 men, who with Pedrarías de Ávila, came to Cuba from the mainland. However, there was no land to challenge us. Now that everything is peaceful in the lands which Vasco Núñez de Balboa has conquered, the place became too small for us. Much time has passed since we returned and we do not have Indians or land, nor have we been able to accomplish anything constructive."

"I understand your impatience, my good Bernal, but tell me, in what way may I help you?"

"We are confident that the generosity of Your Grace will help us with money, vessels, arms—or anything else you think we need. We would be most grateful."

"Not so fast, my good Bernal. Who will be the Captain of this undertaking, and what are you trying to accomplish?"

"The expedition will be headed by *Don* Francisco Hernández de Córdoba, a rich man who has plenty of Indians. We have an agreement with him to organize an adventure to search for and discover new lands. We already have three ships, one of which Governor Velázquez has lent us. We hope to explore the area toward the west and set sail, with God's will, in February of this year. The governor has authorized us to gather gold from the mines there."

"You are quite charming, young nobleman," Cortés said, "but among my interests are none so risky as yours, especially when I am not in charge of an expedition. I am devoted to my work here and to my farms and am truly sorry I cannot help you. But there are other men of wealth who may be interested in joining such an adventure."

"Please excuse my impertinence, *Don* Hernando. I am certain there will be other occasions on which I may better serve you."

Fifth Omen

The lake churned with unbridled turbulence; as it continued its seething violence, the wind lifted it even higher. The waves roiled the surface—back and forth—back and forth—until spray filled the air. The force of the mighty waves crashed against the very foundations of the houses until they crumbled and sank to the bottom of the lake. All that occurred in the lake next to us.

Hernández de Córdoba

Hernández de Córdoba's expedition was a disaster. He discovered Yucatán; but the gold he extracted was very poor quality. His party was attacked and would have been annihilated if the Spanish gunpowder had not surprised their attackers. Those of the party who were not killed were wounded. Later on, as they returned through Florida, still others were injured. Finally, they arrived in Cuba, in the area we know now as Havana, where Hernández de Córdoba succumbed to his wounds.

Diego Velázquez, disappointed by the failure of the Córdoba expedition, but anxious to claim the newly discovered lands, quickly recruited soldiers and organized a new attempt. He himself would head an organization of the usual adventure seekers and eccentrics with more conventional freebooters, whose expeditions were conducted at their combined own risk and expense, but always to the ultimate benefit of the Crown.

***

"The *Alcalde*, *Don* Hernán Cortés, may enter," said Diego Velázquez to his doorman.

When Cortés entered his office, Velázquez said, "Before dealing with our agreement and the question of your position as *Alcalde*, I would like to speak about another subject. As Your Grace anticipated, Hernández de Córdoba's expedition ended in tragic failure. The details about a certain Díaz del Castillo are unpleasant, too. But one thing is certain: toward the west, there is land; people live in great cities, with great riches. We must ensure our right of discovery, extract the gold, and perhaps populate the region."

"Certainly, *Don* Diego. That expedition was doubtful from the onset, organized by inept men. They took unnecessary risks so they might have fresh water, yet they didn't even have the proper containers in which to store it. Regardless, Your Grace is correct. It is urgent to confirm the rights of our government over these discoveries. No doubt you have thought about organizing another expedition, better equipped, and under your direct control."

"That's it, precisely, Hernán. Although I know that you still resist participating in adventures that may not be amorous or that would take you away from your farms and cattle, I propose that you command this one. For my part, I will lend two of my own ships. I will also make available to you the supplies that accompanied the other two ships, which carried soldiers and officers with provisions, ships-stores, arms, and horses."

"The officers will have to be capable and proven in battle. Has Your Grace designated them yet?"

"I am in the midst of that, *compadre*. In command, a relative of mine, Juan de Grijalva, will be the captain. Pedro de Alvarado, a brave and gentle nobleman, will command one vessel; Francisco de Montejo will command another, and I reserve for yourself the fourth, provided you accept the obligation and agree to contribute to the expedition."

"Pardon me, sir, Your Grace knows that I have resisted adventures that I do not personally control. Simply put, and no offense to Your Grace, but I will not risk my fortune on insecure enterprises. Grijalva, a good friend of mine, valiant and discreet as he is, is far too young to command an expedition like this one. I feel most uneasy placing myself under his command. Perhaps I shall be proven wrong, but this expedition is doomed to turn out like Hernández de Córdoba's. I have heard Bartolomé de Las Casas say that Grijalva will make a good priest. Think about that, Your Grace!"

"Shut your mouth, you bad-luck bird," *Don* Diego shouted. "Your excessive prudence and the thousand twists and tricks you display disgust me. I was foolish even to invite you here. But do not worry. Anticipating your refusal, I shall ask Alonso Dávila to captain the ship."

Cortés stared evenly at Velázquez. "I have no wish to cause Your Grace distress," he said. "I have only given you my own opinion. To demonstrate that I am not merely obstinate, I propose to lead the enterprise and risk my own fortune, if you will allow me."

"Look, *compadre*, that offer comes too late. I have decided already. Perhaps another time," *Don* Diego sniffed.

"I am always at the command of Your Grace." Cortés bowed deeply before departing.

Sixth Omen

Many times it was heard: a woman crying, shouting into the night; she went about wailing.

"My little children! Now we must go far away.

"My little children! Where shall I take you?"

Grijalva's Expedition

n the 25th of January, 1518, the armada with Grijalva in command left the port of Santiago, Cuba. Velázquez, plumper than ever, bid him goodbye with these words:

"Gentlemen and friends, relatives and servants, before now you have understood that my principal goal and motive in spending my fortune in a similar enterprise has been to serve God and my King. Both will be well served by our efforts to discover new lands. The natives, who by our good example and doctrine, are captivated by our Holy Faith, are the flock of sheep and the herd of the chosen ones. The means by which this noble enterprise will succeed are: each one do what he should, without considering any immediate interest, because God, for whom we undertake such arduous and important work, will favor us at the very least, with great riches."

Bernal Díaz del Castillo, a member of the expedition, smiled and winked at his soldier-companions and spoke up with malicious intent:

"Ah, my Governor, talking about great fortunes! We know well that you instructed Juan de Grijalva to retrieve all the gold and silver he could find. And, if it was prudent, to found a colony or to settle one. If not, he should return to Cuba."

Díaz added, "It's all well for the flock of sheep and the herd to whom we should be the example. Fine. After all, what are gold and silver?"

The armada left Santiago amidst tears, shouts and cannon fire, tinkling music, and the sardonic smile of Hernán Cortés.

Grijalva's expedition was even less fortunate than Córdoba's. Disembarking at Cozumel, Grijalva took formal possession of the island. Then they sailed to Yucatán, where they were careful not to disembark, first from fear of the Indians who had defeated Córdoba, and further because Grijalva had noticed ill will among his crew, who refused to treat the Indians as they had been ordered, according to Las Casas' account.

Persistently and arrogantly, Grijalva's crew openly spurned his command. Alaminos demanded autonomy in navigation and Grijalva submitted. Finally, he disembarked in Yucatán where there was combat and Spaniards died; an arrow knocked out three of Grijalva's teeth. Later, he sailed for Tabasco and named the river he discovered there the 'Grijalva.' The Indians were ready to resist when he finally located an area where there were peaceful natives, who told him about the riches of Culúa in the high plains of Mexico.

In June, looking in from the sea, the expedition saw snow on the Citlaltépetl mountain peaks (Pico de Orizaba). Without realizing it, the Commander received Moctezuma's messengers, who thought the Spaniards were Quetzalcóatl's vanguard, which explained why they were greeted so peacefully. However, the Spaniards sought only to find gold and to bring it home as quickly as possible, so the adventure lost its zeal. Their bread supply became moldy; some were wounded, and many were exhausted. Alaminos could not go on. Dávila and Montejo had no wish to found a colony. In Coatzacoalcos, they recovered six hundred copper hatchets they thought were gold.

Velázquez Prepares Another Expedition

Impatient for news of Grijalva's expedition, Velázquez decided to send a ship to look for them. As captain, he named Cristóbal de Olid.

In Government House, Diego Velázquez met with his secretary and accountant, discreet, confidential confidants who were also sympathetic to Hernán Cortés.

"I am very much concerned, dear friends, that there has been no news of the expedition which we entrusted to the young Juan de Grijalva."

"You should be concerned, Your Grace. He has not sent us reports of the expedition as he promised. We only hope it is not in the Lord's plan, that so many good men and so much valuable equipment are lost."

"All right, then, I have decided that Cristóbal de Olid, a valiant and vigorous man, should captain the ship I have sent him to search for the expedition. Moreover, my good Lares, arrange whatever is needed to organize a better-equipped expedition, so that Cristóbal de Olid may leave immediately to secure those lands for His Majesty, and after that, under the jurisdiction of this government."

"We already told you, my good sir, that Your Grace should not have entrusted that expedition to a nobleman as young as Juan de Grijalva. In Cuba, there is another gentleman who is a most efficient leader and close to you," Lares declared.

Then, de Duero interjected, "We remind Your Grace of the need to assure for Cuba the rights to new discoveries, because *Don* Diego Columbus was most anxious to retain them under his command. Moreover, from an excellent source, we have heard that the Jamaican government is making overtures to the Spanish court for one Francisco de Garay, who is trying to make further discoveries on the mainland."

Velázquez threw up his hands in resignation.

"You are right, my friends. I have thought about sending Chaplain Benito Martín as a delegate to the court of His Majesty Carlos V, to negotiate my designation as *Adelantado* (governor of a province) in these new lands. In that way, we can halt Columbus' efforts to usurp our own plans. Get hold of the Chaplain and arrange his urgent trip to Spain."

"Immediately, Your Grace," said de Duero. "We agree the Chaplain's mission is extremely urgent."

36

Cortés: Captain of the New Expedition

After executing the orders, Velázquez's aides joined Cortés at the inn.

"Events move ahead as we had anticipated, *Don* Hernán. The Governor is impatient because there is no news about the expedition and he is sending a ship to locate it."

"Who is commanding?"

"Cristóbal de Olid."

"He might as well send no one. I am well acquainted with the fair-haired Olid. If he were as intelligent and prudent as he is robust, vigorous and valiant on horseback, then, he would be a consummate man. However, he is not so much a leader, as a follower. Even so, I would very much like to have him under *my* command. On his own, he is incapable of making decisions and I am sure he will not succeed."

"I shall leave immediately," vowed Duero.

"Hold on, my friend. It is not that urgent," said Lares. "Our robust governor, anxious and impatient as he is, following your suggestions, sent the chaplain Martín to assure the title of *Adelantado* for the lands yet to be discovered and declared his determination to organize a much stronger expedition. In this case, to search for Grijalva and consolidate the power of his Royal Majesty in that land."

"Magnificent!" said Cortés. "I should like to lead that expedition, my good friends. Many will debate that decision, but we must act prudently and with skill. I rely on you that I will be named the Senior Captain. You know I will divide the profits with you. For a long time I have had a premonition that I would have great success serving our good King *Don* Carlos and the progress of our people."

"Have faith, *Don* Hernán! Your Grace is the best man in our entire island for this enterprise and we will exert all our influence so that you will be designated Captain. We suggest that you contribute an important share of the money, supplies, and arms in order to convince *Don* Diego that he needs your participation. We do not doubt it will be a significant expedition."

"Then that's what we will do, my good friends. We should be in constant touch. From this moment on, I will prepare plans for a great expedition. I am certain that this is the opportunity we have been waiting for!"

As Cortés had foreseen, Cristóbal de Olid's expedition was a disaster. A cross-wind off the Yucatán coast forced him to drop anchor. But the chains broke and Olid returned in disgrace to Cuba.

Pedro de Alvarado had also arrived in Cuba after locating Grijalva, who sent back the injured of the expedition as well as the gold they had found, for which Velázquez was grateful. In the meantime, the governor had begun to organize a new expedition. De Duero and Lares succeeded in convincing other schemers that Velázquez name Cortés as the Senior Captain.

"Damn!" Velázquez exclaimed in front of Duero and Lares. "Time passes and still I have no word from the Captain I dispatched for information. How stupid Olid is! And that relative of mine, Grijalva! It was bad luck to appoint him commander of the armada. Nothing! Nothing! Nothing! I hope it is not God's will that I lose everything."

"You are right to be concerned," de Duero said. "A lot of time has passed. One of the captains should have returned. If Your Honor agrees, we should send a stronger armada to learn the destiny of the two ships that are lost, as well as to find the six men from Nicuesa's ship-wrecked expedition. Above all, we need assurance that the Cuban government shall take possession of the new lands."

"You are right, Duero. The new armada has already cost me dearly. I need someone who will be associated with us."

"Absolutely, Your Honor; for that fleet you must name—once and for all—a Captain-General who, with his heritage will commit himself to the success of the mission and instill confidence in others to enlist and share in the enterprise," said Lares. "However, I hesitate to suggest to your lordship a candidate for Captain-General. Surely, you have someone in mind among the many you have considered."

"There are so many things to think about," said Velázquez. "But you are right. It is time to designate quickly a Captain for this enterprise. Indeed, I have thought about many gentlemen. Certain noblemen whom I have confidence in have recommended Vasco Porcallo, others say Augustín Bermúdez, others suggest my relative Velázquez Borrego, and even Bernadino Velázquez. But I have no confidence in my relatives who exert personal influence. Because of my relationship with him, I am inclined in favor of Porcallo."

"Even God wouldn't name him!" blustered Amador de Lares. "Remember, Porcallo is related to the Count of Feria and for that reason is most haughty. He glories in his influence in the Court. Pardon my forwardness, but he is the least capable."

"That's true!" Duero concurred. "Think well on it, Your Grace. Lares is correct when he says he has no confidence in Porcallo. It would be a great risk for him to lead the armada. The Captain-General ought to be a man in whom you have utter confidence, someone you like a great deal and one who owes Your Grace everything; who respects spiritual ties and gratefulness; who is the right age and knows how to use his sword and who has refinement; who is a good Christian and capable of investing his fortune with you in this enterprise. Finally, a man tested by Your Grace and well-established in this island, who has a wife and family who will guarantee his risk. . . ."

"Stop, stop, I beg you, for God's sake. You are describing my *compadre* Hernán Cortés."

"My friend, too, of course!" Duero put in. "It never occurred to me, but now that your Lordship mentions it, I believe, indeed, that the captain of the armada should be someone like *Don* Hernán."

"And why not *Don* Hernán?" asked Lares.

"Hernán Cortés!" exclaimed Velázquez. "My *compadre.* Nevertheless, it occurs to me that I always have to convince him to accept responsibility. It was I who insisted that he marry *Doña* Catalina; it was I who urged him to be ship's captain in Grijalva's expedition. He is stubborn and pursues amorous escapades to the very point of scandal—and he's given up on adventure. With his farms, cattle, and mines, he does very well."

"Why don't you try to persuade him?" asked Lares. "We can try, but we have very little influence on him. You must make the effort, Your Honor. He is your man."

After thinking about it, stroking his beard and patting his mighty belly, Velázquez decided.

"You are both quite right! I will speak to him and try to convince him to accept. To save time, dictate the initial instructions to Escalante, the notary public. You know what these are: to search for the Grijalva and Olid expeditions; to find and rescue the six Spaniards who may be held captive by the natives; to explore the lands and inquire about the inhabitants and learn if they have religious orders, beliefs and ceremonies; to discover what animals and riches they boast of; to inquire if there are giants, yet human beings, with long ears and the faces of dogs. And, naturally, how to bring out any gold and silver. As for colonizing, I shall speak to Cortés about that after he accepts. Perhaps twisting his arm—as I did for his marriage—will convince him."

So it was that Velázquez "convinced" Cortés to be Captain-General of the Armada. Cortés complied, adding an important share of his wealth, at least as much as Velázquez.

In the meantime, Pedro de Alvarado arrived at Santiago with the wounded from the Grijalva expedition and the gold jewelry for Velázquez's pleasure. The governor immediately sent the gold to Chaplain Martín to take to the Spanish emperor, since he had asked the king to name Velázquez *Adelantado* of all the lands discovered in Yucatán. Martín did obtain the title for his superior. For himself, he garnered Abbot of Rica Isla. Velázquez ordered that fiestas and games be organized to celebrate the arrival of Pedro de Alvarado.

For the bullfights that celebrated Alvarado's arrival, a corral and seats were constructed in an amphitheatre in the Santiago main plaza.

"My dear *compadre* Hernán," said Velázquez. "I was right to convince you of the importance of my poor relative Grijalva's discoveries. But now he feels humiliated. Before us we have enormous lands to discover with an abundance of gold and many dark secrets. I have already sent Chaplain Martín with gifts and momentoes for our Catholic majesty and I am sure to be designated *Adelantado* of Yucatán and the discovered lands. This is our greatest opportunity and venture, *compadre.*

"That's the way I see it, too, *Don* Diego," Cortés agreed. "You have persuaded me to contribute my own fortune to this enterprise and only you could have succeeded in that. Now I leave my family, my duties as *alcalde*, my farms, mines, and cattle to serve you better. I will add to the coffers all that I can borrow, but I want your cooperation to procure the best and most experienced people. I guarantee there will be no more failures. I should like to meet Pedro de Alvarado in order to learn first hand about the lands he discovered. Perhaps Your Honor can convince him to accompany me on this expedition."

"Call Alvarado. Dazed by those beautiful women, infatuated as a banty rooster, he is busy taking advantage of his fine figure as a man."

When Alvarado arrived, Velázquez said, "*Don* Pedro de Alvarado, I have the pleasure of presenting *Don* Hernán Cortés, whom I have designated Captain-General of the great armada we send to search for Grijalva as well as to accomplish what that fool failed to."

"It's an honor to make your acquaintance, Your Honor, *Don* Pedro. Your enterprising fame is legion as is the fame of your four brothers, whom I should like to accompany me in this expedition made possible by the benevolence, generosity and reputation of *Don* Diego Velázquez," said Cortés formally.

"The honor is all mine, *Don* Hernán. We discovered marvelous lands expansive and full of riches, well populated with savage people, as well as gold and silver.

"There are huge mountains. At a distance, we saw very high peaks covered with snow that blocked our view to the north. We feel deeply about Juan de Grijalva's anxiety and that he suffers so much. I only hope to God he is not lost. The next expedition will need a devoted, vigorous, brave captain who is extremely skilled. To my knowledge this enterprise is one of the greatest any man has ever attempted. I do not doubt, *Don* Hernán, that Your Grace is the man who can accomplish it. I shall speak with my brothers and advise you of our opinion very soon. And now, *Don* Diego, if you please, allow me to continue my chit-chat with the beautiful young ladies. It has been months since I have experienced feminine charms."

"I am well satisfied, *Don* Pedro, that you are my kind of man," said Cortés.

"But none of your excesses, *Don* Hernán," interrupted Velázquez, shaking an admonishing forefinger. "I have strict instructions for you regarding the treatment of Indian women as well as concerning troop behavior. Anyway, *Don* Pedro, go on about your business, as it pleases you. I am confident you will be joining *Don* Hernán in our adventure."

Once Cortés received the title Captain-General of the Armada, the organization of the enterprise was accelerated. Initially, seven ships were supplied with stores and other needs for the crews, especially those who comprised the newest arrivals to the expedition. After Cortés was named Captain-General, he committed his capital as a partner of the enterprise, even though he was actually in debt. Velázquez contributed an important share and other partners did otherwise. The expeditionaries freely agreed to this corporate effort, submitting their will to the royal authority.

During this period, Cristóbal de Olid's ship returned to Santiago, and soon after Grijalva's battered ship arrived bearing gold, much information and knowledge, plus the six hundred copper hatchets which they had thought at first were gold. This "discovery" became the joke of the island.

Velázquez and Cortés went to the docks to inspect the boats for the expedition. In their retinue, a crazy jester warned Velázquez that Cortés would leave unexpectedly with his armada.

"*Compadre*, Your Grace must exert a greater effort to complete the ship's supplies. The expeditions that failed diminished my capital and my resources. Grijalva's return excites me more about his expedition as it confirms the importance of the new lands. Make a greater effort," said Velázquez.

"I am already doing the impossible, *Don* Diego. However, my credit is diminishing. Nevertheless, in order to serve you better, I will borrow all I can. But have no doubt! The armada will soon leave with sufficient supplies. What concerns me is recruiting more people. There are not many gentlemen or peons who wish to take such a risk after seeing the failures of Hernández de Córdoba and the recent arrival of Grijalva. Those with limited capital have no interest in speculating on gold."

Velázquez was going on ahead to speak to a group when he stopped and called to Cortés.

"Then let's spread the word that we are going to colonize, too, not just explore for gold and silver. That way, many who are anxious to own their own lands and Indians will go along with you. You are aware, my *compadre*, that my designation as *Adelantado* has not yet been confirmed by the Spanish Court. While I have little interest in colonizing for Columbus' benefit, I do wish to make up for the losses I suffered in the Córdoba expedition and later and even worse with Grijalva and Olid."

"I do understand your anxiety, *Don* Diego. But you have a wonderful idea, as usual, to spread the word that we aim to colonize. We can even support colonists in some way, perhaps including some flexible clause in the instructions that Your Grace gives me. Then you can be sure that I shall always do what I am ordered."

"Very sound idea," Velázquez winked broadly at Cortés. "I shall instruct de Duero to include in the orders—and I don't mean to offend you—a clause that disallows concubinage, public crimes, and carnal excesses with the natives."

"In good time, *Don* Diego," Cortés grinned. "I will execute those orders as well as the others Your Grace has given me. I certainly intend to explore for precious metals and Your Honor may be sure I will not bring you copper instead of gold as the unfortunate Grijalva managed to do."

"I have severely reprimanded my relative Grijalva for his stupidities and weaknesses. Now he is down in the mouth, grumbling, locked away in his house in Trinidad [Cuba] unable to face me."

"The unfortunate *Don* Juan de Grijalva is better suited for the priesthood than a shipmaster, as Las Casas says! Well, *Don* Diego, since we are now in accord, I shall order a banner and appeal publicly—with trumpets and drum rolls—to the people to join my company."

When the retinue finally reached the two men and the conversation became general, the buffoon who accompanied Velázquez came forward, reciting vulgarities and making gestures, and exclaimed:

> "To the glory, to the glory of my friend, *Don* Diego,
> who has found a Captain here born in Extremadura,
> to lead a great venture
> and set sail the armada.
> But you will be bankrupt, penniless.
> He is a rake, but respectable,
> Diego, you must listen to reason."

These verses caused an angry outcry. Diego Velázquez tried to interrupt the jester, while Cortés shrugged off the idiot. But Andrés de Duero, the secretary, began to slap the clown on the neck.

"Shut up, you crazy drunk," de Duero cried. "Don't be such a mischief-maker. We know very well that these malicious comments—under the guise of wit—do not emanate from you."

Cortés, giving no importance to the incident and in a calm voice said to the irritated Velázquez:

"How sad is the human condition, *Don* Diego. Again, as years ago, long before we were *compadres*, badly intentioned and seditious people wish to create prejudice against me. No doubt you know who they are. They do not understand my proven loyalty. Without the support and the benevolence of Your Honor, I would be nothing."

"That's fine for you to say, *compadre*. But when the river roars, water flows."

"Easy does it, Your Honor. You know I am ready to serve you. But if your distrust offends my devotion for you, I shall withdraw my participation in the enterprise and continue serving you with my farms."

"Oh, it's not all that serious, *Don* Hernán. By my disposition, I am sensitive to these things and that rogue simply took me by surprise. So let us continue. I have complete confidence in your loyalty and your skill."

"As shall be proved in good time, *Don* Diego. But you can be sure that with my good services and with the help of God, in a short time I will make Your Grace an even richer and more illustrious gentleman."

Concluding his visit to the port to evaluate the progress of the expedition, Cortés vouchsafed to Duero and Lares:

"Our friend Velázquez has no confidence. The intrigues of that crazy Juan Millán and the ambitions of others are bearing fruit. I know my *compadre* all too well. He conceals it now, but later he will try to land a blow. So we must anticipate it. Help me polish the wording in the orders, especially that clause about behavior toward women, which may turn out to be very offensive and repulsive. While you are deliberating, your minds will be relieved. For my part, I shall set sail soon, even though all the supplies are not here. Those men who returned with Grijalva will be valuable and so will any other recruits I can muster."

"For our part," Lares said, "we will try to pacify *Don* Diego. We know him very well. He will waste enough time for Your Grace to easily weigh anchor. No doubt with the help of God everything will go well."

"With God's help and with a great effort on my part, tomorrow we will recruit the men with street-hawkers standing beneath the banners that I had made."

To settle the most important matter—recruiting more men—Cortés ordered public criers to stand under the flags and pennants and shout the announcement: "Whoever would like to go in the company of Hernán Cortés to the newly discovered lands to conquer and colonize will be given their share of gold and silver and the riches discovered there, plus a plot of land with Indians after they are subdued."

These hawkers stood under the banners adorned in gold with the royal arms and cross that read: "Brothers and friends. We follow the sign of the Holy Cross with true faith and with it we will be victorious."

Many men gathered around, among them Bernal Díaz del Castillo.

So it was, one night, without official notice and under a seal of secrecy, that Cortés gave orders to set sail immediately. *Don* Hernán ordered Hernando Alfonso, in charge of supplying the meat—for which he paid him with a gold chain that hung from his neck—to deliver the cattle quickly, as they intended to embark before dawn. Turning to Díaz del Castillo, Cortés directed his remarks:

"Bernal, my friend, go immediately and locate the Alvarado brothers, Gonzalo de Sandoval, Juan Velázquez de León, Cristóbal de Olid, and Alonso Hernández Portocarrero. A few are here and the others close by; you will find them. Invite them all to meet me at Juan de Grijalva's house in Trinidad, where I will sail very soon."

"I will do it, Captain," Díaz del Castillo answered, then hurried off.

Cortés Bids Velázquez Farewell

At dawn, the clatter of preparations for the expedition awakened Velázquez. Quickly sensing what was going on, but fat as ever, he dashed half-dressed and panting toward the docks. When Cortés saw him from the ship, he boarded a canoe and asked for his *alcalde* staff. Surrounded by men visibly displaying their guns and cross-bows, the Spanish *conquistador* brandished his symbol of office as he greeted the governor.

"How is it possible, *compadre*, that you leave in such a manner?" Velázquez roared furiously. "Is this a proper way to bid me farewell?"

"Your Honor, please pardon me," Cortés said with a smile. "We made our preparations without thinking. But it was at your pleasure that you sent me. . . ."

"I prefer to send you to a thousand devils!" grumbled Velázquez as Cortés withdrew, making the appropriate gestures of respect that signaled his departure. It was the 18th of November, 1518.

". . . these matters and similar ones, must be achieved rather than thought about . . ."

As soon as he was back aboard ship, Cortés declared: "Alaminos!* Set course immediately for Trinidad! Hoist the sails."

---

* The fleet navigator, Antón de Alaminos, acted as pilot to Columbus on his last voyage.—Trans.

He turned to his lieutenants:

"Make certain we have all the rations and supplies we need. Then let me know how many men remained on the island and how many replacements we must recruit."

Meanwhile, Velázquez, still furious, arrived at the Government House and summoned his secretary Duero:

"You see! How right the crazy one was when he noted 'the river had water.' My *compadre* has sailed away. You and your suggestion! Since Cortés left without sufficient provisions, he will be obliged to secure them in Trinidad. Send a fast messenger to the *Alcalde* there, my brother-in-law Francisco Verdugo, with instructions that Cortés be detained and return the traitor to me under guard. Then order my servant Diego de Ordaz to follow Verdugo so that he may inform me about the armada and if Verdugo is carrying out my instructions. May a lightning bolt strike him!"

"We will comply with Your Grace's orders," said Duero. "Calm yourself, surely there is some misunderstanding."

"His birth may be questionable, but how well he understands his worth."

When Cortés arrived at Trinidad, his friend, Juan de Grijalva, provided lodging. Soon the others whom he had summoned joined them: the five Alvarado brothers, Gonzalo de Sandoval, Juan Velázquez de León, Cristóbal de Olid and Alonso Hernández Portocarrero.

Cortés greeted them.

"I welcome you and my sincere thanks to Your Graces for accepting my invitation, and to you, *Don* Juan de Grijalva, for welcoming us to your house.

"We are about to begin the greatest adventure attempted by valiant men since ancient times. Great lands laden with riches and mysteries await our heroic exploits to better serve God and our Catholic Majesty. We have already heard the story of the unjust treatment of *Don* Juan de Grijalva, although he is Diego Velázquez's relative. Extensive lands with large populations, gold, silver, jewels are there awaiting the thrust of our bravado; the natives on those coasts speak about empires in the interior, Culúa and Mexico.

"I command a strong armada with the contributions of many noblemen who came with us, and mainly with Diego Velázquez's share and my own patrimony we supplied the fleet anchored here in the bay. I need brave, vigorous captains and I offer you glory, fame, power and riches, which, with the help of the Holy Cross we will acquire, as we expand its faith throughout those unenlightened lands."

"Your Grace has spoken emotional and beautiful words," said Juan Velázquez, "such that move my spirit to accept your offer, but, like *Don* Juan de Grijalva, I too am a relative of Diego Velázquez and I have heard that you set sail for this port without his permission."

"You are very well acquainted with your relative, Diego Velázquez and you know well the influence of his will. True enough, I have had minor differences with him that obliged me to leave somewhat precipitately, but I am certain that his judgment, which has been influenced by jealous and unkind people, will be rectified."

"*Don* Juan Velázquez," interrupted Grijalva, "my condition unfortunately precludes me from joining *Don* Hernán. Nevertheless, and perhaps for that very reason, I suggest that one speak with total frankness. You and I, as *Don* Diego's relatives, understand that he can be capricious, suspicious, impetuous and even unjust. His behavior towards me after I had endured the losses in my expedition filled me with indignation. I was suffering and making him rich, while he was awaiting the benefits in the comfort of his corpulence in Santiago. Without listening to me and giving full credence to my libelers, he abused me, humiliating me so that I couldn't bear it any longer. I remind you that nothing good can be expected from *Don* Diego. Even though we are close relatives, tell me how he divided the lands and Indians that we discovered? With him or without him my unfortunate adventure accomplished that which I was unable to finish. I am certain that fame awaits you."

Cortés nodded gratefully.

"You have heard the experienced voice of *Don* Juan de Grijalva. I have instructions signed by the Governor to carry out this enterprise. Here they are. Our actions are legal. Moreover, I tell you that *Don* Diego Velázquez prefers that we recover gold and silver rather than conquer and colonize which will be in detriment to the service of God and our King *Don* Carlos. I invite you to conquer and colonize another world! Do you accept? Here is my hand!"

Each of the captains grasped Cortés' hand. The last was Portocarrero.

"I know," Cortés said to him, "that you do not have a horse. It's unthinkable that such a vigorous Captain does not have a mount. Come with me. Outside is Juan Sedeño, who arrived with his boat full of casaba bread and salt pork and horses that he wishes to sell in Santiago. Let's go and convince him to sell us all the provisions, or better still ask that he join us in the adventure."

They left.

"*Don* Juan Sedeño," Cortés said to him, "it's better to arrive on time than to be invited. How opportune is your presence here. Before we start to talk business, take this gold knot," and he took it off of his suit, "for that mare that you have."

Sedeño's mare for Portocarrero

"*Don* Hernán, honestly, the mare is insignificant for the payment. . . ."

"Nothing is too good for my friend Portocarrero who will favor me by riding that mare when we attempt great heroic feats conquering the unknown lands."

"I am obliged to Your Grace, *Don* Hernán, and I know that I will offend you if I do not accept such a splendid gift. On the back of this mare we will better serve God and our Catholic Majesty, under the command of Your Grace."

"And now, friend Juan Sedeño, let us talk business. We need your bread and salt pork."

"I have to go to Santiago; but if you pay the cost of the mare we can get together."

Sedeño returned jubilantly and said to his subordinates:

"Not only have we sold bread and meats but a boat and crew to *Don* Hernando. Shout the news to our friends that Juan Sedeño is going with Cortés in the adventure, to better serve God and to expand the dominions of His Majesty *Don* Carlos and to extract gold and be given land and Indians. Those who wish to join me will have their share."

"Already we have eleven ships and everything seems to be going well for us," Cortés remarked, smiling at Portocarrero.

"With your winning manner, generosity and gift of speech, *Don* Hernán, everything will fall in place. We will have all we need. You know well how to turn the wheel of fortune that attracts bold, audacious men."

"Well, let's keep it turning with all our good efforts."

Getting together with the captains and soldiers, Cortés said to them:

"We have ten days to get the arms ready. Each ship's Captain make ready the artillery, which consists of ten bronze cannon and some smaller ones. You, Mesa, Arteaga and Catalán, who are good artillerymen, clean and test the weapons. Have ready the cannon balls and gunpowder, and compute the range. Bartolomé de Usagre will help you."

He continued to give instructions. "All of the blacksmiths begin to make iron arrowheads. Each Captain should order the repair of crossbows and strips of leather; be sure that he is supplied with provisions and make arrows and notches for the crossbows and to store everything. Be careful when you aim at the terrain as you test the range of each crossbow. And you, my deputy, buy all of the cotton available and order that all seamstresses and craftsmen construct snug-fitting clothes of cotton, because according to the information that Grijalva has given me, these Indians hurl spears and arrows and fling lances. Since they have no breast plates or shields, they are dressed in quilted cotton jackets that protect them from Indian flints.

"Now, let us complete our supplies: Let each Captain make certain his ship has feeding stalls and mangers and enough corn and dry grass for the horses and that these be divided evenly among all the ships. Later on, we will have a review of the soldiers and discuss how to fight with precision. I have conferred with Grijalva and his men about the way Indians in those lands are accustomed to waging war."

From Trinidad, Hernán Cortés sailed toward San Cristóbal de Havana with his army in nine ships. In Havana they added two more with additional provisions. There they carried out the instructions Cortés gave them in Trinidad and the blacksmiths joined the expedition.

Velázquez, on learning that the *Alcalde* of Trinidad had not dared to detain Cortés and that Ordaz had gone over to Cortés' side, became more enraged and sent instructions to his deputy Barba and to Juan Velázquez de León that they detain Cortés. But once again, the same thing happened as in Trinidad. Pedro Barba, the *alcalde*, wrote to Velázquez that "he did not dare seize Cortés because he was surrounded by strong soldiers."

Fray Bartolomé de Olmedo approached Cortés' ship in the bay. Cortés was reviewing the instructions he had given to his Captains.

"*Don* Hernán, our friend Duero informs us from Santiago about how *Don* Diego Velázquez is raging mad because you were not detained in Trinidad either by Verdugo or by Diego de Ordaz who were already in your 'camp' and now he informs his lieutenant Pedro Barba and *Don* Juan Velázquez de León and others who favor him, and are on the muster, that they detain you and ship you in irons to Santiago."

"Oh, how badly informed is my *compadre* and so stubborn!" Directing himself to an aide who was nearby, Cortés said to him: "Call Barba and Juan Velázquez de León and those who are on this roll to resolve this important matter here and now, in front of our friends."

After they assembled, Cortés said in a loud voice: "My friend Barba, I know about the orders that the badly informed *Don* Diego Velázquez has given to you and other noblemen to arrest me. I want all of you to know," he said raising his voice louder, "that I am waiting upon *Don* Diego to explain to him, one more time, that he has listened to slanderers and those who bear me ill will. I am willing to carry out the pact of our association and the instructions that he gave me. We are resolved to continue this enterprise at the service to God and His Majesty and it will be to his detriment if this group of brave men remains adrift because he has listened to deceitful knaves. Is that not a fact, my friends?"

"Look here, Captain," said Juan Velázquez de León. "We tried to deal with this affair when we were with Grijalva. I am Diego's relative, too, but I do not owe him anything and am free to go wherever I please. You deal with Diego: I will go with you if—as you have offered—you divide your profits with me and the rest."

"That's what I have proposed, and will inform Diego Velázquez what I have said here."

"Well—then, we are with you."

"And you, Pedro Barba, *Alcalde* of Havana, what do you plan to do?"

"Hombre! Hernán Cortés, *Alcalde* of Santiago, what can I do, seeing that Your Grace is so powerful with so many troops? I know that you wish it and I too want you to resolve this with Governor Velázquez! I also will write to him. And may this not tarnish our friendship!"

"You are prudent and a good friend, *Alcalde*, and my heart tells me we shall soon see each other."

"God be willing, Hernán."

Cortés turned to his captains and soldiers. "This matter is resolved. With the help of God and the agreement of all, tomorrow we will set sail in these nine ships to meet in Punta de San Antón with the other two ships which are loading supplies. And from there to serve our King and to expand Spain even further! For *Santiago*!"*

"*Santiago*!" everyone roared.

---

* Santiago! (St. James) the war-cry of the Spaniards on engaging the Moors.—Trans.

Seventh Omen

The seventh fateful omen occurred in Tenochtitlan. Occasionally, something was trapped in the fishing nets, and one day the people working in the water caught an ash-colored bird resembling a crane. They took it to Moctezuma in the *Casa de lo Negro*.

The sun had reached its peak; it was mid-day. There was something like a mirror on top of the bird's head, almost like a shiny disk in the center of its head, as if perforating it.

The sky was in full view as were the stars, the *Masteletes*. Moctezuma perceived it as a bad omen when he saw the *Masteletes* [a group of three stars in Taurus very near the Pleiades]. But when he looked for the second time at the disk on the bird's head, he saw something unusual: In the distance, people in a long line were hurrying toward each other, pushing, warlike, and carrying on their shoulders something like a deer. He immediately called his magicians and sages, saying to them:

"Can you interpret the meaning of what I saw? Something like people, standing . . . agitated! . . ."

Wishing to give an answer they looked everywhere, but everything had disappeared; they didn't see anything.

They Will Come . . . in the Year Ce-Acatl

All the ominous signs that had happened in the previous ten years were studied and analyzed by Moctezuma and his sages. With deep conviction, terrified and discouraged, Moctezuma ended his deliberations and said to his augurs:

"My sages, magicians, diviners, after listening and meditating, this is certain. They will come! . . . They will soon arrive, when the fifty-two year cycle is completed. They will arrive as it is predicted in the *Ce-Acatl*. They are already arriving. It will be the new Sun, the new age. Quetzalcóatl will come to claim his throne, the one that was lent to us. We will be the protagonists; we will be the witnesses to this fatal change. We wait with fear, with fortitude, disposed to accept what will come. . . ."

And that is what he said to the Counselor and his allies. He called Cuitláhuac, his brother, and Cuauhtémoc, his cousin, and repeated to them.

"They will come. . . . They are already coming. They demand their cycle and their throne. Our Lord Quetzalcóatl comes to demand what is his. We will witness it; we will see it. All time passes and arrives at its stillness. No longer will we have the power. The new era is coming; the new Sun. We will see it. It's our turn to witness it."

Cuitláhuac affected an expression of profound concern, so much so that the young Cuauhtémoc appeared displeased and, looking straight at Moctezuma, he said:

"Lord, my lord, great lord; Mexico is strong; stronger than ever. There will always be a Mexico. We have no reason to accept the fact that we have arrived at a place of tranquility. We will struggle, we will continue to be what we are. Do not allow destiny to overwhelm your spirit. We will fight. We will oppose; we. . . ."

Moctezuma interrupted him with a severe glance, and with fatal resignation said to him:

"It will all be in vain, young Cuauhtémoc. We will merely be witnesses to the great new Sun. The resistance and the struggle will be in vain. A new Sun will come. There is no use opposing it! . . . It will be in vain . . . In vain. . . .
"THEY ARE COMING. . . ."

On the Way

n the 1st of February, 1519, after Mass, Hernán Cortés and his armies sailed from Havana. The nine ships anchored there joined two others that had taken on supplies in different ports.

One ship, piloted by a man named Camacho, had on board Pedro de Alvarado and his four brothers, and among others, Bernal Díaz del Castillo, ignoring Cortés' instructions, went ahead of the other ships and prematurely arrived at Cozumel. Pedro de Alvarado attacked the Indians and captured two men and a woman, forty turkeys and jewels of little value. When Cortés got there, he summoned Camacho and Alvarado, but did not reveal his anger to them. Camacho was placed in irons and the other was severely reprimanded. He ordered Alvarado to return everything he had taken.

"In all my soul, I don't understand it! What an error you have committed when you misinterpreted my order, sailing off ahead of the other ships and attacking Indians and taking their possessions."

Then Cortés ordered:

"Lieutenant, put Camacho in irons and have him locked up in his own ship, with the death penalty for anyone who attempts to free him. An exemplary punishment will be given to whoever does not comply with my orders. I hope that everyone understands the need for discipline now that we are responsible for our own actions."

Then he added:

"And you, Pedro de Alvarado, whom I esteem very highly, it seems to me you have more fighting blood than judgment. You do not seem disposed to take into consideration the consequences of your raid. You must understand that conquering a land quickly and taking the natives' possessions is not the way to subdue these lands. In my own mind, I cannot justify that you used a sword to capture three Indians and forty turkeys. I do not. I do not want to have a bad beginning. Ahead of us we have great promises to fulfill, so think before you act. You, yourself, must free the Indians you have captured and return the gold that you took, as well as the turkeys, and then give the natives a gift of some kind."

Bernal Díaz del Castillo commented to his companions:

"Fortunately we now have a Captain who commands so that what happened to Grijalva will not happen to us. If Hernán can dominate the influential Alvarado, this expedition will continue going forward and we will better serve Our Lord."

"I would like all of the Captains to meet me here!" ordered Cortés.

"My lords and companions. On leaving this island, Cozumel, we are exposed to our own fortunes. Those who are here and a few others who have remained in La Española, combined to make up this enterprise in service to our faith and for the greatness of the King, *Don* Carlos. Something happened here that must not be repeated. The Captain's order must be strictly enforced; disrespect to him will cost you dearly. I will prosecute without thinking twice. The number two is infamous. Only one head has the right to command. And that is exercised by the Captain-General. Understand that once and for all and forever. And now, as we have disposed of this matter, call a review of the soldiers. You, Portocarrero, give me the report."

After the review, Portocarrero approached Hernán Cortés and said:

"Captain, your orders have been executed. There are eleven ships. You are in command of the flag ship. Pedro de Alvarado and his brothers have command of *San Sebastián*, a good ship.

"Francisco de Montejo has another good ship. Cristóbal de Olid, another. Juan Velázquez de León, another. Juan de Escalante, another. Francisco de Morla, another. Escobar "*el Paje*" another. The smallest vessel, like a brigantine, is captained by Ginés Nortes. And I, Alonso Hernández Portocarrero, have another ship. Each ship has its pilot and the chief navigator is Antón de Alaminos. We are 508 men not counting the ship's crew and the marine pilots, who number one hundred. The sixteen horses and mares are spirited and fast.

"Among the men, thirty-two are crossbowmen and thirteen are artillerymen. We have ten cannon (with bronze shot) and four small cannon or muskets. Gunpowder and cannon balls we have in abundance and storage for all the arms. This armada will not suffer any damage."

"Castilan." Jerónimo de Aguilar

"Report acknowledged," announced Cortés. Then he noticed a group of Indians in large canoes next to his ship. He asked Melchorejo what language they were speaking. Melchorejo, a native of Yucatán, had been brought back to Cuba by Grijalva and had learned some Spanish.

"Do you know who these Indians are?"

"Captain, they are traders from the mainland and are coming to the island."

"Call Martín Ramos and Bernal del Castillo."

When the order was carried out he said to them:

"Juan de Grijalva as well as Hernández de Córdoba told me that both of you were in their expeditions and you heard the natives they met say 'Castilan, Castilan.'"

"Yes, that is true Captain," responded Bernal. "It was after we discovered Cape Catoche and before we captured these Indians, Julián and Melchor, the one who is squint-eyed that now is their spokesman. They came in a peaceful manner, about fifty Indians in canoes, and made signs with their hands inquiring if we came from the place where the Sun rises. And they said, 'Castilan, Castilan,' but frankly there was no Spanish spoken."

"I have thought about this often," said Cortés, absorbed in thought, "and by chance there may have been some Spaniards shipwrecked in that land. I think that it would be well if we ask these traders of Cozumel if they know anything about them. Ask Melchorejo, who now speaks Spanish, to ask them."

After Melchorejo inquired, in bad Spanish, he informed Cortés:

"These tradesfolk say that white-skinned people with beards are on the mainland, about two *soles* from here."

"Ask them in what condition they are." After he inquired, Melchorejo said:

"They are slaves. With letters, some jewels and ransom they will be allowed to come here."

All of the Spaniards were joyful and Cortés then ordered:

"*Don* Diego de Ordaz, prepare two small boats and a ransom of beads. With twenty crossbowmen and musketeers sail to Cape Catoche. Accompanied by these traders, take a letter I will dictate to the scribe on behalf of our brothers who are captives. Wait there eight days with the larger boat and send back the smaller with your report."

The *cacique** did not read Spanish but the importance of the note did not escape him:

> Lords and brothers: Here in Cozumel I have learned that you are under the authority of a *cacique*. Mercifully, I ask that you may be allowed to come to Cozumel. So that may happen, I am sending a boat with soldiers, and a ransom for you to give to the Indians with whom you live. The boat will wait for you for eight days; but come as quickly as you can. I have five hundred soldiers and eleven ships. With them you shall be well looked after. I shall remain on this island, then take the route to a village that is called 'Potonchan' in the Tabascan language.

Ordaz sailed off, crossed the channel and within two days the tradesmen gave the letter to the Spanish captive, Jerónimo de Aguilar, who obtained permission from his *cacique* to go where the other Spaniard, Gonzalo Guerrero, lived. He, too, read the letter, but because he had many ties, a wife and children, he refused to be ransomed:

"Brother Aguilar. I am married and have three children and the natives consider me a *cacique* and a Captain when we wage war. You go with God. My face is disfigured and my ears pierced. What would my Spanish brothers say when they saw me? And you see how beautiful my children are. To save my life, you give me these green glass beads. I will tell them that my brothers sent them to me from Spain."

Jerónimo de Aguilar argued with Gonzalo Guerrero, saying that, if he wanted to, he could bring his children, but that he should not lose his soul because of an Indian wife. They were in the midst of this discussion when Guerrero's wife brusquely reproached Aguilar, saying to him: "See how rudely this slave speaks to my husband? Go away and do not talk to him again."

---

* *Cacique* is the term usually employed by the Spanish as equivalent to chief or king. It is *not Mexican* but a Cuban word.—Trans.

And she pushed him while Jerónimo de Aguilar went on trying to convince Guerrero, who still remained with his wife and children and would not accompany Aguilar.

The eight days had already passed when Jerónimo de Aguilar returned, so he did not find the ships. Sadly, Aguilar returned to his confinement.

When Cortés learned the two ships had returned without the Spaniards, he was very angry and strongly rebuked the Captain.

"In truth, *Don* Diego, you have acted in a careless way concerning our brothers. I never would have thought that you would return without them. Now we know for certain they are captives on the mainland. Someone more capable than you will rescue them from their sad condition. And you, Berrio, what is so pressing that you must interrupt me when I am investigating such an important matter?"

"*Señor* Captain, some seamen have stolen meat and refuse to return it."

"Oh, what the devil! We must have order and respect in this armada!"

Turning to his lieutenant, he said:

"Investigate this accusation. If the seamen are guilty of theft, they will be flogged. However, if you cannot be certain, then Berrio will suffer the whipping."

The mariners were found guilty and they were whipped publicly despite pleas from their Captain, one of the Alvarado brothers.

After the punishment was completed, Cortés, quite enraged, proclaimed:

"May this serve as a warning. Now there are floggings; tomorrow, the death penalty. I swear, I will tolerate neither theft or insubordination."

Bernal del Castillo commented to his companions:

"There is no room for doubt that we have a Captain in command of everything! Now we know our enterprise will be successful!"

The First Idols Demolished

So it was at this time in Cozumel that the natives made a pilgrimage to the *teocalli* [temple] of idols. In the morning following the previous incidents, many Indians from the mainland came together and burned incense and prepared the sacrificial ceremonies. A priest dressed in long robes climbed to the top of the pyramid and began to invoke the gods.

Through his interpreter, Melchorejo, Cortés was told what the priest was saying, and he interrupted with outcries that Melchorejo translated for the Indians.

"If you wish to be our brothers, give up these devilish preachings and those sacrifices to these horrendous idols that represent evil. You are living in error, making these wicked ceremonies that will take you all to hell. We have come to take you down the path of the true faith, whose symbol is this Holy Cross where Our Lord, Jesus Christ died to redeem our sins. You should worship this Cross and this image of Our Lady and thus save your souls. Sow good seeds in this life and everything will go well for you.

"You, Bernal, take your companions and break those idols into pieces and throw them down the stairs."

Which is what he did.

Indignant, the Indians complained:

"With our ancestors, we adored these gods which are good. You destroyed them and evil will come to you; you will be lost at sea."

"Let us see who loses. Tell these *caciques* that they should whitewash the walls of the temple with lime and make a large cross with the image of the Virgin."

When this was done in front of the startled and fearful natives, Cortés said:

"I entrust the Cross and the Image; you will revere them, too. Keep the altar clean and many blessings will come to you."

Frightened, the Indians said nothing.

On the 5th of March, the eleven ships, upon Cortés' order, set sail from Cozumel for the mainland. The weather was fair, but at ten o'clock in the morning voices and a cannon shot were heard from Escalante's boat.

The armada was alarmed.

In a loud voice, Cortés asked the close-by ships:

"What's happening?"

After inquiring, Luís de Zaragoza told him:

"Captain, Juan de Escalante's ship is taking on water and that is where our casaba bread is stored."

"Please God that we may not have any misfortune. Alaminos! Order the armada to return to Cozumel."

When they arrived, the *caciques* asked the reason they had returned and Cortés answered:

"We have a breakdown in a ship that's taking on water. Please help unload the casaba bread with your canoes while we repair the vessel."

The Spaniards were delighted when they found the altar clean and well cared for.

They were there several days repairing the damage, and meanwhile Jerónimo de Aguilar, sad and without hope, remained in Cape Catoche. He found out from some traders that the Spaniards had returned to Cozumel. Now, he was very happy. With the ransom beads he received, he rented a large canoe with six men. In a short time, they crossed the channel and arrived at Cozumel.

On the 13th of March, the sentries informed Cortés that a large canoe had come from the mainland. After investigating, Cortés learned that Jerónimo de Aguilar—who would later become the interpreter of the Conquest—had been reunited with his own people.

It was Andrés de Tapia who first told Cortés.

Jerónimo de Aguilar comes to Cozumel

"Captain, one of the men on the watch tower advises that a large canoe with seven Indians are disembarking."

When Aguilar saw Andrés de Tapia and his soldiers, in bad Spanish he cried out: "God, Holy Mary and Seville," and ran over to embrace Tapia, whose soldiers ran to give the news to the Captain.

"Captain Hernán. *Albricias*! Oh, happy day! A Spaniard who resembles an Indian is here."

Everyone was delighted. Soon Jerónimo de Aguilar appeared, heavily tanned by the sun, his hair cut like the Indians and wearing a loin cloth. He carried an oar on his shoulder. He was wearing one huarache and the other was hanging from his waist. In an old cloth bundle, he carried a venerable *Book of Hours*.

Cortés did not recognize this apparition as a Spaniard and asked Tapia:

"What happened to the Spaniard? What did you do with him?"

"I am he!" insisted Jerónimo de Aguilar.

"And who are you?"

"Jerónimo de Aguilar, a native of Écija [Spain]. I have been ordained in the gospel. Eight years ago, with fifteen men and two women, we were traveling from Darién to Santo Domingo where a storm threw us off our route and some of us came to these lands. I remained as a slave. I know there is another, Gonzalo Guerrero, but he refused to come with me because he has a wife and children. He is a *cacique* in time of war. Two years ago, when three Spanish ships arrived at Cape Catoche, it was Guerrero's suggestion to attack them and wage war against them. If I look like an Indian, he does even more so with his decorated face and pierced ears."

"Tell me, Aguilar," Cortés said, "do you speak the Indian language fluently?"

"At the moment, better than Spanish, which I have not had the opportunity to use for eight years."

When the natives of Cozumel heard him speak their language, it filled them with joy.

"Well, Aguilar, Andrés de Tapia will give you some clothes and then instruct these natives in the mysteries of our faith and in the care of our Holy Cross and the image of Our Virgin."

"I will do it gladly, Captain. And I thank God for delivering me among you."

En Route to Tabasco

ne day before he sailed from Cozumel to Tabasco, Cortés ordered a general review of the troops so that they might be instructed in the tactics to be used in warfare against the Indians.

"Brothers and friends. From now on, war will be a challenge. Tomorrow we set sail once again for Tabasco where Hernández de Córdoba had a mighty battle. We will likely be confronted by large numbers of Indians and we are just a few. Therefore, you must understand the art of warring against them. Besides your familiarity with arms and artillery, bear in mind what I tell you now; I will repeat it many times.

"Those of you who have no armor or leather breast-plates must wear, in spite of the extreme heat, the quilted cotton jackets. Wear them day and night. Those of you who still have a queue of hair, cut it off. Long hair hampers the fight. The Indians attack in droves and there will be hand-to-hand fights, whose purpose may be more to capture us than to wound us. We must keep our units tight and help each other.

"Bear in mind that in the hand-to-hand fighting the natives have no defense, for their abdomens are usually uncovered. They wield wooden *macanas** which have a sharp flint blade. Because of that, your first blow should be aimed at the stomach. After we have landed, the horses will be ready to mount. We will form lines, three abreast, which alone will let us help each other. We should be able to easily roll back even an army of warriors. Remember! Aim your lances toward their faces, but don't pierce the body and don't hesitate before you strike. The whole idea is to throw them into confusion. Then the foot soldiers will follow up with their round shields to rush them with the point of the sword. Remember! Lances to the face and swords to the stomach."

Cortés was thoughtful for a moment and then he added:

"Shots and small cannon will be fired from the distance over the warriors so the foot soldiers and mounted men will have a chance at second encounters. The captains will order shots over the walls or fences, if necessary. Regarding crossbows and the arquebuses we know their range: One fires while the other loads. There must never

---

* Sword, a flat blade of wood three or four feet long, three inches wide, with a groove along either edge into which sharp-edged pieces of flint or obsidian were inserted. This Indian sword could decapitate a horse with one stroke. This appears later in the narration.—Trans.

be a shortage of provisions or arms. With faith in God and the courage in our hearts we will triumph! As many warriors have said before us: '*Santiago y cierra España!*'"

"*Santiago y cierra España!*" the chorus of men repeated.

The following day they set sail for Tabasco. On the 22nd of March, 1519, they arrived at the mouth of what the Indians called the Tabzcoob River, which Juan de Grijalva has previously named the Grijalva.

Facing the Grijalva River

rijalva! The Grijalva River," cried Antón de Alaminos, the chief navigator, who was with Cortés in the captain's quarters.

The eleven ships were close to each other.

"Captain, we are at the mouth of the Grijalva River. The sand-bar prevents us from entering with boats because of the draft of the vessels. When Grijalva's men disembarked at Palmares Point from the small boats and launches, they made a poor effort to take out gold. At first the Indians were hostile, then received them peacefully. You can see the land here is very swampy and of little use."

"From now on, nothing is of little use, Alaminos. We will not leave here without knowing the secrets in these lands. Make ready a small brigantine and the boats and launches for all the soldiers. The seamen and guards will remain on board the ships. When they are ready to disembark, transfer the horses to the boats."

All the soldiers crowded aboard the vessels. The boats advanced up river until they came to Palmares Point where the troops encountered thousands of Indian warriors, beating drums and blowing their shell-horns with a great outcry. Hostile Indian warriors in large canoes crossed back and forth in front of the Spaniards, threatening them.

"Ask them why they are up in arms against us," Cortés said to Aguilar. "We did not come here to harm them. Two years ago they received our brothers in peace. We have come in peace and they should not begin a war that may cost them dearly."

Aguilar, directing himself to a large canoe with some officials, translated what Cortés said. After wrangling with them a bit, he said to Cortés:

"They said we should not continue ahead and that we should not dare to disembark, as they will kill all of us. They are prepared and well fortified. This time will not be as it was two years ago when they didn't fight our brothers. The traders ridiculed and jeered them."

"Please insist that we come in peace and that they must allow us to disembark in order to find water and replenish supplies and also so that we can sleep, as there is not enough room in these launches. We do not want war nor do we wish to do them any harm."

Aguilar repeated Cortés' words and tried to convince them, but the Indians became more agitated and shouted and gesticulated.

"It is useless, Captain. They say that we should leave here and if we disembark in those swampy lands they will attack us."

"Fine!" answered Cortés. "We will go ashore on those sandbars and early tomorrow morning we will contend with them."

When they were ashore, Cortés ordered:

"Captains, put the cannon in the bow of the vessels so that we can fire when necessary. Divide proportionally among the launches and vessels the crossbowmen and the musketeers. You men who were in Grijalva's expedition, do you know or do you remember if that road that we see leads to the village of Tabasco?"

Those men, including Bernal Díaz de Castillo, consulted each other and the latter spoke:

"We remember that it leads to a town."

"Alonso de Ávila," Cortés said, "tomorrow at daybreak you will command two hundred soldiers, among whom will be ten crossbowmen. You will lead your men down that narrow road that leads to the village, while we in the boats will take the front. Wait for our shots before you enter the village."

Very early on the 23rd of March, after celebrating the Mass, they set out as Cortés had planned. Ávila and his men disembarked at the narrow road and with the dawn light, the rest of the soldiers, under orders from Cortés, continued up the stream. The Indians could see them from the mangrove plantations. The canoes closed in around them while the blare of trumpets, shell-horns and small kettle drums sounded.

They shouted to Aguilar:

"Don't set foot on our land! We will kill you! Go to your own land. This time it will be different. Go! Go!"

To which Cortés replied:

"We will stop. No one discharge weapons. Let's try to settle matters with the chief of command, the Indian Council! Diego de Godoy, scribe of the King, use Jerónimo de Aguilar as your translator and proceed to make an official summons to these Indians. If they deny us the right to come ashore to take on water and provisions and if we must fight them to defend ourselves—then it will be their fault, not ours. Tell them about God's work and about His Majesty the King."

From the ship's bow, Diego de Godoy, Bible in hand, dictated to Jerónimo de Aguilar the Official Summons:

"Natives of these lands, you should know that God has made a man and a woman whose progeny has been dispersed throughout the world. From all of these people, God, Our Lord, gave the burden to one whose name is Saint Peter, so that he, of all men in this world, would be the Prince, Lord and Superior whom all obey as he would be the head of all human lineage. This person is called the Pope. One of the past popes made a gift of these islands and lands that border on the great ocean to the Kings of Spain. For this reason, I request that you resign yourselves as subjects of the said King *Don* Carlos, inasmuch as you are bound to him. Understand well what I have said and take time to deliberate about it. If you consent, His Highness and I, in his name, will receive you with love and benevolence and will not covet your women, children and possessions. We will free your slaves so that they and you may live freely, and we will not demand that you accept Christianity until you are informed of the truth and wish to convert to our Holy Catholic faith. If you do not accept or if you resist us, you may be sure, with the help of God, that I will go against you with all of the might of my army and weapons. And you will be subjected to the yoke and obedience of the Church and His Highness. I will make slaves of your people, your women and children, and confiscate your possessions. And if in accomplishing this feat, there are deaths, the fault will be yours, because you resisted the *Summons*."

The Indians listened, at first confused; then they answered with loud hisses and whistling.

When a few minutes passed, Godoy repeated the *Summons*. This time, the comment of the Tabascan Indians was not hisses, but arrows.

Pedro de Alvarado, who was in a boat close to Cortés, said smiling:

"*Señor*, it seems to me that these Indians do not want to listen to the theology of the *Summons*, nor have you anyone to convey its meaning to them. Your Grace should order a defense until we have one of these Indians in a cage so he can slowly learn it and the Bishop help him understand the text."

"What you suggest is impractical and a waste of time, Alvarado. But I know something about law, about the importance of following orders and maintaining the status quo. In every aspect of this Conquest, we must respect the demands of his Catholic Majesty and the Council of the Indies."

As soon as Godoy finished the second Summons, Cortés ordered:

"Repeat it for the third time, Godoy."

As he did, he and Aguilar, his interpreter, were protected by shields from the many arrows the Indians launched at them from a distance.

When the third reading of the Summons ended, Cortés ordered an advance against the canoes that surrounded them, and took the route to the beach where there were also many warriors. Arrows, shouts, beating drums, and screeching shell-horns were everywhere.

"Advance in rows! Row toward the beach and break through the center of the canoes; our rowing oars are more powerful. Come close to the beach and when the canoes are grouped close together and there is a multitude of warriors, I will call out to shoot. Then row faster. Crossbowmen and musketeers, wait for the signal and shoot at your own discretion. When we are on the beach, we will go ashore with our swords in hand. And remember—the blow of the point to the stomach! *Santiago y cierra España!*"

This expression became the battle cry of this skirmish as well as those that would follow.

Shouting courageously, the Indians used their canoes to resist the passage of the boats. At Cortés' order, his men fired their guns, opening breaches and creating great confusion among the boats and the warriors on shore. As the ground was marshy, not all the boats could reach the shore and many men disembarked in water up to their waists. The Spaniards, taking advantage of the confusion caused by the cannon fire and the shots from the crossbows and musketeers, left their boats quickly. Cortés lost a shoe and was stuck briefly in the mud; even so, he continued to fight alongside his men.

The Indians withdrew to some trenches and bulkheads where with great courage they mounted a defense.

"Advance, advance," shouted the captains, including Cortés. "*Santiago y cierra España*!"

"*Al calacheoni! Al calacheoni!*" shouted the Indians.

"What does that mean?" someone asked Aguilar.

"The Captain! The Captain! That they kill him or capture him."

"You men," shouted Cortés, "make an opening in the enclosure while the crossbowmen protect you!"

As their tight circles opened, the Spanish foot soldiers rushed forward with their swords and attacked the Indians, who resisted fiercely.

At this point, from the rearguard, Alonso de Ávila's soldiers appeared, something the Indians did not expect. The latter took refuge in an orderly manner and, without turning their backs to the Spaniards, they shot arrows and hurled spears until the Spaniards reached the great ceremonial plaza where there were two pyramids and three temples. Then, obeying a command, the Indians retreated at full speed.

"Stop! Halt!" shouted Cortés. "We go no further. The enemy has fled!"

Once the battle was over and the Spaniards had rested, Cortés said:

"We must be alert. These people will not go away defeated. They never turned their backs in the battle, but withdrew efficiently and orderly. No doubt they will regroup. Captains, change the guards and the lookouts and send some scouts to keep an eye on the Indians' movements. And you, Alonso de Ávila, why did it take you so long to arrive? We were quite exhausted."

"Captain, we were unexpectedly delayed by the marshes! The shallows made it difficult for us to pass. Still, we came as fast as we could."

"Very well. Now, listen. The Indians are not defeated and are probably regrouping to counterattack. *Don* Pedro de Alvarado, get ready to lead a group of one hundred soldiers, among them fifteen crossbowmen and musketeers. Tomorrow at dawn, you will go to scout out the area inland about two leagues. Take Melchorejo as your interpreter. And you, Francisco Lugo, with another one hundred soldiers, including twelve crossbowmen and musketeers, go by this direction for two leagues. Take Jerónimo de Aguilar as your interpreter. Now let's all return to sleep at the camp. We will stay in touch so we can assist you if there are any surprises."

Finally, Cortés added:

"And now, as we are assembled, I am going to take possession of these lands for His Majesty, in his royal name."

Then Cortés unsheathed his sword, gave three cuts as a sign of possession on a large ceiba [cottonwood] tree that was in the ceremonial plaza and shouted:

"I am taking possession of these lands in the name of His Royal and Catholic Majesty *Don* Carlos. If there is any person who opposes me, I will defend my right with shield and sword."

A chorus of the men echoed:

"All of us will defend it."

When the ceremony was concluded, Cortés ordered the Royal Scribe:

"Write out an ordinance of possession and certify it."

Before dawn the next morning, Cortés watched Lugo and Alvarado prepare for departure. Alvarado said:

"I have news, Captain. Melchorejo fled last night, leaving behind the clothes we gave him."

"Then leave without him," Cortés shrugged.

The two expeditions departed. About one league away, Lugo faced formations of Indians, their captains leading them. There were many bowmen, others with lances and shields and musical instruments. All the foe were adorned with feathers. They came straight toward the Spaniards, shouting and hemming in the company with a rain of arrows.

Jerónimo de Aguilar, his voice in his throat, shouted at the Indians:

"Don't be crazy! Why do you wage war when we come in peace? Be calm! We will surely kill you if you come with the sound of war."

They answered with more arrows and shrill whistles. A large band of warriors attacked Lugo's command, which had formed into a square to defend themselves. A scout ran to Alvarado with the news of Lugo. Alvarado and his men came to Lugo's aid, breaking through the ring of Indians and driving them away. Then, the Spaniards returned to camp in the afternoon.

"Captain Cortés," reported Alvarado, "about a league away numerous squadrons of Indian bowmen attacked Lugo's command and encircled them. I had to go to his aid and after breaking the circle we retreated back here. We have many wounded. An Indian prisoner told Jerónimo that it was Melchorejo who suggested the idea of war and warned the *caciques* not to be afraid of us. He told them that we are mortal men and few in number, and they alerted all of the provinces to join them in a war that would kill all of us."

"Obviously, they are planning to attack us. All right, we will need the horses and all the ammunition and small cannon. Portocarrero! Arrange to unload the horses as soon as possible. Be sure they are protected by breast plates with bells,"* ordered Cortés.

"Captains. I would like all of your crossbowmen and musketeers, even though they may be wounded, to be ready with their arms. You, Diego de Ordaz, will be captain of the foot-soldiers, crossbowmen and musketeers. Mesa! Prepare the artillery." Then he added:

"We will go mounted. Cristóbal de Olid, Pedro de Alvarado, Hernández Portocarrero, Juan de Escalante, Francisco de Montejo, Alonso de Ávila (who will mount Ortiz, the musician's horse), Bartolomé García, Juan Velázquez de León, Francisco de Morla, de Lares (the splendid horseman) and Gonzalo Domínguez. You all know the rule: lances to the face. Ride in rows three abreast, and I will indicate the turning points for the foot-soldiers. Again, I recommend a blow to the stomach.

---

* The bells were important. When the sixteen horses pranced, it produced a sound foreign to the Indians.—Trans.

66

"Tomorrow morning we will march out to find the enemy. The best defense is to attack. We may be a few, as Melchorejo said, but remember the way these Indians fight; attacking in large numbers, instead of impeding us, helps us.

"Maybe we will have to fight one on one. With the help of God, we will be victorious!"

The following morning, the 25th of March, after hearing a Mass chanted by Fray Bartolomé de Olmedo, everyone assembled. The foot-soldiers marched toward the large, open plain where the first battle was fought.

The cavalry set out from its position to the beach where they exercised the numbness from their horses, which were all harnessed with trappings and bells, producing a piercing and frightening sound.

"Bring up the horses, Captains," shouted Cortés. "We will fall back to the rearguard. Let us hurry, because the scouts told me that there are many marshy places along the road. And remember! The lance to the face! Do not stop when you throw the lance. We will break up their units with the turns and gaits of our horses. Rows of three!"

Next to the Zintla Village, the Indian companies were organized in a line that covered the entire long plain. Seeing that the Spaniards had taken the initiative, the Indians advanced furiously and encircled the Spaniards' defensive squadrons. They threw arrows and poles, wounded seventy and continued fighting. One arrow entered a Spaniard's ear, and he died on the spot. Then the Indians began hand-to-hand blows with their *macanas* matching blows from the Spanish lances. As the sword points injured them, many withdrew so that they could shoot their arrows more effectively.

Ordaz ordered Mesa to fire his cannon at the Indians when they opened their lines. As soon as the cannon fired, the Indians closed up their lines while the artillery reloaded. In the midst of the massacre, there was much confusion; but soon the Indians recovered and continued their attack with arrows and lances, and with less hand-to-hand fighting. The Spanish defense squadrons held. Bernal Díaz del Castillo found Diego de Ordaz and said:

"It seems to me that we are only able to assault them one on one because they truly feel the point of our swords and the thrusts. Then, fearing our weapons, they turn away from us and take aim with their arrows, forged rods and so many stones that they seem like hail."

Ordaz responded:

"I'm afraid it's a losing cause. For every one of us there are three hundred Indians and we are unable to attack such a great many. We should remain here, forming squares until the cavalry arrives. God knows, I expected them sooner. Let us stab those we can reach. Leave with discipline and return after each thrust of the rapier."

As a result of this tactic, the Indians (Mayas and Zoques) withdrew across the large plain.

Then Ordaz remembered that by avoiding the marshes the artillery could fire over the heads of the squares. After each shot there were loud whistles and drums from the Indians, who tossed dry grass and dirt into the air so the Spaniards would not be aware of their casualties. As they did, they shouted: "Alala, Alala!"

They thought that the horse and rider were one piece. . . .

Now, from the rear guard came the men on horses, utterly surprising the Indians. The field was flat, and the better horsemen who were bold and enjoyed galloping, made a shock attack on the Indians, who had never seen horses. Confused, they thought horsemen and horse were one being.* The Spanish foot soldiers took advantage of the Indians' astonishment to rush the marsh and complete the destructive work the horses began. In panic, the Indians fled toward some hills and the field was left in Spanish hands. Cortés, coming up to Ordaz, said:

"We had a lot of trouble crossing the marshes and had to finish off the Indian units who were impeding our passage. We were afraid we'd be too late to help you, but thanks to *Señor* Santiago, ours has been a great victory, in this first war of this land. We will have to call this village Santa María de la Victoria because this is the day of Our Virgin."

"Captain, we are exhausted from thrusting our weapons and we have suffered badly from their arrows. Without your horsemen, we would not have achieved the victory. Thanks be given to the Virgin Mary."

"Count the dead and tend to the wounded and to the horses."

"Captain, we have nothing with which to treat the wounds, only cloths to cover them," said the ensign.

"Brave injuries deserve brave remedies. Take one of the fat dead Indians, render the fat from his body and apply it to the wounds of the men and the horses."

So that is what he did.

The ensign returned and said:

"Captain, two Spaniards have died, more than seventy have been wounded, not counting those with head injuries; eight hundred Indians are dead from sword thrusts, many were wounded and five horses were hurt."

"Just do as I told you! Ours was the victory of God's work. And take extra care, captains. Be sure to post night guards and sentinels."

---

* The Aztecs had never seen a horse. When they saw the Spaniards mounted on the animals, they said they were four-legged monsters with human bodies issuing from their backs.—Trans.

Doña Marina, La Malinche

The morning of the next day (the 26th of March, 1519) the *caciques* and authorities of the Tabasco village appeared with great demonstrations of respect and reverence. As presents they brought to the Spaniards golden jewelry and beautiful cotton cloths, but even these did not compare with the twenty Indian maidens, among whom was a beautiful young girl who later would convert to Christianity.

Cortés met with the Indian *caciques* and officials and through Jerónimo de Aguilar's fluency in their langauge, he said to them:

"I thank you for the presents that you brought to me. Remember that we come here as friends and in peace. It was your fault that so many died. Three times we requested that you not wage war, yet you did. Why?"

"My brother the *cacique* from Champotón advised me to do it," said one of the *caciques*. "Otherwise, they would say we are cowards. He accused me of that two years ago when we did not attack the Spaniards, but received them peacefully. Now, we know that was Grijalva and his men. Another native, who was your interpreter, advised us to do the same. We sacrificed that one to the gods for his evil judgment."

Cortés nodded. "If you wish to be our friends, in two days we will return to colonize this village with your women and children. In this way you will know that you are in peace with us."

"Then that's what we will do, Captain."

"Furthermore," said Cortés, "when we settle in, you must destroy your idols and no longer sacrifice human beings. You must listen to Jerónimo de Aguilar, who will instruct you in the true faith of Our Lord, the only true God.

"He will show you a devout image of Our Virgin with her Son in her arms and will make known to you her reverence."

"Well then, it seems that this Teotlcihuatl, the Indian virgin, must be a very great *señora*."

"You will worship her as the mother of God," Cortés said. "I would like the carpenters, Alonso Yáñez and Álvaro López, to fashion a great crucifix and to build an altar. Finally, you must tell me from what area you found this gold and jewelry."

"Where the sun sets, in Culúa, Mexico," the *cacique* said, gesturing.

"And where is that?"

"Far, far, where the sun sets."

"We will go there; there we will go," answered Cortés.

The next day, the altar and cross were built. Bartolomé de Olmedo chanted the Mass and proceeded to baptize the twenty women, among whom was one most outstanding in beauty and dignity, Malinalli.*

Aguilar preached in the Indian language to the recently baptized, the first Christians of what would be New Spain. Malinalli was baptized as Marina.

Then Padre Olmedo said:

"Malinalli, I baptise you in the name of the Father, the Son and the Holy Spirit, as Marina."

Malintzin. Marina. La Malinche.

Bernal came over to Jerónimo de Aguilar who said:

"*Doña* Marina must be a daughter of a *cacique*. She is a truly beautiful woman and has the appearance of a great lady."

With great dignity, *Doña* Marina accepted her new conditions. Throughout the ceremony, she glanced with special attention toward Captain Cortés. Once the

---

* The Indian *cacique* delivered to Cortés twenty Indian maidens, richly dressed, wearing collars and gold ornaments, with a number of female slaves to wait on them. They were the daughters of the principal chiefs and the *cacique* requested that the Spanish captains take them as their wives. Perhaps it is appropriate to clarify the Spanish social custom of accepting these Indian maidens as their *barraganas*. Whoever thinks that the attitude of the Spanish captains toward those young Indian maidens, whose fathers delivered them to the Spanish officers, was limited only to sexual satisfaction is mistaken.

In that period in Spain, there was an institution whose purpose was to combine the sanctity of matrimony with those polygamous tendencies of the race; *barraganía* became a sort of offically recognized concubinage. These Indian girls became wives in every sense of the word except the actual marriage vows. The men referred to them as *doñas*, a symbol of nobility which implies respect and deference toward them from the rank and file soldiers. They were not slaves, but *señoras*. The Spaniards considered them as their Indian *barraganas*, which included all honors and privileges, and treated them with absolute social and racial equality. (Madariaga, Salvador, *Hernán Cortés*, Madrid: Espasa-Calpe, 1975, 178–80.)—Trans.

women were baptised, Cortés himself divided the ladies among the men. As he approached *Doña* Marina, he addressed Alonso Hernández Portocarrero.

"And for you, *Don* Alonso, I have retained this beautiful and great lady whose name is now Marina. She is proof of the affection that I profess for you."

Cortés took Marina's hand. She, feeling the contact of his flesh, began to tremble. Cortés gave her to Portocarrero, who was smiling and flattered. Marina did not understand what was happening. On being received by Portocarrero's hand, her expression revealed total confusion. She continued to stare at Cortés, who looked into her eyes, then turned away.

"I am much obliged to you, Captain Cortés," said Portocarrero who, when night came, led *Doña* Marina to his quarters.

Without physically rejecting the Spaniard's caresses, she was totally unanimated, which caused Portocarrero to complain:

"For God's sake, you are as cold as you are beautiful."

Before the armada again set sail, five days lapsed while wounds healed, soldiers rested and Cortés preached to the neighboring *caciques*. The scribe noted that the *caciques* had declared themselves subjects of His Catholic Majesty.

In Zintla, where the battle took place, Cortés ordered that a cross be placed in the blaze-marked ceiba tree. Since the *caciques* had sworn allegiance and become His Majesty's subjects, he ordered that the Indians assist with the ship loading because it was Palm Sunday. The Spaniards were planning to pray before the Eucharist, so they requested that provisions be brought.

On the 17th of April, Palm Sunday, after a procession in which Indians and Spaniards walked together for the first time in a common religious ceremony, Cortés bade his new friends goodbye.

"We leave in peace and I leave you as His Majesty's subjects. Now you possess the true faith. I entrust to your devotion the Cross and image of Our Lady."

Early the following day they set sail.

Bound for San Juan de Ulúa

oña Marina and the other Indian maidens were given to Cortés' captains. While Portocarrero accompanied Cortés, *Doña* Marina was put in the lead ship, where she arranged her possessions close to the stern in the aftercastle. No special cabins were provided for the women. When the voyage began, Bernal Díaz del Castillo, who was also on board, approached Jerónimo de Aguilar and proposed:

"Good Jerónimo, please come with me to speak to the beautiful Indian *señora*. Portocarrero is indeed fortunate. I don't know why Cortés gave her to him."

"If a good Captain would be first, he must be last and a servant to all of his men, Bernal."

"It must be a shame for any man to be less than last," nodded Bernal.

The two men approached *Doña* Marina who, with two other Indian maidens, was leaning demurely on the railing and gazing toward the land.

"What are you regarding so intently, *señora*?" Aguilar asked.

"That land where they made me a slave."

"Were you not born in Tabasco?"

"No. I was born far from there, in Copainalan, the place where the serpent went, where the Coatzacoalcos River was born. The place from which Quetzalcóatl departed toward the East."

Although *Doña* Marina was speaking in Mayan, she pronounced "Quetzalcóatl" as a Náhuatl speaker might. In Mayan, the word was "Kukulkán."

Puzzled, Aguilar asked, "Quetzalcóatl? What word is that? In what language?"

"Kukulkán is in the language you understand; 'Quetzalcóatl' is our word for it in the tongue spoken where I was born: the region of the serpents that worshiped the god."

"And who were your parents? Bernal here thinks you must be a queen. He can't understand how you came to be a slave."

Doña Marina looked at Bernal serenely and smiled.

"I am the daughter of the Lord Tlatoani of Copainalan. When my father died, my mother remarried and gave birth to a son whom they wished to be a *cacique*. So that I would not be in the way, they sold me to the Xicalango traders who, in turn, gave me as tribute to those in Tabasco."

"Your instincts were correct, Bernal," Jerónimo said, turning toward him. "She *is* an important *cacica* and a titled lady."

In Tenochtitlan

Moctezuma, seated on his royal *icpalli* [throne], addressed the noblemen:

"Come here, knights of the tigers and knights of the eagles!* Once again it is said that our Lord Quetzalcóatl has departed for our lands. Two years ago, in 13-Conejo, we heard that three very large houses, such as man has never seen, were going about on the sea. There in Xicalango they stopped quietly and out of these houses there came strange white men with beards who brought certain gifts, which we keep now in the treasury. These men were the emissaries sent ahead by Quetzalcóatl, but they did not wish to come ashore. At that time, I commanded: no one had permission to open his lips or utter a word about the event; no one could write about it, except among ourselves. . . . But now, in this year Uno-Caña, at that new union of time, our seers inform us that eleven floating houses are close to the shore at Xicalango. The god, their lord, says he wishes to become acquainted with us. So go and meet him; listen well to what he says.

"Here is how you will welcome our lord:

This is the treasure of Quetzalcóatl:

Quetzalcóatl's surcoat

I give you also Tezcatlipoca's ornamental finery

And also that of Tlalocan Tecuhtli.

These are divine raiments,

Take them to the god. Go at once; do not delay.

Make an obeisance to our lord, the god.

"Tell him:

"'Your deputy, Moctezuma, sent us here. He sends you these gifts as a welcome to your home in Mexico.'"

"Take with you the portrayers to draw pictures of the gods, their faces, and everything about them."

---

* The elite military corps.—Trans.

San Juan de Ulúa

Making good time, the armada sailed toward San Juan de Ulúa. Aboard were men who had been in Grijalva's expedition, among them Bernal, happy to be once again in familiar surroundings.

"There is *la Rambla*, which in the Indian language is Ayahualulco. And there is Tonalá and over there the great Coatzalcoalcos River."

Doña Marina, standing close to Jerónimo de Aguilar, said,

"From there Quetzalcóatl left our land and will return in the year *Ce-Acatl*, in the year it was foretold."

As she spoke, she studied Cortés intently.

"And there, far away, one can see the Sierra Nevada," said another seaman. "And over there is the Alvarado River, so named because he was the first of Grijalva's expedition to enter it. And there is the Banderas River where we recovered sixteen thousand pieces of gold. And there is White Island and Green Island."

Close to the shore, they spotted Sacrificios Island.

In good humor, Alonso Hernández Portocarrero came over to Cortés. "It seems to me, *señor*, that these caballeros have seen these parts twice before." He broke into a sailor's ditty:

"Look at France, Montesinos
Look at Paris, the city;
Look at the waters of the Duero
that flow out to the sea."

When he finished, Portocarrero laughed loudly. Still grinning, he said, "I say Captain, that you, seeing these rich lands, already know how to govern them well."

Cortés nodded gravely. "May God grant us good fortune in arms, like the paladin, Roland, among others. Your Grace and the other *caballeros*, will know what I mean."

The 21st of April, Good Friday, 1519, the entire armada arrived at San Juan de Ulúa.

Just then, Alaminos, the navigator, ordered, "Drop anchor here so we are protected from the north wind. From this flag ship hoist the royal banners and standards. From the others, fly the streamers."

Indians on Board. The Culúa Reception

I t took them about a half hour for all the ships to drop anchor. As soon as they did, two large canoes with many Indians aboard headed for the Captain-General's ship, which they had recognized by its trappings. On arrival, they began to speak to the crew in Náhuatl. Jerónimo de Aguilar, accompanied by Marina, came to hear them, but did not understand their language.

Aguilar said to Cortés, "This seems to be the language of the people whose land borders the Coatzacoalcos River around these parts. It is the language of the Culúas or the Mexicans. I don't understand it, but *Doña* Marina does. She is a native of these lands and the daughter of an important *cacique*. She tells me the men in this canoe are natives from Chalchiuhcuecan in the Aztec nation of the Culúa Empire. They are asking for the *tlatoani*, the Captain."

Cortés looked curiously at *Doña* Marina, taking in her beauty.

"A beautiful woman and she seems illustrious as well. How fortunate Portocarrero is to have her. Ask her, Aguilar, if she will interpret for these Indians. You, in turn, will tell me what they say. Then they may come aboard."

And that is how it went. The Indians, seeming to understand the gist of Cortés' remarks, spoke with *Doña* Marina in Náhuatl. She translated into Mayan and Aguilar translated her words into Spanish for Cortés.

The Indian visitors' spokesman proclaimed: "We welcome you to Chalchiuhcuecan in the name of the great Moctezuma who sends us to find out who you are and why you have come here. Should you need anything for yourselves or for your ships, just tell us. We have been instructed by the great Moctezuma to satisfy all of your wishes."

"The god says," *Doña* Marina translated through Aguilar, "I am grateful to the great Moctezuma for the good disposition and welcome that they greet us. Please come into our ship, and eat and drink as our guests whom we wish to honor."

So they all ate, drank, received some blue beads and were quite satisfied. Then, *Doña* Marina, again through Aguilar the intermediary, translated for Cortés.

"This *teule* says: 'We come to see you and learn the secret of your land, as the fame of the great Moctezuma travels very far. We come seeking peace and trade with you, and do not wish anything but friendship. Tomorrow, on land, we will continue our conversation.'"

Quite contented and slightly tipsy, the Indians boarded their canoes and returned to shore.

On Holy Saturday, the 22nd of April, the Spaniards disembarked and set out for San Juan de Ulúa. They unloaded the artillery and horses onto the sand-banks of Chalchiuhcuecan, afterwards called San Juan de Ulúa. They wasted no time erecting an altar, and some crude shelters and huts for Cortés and his captains, while the soldiers collected wood and branches and built their own. While they were in the midst of this, numerous Indians appeared with cloths and provisions. They said to *Doña* Marina:

"Teuhtlilli, the lord of Cuetlaxtan, the chief of these lands, sent us with these cloths so we may adorn the lodging of the gods. We are to provide for you everything you need. Cuitlalpitoc will come in person—as an emissary of the great Moctezuma."

On the 24th of April, emissaries from Moctezuma arrived with great solemnity in Cortés' camp. As a demonstration of their respect, one of the group put his hand on the soil, raised it in reverence, and then lifted it to his mouth. This display was in front of Cortés' hut. Both Jerónimo de Aguilar and *Doña* Marina inquired:

"Who are you? Where do you come from?"

"I am Teuhtlilli, lord of Cuetlaxtan, and he is Cuitlalpitoc. We come from Culúa."

"It may be that you come from there, or perhaps you invent that tale. Tell me, who is your lord?" asked *Doña* Marina.

"The great Moctezuma."

Then the two chiefs went over to where Cortés was seated in his easy chair under a cloth covering. Through *Doña* Marina the messengers said:

"Moctezuma's deputy comes to pay you homage. He has in his charge the city of Mexico. He says that you must be tired; that the god is exhausted. So receive this treasure. Allow us to adorn you as you deserve and to give you these ornaments."

Before Cortés they placed a mask of turquoise with a crosspiece of *quetzal* feathers, a decorated short jacket and a petal necklace of emeralds. Not quite forward enough to remove Cortés' shoes, they placed at his feet golden sandals with gold bells and gave him a wand of authority with a gold cross-bar and mother-of-pearl shell, its fringes and streamers covered in *quetzal* feathers. Other finery and divine treasure they placed with much reverence at his feet.

Doña Marina translated Cortés' remarks:

"The god says: 'Are these the gifts you usually give to welcome guests?'"

The Indians answered: "This is all, only with these gifts we came, our lord."

The Spanish soldiers who witnessed the scene eyed the treasure greedily.

Through his interpreters, Cortés then said:

"The god says: 'I am indeed grateful to the great Moctezuma for his gifts. Tell him we wish to have him for a friend and we wish to see him. Wherever he chooses, we will meet.'"

To which Teuhtlilli responded somewhat arrogantly:

"You have only just arrived and already you wish to speak to Moctezuma. Receive these presents now, which we offer you in the name of our lord, then tell me how we can be of service."

Quetzalcóatl's insignias

Cortés commented:

"These men, Tendile and Pitalpitoque, are arrogant. We shall discourage that. Tie them up and put their feet and necks in irons."

When the order was carried out, they rolled out the great cannon and shot a few rounds. When the shots were fired, Moctezuma's emissaries fainted dead away.

At once, the Spaniards released the shackles and comforted the Aztecs with glasses of wine.

When they recovered their faculties, Cortés approached the emissaries and said: "You must understand that I was trying to ascertain whether you are who you say you are. You should not assume such arrogance when you refer to Moctezuma. Excuse me now, please. After we attend Mass, we will talk."

He invited them to hear the Mass sung by Fray Bartolomé de Olmedo and Padre Díaz. After the Mass ended, Cortés, his captains and Moctezuma's representatives ate together. The dogs, greyhounds and mastiffs, some tied and others eating from their masters' hands, Cortés among them, panted and barked at their sides.* As the Aztecs ate, they watched everything with great uneasiness; nearby, the Indian portrayers continued to sketch the events.

One of the soldiers had a bronze helmet. Teuhtlilli caught sight of it and said to Cortés:

"That helmet looks very much like one of ours, which our ancestors left us from their lineage. It is an example of where we came from and we have it placed on our god Huitzilopochtli. Our Lord Moctezuma would be proud to see it."

Cortés gave him the helmet and said:

"We would like to know if the gold from this land is like the yellow metal we take from our rivers. You should return the helmet filled with gold so that we may send it to our Emperor, *Don* Carlos."

---

* The Spaniards brought several breeds of dogs: greyhounds, mastiffs and the ferocious lurcher, the English cross-bred dog which hunted silently.—Trans.

And he added:

"Deliver to Moctezuma this chair, these beads (imitation pearls) which have a light fragrance and this string of diamonds (glass beads) along with this shirt from Holland, these stockings and this red velvet hat on which is a medallion of St. George. All of these gifts are a sign of our friendship."

When they left the dining area, they walked toward the beach and there Cortés ordered the lombard guns be fired. The trees they hit were shattered. Likewise, he ordered Pedro de Alvarado to organize a contest among the calvary in which Cortés himself participated. All of this, of course, was designed to impress and perhaps to frighten the Indians.

Skirmish on the beach of San Juan de Ulúa

As Cortés dismounted, he directed his remarks to the Indian emissaries and said to them:

"I have been told that the Mexicans are very strong and powerful soldiers and that a single one can route numerous enemy warriors. I would like to convince myself to test how strong you are, how brave you are. Early tomorrow morning, at dawn, we will have a tournament in pairs to see who falls to the ground first."

"Listen, my lord," said the Indians with great dignity. "Moctezuma did not send us here for such a contest. We came with the sole commission of greeting you. We are not obliged to accept your challenge. However, that would be a sport the boys from the Calmecac school would enjoy. If we would do such a thing, we may displease Moctezuma, and he would kill us. With your permission, let us return to give the great Moctezuma an account of everything we have witnessed here."

Prudently, they stood up and left.

In Tenochtitlan

When they were sure the Spaniards could not see them, the Indians hastened their steps and said to one another,

"We'd better hurry. We cannot afford to have anything happen to us before we report to the great Moctezuma all we have seen. These events were truly terrifying; they are unlike anything we have seen before."

Without resting, they hurried on to Mexico and arrived at night. When they reached Moctezuma's palace, they told the guards:

"Tell the Lord Moctezuma that those whom he sent to the sea have returned."

Moctezuma, ever vigilant, had been unable to sleep. When the guards advised him of the emissaries' return, he said: "I don't want to see them here. I will go to the *Casa de la Serpiente* to receive their report. Tell them to go there"—and after a pause—"take two captives and prepare them to be covered in earth."

They all went to the *Casa de la Serpiente* and when they came together Moctezuma ordered the two captives sacrificed. With their blood, the priests sprinkled the emissaries while Moctezuma said: "Receive this blood, because you have had a very difficult journey; because you have seen the gods; because you have seen the eyes in their faces; because you have spoken to the gods."

To continue on, the messengers, helped by the artists' drawings, told Moctezuma everything they had seen and heard.

"And when they lighted the shot, something like a ball of rock emerged from its entrails, soaring, raining fire and sparks; the smoke that came forth smelled putrid, like rotten mud. It penetrated our very brains and made us feel ill. And when they aimed at a hill, the shot moved through it, splitting it, and when they aimed at a tree, it shattered into splinters, as if blown to pieces from inside," said one.

"All their weapons are made of iron; they are dressed in iron; the helmets on their heads are made of iron; their swords are iron; their bows are iron; and their shields and lances. On their shoulders they carry their deer which are as high as the roofs," explained another.

"Their bodies are entirely covered; you can see only their faces. They are as white as if painted with lime. Many have yellow hair; but some have black. Their beards are long and yellow, as are their moustaches. Some have very fine hair; others rough-textured," said another.

"As for their food, they eat what humans eat, not foods of the gods: they eat large portions, soft and light as if they were eating hay. The flavor was odd, like wood from corn stalks, like a substance of cane with the flavor of corn. It seemed sweet daubed with honey; they eat their sweet food as if it were honey. And their dogs are enormous; some have flapped ears, others have flat ears, and their large tongues hang out of their mouths; they have eyes that shoot fire and emit sparks. Their eyes are yellow, intense yellow. Their hollow stomachs are extended, fluted. They are very strong and robust; they are never still, but go about panting, their tongues hanging out. They have spots like a tiger. The strangers communicated with signs that we should return with the helmet full of gold. We believe this helmet is just like the one in the Huitzilopochtli treasure."

"Yes, it is identical," said Moctezuma, uneasy. "There is no doubt. It is they. And the Captain! What did he look like?"

"Like the rest. He looks very much like Tizonahuácatl Quetzalaztatzin except in his color and beard. He is ferocious and although he embraces you, he is arrogant. He tied us with irons before he gave us something to drink in order to demonstrate his strength."

When he heard all this, Moctezuma became frightened and felt as if his heart would sink. He stood up murmuring and retired from the area: "What will happen to us? Who can truly withstand this? In other times I went! . . . Near death is my heart as if it were immersed in a potion of *chile*! How I torment myself! Much in me burns! . . . Where to, oh lord?"

In his palace, Moctezuma, greatly disturbed, could not sleep, walking from one hall to another. At dawn, he ordered: "Please call for a Tlatocan reunion; call Cacama from Texcoco and Totoquihautzin from Tlacopan. I would like Cuitláhuac and Cuauhtémoc to join us. Also the spiritual ones, diviners, wizards, and also Quetzalaztatzin. Have the captains who lead our armies come, too."

When the warriors arrived, he said to them: "Take everything they need to the gods who arrived from the heavens, food and gifts of gold for the greedy ones. Take the helmet full of gold ore so their hearts may be satiated. Make them understand it is a most fatiguing trip to come to the City of Mexico and they do not have to attempt it." He added: "And you priests, if by chance the gold does not satisfy them, take some captives and give them their blood to drink, for if they are gods they will wish it. . . . And you, wizards, if they are not gods you must create some sorcery. But they are not to come here, or penetrate our lands. Quetzalaztatzin will go with you, for he resembles their Captain very much. Steal their souls with the Náhuatl ceremonies; blow air at them until it hurts. Bewitch them. But I do not want them to come here; they are not to come here."

"My lord, my great lord," said Cuitláhuac, "if you don't want them to come here, why don't we attack them now? Do not permit anyone to enter your house if he wishes to evict you."

Cuauhtémoc dared to say:

"Let us attack them now, before their seeds take root and sink into the ground."

"If they are gods, it will be futile. They have been foretold. Do as I have told you," Moctezuma concluded.

So the expedition, much larger than the first, set out with supplies and instructions.

In the Spanish Camp

In their camp, the Spanish army rested. Each day more Indians came to see them, bringing food. Many came with a small amount of gold to exchange for the glass beads from the soldiers, as they had learned from the Grijalva experience. The soldiers who did not have Indians to help them, fished and foraged for food, envious of the officers who were so well looked after.

One morning, early in May, Teuhtlilli arrived with a great number of Indians and warriors. From the time they arrived and first saw the Spaniards, they went about saying "Cortés, Cortés." Accompanying him was Quetzalaztatzin, who, it was said, resembled Cortés. He accentuated that resemblance by combing his hair and decorating his face to look bearded.

On approaching Cortés, Teuhtlilli kissed the ground and ordered the wizards to put in front of Cortés braziers with burning incense. They made signs and invocations and put their magic potions into the flames. But the wind changed and the thick smoke covered the magicians, who withdrew, quite frightened. A few young puppies, running loose, came too close to the braziers and knocked them over.

Doña Marina, alarmed, said to Jerónimo de Aguilar: "These magicians want to bewitch the god [Cortés] but the wind has become angry and frightened them. We must watch them carefully, for no doubt the one that resembles Cortés—wishes to steal his soul. Stir up the puppies again, Jerónimo."

Teuhtlilli then ordered Quetzalaztatzin to come over. He had been walking around, summoning the Spanish soldiers. He introduced him to Cortés who acknowledged the greeting, smiling. The wizards came closer to Cortés, still standing by the Indian who resembled him; with flowers and bundles, they tried to encircle them, but the small dogs, frightened by Aguilar and playful as they were, tugged at the wizards' tunics and made them spill their magic preparations. Disconcerted, the enchanters withdrew, but continued their sorcery from a distance, even though no one was paying any attention to them now. Finally, Teuhtlilli dismissed them.

Next came the priests, with great ceremony, bringing Cortés earthen pots of food sprinkled with human blood, and jars full of rancid-smelling blood.

Cortés' lieutenants did not allow them to come too close. Through *Doña* Marina and Aguilar, they asked: "What are you bringing here that smells so bad?"

"Food of human blood, because the gods who came from the heavens may by chance want to drink it."

Disgusted, spitting and slapping their hands, the lieutenants shoved the priests away.

"Go! Go with these things from the devil!"

¡Idos! Estos teules no comen carne ni beban sanpre de humanos.

"Go away! These gods do not eat human flesh nor drink the blood."

Doña Marina said to the priests: "These gods do not eat human flesh nor do they drink blood. Go! Go!"

Humiliated, the priests asked among themselves:

"What kinds of gods are these that disdain their food? In truth, who are they?"

"That is what I ask," said *Doña* Marina.

Then Teuhtlilli, who had observed everything closely, decided the time had come to deliver the rich presents to Cortés.

On straw mats covered with cotton cloths, the Indians displayed their gifts. The first was a wheel of very fine gold in the shape of the Sun and another of silver made in the shape of the moon.* Then they brought forward the helmet filled with gold that looked as if it had just been mined. The Spaniards' eyes widened with astonishment and greed.

Teuhtlilli, delivering the treasure, said:

"My great lord Moctezuma has sent you these gifts. Receive them with great pleasure as my lord has pleasure sending them, and distribute them among your gods. Moctezuma takes satisfaction that such vigorous beings come to this land; he sends gifts for the one whom you say is your Emperor. Before you leave we want to be sure you have all you need; for your return, we will supply everything your hearts' desire. As for going into the interior to see Moctezuma, he asks that you do not insist. The journey is quite hazardous and he is not disposed to see you."

---

* The first was as big as a cartwheel, with many sorts of pictures, probably the Aztec calendar all of fine gold. The second was of even greater size, probably the astrological or lunar calendar.—Trans.

Cortés answered: "Please thank the great Moctezuma for these rich presents that truly satisfy our hearts. For you, here are these shirts from Holland and for the lord Moctezuma, this glass goblet made in Florence. Tell him we have traveled over many seas and remote lands just to see him and speak with him in person, and if we returned without such a visit, our great King would not be pleased. No matter where Moctezuma is, we wish to see him."

"We will tell him what you said. But a visit is out of the question. The road is very treacherous and Moctezuma would not be able to see you."

At that, the two principal Indians and the others left. The one the Spaniards called "Pitalpitoque" (Cuitlalpitoc) stayed behind to see that the Spaniards' needs were met.

Dissensions

The followers of *Don* Diego Velázquez, awed by the opulence of the gifts Cortés had received, said among themselves: "These gifts and riches the Indians have given us are magnificent. This was a much more valuable expedition than the others. We should return to Cuba now with this gold and the information we've gathered. We must insist that Cortés do this."

"We have tried to convince Cortés," some others replied, "but he insists on discovering the secret of these lands. He has even ordered two ships commanded by Francisco de Montejo to reconnoiter the coast ahead along Grijalva's old route to look for a safe port protected from the north wind, one without mosquitos, far from the swampy lands and closer to the populated areas."

"It seems as if Cortés wishes to colonize. But that is against the orders of Velázquez, who only wishes us to extract treasure. It will be hard to convince Cortés to change his mind, but we must go back. If necessary, we must combine our influences, for there are many of us who feel the same way. We can warn him that we will not sail with the armada any longer."

In Tenochtitlan

After dark, once again in the House of the Serpent, the emissaries—with Teuhtlilli in charge—met with Moctezuma.

Teuhtlilli said to him: "Lord, great lord, my lord. Your commands have been carried out. We went and we have returned. The news is this: THEY HAVE ALREADY ARRIVED. . . ."

Moctezuma became terrified. Frightened and shaking, he asked:

"And what of the wizards' magic?"

They answered: "We worked our craft, as you charged us, but we could accomplish nothing. We were no match for them."

"What happened when the priests brought the food that the gods eat?"

"They felt nauseated, they spit, rubbed their eyes, closed them. They shook their heads with contempt and pushed us away. We cannot understand why these *teules* [gods] [Spaniards] do not want to eat the foods of the gods. They appear to be human, but they are different from us."

"And the beautiful presents I sent: Did these not satisfy their hearts so they would return to their own land?"

Teuhtlilli answered: "They received them with repugnant greed; their eyes and teeth were shining. That seems to be their real 'food,' the gold which so many asked about. They insist on coming here to meet you and they asked many questions about you. They insisted they would meet you anywhere you designate.

"With them was an Indian woman of our region who speaks Náhuatl and always accompanies them. Her name is Malintzin; her birthplace Tectipan. They came upon her somewhere on the coast. She insisted they come here, that their coming was foretold a long time ago. . . ."

Frightened and dismayed, Moctezuma erupted: "Where will I go? Where can I hide?"

His servants and advisers answered: "The place of our ancestors is known; the House of the Sun and the Land of Tláloc and the House of Cintli. That's where you should go. Wherever may be your good will."

"I will go to the House of Cintli. But no; even that will be useless. I have nowhere safe to go. I must abandon the House of the Elders, the great royal house; I will go to my own noble house. I will await them there. My heart reels in great circles. They are coming. And there I will await them. Although my heart is resigned, I will moderate my passions. Whatever happens, I will compose myself so I may see and admire what is ordained, what is going to happen."

Soon it was heard among the people: "The great Moctezuma is downhearted, he is fearful, and he has resigned himself to fate. He will depart the royal palaces and go to his own."

The news spread all around.

They are Coming . . .

ow it was the year of *Ce-Acatl*. The year ordained. Therefore, there was great fear. People spoke of nothing but these events, and talked constantly about what had happened.

There were meetings, discussions. Cabals were formed. In the streets, weeping was heard. The people went about crestfallen, with their heads down; greeting each other amid floods of tears trying to cheer one another; they caressed each other and petted the children.

Fathers said: "Oh, my darling children! What will happen to us? Oh, you will witness what was forecast would happen!"

The mothers said: "My dear little children! How can you foresee the unknown that will happen to you?"

At night again the voice was heard: "Aaay, my children! . . . "

Founding of the Villa Rica de la Vera Cruz

There were cliques in the Spanish camp and they were making demands on Cortés.

Some had as their spokesman Pedro de Alvarado:

"We demand that we make inroads into the country, to discover these populated lands where fortune favors us. We cannot stay in these marshy areas, eaten up by flies, mosquitos, small and large. Here, even our casaba bread has rotted and is moldy and full of weevils. It is difficult to find food, and worse, Pitalpitoque has not sent food or supplies with the natives, so we have very little left."

Others, through Juan Velázquez de León, said: "We demand that you, Captain, return to Cuba and give Diego Velázquez an account of the gold recovered. We left home a long time ago, abandoning our haciendas and Indians, and in this camp some thirty-five have died from battle wounds suffered at Tabasco, and of sorrow and hunger. These lands are vast and heavily populated and one day soon the natives will attack us. We wish to return to Cuba."

After hearing both sides, Cortés called a meeting. "I have thought about the suggestions you have given me. Some of you wish to continue on and penetrate the land; others wish to return to Cuba. I myself believe that, so far, no one has any cause to complain about the fortune that has come to us. We ought to thank God He has helped us in war as well as in peace with the Indians. It's true that some have died, but that happens in war and in work; it's the human condition.

"We would serve badly our Catholic Majesty if we did not learn the secrets of this land, so I do not think it is a good idea to go back home now. Let us travel further to the north, to the village Montejo and Alaminos saw where there are no mosquitos and where we can eat corn and obtain a good supply of provisions from the Indians there. Since nothing stops us we must do it."

When Cortés' decision was accepted by the first group, it appeased the others somewhat. Although they continued to demand the return to Cuba, they went along with the others.

After nightfall, Cortés met secretly in his tent with Alonso Hernández Portocarrero and Pedro de Alvarado and his four brothers—Jorge, Gonzalo, Gome and Juan; also Cristóbal de Olid, Alonso de Ávila, Juan Escalante, Francisco de Lugo and Francisco de Montejo.

"Captains," Cortés said to them, "it seems to me that Diego Velázquez's followers, headed by Juan Velázquez de León, Diego de Ordaz, Pedro Escudero, and "the Page" Escobar, are encouraging the soldiers to demand that we return to Cuba and that we deliver the gold we have received to the Governor, whose avarice we are all well aware of. I would like your views on this point."

"We have no doubts at all, Captain," said Pedro de Alvarado. "We hold that we ought to penetrate the country and colonize—even break relations with Velázquez altogether and make his sympathizers submit to us, even subdue them, if need be."

The other Captains nodded agreement.

"I agree with you," Cortés said, "except I do not suggest we resort to violence, which will certainly divide and weaken us if we have to fight the large numbers of Indians we are facing."

"What do you recommend then, Admiral, if not the sword?"

"The law, Alvarado. Respect for civil formalities and for the law."

"But how is that possible if all the authority belongs to Velázquez and he has the law [on his side]?"

"Quite simple. We form a government as the equals that we are. We establish a town that relies upon the Emperor, to whom we will send, immediately, the Royal fifth of all the gold we have collected. By mutual accord, we will name a Captain-General, a high constable, mayors and magistrates, and fill all the offices a town calls for. These men will continue in authority until confirmed by the Emperor, to whom we will send solicitors to ascertain their confirmation. That step will protect us from any misfortunes Diego Velázquez may call down upon us. As Spaniards, we have a right to enter territory and to colonize—a right confirmed by the Papal Bull of Alexander VI, which, from the 4th of May, 1493, gave to Spain dominion over these lands."

"I agree that seems to be a better solution than the sword," said Portocarrero. "Are you not of that same opinion, Captains?"

Alvarado said: "Let's put words into action. We, the captains, name you Chief Justice and Captain-General and. . . ."

"Slow down, Alvarado," Cortés said. "We must do things wisely and prudently. We must be the men that the others demand of us and we have to pretend at least to consider this step. As is said in the adage 'You have asked me to do what I have already made up my mind to do.'"

Then Cortés added: "I will speak personally with the soldiers who are already on our side and even with some partial to Velázquez, such as Díaz del Castillo who served Diego de Ordaz—he actually feels as we do. In less time than you think, everything will be resolved."

The Captains left to carry out Cortés' instructions.

That night, Francisco de Lugo, a relative of Bernal Díaz del Castillo, came over to his tent and said, "Ah, *Señor* Bernal Díaz, come out with your arms and let us make rounds. We can accompany Cortés, who is just now going the rounds."

Once Bernal was outside, Lugo said: "Listen, *señor*, I have a little matter to discuss with you in secret. Your companions will not approve, as they are on the side of Diego Velázquez. It seems to me they have tried to fool us. You remember in Cuba there were proclamations by criers announcing that we were coming here to colonize and now it seems these others want us to return to Cuba to deliver the gold to Diego Velázquez. You, Bernal, who have been here three times, spending your money, risking your life, suffering wounds, what do you think about it?"

"I think we should conquer and colonize the land," Bernal replied quickly.

"Well then, we will convene in order to found Villa de la Vera Cruz and we will elect as Captain, Hernán Cortés. Thus will we free ourselves from Velázquez's poisonous authority."

"That suits me," Bernal answered.

In the same way, the other Captains spoke to their men that night and the *Ayuntamiento* [municipal government] was convened the following day.

Soon after dawn, all the soldiers and captains assembled in front of Hernán Cortés' tent amidst a great outcry.

Cortés came out and shouted: "What a disturbance! So much shouting and disorder! What do you want? Let's see. . . . Diego de Ordaz, you speak first," Cortés pointed his finger at the dissenter.

"I say this: You have been too crafty about remaining in these lands without making a report to our Captain, Diego Velázquez. I don't think that's right. We ask to return immediately and for an end to your roundabout ways and secrets with the soldiers. There is no food here, no people, and no possibility for colonization."

Cortés listened attentively. Without anger, he said: "And you, Juan Velázquez de León, what do you say?"

"The same! It's time that we went back without listening to any more of these suggestions and petty intrigues."

Those allied with Diego Velázquez supported his words and shouted: "Return! Return! To Cuba! To Cuba!"

Meanwhile, the Alvarado brothers were organizing the followers of Cortés and admonished them: "Be calm! Let Cortés handle it."

Without rancor, Cortés spoke. "I am pleased that Captains Ordaz and Velázquez have spoken so frankly. And I have noted the shouts of support from the soldiers. As that seems to be the general consensus, we will not oppose the instructions of Diego Velázquez, who ordered that we take out all the gold we could find and return. Therefore, I proclaim publicly that tomorrow all of us will board the ships, each in the ship he arrived in."

Then the Alvarado brothers motioned to their supporters.

"No! No! We want to colonize! We wish to remain here! Let those who wish to return, go! May Diego Velázquez's 'servants' return! We will stay!"

"Order!" shouted Cortés. "Let one soldier speak."

Francisco Lugo proposed: "Let's hear from Bernal Díaz del Castillo."

"Yes! Yes! Yes!" joined in the others.

"Captain Cortés," Bernal said respectfully, "we have been speaking among ourselves and we think it has not been proper on your part to bring us to these lands under false pretenses. As you know, in Cuba it was announced by public criers that we would come here to colonize and it was for that reason that many of us signed on for the expedition. We knew well how little gold each soldier had brought out in the two prior expeditions. Most of the benefits went only to the Governor, who always has been opposed to colonization."

"That's true!" shouted some.

"So I request, Captain, in the name and service of God and His Majesty, do not forsake us! Be our leader in establishing a colony for all who wish to remain, and be our Captain. The natives have allowed us to come ashore. What will follow, who knows? As for those who wish to return, in good time they may leave. We who remain hope Your Grace will lead us."

"Yes! Yes!" shouted the soldiers from Bernal's group while the others stirred restlessly.

"Accept, Cortés! Accept the assignment! We wish to colonize! We wish to remain here. Let the others leave."

Pedro de Alvarado took the stand. "We will stay here to colonize with Your Grace! It is not fair to fool such loyal and brave soldiers."

Cortés feigned a loss for words. "I understand the reasons; but Governor Diego Velázquez's instructions! . . ."

"Excuse me, Captain," said Portocarrero, "here we are, Spaniards who wish to colonize. We have a right to establish a town and to name as officers men who are not obliged to take instructions from an avaricious governor."

"That's true! Yes! Yes! Establish a town! Vote! Vote!" shouted many of the men.

Cortés raised his hand to restore order. "I have listened to your demands and they seem reasonable. Never would I oppose the establishment of a town, certainly not when it will benefit His Majesty. I ask then, who is in favor of establishing a town?"

"I! I! I!" a considerable number of soldiers raised their hands.

Then Cortés ordered: "Come over to this side! Diego de Godoy! Scribe of the King! So that His Catholic Majesty will be aware of it, write an ordinance stating that this day those who are here wish to establish the Villa Rica de la Vera Cruz.

"And, as my title of Captain-General comes from Velázquez, I place it here, for it is worthless. I hereby free the members of the town to elect their own authorities! . . .

The founding of Villa Rica

"For those who wish to return, soon we will ready some ships for Cuba. Now, to important matters: Let us elect our new authorities."

While the Captains organized the voting process, Cortés sat down with Diego de Godoy to write the ordinance.

At the same time, many soldiers, once allies of Diego Velázquez, began to join with the founders and their departure diminished the forces of those supporting Juan Velázquez de León, Diego de Ordaz and the rest.

Eventually, the results of the voting were read and certified by Diego de Godoy:

Chief Judge and Captain-General: Hernán Cortés

Mayors: Alonso Hernández Portocarrero and Francisco de Montejo

Captain for the *Entradas*: Pedro de Alvarado; quartermaster, Cristóbal de Olid; high constable, Juan de Escalante; treasurer, Gonzalo Mejía; accountant, Alonso de Ávila; ensign, Juan Corral; constables and storekeepers, Ochoa (the Biscayan) and Alonso Romero.

Cortés ordered that stocks be placed in the plaza and outside of the town, a gallows.

By now, Juan Velázquez and his followers, their numbers much reduced, went around muttering: "Shyster! Bamboozler! Cheat! Sneak!"

They Enter the Mainland. Cempoala

The following day, Cortés met with his captains.

"Regarding colonization, we must do it as quickly as we can. We will march inland and leave these sand dunes behind. You, Pedro de Alvarado, go to the area that they call Culúa, where the natives are subjects of Mexico. There is a village, Cotasta. Occupy it and we will advance toward Quiauiztlan, which is the village Montejo told us about."

Portocarrero said to him: "And what should we do with Diego Velázquez's supporters, who are furious and beginning to put together factions and schemes? They even speak disrespectfully of Your Grace."

Cortés answered: "I have already said that I will not keep anyone here by force. Those who wish may return to Cuba, but in the meantime, and as of now, Juan de Escalante should order them to accompany our men as we march inland."

Escalante delivered the message, but soon came back. "Captain! They refuse to obey you and even mouth arrogant words against you."

"My Captains," said Cortés, "it's not a good idea to allow these obstinate men to stay behind. As chief justice of this village, I hereby order you to arrest and put in chains under guard the following men: Juan Velázquez de León, Diego de Ordaz, Escobar "the Page," and Pedro Escudero. Constables! Carry out this order! They are to be held on the flagship and guarded."

After the constables left to carry out his orders, Cortés resumed. "Let us go inland to the Culúa territory and lead the armada to the secure location Montejo described. Three hundred will go by land and one hundred and fifty, with the artillery, will travel by sea and we will be in constant contact."

Without taking time to eat, the expedition spent the night in Cotasta. The following day, they continued to advance through the savanna, where deer were grazing. On his sorrel-colored mare, Pedro de Alvarado galloped toward a deer and thrust his lance but missed it. At that very moment, twelve Indians appeared. Through the interpreters, they said they brought turkeys and "pan de mar" that their *cacique* sent. They invited the Spaniards to visit their village.

In many areas the Spaniards passed through there were examples of cruel acts of human sacrifice.

One day, Bernal Díaz del Castillo was on watch with a companion, when in some sand dunes he saw five Indians dressed in a style not seen before with great ear pieces and mouth adornments. They spoke a language that neither Malinche nor Aguilar understood, but she called out to them in her mother tongue, and the one who was nearest to her answered in the language of the Totonacas. With the confidence of her Indian heritage, she translated what they said, then led them to Cortés and said to him: "*Señor Capitán*, these five natives are Totonacas, which is a very large kingdom in this region. They say they come from a village called Cempuallan and that their *cacique* wishes to speak with you. Some time ago, Moctezuma's Mexicans conquered them. With great cruelty they subdued them and demand that they pay tribute to Moctezuma. The *cacique* wishes to speak to you about this."

"Tell him," Cortés said to *Doña* Marina, "that with pleasure we will go to discuss with their *cacique* whatever matters he wishes to confide in us."

Portocarrero and Pedro de Alvarado were close to Cortés and to them commented: "By my conscience, noblemen! This is a pronouncement from heaven itself! It seems to me that in these lands the Indians are divided and there are strong feelings of rancor among them. Remember, it was Caesar who said 'divide and conquer.' Well, they are already divided and we would be idiots if we failed to take advantage of their differences. So let us visit this *cacique* as soon as we can to confirm what these visitors have told us. Let us make haste to conquer this land as we come face-to-face with these people on their own soil. On to Cempoala!"

Moving along the road on their horses, Cortés said to Portocarrero: "Alonso, I may have hurt your feelings when I took as a free Indian servant *Doña* Marina, who has been most useful to me as a translator and who now spends more time in my company than in serving you."

"Don't worry about it, Captain, she is a very cold and contemptuous woman and it is not possible to have the relations with her a man should have. Keep her. She will serve you well; she is always looking at you."

"I will make up for this favor, Alonso. You will be well compensated."

The change of scenery was remarkable to the Spaniards—from the sand dunes of San Juan de Ulúa to the tropical meadows; a savanna filled with life and in the distance the snow-capped peak of Citlaltépetl.

Cortés' military group, even in these friendly lands, was well organized, with scouts, reconnoitering patrols, the main body of the army and the rear guard.

A short distance from Cempoala, twenty of the town's officials came out to receive the Spanish army with huge bundles of flowers. From a distance some of the Spanish soldiers thought the houses were made of silver—they were whitewashed and in the sunlight shined like silver. They ran up to Cortés, who was mounted on his horse.

"That city is made of silver, Captain!" they shouted.

When Marina heard the man, she explained to Cortés: "It is not silver or anything like it. The whitewash paint makes it shine so brightly."

The illusion became a great joke among the foot soldiers.

In the midst of a joyful multitude, the Spaniards entered Cempoala, the first large city they had encountered: It was so beautifully laid out and had such wonderful gardens that even Cortés commented: "To me it looks like Seville!"

The troops were saying: "That one looks like the house of the Duke of Medina and the other like the Duke of Arcos."

Upon receiving Cortés, the chieftains said that they came in the name of the *cacique* who could not come out to greet them as he was very fat and the walk would fatigue him. However, after the Spaniards had dined as they deserved and their stomachs were content, the *cacique* appeared in person to visit Cortés.

In a litter carried by many Indian officials, he arrived at the house where Cortés had his headquarters. In good humor and with great joy he greeted the visitors. "Welcome, my lords, to the lands of Cempuallan, the capital of the Totonacapan province, the land where until a short time ago we lived and ate very well as I hope you have done. But a short time ago, a great misfortune befell the Totonacas."

Puffing mightily, the bearers lowered the *cacique* from the stretcher. He waddled into Cortés' quarters, where the other Indians brought in an enormous chair made of wicker with a leather seat and back.

Ceremoniously, Cortés stood up and tried to give the *cacique* an *abrazo*, but the immense stomach of the man made it impossible.

It was impossible to embrace the *cacique*

The *cacique* roared with laughter at Cortés' confusion. "I'm afraid what you attempt is impossible, Captain. Let us demonstrate our signs of respect with our hands."

As they formally shook hands, Cortés said, "Cempoala is beautiful, so much so that it reminds us of Seville, one of the most beautiful cities of our homeland."

The *cacique* frowned bitterly. "It would be even more beautiful if it were not for the abuses and bad treatment the Mexicans impose upon us. Ever since Moctezuma ordered our lord to renounce the treaties we had made with them. A few years ago," even his smile disappeared now, "after they waged damaging wars against us, they demanded tributes and oppressed us.

"If we do not give them what they demand, they raze fields that have been recently sown and carry off our women and children to violate them in front of their families. They abuse everyone and if we do not give them our possessions, they steal them and beat us."

The *cacique* began to cry. ". . . and they kill our people or take them alive to be sacrificed to their gods. All thirty Totonaca villages suffer such oppression from the Mexicans."

"Why do you not oppose such atrocious tyranny?" Cortés asked.

"Because Moctezuma is a very powerful lord who has become lord over everything: He is as strong as he is cruel." The *cacique* sighed impatiently.

Cortés nodded sympathetically.

"It hurts us very much to hear your afflictions. But do not worry any longer as we have been sent here by the most powerful king in the world precisely to prevent such stealing and grievances. We will free you from the abuses and the authority of Moctezuma. If you wish to have our aid, you must understand that our God does not condone human sacrifices and the adoration of your idols that resemble Satan, himself. You must hear Fray Bartolomé de Olmedo speak the truth in which we believe so we may be able to help you."

"As you wish; as you wish; but help us to loosen Moctezuma's claws and get rid of the cruel treatment we have been subjected to."

The Calpixques [Tax-collectors]

As they were talking, some Indians of the village came to inform the *caciques* who were meeting with Cortés that five Mexicans who were Moctezuma's *calpixques* had arrived. After they heard this news, the color drained from the Totonacas' faces and they began to tremble from fear. Quickly, they left Cortés and went to greet the Mexicans.

Frightened, the fat *cacique* stood up from his chair with all the haste he could summon. All he said was: "The Mexicans, the Mexicans!"

With great dignity and composure, the Mexicans walked past the Spaniards without acknowledging them until they came to the fat *cacique*'s palace. The Mexicans were dressed in beautifully embroidered cloaks and loin-cloths and their straight shiny hair was gathered up as though tied on their heads. Each one held a rose, which he was sniffing. They were attended by servants carrying flywhisks. Each of the five displayed the insignias of their rank and each held a staff of authority. Accompanied by groups of submissive Totonacas, they arrived at the *cacique*'s palace. The Totonacas left when the Mexicans were served their meal.

The fat *cacique* wished to speak to them, but they would not allow him to enter the room until they had eaten. By now the *cacique* was sweating and shaking with fear, because from time to time Moctezuma's emissaries glared at him. When they had finished their meal, the Mexicans allowed the *cacique* to enter the room. Immediately, they began to berate him and to tap him disdainfully with their staffs.

At the end of this humiliating scene, Cortés asked the fat *cacique* to appear before him. Laconic, grieved and exhausted, the dripping, defeated *cacique* came in with some other officials.

"I have been advised that you permitted the Mexicans to deal severely with the *cacique* in your own palace and in your presence," said Cortés.

"Captain," answered one of the officials, "the *calpixques* are very angry because we have received you hospitably, giving you lodging and food without Moctezuma's permission. They also object to the gold jewelry that we have given you and even that we spoke with you. In order to make amends to their gods—more than an ordinary tribute—they demand twenty male and female Indians for sacrifice."

The fat *cacique* was beside himself. "Twenty of our women and among them some from my own family. Now, great lord, you can plainly see the tyranny we suffer. What can we do to oppose Moctezuma's anger?"

Embajadores de Moctezuma llegan a Cempoala

Moctezuma's ambassadors arrive at Cempoala

Cortés allowed a moment of silence to pass.

"It's only a small thing that has frightened you. I have told you that the King, my lord, has sent us here to punish offenders and we will not allow sacrifices or stealing. We are here to defend you. To that end, I order your guards, immediately and in front of me, to seize and tie up the tax-collectors so that Moctezuma may learn the reason, how they come to rob and carry away as slaves your children and women and commit other misfortunes."

When the *cacique* vacillated, Cortés reproached him, shouting insistently, "Do it! I order it!"

Reluctantly, the fat *cacique* complied and the *calpixques*, much to their astonishment, were seized and cords were bound around their necks, hands and legs, then tied to heavy posts.

"We have obeyed your order," said the fat *cacique*, "but what will happen to us now? All the Mexicans might well rise up against us. If so, they will kill us and destroy our city."

Unruffled by the *cacique*'s nervous expressions of fear, Cortés reassured him. "My good friend, do not be afraid. I have already told you we are here to help you. My brothers and I will defend you from all of Moctezuma's forces and we will kill anyone who even tries to harm you and your people. Before we fulfill that commitment, however, you, your village, and the entire Totonaca nation must pledge obedience to *our* Emperor. And all of these villages and *caciques* must promise they will side with us in whatever we ask of them. They must promise to join forces with us against Moctezuma."

Cortés asked for the scribe, Godoy. In his presence, the Totonaca *caciques* pledged their oaths of allegiance to King Carlos of Spain.

Cortés demanded that the Indians send a notice throughout the Totonaca territory that the tribe would no longer pay tribute to Moctezuma. The results of his message were immediate. The Totonaca people began to say:

"Truly these white men are *teules*."

From that time on in the Indian villages, the people began to call the Spaniards *teules*.

The fat *cacique* discussed with Cortés the fate of the captured *calpixques*.

"We will sacrifice them at once so our gods will favor us and aid us in the wars Moctezuma will now wage against us. Besides, if they are dead then they can't tell Moctezuma what went on."

Cortés was livid. "Absolutely not! Human sacrifices are the work of the devil himself. Such things violate our beliefs. Soon we will speak to you about The Truth. For now, though, there will be no sacrifices of the *calpixques*. They will remain in my personal custody and our guards will watch over them."

At midnight, the Spanish guards released two of the *calpixques* and brought the men to Cortés' quarters. The Captain-General greeted them with great interest. Smiling, he asked them through his interpreter, *Doña* Marina: "What happened to you? Who are you and why are you being held?"

"We are ambassadors or, really, tax collectors from the great Lord Moctezuma. We came to collect the tribute these Cempuallans owe us. Apparently, these Totonacas became demented by your presence and took us prisoner. We have been humiliated. Soon, Moctezuma will learn about this incident and that will mean the end of the Totonaca nation."

Cortés smiled warmly. "How sorry I am about the affront committed against you. I doubt the Totonacas planned it, but they probably think it will put pressure on you. But do not fear. Because of Moctezuma's reputation, we have come from a distant land to make friends with him. You must go immediately to Mexico to send my greetings and give him the message that I want his friendship. Now that I have freed two of you, I will personally guarantee the well-being of the other three who remain prisoners. Please tell Moctezuma that is but one example of my friendship."

The two *calpixques* left at once. The following morning, when the Totonacas learned of their escape, they hurried to Cortés to complain.

"Captain, no doubt your guards must have fallen asleep and two of the five captives have escaped. Soon word will reach Mexico about this grave affront we have committed against Moctezuma."

Cortés glared at the Totonacas. "I don't know if the guards fell asleep or if some of Moctezuma's secret supporters or others fearful of his anger helped them. In any case, I will punish the guilty. So that such a despicable escape does not happen again, the Mexican prisoners wlll be confined in one of our ships. Take them to Alvarado's ship."

After the prisoners were taken away, Cortés met with all his captains, except for Diego Velázquez's friends, who were still under arrest.

"That was a splendid piece of work you accomplished with these Indians, Captain," Alvarado began.

"All to advance our cause, my friend. Here we are, brave men who wish to continue inland to colonize this land, which each day seems more marvelous than before. As if signs from God, the divisions and rivalries among the Indians have been revealed to us. They have not one, but many nations among them."

"Well, that's the way it looks, at least," said Portocarrero. "Not only do the natives of Cempoala fear and hate the Mexicans, but as we have learned through *Doña* Marina, there are internal conflicts between Temistitan,* where Moctezuma governs, and certain villages who report there is even friction between Texcala and Huejotzingo and others whose names I cannot even pronounce."

"With God's help we have made an alliance with Cempoala and so as not to anger Moctezuma we have freed his ambassadors. When I order it, Alvarado, release the other three who are being held in your ship, too. Let them go a few leagues north of here, where there are no Totonacas, so the three may return and make Moctezuma happy."

Alvarado roared with laughter. "Captain, oh, captain, you must have heard the old saying, 'all's fair in love and war.'"

"Perhaps so, Alvarado. But we would be idiots if we began our advance into the interior only to clash with Moctezuma's forces. As long as we seek alliances, things will go more easily. Nevertheless, I am convinced, captains, that we can penetrate this territory. Before we do, though, we must fortify our Villa to make sure our rear is protected. Then we will see who really wishes to go back to Cuba. Every day the number is fewer. And in a short time, through the will of God, we will greet in person the elusive Moctezuma."

The captains cheered.

---

* Cortés and his men could not pronounce the names in the Náhuatl language. Instead of *Tenochtitlan* (Mexico), they said *Temistitan*. (Letter from Lic. José López Portillo to Beatrice Berler, April 4, 1988)—Trans.

In Villa Rica

With the point of a lance Cortés drew in the sand the layout of Villa Rica. Here, the site of the fortified church; there, the municipal council hall, the jail, the arsenal, warehouses and the slaughterhouse. As an example to the others, he took off his armor and went to work making the foundations, digging out rocks and carrying them away. Soon, all the other Spaniards were working, too. Then the work was speeded up when the *cacique* of Cempoala sent laborers and artisans to help.

Seated under the shade of a tree, the translators, *Doña* Marina and Jerónimo de Aguilar, were chatting.

"Tell me, Aguilar," she said fervently, "what kind of man is Captain Cortés? Who is this one who arrives like a god in the year that was announced and yet who works like a man? Is he by chance Quetzalcóatl? Who is he? His son? His brother?" She kept repeating the phrases as she stared at Cortés with admiration. "What is he? Who is he? I am so confused!"

"What do you mean 'the year it was announced,' *Doña* Marina?"

"Our forefathers predicted that in the year *Ce-Acatl*, which we are in now, Quetzalcóatl would come from the East, that he would return with his white brothers. Now, here he is, but I do not really know who he is."

"Ask him yourself, *Doña* Marina. I know him to be a captain from Extremadura, but only he knows for sure. Go ahead. Ask him."

"I will, but only when I speak the language of Castile more fluently. I will tell him I am Malinalli, born on the day of Malinalli Xóchitl, the enemy of Quetzalcóatl's enemies and to the god I was pledged, destined. I want nothing more than to serve him [Cortés] forever. But I don't want to stay with Portocarrero any longer." She began to weep.

"Come, come, *Doña* Marina, soon you will be able to speak to him. Calm yourself."

While the Spaniards were building the structures of Villa Rica, new ambassadors arrived headed by Moctezuma's two nephews. Reposing in his easy chair, Cortés received them, surrounded by his captains, *Doña* Marina and lieutenant standard bearer—each restraining the guard dogs with leather straps. Cortés made the Mexicans wait. The nephews had brought gifts of gold and beautiful cloths. After exchanging formal greetings, they spread the gifts on the rugs in Cortés' hut.

The older spoke. "Our lord, the great Moctezuma, once more greets you with respect. He is grateful because you freed two of the five tax collectors captured by the Totonaca's rebels. He is sorry that the Totonacas rebelled, thinking they had found favor with you, the gods. For the present, and out of deep respect for your gods, I have not dispatched my soldiers to punish the Totonacas as they deserve. But some day I will."

Gravely, Cortés responded. "Without our knowledge, the Totonacas took the great Moctezuma's ambassadors prisoner. When we heard about it, we freed two of them at once. The other three are safe on one of our ships, but before you leave we will entrust them to you. The great Moctezuma may be assured of our friendship despite the fact that Governor Pitalpitoque abandoned us and did not supply the food we had been promised. Only for that reason did we invade this territory and make an association with the Totonacas who are now subjects of His Majesty, King Carlos. It would be wise for Moctezuma to pardon their foolishness until we can meet with him in person."

"We will tell Moctezuma what the captain has told us. As for meeting him, that is not possible because the journey can be very difficult."

With that, the nephews departed.

The Totonacas, amazed, saw how tenderly the Mexicans were treating the Spaniards with gifts and fine words. Some of them remarked to the corpulent *cacique*: "In truth, these are gods."

Once the emissaries of Moctezuma were gone, the fat *cacique* visited Cortés. "How good it would be if all Mexicans were as nice as these and had such good manners."

"How have they been treating your people?" Cortés asked.

"The Mexican garrisons in Cicapatzingo have stolen and destroyed our crops and carried off the women. We would like the gods to help us against them."

"We are allies in order to help you in every way. You can count on that," Cortés said firmly.

After the *cacique* left, Cortés grinned broadly. He told his captains: "You know, my lords, it seems to me that throughout these lands we are known as courageous men; they believe we are gods or their idols. If they are so sure that one of us is strong enough to destroy those other Indian warriors—their enemies—then we should send Heredia—'the old man.'"

Cortés demanded his presence. Heredia, the Biscayan, had a bad twitch on his cheek, a huge beard, a face full of scars. He was blind in one eye and lame in one leg.

"Heredia, you go with these *caciques* to the river. When you arrive, pretend to drink and wash your hands, then fire a shot from your musket. I will send an order to call you back. I wish to do this because these people think we are gods. Since you are quite ugly enough, they will believe you are an idol."

To the *caciques*, Cortés said, "I am sending this brother of mine with you to kill or expel all the Culúas from the village you speak of and to bring me as prisoners all those who refuse to leave."

The *caciques* looked at him with astonishment. They did not know whether to believe him, but seeing that Cortés was serious, they did as they were told. At the river, Heredia fired his musket, which frightened the enemies in Cicapatzingo.

Then, Cortés sent an officer to summon Heredia and said to the *caciques*: "I have thought of a better idea. Tomorrow, I will go myself with my own 'mouths of fire.'" Then, Cortés ordered the *caciques* to provide *tamemes** to pull the cannon.

And to the ensign, he said:

"Convene the other captains and the soldiers. Tomorrow, we will raid Cicapatzingo territory."

The following day, the army was in formation and about to march away when seven of Diego Velázquez's supporters broke ranks. Through a spokesman, they announced, "We, and many more like us, are not marching into the interior. Captain, you have brought us here under a false pretense, thinking we are fools, which we are not. You have promised us a ship to take us back to Cuba and that is what we wish to do. You have yet to keep your word on this."

Cortés addressed the rebels easily. "I did promise that, but now I have further responsibility for His Majesty's subjects. You who abandon their Captain's flag are making a big mistake. Alaminos, please prepare a ship, well supplied, so these men who wish to leave may do so. And we will delay our march to the interior untll we know for certain how many will honor the flag."

With that, Cortés withdrew to his quarters, where the officials and magistrates of Villa Rica found him. They were both troubled and angry.

"Captain," said Alvarado, "we think it is bad judgment to have delayed the march inland because of these traitors. If we give into them now, they will soon destroy all of us."

"Do not worry yourself, Alvarado," Cortés said lightly. "This is the chance, once and for all, to finish off these bastards. Listen well to my plans. This is an official session of Municipal Council and we will decide right here and now what to do about those who beg to return."

"They will not return," said Alvarado.

"There can be no retreat!" yelled the other captains.

"All right," Cortés said, "the Municipal Council, under threat of death, prohibits any man from abandoning the Captain's flag during the march to the interior to aid His Majesty's new subjects."

"That order has the full approval of the Municipal Council," agreed all the Captains.

The following day, the army began its march accompanied by the subdued and frustrated rebels. The cannon were hauled by the *tamemes* and more than a thousand armed Cempoaltecans accompanied the Spanish army.

When the force arrived at the banks of the river, near Cicapatzingo, Cortés was greeted peacefully and the people there asked to meet with him.

---

* *Tamemes*, humble Indian porters who carried supplies weighing up to fifty pounds for a distance of eighteen or twenty miles. The Mexicans had not invented the wheel nor did they have domesticated animals that could carry a load. It is curious to note that they had toys with wheels.—Trans.

"Captain," they said with tears in their eyes, "the Mexican garrisons withdrew from this area when you freed the two *calpixques*. These Cempoala people came to fight because of some old grudges and they wish to sack our farms. We beg you to stop them."

"Alvarado! Olid! Do not permit the Cempoaltecans to advance. They must not cross this river or enter that village. Bring their *caciques* here to me."

When they appeared, Cortés said in a loud voice full of fury: "You have tricked me and made me very angry. I do not see any Mexican garrisons. You came here with me only to settle old disputes and to plunder for the spoils of war. That is not how brother villages and subjects of His Majesty King Carlos treat each other. You must return at once everything you have taken from them."

Meekly, the Cempoaltecans complied.

"Now, give them your hands and *abrazos* as a sign of peace and harmony, as we all serve the same King and we must fight against the common enemy, not among ourselves. Let us return to Cempoala."

Upon entering a village on the road back, Cortés noticed a disturbance. A soldier was stealing two turkeys from some Indians who were trying to stop him.

"For God's sake!" roared Cortés, "we have just ordered the Cempoaltecans to return the booty they took and one of our own men against all my orders steals two turkeys. That is intolerable! I have warned you against such a breach of discipline. Hang that scoundrel from this branch."

The order was quickly obeyed. As the rope tightened, Cortés winked at Alvarado who was close beside him. Alvarado moved his horse toward the dangling man and with a mighty sweep of his sword, severed the rope. Cortés glared, then grinned broadly. "All right, men. Now, each of you has had an important lesson. But next time, Alvarado's sword may not be there to save you."

La próxima vez no habrá espada de Alvarado...

"The next time we will not have Alvarado's sword."

103

More Idols Demolished

When the events of the campaign were related to the fat *cacique*, he received Cortés with great signs of reverence and understanding and said to him, "We have learned that your justice is fair and good. You judge us precisely as you do your own. We wish to be not only your friends, but your brothers. We beg you to accept our daughters and kinswomen to beget a new generation."

The *cacique* ordered eight Indian maidens to serve Cortés and his captains. Then he said to Cortés, "Lord, these seven girls are for your captains. The eighth, my niece, is for you. She is a titled lady over the villages and subjects."

The *cacique's* niece was as fat as he and just as ugly. Cortés hardly reacted at all. He said, "It is a great honor you have given me and my Captains. But before we accept them as you suggest and consider ourselves your brothers, you must no longer believe in or honor those horrible idols." Cortés pointed his finger toward those on the pyramid.

"Furthermore, you must not sacrifice any more human beings or follow that rite, because it is the work of the devil. Then you must become Christians. Tomorrow, we will meet in this very place to receive the maidens in the baptismal ceremony in which you will abandon your idols and lewdness."

Encouraged by the other chieftains, the *cacique* approached Cortés. "We give you our women as a sign of brotherhood, but we cannot consent to renouncing and destroying our idols. These gods have made it possible for us to live and have good crops. We cannot merely disregard our gods, nor can we cease sacrificing humans, because that will anger our gods. If that happens, they will destroy our village along with you and your men."

Turning his back on the *cacique*, Cortés spoke to his men with great emotion. "From the moment we arrived here in love and friendship, we have witnessed many cruelties and other disgraceful acts that we will no longer tolerate. How can we even attempt to do any good deeds if we do not direct our cause for the honor of God. If we do not serve Our Lord, we deserve nothing—not honor, conquest, or gold. We will be condoning evil if we do not stop the human sacrifices performed before these idols. So, gentlemen, right now, we are going to destroy them. Let happen what may happen! Be alert in case the Indians try to defend their idols, but when I give the order, topple them, in the name of service to God."

To Marina, who now understood and spoke a little Spanish, he said, "Tell the fat *cacique* that I am ordering these idols destroyed because there is no other way we can become brothers."

The *cacique* ordered his people to be ready to fight, then he shouted to Cortés, "Do not dishonor our gods, for we all may die."

"I have already told you that you must no longer make sacrifices to those evil idols. Do not ignore my orders. So that there will be no more misunderstandings, your devils are about to collapse."

Cortés turned to the troops. "Soldiers, climb the steps and knock those idols to the ground. Olid, you and your troops seize and bind that fat *cacique* and his chiefs and threaten to kill them if their warriors dare attack us. Through *Doña* Marina tell them that if they continue to thwart us we will leave them to the tender mercy of the Mexicans."

One troop of Spanish soldiers stood guard at the base of the pyramid while the others climbed up to where the idols were placed and toppled them down the steps. Completely disconcerted, the Cempoaltecan warriors did not attempt to oppose the desecration. Bawling loudly, the fat *cacique* covered his face with a cloth so he wouldn't have to witness the destruction.

"It is without our consent," he managed between sobs, "that you are destroying our gods. Because you are gods, you may be stronger than they, but perhaps, you too will die because of your boldness."

Violently, the Spanish soldiers hurled the idols, which crumbled as they bounced off the steps of the pyramid. The Totonacans shrieked and wept and covered their eyes.

They shouted: "We are innocent of this desecration! It's the gods who are guilty! The same ones who say they will defend us from the Mexicans."

The Cempoala idols are demolished

When some of the warriors aimed arrows at the Spaniards, Cortés had Marina warn them:

"If you shoot even one arrow, your *cacique*, his chieftains, and the priests who are our captives, will all die."

After the tumult had passed and the broken idols had crashed onto the plaza, the dust finally settled.

Cortés said, "Your devils are destroyed and lie helpless in the dust, yet nothing evil has happened. This should prove you have been deceived. You were mistaken to worship these bundles of wood, stone and rock that we are about to set afire."

Quickly, he ordered the soldiers to "take these broken idols and burn the horrible objects." Then he added, "Untie the *cacique* and his chieftains!"

Without blinking, Cortés said: "Now we may be brothers. Now we will defend you against Moctezuma and whomever else might wish to harm you. But remember this—not on the highest points of your temples or in any other location will you be allowed to restore these demons. I will replace them with our symbols of Truth so you may worship them even as we do."

He motioned to the padre. "Fray Bartolomé de Olmedo! Provide whatever is necessary so this temple may be cleaned and white-washed to become a suitable home for the Christ, Our Lord, and his Most Revered Mother. Get the carpenters to help you."

Fray Bartolomé supervised Spaniards and Indians as they worked. First they cleaned, then they painted the walls with lime. The men erected an altar and ordered the women to bring flowers to adorn the area under the Cross with the image of the Virgin. Supervising the work were armed and alert Spanish soldiers.

At nightfall, the priest went to see Cortés. "I have followed your orders and have already begun to preach to the natives. Because this city is the largest we have encountered so far, I would like your authorization to leave behind old Juan de la Torre as the head of this mission. He limps, as you know, Captain, so his usefulness as a soldier is limited. I have selected eight Indian priests to help with the converts and they will assist him."

"Yes, but cut off that foul-smelling hair full of dried blood that is hanging down their faces. Then dress them in white robes so they may at least appear devout."

"I will do as Your Grace ordains," Fray Bartolomé said.

Cortés raised an imperious hand. "Not yet, Father. For the crowning glory, tomorrow you chant the Mass and baptize those Indian maidens they gave us. We must strike while the iron is hot."

Next day the Mass was celebrated and all the *caciques* were invited to witness the baptism of the Indian girls. For his sermon, Fray Bartolomé de Olmedo preached against the idols.

Among themselves, the Totonacans nodded and whispered, "These gods are stronger than the others."

After the ceremony, Fray Bartolomé said to Cortés, "The Indian maidens are now Christians. You may receive them."

"Tell the *cacique* their fathers or uncles may bring them to us."

The ugliest and fattest one, the niece of the *cacique*, was named Catalina. They led her to Cortés and he received her with kindness despite the soldiers' rude comments.

The most beautiful, *Doña* Francisca, was given to Portocarrero, and the others were divided among the other Captains.

When he led the beautiful Indian maiden to Portocarrero, Cortés said, "You deserve this beautiful Indian, old friend, as *Doña* Marina, my translator, is with me more than you. She is most useful to me in all circumstances in this land."

Portocarrero demonstrated his gratitude with a gesture and a smile.

Doña Marina, satisfied now, witnessed the scene and said to Jerónimo, "Aguilar, now we are closer to the day when I will be all to my love and lord. . . ."

Cortés and his men took leave of the obese *cacique*, leaving that same day for Villa Rica de la Vera Cruz.

"We leave you our altar. Juan de la Torre will be in charge. You must help him in all that he asks. Soon we will be back to explore further the Mexican territories, so you should prepare extra warriors and *tamemes* to help us."

"Without doubt, powerful gods you are," said the fat *cacique*. "Now we have no other gods but yours. And we will honor them. At last, we really believe we are your brothers, because you take our women away with you. Go contented. We will await your return."

The Report to the King

When the troops returned to Villa Rica they found the construction quite advanced. The whole village was bustling with activity.

When Cortés arrived, Captain Escalante, who had been in charge of the garrison, reported. "Everything is in order at the Villa, Captain. We need only to roof the buildings and lay the floors. The other news is that a ship arrived under the command of Francisco de Salcedo with supplies, ten more soldiers, a horse and mare, some arms and news from La Española."

"Thank you for your report, Captain. Tell Salcedo I would like to see him."

"That fellow Salcedo," muttered Bernal Díaz to his companions, "whom we call the 'fastidious' one, brags all the time and always goes about in clean, neat clothes in the height of fashion."

Cortés greeted him cordially. "Welcome, Francisco de Salcedo. It took you a long time to get here, but your arrival is indeed timely."

"The ship you bought in Santiago required more time than we expected to repair her hull, but we set sail when Velázquez least expected and his men were unable to stop us."

"How is my *compadre, Don* Diego?" Cortés almost sneered.

"Still ranting and raving about you. But he is a bit happier since he was appointed *Adelantado* of Cuba, with powers to trade and extract riches and colonize in Yucatán."

"Governor of Cuba! So my dear *compadre* now has powers contrary to mine. Hmmm. We will have to put things into action."

"Besides that, Captain, when we left, it was rumored a well-supplied armada was being organized with many men, at the command, it was said, of Pánfilo de Narváez whose orders were to capture and punish you."

"Pánfilo de Narváez! Strong and robust, but frequently sleep overcomes him," remarked Cortés smiling. "Thanks, Salcedo. You are the same natty dresser I remember."

Quickly, Cortés summoned his captains and told them the news.

"Gentlemen, we must act quickly because of what I am confiding in you. Diego Velázquez is now Governor of Cuba, with the authority to colonize the Yucatán. Now, he is organizing an expedition under the command of Pánfilo de Narváez to humiliate us."

"So we will stop him," Alvarado shrugged.

"This is more serious, because now he has the law behind him!" said Portocarrero.

"Yes, but we have the achievements," said Cortés. "We are already here, acquainted with the land and we have riches we can exhibit to His Majesty. Finally, I propose to act as follows. First, we will dispatch to the Spanish Court two proctors with a letter from the Municipal Council in which we describe everything that has taken place in these lands from the failures of the Hernández de Córdoba and Grijalva expeditions up to our actual victories, and relate how Velázquez wanted to keep material wealth for his own benefit without colonizing. We will also tell His Majesty it was the will of these brave Spaniards to found a Villa and to elect authorities who would colonize, according to the Bull of Pope Alexander VI, to better serve God and His Majesty. We implore His Majesty's permission to confirm authority over what we have conquered and His gratitude for the peace we have brought to this country."*

Cristóbal de Olid interrupted. "Also be sure to say that Velázquez only put up one-third of the expenses for this armada and that he spent more of that on wines and clothes and other useless things for us to sell here at double and triple his cost."

Alvarado added, "That and more, and especially you must beg His Majesty not to grant any authority to Velázquez here and to confirm those members of the Municipal Council whom we elected."

"And don't forget," put in Portocarrero, "when we dispatch the gold we have obtained and Moctezuma's presents, besides the Royal Fifth, the King will gain advantage over Velázquez's greed and that will demonstrate our devotion to His Majesty."

Cortés smiled his agreement. "Very well put, my friends. We will begin to write the Report of the Municipal Council as we all have agreed. I will go instruct Godoy. You, Portocarrero, and Sandoval will add your thoughts as will the captains and ten of the best trained soldiers who wish to settle this land.

"But that won't be enough, men," Cortés said. "We must go inland to locate Moctezuma and his kingdom, but we can't afford to leave the Villa unprotected."

"May I remind you, Captain, that the followers of Velázquez who wished to return to Cuba are once again inspired to revolt now that he has been named Governor."

"Gentlemen, I am formulating a plan that will finally resolve that question. I urge each of you to encourage your soldiers to accept my decision to explore the Mexican territory and you must secure the men's consent to donate their share of any treasure to the King."

---

* In a letter to the emperor, Cortés gave a full account of everything that had happened since his departure from Cuba. This was the FIRST LETTER. No one has ever located a copy and it has eluded every search for it in the libraries of Europe. (*Señor* Lic. Francisco Porrúa gave this datum to the translator, July 10, 1990.)—Trans.

Conspiracy

The Captains agreed to Cortés' terms and left him while he began to write the communique. A few moments later, an aide interrupted to tell Cortés that Bernardino de Coria wished to speak to him confidentially.

"All right. Have him come in while I finish this page."

Cortés looked up from his parchment. "What brings you here, my good Bernardino, at so late an hour?"

"First, Captain, I ask your word of clemency in recognition of our old friendship in La Española."

"So granted, Bernardino. Your cause must be very serious. You seem very disturbed."

"It is serious, Captain, and by your clemency I hereby withdraw from a conspiracy I was involved in with Diego Velázquez's supporters to steal a ship and return to Cuba so we could inform him about your activities and all that has taken place here."

"Who else is involved in the conspiracy?"

"Here is the list, Captain."

"Which is the leader?"

"Both Escudero and Cermeño. With them are Gonzalo de Umbría, the two Peñete brothers, and even the priest, Juan Díaz, who encourages them. I think there are a few more. They asked me to sneak some provisions from the ship "El Pulido," taking advantage that I had been drinking a lot. But I could not sleep thinking how I might lose your valued friendship."

"Which Escudero?" Cortés asked.

"Pedro, the one who was held prisoner on the flagship with Velázquez de León and Diego de Ordaz. He escaped from there to organize this conspiracy."

"Don't worry about it. When do they expect to put his absurd plan into action?"

"Later tonight, before dawn."

"We must stop them."

Cortés called in Cristóbal de Olid and Portocarrero.

"Get your troops together. A bunch of Velázquez's followers plan to steal a ship and desert from La Villa."

Together, they went to the port, where Cortés posted guards. When the conspirators arrived, they were seized.

In his strong husky tones, Cristóbal de Olid reproached them, "Where do you think you are going, deserters?"

The traitors tried to resist the guards, but they were soon subdued.

"Do you admit you were going to steal a vessel and desert the Villa?" Cortés asked as Chief Justice.

Escudero answered:

"That is true, Captain, since you never carried out your promise to those who wished to return."

"Quite so. I gave my word to you, but under the death penalty the Municipal Council ordered that no one could leave. Particularly since we are now at war. And now you plan to steal a ship and leave under the cover of night. Olid, find out who the leaders of these rebels are."

After questioning and contending with the conspirators, Olid reported:

"Cermeño and Escudero have admitted they are the ringleaders. Umbría and the Peñete brothers are allied with them."

"Present them before the Chief Justice of the Villa Rica de la Vera Cruz."

When the deserters were in front of Cortés, he said: "Do you admit you have led a rebellian against a legal order of the Municipal Council and that you wish to desert this land by stealing a ship to go to Cuba?"

"We do," they said as Olid prodded them.

"In view of the gravity of your crime and as Chief Justice, I condemn the two leaders to die by hanging. For Gonzalo de Umbría, his legs shall be cut off. The Peñete brothers shall be flogged and I will personally punish the priest," Cortés said.

"Hang them."

The orders were carried out.

Umbría's legs were hacked off and the Peñete brothers were lashed.

Then, Cortés ordered Cristóbal de Olid: "Awaken the other captains and convene them in my quarters, while I go to the flag-ship to deal with the prisoners Juan Velázquez de León and Diego de Ordaz to see if they are willing to join us when we head inland to seek treasure and fame. Ask if they wish to remain prisoners, at the risk of death, if we prove they were part of the conspiracy."

At midmorning, Cortés met with the captains in his quarters, accompanied by Juan Velázquez de León and Diego de Ordaz. The Chief Justice said: "Captain, these gentlemen have decided to join us because I have convinced them they will better serve God and His Majesty as we explore this Culúa territory to conquer and colonize. They have given me their word as gentlemen that they were not involved in this latest conspiracy. They wish to forget about their 'games' and conspiracies to return to Cuba and will now obey their captain's orders."

"Captain Hernán Cortés," said *Don* Juan Velázquez de León, "has been very persuasive and most generous with us. He told us our share in the division of the treasure will be recognized despite our rebellion."

"With your authorization, gentlemen, we will send your gold to His Majesty, along with the precious metal from the other men. Gifts crush boulders," said Alvarado cheerfully.

111

When Cortés noticed the freed men were confused, he told them, "We will explain it to you later."

"With all good fortune," said Montejo, "welcome once again to our arrangement, brave captains."

"Welcome!" they all cried.

"Men," Cortés said, "in view of the misfortune of Cermeño and Escudero, we must not only remain firm, we must act quickly to launch our conquest of these lands. My letter with our Report to the Municipal Council is almost finished. With it will go another from me to my father, Martín Cortés, for him to deliver to the Emperor. The letter has been drawn up by the members of the Municipal Council and ten soldiers." He added, "It is urgent now to dispatch the report. As we are all congregated here, I propose the following two men be sent as our representatives to Spain: Alonso Hernández Portocarrero and Francisco de Montejo. We have the best ship to make this journey, qualified and commanded by Antón de Alaminos. They will sail the 16th of July in this year of 1519, the day after tomorrow. I urge that you ask your soldiers to express their desires concerning the movement into the interior as well as their consent to offer their share of the gold to His Majesty and to accept as proctors Portocarrero and Montejo. My friends, captains, go and speak to your soldiers."

The next day, the captain, the two emissaries and the troops assembled in front of Cortés' quarters.

Portocarrero turned to him and said: "It is fitting, Captain Cortés, that you heed what these soldiers have to say. They have selected Bernal Díaz del Castillo to speak for them."

"Step right up, Bernal, the indispensible."

"Captain, we have been in this Villa for three months having no more to do than building the fortress, the other buildings and houses that are now ready for roofs and floors. It would be a good idea to learn about the great Moctezuma and to pursue our lives and our fortunes. But before we take this road, let us send our emissaries to kiss His Majesty's feet and give him an account of everything that has happened since we left the island of Cuba. I also would like you to know that all of us are in accord regarding the gold for His Majesty. We wish to give all that we have acquired as well as the gifts that Moctezuma gave us."

"Officers and soldiers," replied Cortés, "I agree with everything you have said. What pleases me most is a thought that comes to mind. It is almost as if I had known beforehand what you, Bernal, just told me. I had discussed this matter with several of the officers, whether there might be some soldiers who would rather keep their share. If it were divided, then there would be very little to send. Therefore, I appointed Diego de Ordaz and Francisco de Montejo to go from one soldier to another of those whom we suspected would demand their share of gold and ask them to read and sign this paper. If they agree, the emissaries will leave tomorrow.

"Men, you know that we wish to make a gift to His Majesty of gold that we have gathered here, and since it is the first sent from these lands it must be much more than the traditional Royal Fifth. It seems that the rest of us are contented with the share we received. The other officers and soldiers who have signed the paper have done so as a sign that we do not want our share of the gold, but wish only to serve Our Majesty because he grants us his favors. If any man wishes to keep his share he will not be denied. Anyone who wishes to donate his share, please sign here. My last request: We must agree that our emissaries will be Alonso Hernández Portocarrero and Francisco de Montejo."

The following day, Ordaz and Montejo appeared before the Municipal Council. Cortés, the captains and the soldiers were present.

"Captain Cortés," Montejo said, "all of the soldiers signed the account and have accepted the emissaries you appointed to deliver the letters and gold to Spain."

"May the Treasurer of the Municipal Council be protected," answered Cortés. Directing himself to the rest of the men, he said: "May the Father of Mercy chant the Mass and then the emissaries will board with the gold and the letters and some natives* and products of these lands, in order to amaze the Spanish Court."

"When you arrive, don't forget to tell them in a vibrant tone, my friend Montejo," said Juan Velázquez de León, "that 450 soldiers stayed behind—in great danger among the multitude of Indians and war-like people and other ferocious warriors—to serve God and the Royal Crown and that they be merciful for what we ask—and that many of us feel we deserve their support more than those who hold offices and foment only commerce with these ventures."

The ship set sail on the 16th of July. Cortés and the men stayed on the beach for a long time. Finally, when they turned to leave, Cortés took *Doña* Marina's hand. "Alonso, my good friend, is gone. Now, you will come with me."

Goodbye to Portocarrero

---

* They freed from a cage five natives who were ready to be sacrificed.—Trans.

Cortés and Marina

With dignified joy, *Doña* Marina agreed and walked by Cortés' side to his quarters.

There, Marina, in her halting Spanish, asked Cortés: "May I help you, *señor*?"

As she helped take off his armor, Cortés regarded her lustfully. Once the iron was removed, he drew her toward him into a passionate embrace.

"Lord! Oh, my lord!" said Marina.

"Now you are mine; only mine," Cortés said.

"So I always have been, my lord. I was born Malinalli, on the day of Malinalli Xóchitl, the enemy who fought against Huitzilopochtli, the enemy of Quetzalcóatl, my lord, my great lord. As I was his, I am yours. I have been since I was a child."

"I don't understand all that, Marina. You can explain it to me later."

They slept with their arms locked in a warm embrace.

Destroying the Ships

"Men," Cortés said the following morning, "let us waste no time. As we agreed, we must begin our march inland immediately. I will leave promptly for Cempoala to prepare for our advance with the *tamemes* and the Cempoaltecan warriors that the fat *cacique* will supply. The Alvarado brothers, Gonzalo de Sandoval, Cristóbal de Olid and Juan de Escalante, will accompany me. Meanwhile, the rest of you get ready for the journey and wait for further instructions."

Along the road, Cortés and his officers chatted.

"I understand, *señores*," the Captain said, "that we are resolved to begin our march to search for Moctezuma to better serve God and His Majesty."

"Right," said the officers.

"Once we have begun our adventure, there will be no turning back. Agreed?"

"Absolutely."

"I will now confide in you an intimate thought: As we have seen, the ships are expendable—they are a temptation for those who might want to leave and there are many who would risk their lives to steal them. As long as they are anchored in the port, we can expect desertions. As it is, our numbers are too few to attempt this great adventure."

"What can we do, Captain?" asked Olid. "What do you think?"

"I am thinking of a bold stroke, something that any well-intentioned, audacious man would attempt. We must damage the ships so no one can return. But, to do that, I need your opinions and your determination."

They rode along silently for a short while, then Cortés said: "Well, if you are afraid to risk it. . . ."

"No, it isn't that," said Pedro de Alvarado. "You are proposing an action that respectable men would venture and I am with Your Grace. There is no doubt that this undertaking should go forward."

Juan de Escalante put in: "Captain, like Alvarado, I agree with you and no doubt Sandoval and Olid, as valiant and audacious men, would, too. Although he is not here, I can guarantee Ávila would also have the same opinion. I don't know how Juan Velázquez de León or Diego de Ordaz would view it since they have been Velázquez's followers."

"I agree with you, Juan," said Cortés. "I have the same conviction. For me, your agreement is enough. But since the risk is high we must act with great caution."

"We know you are a prudent man," smiled Alvarado. "Tell us your plan."

"You, Juan de Escalante, along with Alvarado and Olid, go back to the Villa and tell Velázquez de León and Ordaz to come immediately to Cempoala with two hundred of their best soldiers. Be sure Jaramillo and Díaz del Castillo are among them. Coach them to beg me to intercept anyone returning to Cuba even if we must destroy the ships."

"Of course!" said Alvarado, smiling. "Once again, 'You ask me to do what I have already made up my mind to.' I understand."

"Once they are here, that very night, take men in whom you have total confidence, then you, Escalante, scuttle the ships. Spread the news that they thought it was only a joke. You will take command of the garrison at the Villa. Choose a hundred soldiers, the wounded, the old, the exhausted, plus any sailors who do not choose to become foot soldiers. You, Alvarado, Sandoval and Olid, with the rest of the men—once you are sure there is no serious unrest because of the damaged ships, leave Escalante in the Villa and come back with all the men to Cempoala as I do not want to lose any more time before beginning our march inland."

"We will do as you have ordered," the captains said, and left at once to carry out Cortés' instructions.*

The ships capsized and sinking

---

* There are many versions describing the destruction of the fleet. Some say Cortés consulted with his officers; others say he did not, but there is no doubt that "Cortés' destruction of his fleet . . . is, perhaps, the most remarkable passage in the life of this remarkable man. History, indeed, affords examples of a similar expedient in emergencies somewhat similar; but none where the chances of success were so precarious, and defeat would be so disastrous. Had he failed, it might well seem an act of madness. Yet it was the fruit of deliberate calculation. . . . There was no alternative in his mind but to succeed or perish. The measure he adopted greatly increased the chance of success. But to carry it into execution, in the face of an incensed and desperate soldiery, was an act of resolution that has few parallels in history." (Prescott, William H., *The History of the Conquest of Mexico*, New York: Modern Library, 1936, 203)—Trans.

Once Juan Velázquez de León and Ordaz with the two hundred soldiers had left the Villa on the way to Cempoala, Escalante began to plan how to scuttle the ships. He decided to invite the guard on each ship to come ashore to celebrate the march inland, then make sure they got drunk. At night, with a select group of men, he bored holes in the hulls of the ships, which made them list and topple sideways in the water. The next day, everyone saw a remarkable sight: All ten vessels were resting on their sides in the harbor.

"Our old ships!" cried Escalante.

"Yes," said a sailor, "old and dead all at the same time. This is some of Cortés' work!"

"Shut-up, you crazy fool! When things go bad, it is better to smile."

Directing his remarks to the ship captains, Escalante ordered: "Save everything useful: Pieces of iron, nails, cordage, cables and anchors, sails and instruments and anything else we can use. And gather it quickly instead of just standing around grumbling!"

Alvarado and Olid left Escalante in charge of the garrison and departed for Cempoala with the rest of the soldiers—some distrustful, others merely frightened, some few cursing bitterly and the rest delighted.

"Just look at that tragedy," Alvarado smiled when he said goodbye to Escalante.

"By my faith!" Olid declared boisterously, "now we shall have to look ahead."

The day before, Velázquez de León and Ordaz had arrived in Cempoala with the two hundred troops. When Cortés greeted them, he said, "As we all had pledged, as soon as we are ready, we shall march into the Culúa territory in search of Moctezuma. I invite you captains to ask the fat *cacique* and his chieftains about the best route to take and how to provide for our needs in the march. Also, figure out some way to maintain contact with Escalante."

Velázquez, Ordaz, Ávila, as well as Gonzalo de Sandoval met with the obese *cacique* and his officers. Among the contingent was *Doña* Marina with Jerónimo de Aguilar. By this time, she could speak passable Spanish and he was nearly fluent in Náhuatl.

"So we may better defend you, as you are now loyal subjects of His Majesty, we have decided to march into Culúa territory to find the great Moctezuma."

"Ya! Only the gods would dare attempt that," said the fat *cacique*. "There are a great many valiant Mexicans."

"Well, we are not afraid of the Mexicans. With God's help and our own strength, we will confront them. We ask you Cempoaltecans to tell us which is the best route to take."

The corpulent *cacique*, after consulting his advisors, said: "The best road is through the province of Tlaxcala, because they are the mortal enemies of the Mexicans, who have never been able to subdue the Tlaxcalans. But they have rendered them powerless, taken over their paths to the salt mines* and thus deprived

---

* The Aztecs controlled all the salt mines in the country. The Tlaxcalans, as enemies of the Aztecs, were deprived of salt for many, many years—until after the Conquest.—Trans.

them of this staple for more than forty years. Moreover, they are our friends and perhaps we can convince them to be yours."

"Will you supply us with guides?"

"I have forty chieftains ready with Teuch, Mamexi and Tamalli as the leaders and one thousand warriors to guide and accompany you and to speak to the Tlaxcalans."

"We will also need load-bearing Indians."

"We have two hundred *tamemes* ready to go with you."

"We will need a contingent to maintain communication with our garrison."

"We will do what we can."

"Ordaz," said Cortés, "speak to the chieftains about carrying out these arrangements we have made with the *cacique*."

Leaving the meeting with the *cacique*, Cortés, Velázquez de León, Sandoval and Ordaz were approached by a large group of soldiers, among whom were Jaramillo and Díaz del Castillo.

"Captains," said Jaramillo, "if Your Graces allow it, we would like to offer you our advice."

"Speak up, Juan," said Cortés.

"We are in favor of going inland to discover the mysteries that may be found, as the captain has said. And we are excited about that adventure. But we also feel fearful. Why don't you explain it to him, Bernal?"

"We are afraid," began Bernal, "that the ships anchored back in the bay will always tempt any cowards who might want to desert, which has already occurred. We are a few men now and there would be even less if some deserted."

"What do you propose?" asked Cortés.

"Well . . . we have talked about it among ourselves and those who are your friends thought the best thing to do would be to burn the ships."

"That would even be an advantage to us," interrupted Jaramillo, "because we could have the ship-masters, pilots and sailors, about a hundred men, as lookouts and soldiers instead of staying behind in the port with nothing much to do."

"Although that feeling is not unanimous, we would all be free of hindrances and temptation, then we could better serve the cause of God and His Majesty," concluded Bernal seriously.

Cortés smiled. "I appreciate your friendship and good advice. I am sure there are some who do not agree, but I like your idea."

The next day, Alvarado, Olid, and the rest of the soldiers arrived. Alvarado rode ahead until he found Cortés.

"We bring you the news, Captain Cortés, that the ships have been scuttled—at first it was taken as a joke—but they are on the bottom of the bay."

There was an outcry of shouting among the soldiers.

Bernal nudged his supporters. "Taken as a joke! Oh, sure, a joke contrived by Cortés so they could beg him to do what he already wanted to do. Not only is he enterprising, he's able and full of crafty ideas."

"Ah, my friend, to have learned about this grave misfortune . . ." Cortés said to Alvarado with a secret wink. "Tomorrow, God willing, after the Mass, I wish to speak to everyone, the cavalrymen and the soldiers."

The next day after Mass, there was a muster of Spanish forces in the main plaza of Cempoala. From the steps of a pyramid, Cortés addressed his companions. "As a favor I ask that you listen to me with strict attention, as there are important matters to be dealt with. All of us have understood and accepted the journey we are about to undertake into this Culúa territory. Through the mediation of Our Lord, Jesus Christ, we will win all the battles and skirmishes. We will have to be as diligent as possible, because anywhere we are defeated, which, God willing, will not happen, we cannot lift our heads to ask for help because we are few in number and we have no other assistance or aid but God, except our expertise as soldiers and our strong hearts.

"We no longer have any ships in which to return to Cuba. There is no way back. So we will have to fight not only for God's sake and His Majesty's, but for our very lives. We are like Caesar before the Rubicon. And if those Romans were vigorous and could accomplish by their valor such great victories, we will do even better, because we come to this enterprise with the will to serve our Holy Faith and our Emperor in the greatest undertaking of all time. We are a band of impassioned men who feel more strongly about invading this land than about fleeing like cowardly and meek men. We have a flag and a land to protect!"

Finally, even more spiritedly, Cortés said, "With luck we can cast our own fortune! Now, we are *conquistadores* who dare to venture wherever we choose!"

Waving the banner, he cried, "With the help of God we shall succeed. *Santiago y cierra España*!"

All the soldiers applauded and took up the cry. "Onward! To our adventure! You command, we will follow. We can cast our own fortune! Lead us! *Santiago y cierra España*!"

Cortés asked them to bring forward the fat *cacique*. Before the entire army, he said to him: "Tomorrow we undertake the march and we leave you in charge here. We remind you to revere the Church and the Cross. We will warn Moctezuma that he must not steal your crops or possessions or perform human sacrifices. Tomorrow, have ready for us the guides, the warriors and the *tamemes*."

"Only the gods can fight other gods and the Mexicans, too. We will provide everything you wish."

While all this was going on, a messenger on horseback arrived with an urgent note from Juan de Escalante at the Villa.

Cortés stepped aside to receive it.

"Captains!" he shouted.

Governor Garay's Men

ortés' expression was sober.

"Escalante has just informed me a ship has anchored off shore and someone on the beach is making smoke signals and waving a red cape, urging them to come into port, but so far they have refused. Plainly, there is something most strange here. I hope it is not Velázquez's people. I've decided to delay our march until we can learn more about this ship."

He turned to one side and raised his voice. "Alvarado! You and Gonzalo de Sandoval are in charge of the army. Gather fifty of the most able soldiers and four cavalrymen to come with me while I investigate this matter."

About noon, after a hurried march, Cortés and his contingent arrived at Villa Rica. Escalante was waiting.

"What more do you have to report, Escalante?" Cortés asked.

"It seems that this crew is under the command of Francisco de Garay, lieutenant and governor of Jamaica. That is what they shouted when I rowed out in the only skiff that we have left. I wanted to get as close to them as possible," Escalante said, "so I yelled out that Hernán Cortés has colonized this village and that I would be glad to guide them to the port, but they did not pay much attention. I am not sure they even heard me."

"Where is the ship?" Cortés asked.

"About three leagues from here, but no one has come ashore. I think it would be a good idea to go out there tonight, before they can set sail," Escalante suggested. "Why don't you rest, Captain, and have something to eat? I will go out with twenty soldiers."

"A lame goat has no time to rest, Escalante. I, personally, will lead the soldiers who came with me. Follow me, men!" Without pausing to rest or eat, Cortés rode up the beach.

About two leagues along the coast, with the ship in sight, Cortés and his men met four Spaniards.

"By the grace of God!" Cortés greeted them.

"And may you have the same," they replied.

"I am Hernán Cortés, Chief Justice and Captain of the Villa Rica de la Vera Cruz in whose jurisdiction you find yourselves. How may we be of help to you?"

120

"We came here looking for you, Captain. I am the Notary, Guillén de la Loa, and these are my witnesses, Andrés Núñez, a shore carpenter; Pedro del Arpa, master; and Felice Arce, a sailor."

"What is it you intend to witness, my good Notary, if you will be kind enough to inform me?"

"Taking possession of these lands, in the name of Francisco de Garay, Lieutenant Governor of Jamaica, which were discovered by his deputy, Alonso Álvarez Pineda, from here to the mouth of the Pánuco River and northward," de la Loa said officiously.

Cortés smiled coolly. "What titles can the Governor de Garay present that gives him such a right? We have already taken possession of these lands in the name of His Catholic Majesty and we Spaniards have founded a village here."

"The grants have been made by Bishop Fonseca in charge of the affairs of the Indies, who named Garay governor of everything he discovered toward the north."

"Another governor!" Cortés chirped, clapping his hands gleefully. "You realize, I hope, Notary, that these lands are not only well discovered, but colonized as well. I must consult with your Captain about this confusion. Please ask him to sail into the port. Inform him that I wish only to serve the King and that I will help him in every way that I can."

De la Loa ignored Cortés' request and continued doggedly. "I am empowered to enact an arrangement with you concerning the boundaries of your discoveries, which may be from Nautla to the south."

"I must agree, but there are many questions that only your Captain and I can resolve. Meanwhile, I invite you and your witnesses to the Villa, while your captain makes arrangements to come ashore. There we can spend the night, as it is getting late, and we can enjoy our meal more comfortably than among these sand dunes."

"You are too kind, Captain, but my orders are to return to the ship. Under no circumstances do I think the Captain will come ashore or anyplace else you may be. I have clear instructions and full power to deal with you."

Cortés smiled ominously. "I must say that's a peculiar way for a discoverer to negotiate matters and to register his discoveries. Has anything improper occurred in the land?"

"Oh! Don't think that, Captain. I am merely executing my directions as prudently as I can, given your fearless reputation, which is well-known ever since you left Cuba without Governor Velázquez's permission."

"I don't know if I should laugh or become furious at that remark, Notary. You know very well that my sole purpose is to serve better the Emperor our King as we all are his subjects. But let us not quarrel about your impertinence. May I have a look at your papers under the torch, as it is now quite dark?"

While the torches were lit and a supper was prepared, Cortés said, in an aside to Escalante:

"Juan, this episode with Garay causes a potential problem for our rear guard. It seems these people have claims to colonize. Even though he may resist, we must insist the Captain come ashore." Cortés paused for a moment in deep thought. Then he grinned broadly. "I have an idea."

"At dawn we will pretend to leave with our men. Then four of our soldiers will capture Garay's men and force them to change clothes with them. Our men will go out on the beach and make signs to their comrades to come ashore. When they do, we will take them prisoner."

Cortés stroked his chin. "No doubt they will be cautious. It will be difficult to make them fall into the trap, but this plan is better than nothing."

At dawn they carried out the scheme as Cortés had suggested. Ostensibly, Cortés, his horsemen and soldiers set out for the Villa in their usual form, leaving four soldiers dressed in the clothes of the recent arrivals on the beach. Cortés and his men hid behind a sand dune while his men on the beach signaled with their capes, beckoning to those on the ship to come ashore. The crew was skeptical at first, but eventually they sent in a launch with twelve men. Only four debarked and they did so very cautiously.

Disgruntled, Cortés turned to Escalante: "Well, you were right. Our maneuver did not turn out so well, but if we do not capture this lot, at least we will frighten them. Let's get them!"

With the soldiers behind him, Escalante ran to the beach to capture the four sailors. One tried to shoot Escalante, but his pistol misfired.

Very frightened, the eight soldiers in the launch rowed quickly back to the ship, which was already hoisting its sails when they arrived.

"Well, Escalante," said Cortés. "This episode wasn't too successful. It is most important that we induce the Totonacas and even the Culúas to intercept Garay's men and to keep me informed during our expedition into Moctezuma's territory. You will command at the Villa with one hundred men and three horses. Keep in touch with the chiefs in Cempoala and be sure they take good care of the altars. We will exchange messages as best we can."

Cortés returned to Cempoala to spend the night. When he arrived at camp, *Doña* Marina was waiting for him with warm water in a big tub, so he could bathe and change into clean clothes.

"Welcome, my lord!"

"Marina!" said Cortés, kissing her warmly.

"This is a very good Mayan custom. To bathe in herbs that will relax you."

While he was bathing, Marina remarked:

"You seem troubled, my lord."

"Everywhere there are problems, Marina. Some Spaniards have arrived unexpectedly and there appears to be a dispute about these lands."

"Don't worry. This land is yours, just as I am."

Cortés grinned at her passionate loyalty.

"Soon we will be going inland, Marina, and I will need you even more."

"I will remain with you forever, my lord. Whether in danger or in the delight of a bath. Always I shall be with you."

Route to Mexico

On August 16, 1519, the Spanish army set out from Cempoala for Mexico, by way of Tlaxcala.

"Gonzalo de Sandoval, let's have a review of the troops," Cortés said on the morning of the march.

16 de Agosto. 1519
Rumbo a Tenochtitlan.

16 August, 1519. The route to Tenochtitlan

"Captain, we are four hundred Spaniards counting cavalry and soldiers. Of the four hundred, thirteen are horsemen, with that many horses, thirty-two are crossbowmen and thirteen are musketeers. We have ten cannon and four small cannon, cannon balls and gunpowder in sufficient supply. We also have about one thousand Cempoalans, among whom are chiefs, *tamemes*, and warriors."

"Pedro de Alvarado! Give the order! The patrols will lead with four scouts from the main body. Then assemble the horses, the foot soldiers and the dogs. After them will come the main body, with five more horses; then the baggage and a rear guard of fifty foot soldiers and four horsemen."

"Forward! *Santiago*!" Cortés cried, drawing and brandishing his sword.

The army responded in unison: "*Santiago*!"

Cortés rode on horseback along with the main force. By his side walked *Doña* Marina who now wore Spanish shoes instead of *huaraches*. Next to her were some Cempoalan chiefs.

Teuch, a Cempoalan, commented: "We go first to Xalapa, whose people are our friends, until we reach the very high mountains."

After crossing the low Cempoalan mountains in the midst of the humid tropics, the army descended to coastal plains of grasses and verdant tropical vegetation. Passing through villages, they noticed the skulls of sacrifices. Each time, Father Bartolomé de Olmedo gave an oration and *Doña* Marina translated.

"Rid yourself of your false gods and these horrible human sacrifices, which are the work of the devil. Love the One God and His Son Jesus Christ and His Divine Mother. We are servants of the Emperor *Don* Carlos, who directed us here so there would be no more human sacrifices or stealing from one another."

In each village they placed a cross, explaining that it was a symbol of Jesus Christ, the Son of God, who died to save the world from sins.

As Teuch had suggested, the army penetrated deeper into the countryside, ascending the sierra. There, the temperature became quite pleasant. When they got to Xalapa and Xico, the Cempoaltecan said to Cortés: "Up to this point we have been among friends, those whom you ordered not to pay further tribute to Moctezuma. But from here onward, the sierra is steep and difficult to climb."

After resting, the troops strung out in a long line as they began the ascent of the sierra. *Doña* Marina was still at Cortés' knee and at times the path forced her to grab the horse's mane or onto some part of Cortés' trappings.

They ascend the sierra

Halfway through the mountains, they were startled by a storm with strong winds and hail, which kept them from continuing. Soon after, night fell. Only a few were able to build small fires to keep warm. The cold was so intense, a few Cuban Indians, raised in tropical warmth, died. Even some of the Spaniards, by now generally accustomed to a warmer climate, became ill. Cortés wrapped his cape around *Doña* Marina and himself.

"I haven't been so cold since I was a boy in Medina del Campo, but there I had a coat and not this cursed armor which only makes me feel colder," grumbled Bernal Díaz del Castillo.

"Sure, it's cold, but don't forget, amigo, you were one of those making fun of me sweating because I wore this quilted cotton *escaupil* [doublet], thickly stuffed with cotton. Not only will it protect me from the arrows and stones, but from these icy winds," said Bernal's friend.

"We are all suffering, but those who suffer the most are the Cuban Indians. I saw some in a death trance," said a soldier.

"In the morning, things will improve," said Bernal.

The storm ended the next day and Cortés gave the order to proceed.

His lieutenant said to him: "The news, Captain: Four Cuban Indians died from the cold and many others are frost-bitten."

"The march will soon warm them."

The army struggled up the steep sierra until it came to the village of Ixhuacán. On passing through the gates, Cortés, with Marina at his side, halted his tired horse, a veteran of so many treacherous passages. To rest the exhausted animal, Cortés dismounted and began to walk, leading his horse. The other riders quickly followed suit.

One soldier suggested, "Let us call this village, the first that we encountered since we left the coast, *Puerto del Nombre de Dios*. Truthfully, it is so high and there are so many rough areas, I don't believe there is a more difficult mountain pass in all of Spain."

"The air is so thin that the body suffers. One must hold on tight to catch his breath," muttered Gonzalo de Sandoval. "I don't remember any mountains as high as this. Look," he pointed, "there is a snow-capped sierra and over there a curious formation, just like a big box."

Bernal heard the comments as he approached the officers. In a festive tone, he remarked: "It looks like the trunk of Perote (Pedrote), the Biscayan."

His gibe passed quickly through the camp until it reached Perote, a gigantic soldier, who needed two *tamemes* to carry the mighty trunk in which he planned to store his treasures.

"It's a good idea to name this mountain the *Cofre de Perote* and be certain that I will come back here to establish an inn to fill my trunk with treasures. I haven't seen any others in these rough mountains."

When they began to descend the high plain, the journey became less arduous. Beyond the last pass lay a cold, sterile valley, a spur of the main mountain range. The summer rainy season had begun in Mexico.

In Tenochtitlan

I n his palace Moctezuma, deeply distressed, from time to time received news of the Spaniards' advance.

"They have left Cempoala and are marching toward Tenochtitlan. With them are Totonacan warriors at the command of Teuch and Tlacocheacatl. *Tamemes* carry their artillery. They all march in an orderly manner," the reports announced.

". . . They have arrived at Xalapa and are beginning to ascend the sierra. There is a lot of rain."

". . . They have crossed the sierra and continue to place crosses and to steal food."

". . . Tlacocheacatl is guiding them. They take one path and then cross over to another."

The March Continues

The Spaniards marched through villages that were small, and with little food for the army, which suffered as a result. They pressed on into the valley of Caltanmic and the village of Xocotla, where many of the stone houses were painted with lime, similar to those in Europe. Giant pyramids were prominent.

"Indeed," said a Portuguese soldier. "That Indian village with the stone houses painted with lime looks like Castil-Blanco in Portugal."

"Then Castil-Blanco we shall call it," said Bernal Díaz del Castillo to his companions.

"Tell the vanguard to wait for us before they enter the village," Cortés ordered a lieutenant, who left immediately.

As the army assembled before entering the village, Cortés directed his remarks to the Cempoaltecans.

"You tell me that this great village is subject to Mexico, and is a loyal vassal."

"That's right," said Teuch, the *cacique*. "We think two of us should go first as your ambassadors, announce your arrival and explain that we need housing and food."

"If you would be so kind."

An hour later, the two Cempoaltecans returned.

"Captain, we have spoken in your name with Olintetl, the *cacique*, and he gives his consent to enter the village in peace and friendship."

"That's good," said Cortés.

"In honor of your arrival, he has sacrificed fifty captives."

"That's bad," said Cortés. "But let us replenish our provisions, anyway. Proceed!"

Xocotla: Castil-Blanco

The Spaniards gathered before the village portal, where the *cacique* Olintetl and his officials awaited them. Olintetl was almost as fat as the *cacique* in Cempoala and as he moved about his flesh quivered.

Observing this phenomenon, Bernal commented to his companions: "It seems corpulence is a prerequisite for *caciques*. Look how his flesh trembles. We should call this one the 'Trembler of Castil-Blanco.'"

"I welcome you to Xocotla," said Olintetl, "even though I do not know who you are or what you wish here. We will speak later about that after you have gone to your lodging and eaten."

They enter Xocotla. It seems that corpulence is a prerequisite for a *cacique*.

The army entered the village, found lodging in various houses, and was fed.

Said Bernal to his friends: "Not very much or very graciously have they fed us. No doubt these are mere scraps from 'The Trembler's' table."

After the meal, which he took in silence, Cortés asked the *cacique*: "Tell me, are you Moctezuma's subjects?"

Olintetl studied Cortés without replying, then lowered his eyes and seemed absorbed for a few seconds.

Cortés' impatience was clear and he was about to repeat the question, when the *cacique* replied:

"Who is not a subject of Moctezuma?"

"In the world I come from there is an Emperor more powerful who rules over kings and sovereigns and it is he who has sent me to see Moctezuma."

The *cacique* shuddered, horrified. "Well, you will not see him unless he gives you permission. He is very powerful, with warriors as well as his fortress in Tenochtitlan. He rules over whomever he wishes."

"Warriors, you say?"

"Yes, thousands. The Lords *tigres* and the Lords *águilas*—the elite command of the military units. There are many more thousands of men than you have. Some are in the great city, others on the borders and many in the territories."

"What makes Temistitan so strong?"

"The water!" answered Olintetl. "It is built in the middle of a lake and one can only enter by three causeways easily defended because there are bridges that can be removed and you cannot even pass from one house to another except by bridges or canoe. There are also trenches and many other defenses. It is a nation that everyone pays tribute to and it is very rich."

"What sort of riches does Temistitan have?" Cortés asked.

"Lots of gold, silver and *chalchihuites** and precious feathers that are impossible to count and every kind of riches from the earth—that is what the great lord Moctezuma possesses and he is the greatest king who has ever ruled and from everywhere we send tribute and captives to be sacrificed."

The Spanish soldiers, sitting around the table where the two men were talking, were attentive but excited.

In an aside, Bernal commented to his friends: "It sounds like adventures in the chivalric tales."

"How I would like to be there already!" said Jaramillo.

"How true," replied Bernal. "Since we are such great Spanish soldiers, we would all like to be experiencing the adventure of those causeways and against such brave warriors."

"I don't think," Olintetl concluded, "that Moctezuma will be very pleased when he learns about your visit to this village, that we gave you lodging and food without his permission."

"Gave us food!" murmured Bernal.

"Don't worry, Olintetl," Cortés said. "I want you to know that we come from far-off lands ordered by our King and Lord who is the Emperor *Don* Carlos. He has as his subjects many important lords and he sent us to order your great Moctezuma that he must not sacrifice or kill any Indians or steal from his vassals or take away any land and to swear obedience to our King and Lord. And now I tell you the same thing, Olintetl, and to all the other *caciques* who are here. You must not sacrifice the

---

* *Chalchihuites* resemble emeralds. Aztecs claimed each was worth more than a load of gold. Only nobles were allowed to wear them—usually on their wrists.—Trans.

natives or eat the flesh of your fellow creatures or commit the other crimes you are familiar with because Our Lord, God, who is the one we worship and in whom we believe, who gives us life and death and leads us up to heaven, forbids it."

Olintetl and other officials looked at Cortés, lowered their eyes and remained coldly silent.

Since they did not comment, Cortés turned to his men.

"It seems to me, *señores*, there is nothing else left for us to do but to erect a cross."

To which Father Bartolomé de Olmedo responded:

"To me it seems unwise to erect a cross here and leave it in the care of these villagers as they are impudent and fearless because they are Moctezuma's subjects. They might well burn it or do other harm. What you have told them, Captain, is enough until they have more knowledge of our Holy Faith."

Cortés nodded and a cross was not erected.

"Regardless, Fray Bartolomé, even if we do not place a cross here, let us show them a few of our strengths."

They all left the lodgings and went to the great plaza. Cortés called for a horse race.

"We believe that the creature is one with the man," commented the Xocotlans to the Cempoalans, who answered: "They can dominate anyone they wish."

Cortés ordered the cannon fired.

"That seems like the force of a turbulent sky," cried the Xocotlans.

"With their steel balls and stones these strangers who came from the East can kill whomever they wish wherever they find them," said the Cempoalans.

Then the Spanish *caballeros* brought forth a large greyhound.

"Is that a tiger or a lion?" asked the men from Xocotla.

"They bring it along so if anyone makes them mad, that beast kills him," said the Indians from Cempoala.

"Well, if this is how they act, these white men with beards must surely be gods," concluded Olintetl and his chiefs.

"Well, now you see them," said the Cempoalans, "and it is wise not to engage in anything evil that will anger them because they can divine what you are thinking. These *teules* tied up Moctezuma's *calpixques* and ordered us to stop paying tribute to him. They defeated the Indians in Tabasco and Champotón and are so clever that they made friends between us and the people of Cingapatzingo. Now Moctezuma sends them gifts and we notice that since they arrrived in your village you have not given them anything. You had better go and get some presents."

The chief of Xocotla brought gold jewelry and four Indian women to grind corn and make tortillas.

Cortés received them with joy and good will.

The soldiers dispersed and as they walked about the plaza, they saw at the furthermost point the *Tzompantli* [rack of skulls] and putrified heads hanging from the eaves, all in the care of the priests. They were horrified, but took no action.

At nightfall, Cortés met with Olintetl. "*Cacique* Olintetl, tomorrow we will continue on our way to Temistitan. We would like to know the best way to get there."

As always, Olintetl paused first, then, he said: "Cholula is the best road; it is closer and is a very large village where you will find everything you need."

That night, in his quarters, Cortés asked *Doña* Marina: "What do you think about the road this *cacique* Olintetl recommended?"

"I do not think my lord should go by way of Cholula. They are very false people. Do not distrust the Cempoalans, either. Moctezuma has garrisons of warriors. We should go through Tlaxcala, even though it is farther, because its people are friendly with the Cempoalans and are mortal enemies of the Mexicans. We can convince them you come in peace and friendship."

"Then we will go by way of Tlaxcala," said Cortés. "What do you think about putting crosses here?"

"I agree with Father Olmedo. You gain nothing if they do not want them."

Before retiring, Cortés gave the last order: "*Doña* Marina, tomorrow ask Olintetl to send twenty warrior chieftains with us."

Then he kissed her.

Route to Tlaxcala

Early the following day, the Spaniards left on the road to Ixtacamaxtitlan. Cortés told his captains: "We will end our day's journey in this village of Ixtacamaxtitlan. Our friends the Cempoaltecans have suggested—and it's good advice—that we send ambassadors to Tlaxcala to ask their friendship and to receive us. We will wait here for their return."

He turned to the Cempoaltecans. "As you have suggested, four of you will go as our ambassadors to ask the Tlaxcalans for their friendship and to allow us to pass through their territory on our way to Temistitan. Take this letter, which I am sure they will not understand, but it is an indication of our intentions, as well as this Flemish red hat for their chief."

Dressed in appropriate garments and insignias which announced their respected position, the four ambassadors left. When they arrived at Tlaxcala, they were well-received, fed and rested. They exchanged their insignias, for flowers. With their eyes cast down, they were directed to the Senate Chamber of Tlaxcala, where the Council of Four that governed Tlaxcala was in session. Each of the four represented a dominion: Maxixcatzin was in charge of Ocotelco. Xicoténcatl, the elder, almost blind, was from Tizatlan. Tlehuexolotzin oversaw Tepectipac, and Citlalpopocatzin, Oniahuiztlan.

Each chief was seated on his special throne, wearing a ceremonial robe, and displaying his insignia of office.

Reverently, the ambassadors entered and in the center of the hall seated themselves on the ground, covering their finery with the customary tattered cotton cloaks.*

Maxixcatzin motioned for them to speak.

Courteously, in a low voice, the Cempoalan ambassador, who had brought Cortés' letter rolled up in a reed, said: "You know, Chieftains, as it has been predicted, many white men with beards would come from the East with light eyes and yellow hair, who seem to be gods. They have freed the Totonacan villages from paying tribute to Moctezuma. We Cempoalans suggested that these gods make an

---

* The ambassadors covered their elegant clothes with ordinary, threadbare cotton cloths before making an appearance before the august presence of the chieftains.—Trans.

131

alliance with Tlaxcala on their way to Mexico and be received in peace and friendship, and that you permit them to pass safely through your territory. This is the message they have asked us to bring to you."

Los Cuatro Tlatoanis de Tlaxcala Reciben la Embajada de Cortés.

The Four *Tlatoanis* of Tlaxcala receive Cortés' legation

He handed the letter to them.

The four listened attentively. They remained silent for a brief time and then Maxixcatzin said: "You are welcome, respected ambassadors. While you are among us, you will be treated as you deserve. We understand you no longer pay tribute to Moctezuma. You must wait for our answer because it is our law to deliberate and determine the opinion of the majority. You may leave now."

After the ambassadors left, Maxixcatzin opened the debate: "We have heard the gods' demands: We ought to receive the *teules* as friends and allow them to pass through our land on the way to Mexico. If they are gods, they will pass through anyway. If they are not, they seem to be Moctezuma's enemies and as such, we ought to welcome them."

Xicoténcatl, the elder, almost blind, said, "If we believe what is said about these strange creatures, they are not men but monsters who have sprung from the ocean foam itself riding on gigantic deer. They eat the very earth and are greedy for gold. They sleep on cotton cloths and enjoy every kind of delicacy. For that reason, the sea, satiated with them, has cast them onto the earth. It will be a great error to greet these gods."

Tlehuexolotzin said: "I propose we send ambassadors to the strangers inviting them here. Meantime, Xicoténcatl, the Younger, with all the Otomie warriors and ours, will attack them. If Xicoténcatl triumphs, we will know they are not gods and everything will be resolved; if the strangers are victorious, then we will blame the Otomies and receive the creatures as they request."

The four chieftains agreed to this plan.

They sent for the Cempoaltecan ambassadors. Maxixcatzin said to them: "I hope you have rested from your journey. Go to the strangers and tell them that soon we will send our ambassadors to conclude their welcome to Tlaxcala."

The Cempoaltecans returned, satisfied, and told Cortés: "*Señor*, There is an arrangement being considered in Tlaxcala to welcome you as you deserve. They will soon send ambassadors to work out the details of your entrance to Tlaxcala, as friends."

The Ambassadors Do Not Arrive

 few days later, when the Tlaxcalan ambassadors had not arrived, Cortés consulted his captains and the Cempoaltecans and decided to continue along the river-bed toward Tlaxcala.

"I am going with the vanguard," he said. "Two cavalrymen will follow me, leaving six as scouts to see what might await us."

Traveling with the advance troops, Cortés was the first to spot the fortifications that protected the Tlaxcalans.

There was a stone wall more than nine feet high and twenty feet thick with a parapet eighteen inches wide. In the middle was a single opening, created by two semi-circular lines of wall overlapping each other for forty paces, affording a passageway ten paces wide and designed so as to be perfectly defended by the inner wall. It was constructed of immense stone blocks fitted perfectly together without mortar. It reached from sierra to sierra, and to pass, one had to make many turns.

The Spaniards' advance guard halted in front of the wall. They awaited the foot soldiers, followed quickly by the cavalry, among whom was Bernal, who commented to his companions: "This great wall gives one much to consider."

On hearing Bernal's remark, Cortés understood the effect the fortification would have on his men. In a tone loud enough for all to hear, he said, "Here we fight might and craft. Pass through this wall if you dare, strangers, but before you do, consider well whether you can exit."

After pausing to let his words register, he went on. "Sirs, let us follow our banner which bears the sign of the Holy Cross. With its help, we will conquer."

A great shout erupted from the men. "May good fortune await our advance, for in God lies the true strength!"

Cortés ordered Ensign Corral to display the flag and they began to pass through the fortification. On the other side there was no one. The Spaniards continued on through the valley, puzzled and silent.

Cortés waited until his army was reunited inside the wall. "Always be alert, as I have told you. Those who are mounted, proceed at half rein with your lances slanted down and three abreast. Break ranks without stopping to hurl the lances at any foot soldiers in closed ranks. Aim your lances at their stomachs. Crossbowmen and arquebusiers, alternate shooting and loading. Let's see tongues of fire from your squadrons; open to fire and then close ranks."

The Tlaxcala Wall. "When you are entering figure out if you can exit."

"I remember everything very well," said a soldier, "but I don't see the enemy."

When Cortés heard him, he said, "Listen, men, we are very few in number. But you must be prepared, not as if you were going to battle, but as if you are actually in the midst of it. I know that you need no instructions in battle but you have my best wishes that you will fight more courageously."

As they continued on, they approached some hills and tall pine groves. Stretched across the road were some strings, and from them hung certain papers.

"What mysterious strings and papers," commented Cortés wryly as he went up to the vanguard.

"Those are bewitchments the Tlaxcaltecans placed warning you not to go forward," *Doña* Marina said to Cortés.

"A minor impediment," Cortés snorted.

"These signs can do you no harm because you are gods," *Doña* Marina reassured him.

"Among us there are gods and mortals. Send the dogs ahead to search for the spies or ambushes in these holes and thickets," Cortés ordered.

When the mounted troops advanced into one area, the dogs began to bark and run faster, discovering a group of fifteen Indians in feather head-dresses and war regalia. When the Indians spotted the dogs, they ran to the bottom of a hill.

Two cavalrymen turned as Cortés approached. "Captain, there are Indian warriors ahead," they said.

War with the Tlaxcaltecans

lvarado and Gonzalo de Sandoval, direct the soldiers into combat order by squadrons and follow me. You four horsemen come with me; I smell an ambush," Cortés grunted. At a gallop, they went to meet the enemy.

Lares had gone on ahead and followed the fifteen Indians, killing two of them. The others scattered to hide in the underbrush.

As the four horsemen and the vanguard continued their pursuit, the dogs were barking furiously in a bend of the road, where soon again appeared the Tlaxcaltecan soldiers dressed in their armor and plumes of war. The advance cavalry charged them.

"Stop! Stop! It's an ambush!" Cortés yelled uselessly from afar. "You eight, wait for the soldiers and advance with them!"

Cortés spurred his horse, galloping ahead in an effort to keep his companions from continuing their pursuit of the fleeing Indians. Coming to a clearing, thirteen Indians gave great war yells and closed together in a surprise move. They first attacked Pedro de Morón's horse. His lance defended him from two of the Indians, but the others seemed impervious to the blows, and began to grab at the horse's hooves. Then with one blow of a *macana*, they decapitated the animal. Morón fell to the ground, defending himself with his sword while Cortés and his companions tried to help him.

With great outcries, from the top of the small glen hundreds of Indians wearing white and red feathers descended in screaming waves. In a concerted effort, they advanced against the Spanish horsemen who thrust their lances at them, while Morón, wounded, lay in agony on the ground.

The rest of the Spanish army charged ahead quickly. In the front line were the eight horsemen who came to Morón's aid and saved him. It seemed the Indians were more interested in dragging away the horse they had killed than continuing the skirmish.

Now the horsemen, with Cortés in the lead, entered the fray and emerged, organized in a row. The Indians began to withdraw, carrying away the dead horse and leaving their dead companions behind.

When the main body of the Spanish force and the horsemen were reunited at the end of the road, two ambassadors with Tlaxcaltecan insignias appeared. They came over to Cortés. "The four Tlaxcalan chiefs say they are sorry that these undisciplined

Otomie tribes have attacked you. We greet you and say that we will pay in gold for hurting your rider and the dead animal and whatever other damages you suffered."

"I am grateful to the chiefs of Tlaxcala for this fine gesture," answered Cortés. "Tell them that they owe us nothing; they are not responsible for the rebel attacks. The horseman will not die and we are expecting more horses. What is important to us is to make peace and friendship with Tlaxcala."

The envoys nodded graciously. "We will give the Chiefs your message. Tomorrow other ambassadors will come to inform you how you may enter Tlaxcala."

Then they left.

"This business of ambassadors does not smell right to me and the offer about the horse smells worse. It sounds like they are preparing another ambush," Cortés said, then ordered: "Let us leave this little valley and continue on ahead to complete one day's march."

The army marched ahead and eventually camped on a much larger plain, taking maximum security precautions.

Under the canopy of his tent, close to his saddled horse and still armed, Cortés rested his head on *Doña* Marina.

"What do you think about these Tlaxcaltecans, *señora*?"

"They are a fearless people. They wish to wage war to see if you are really gods. So be ready!" A little later, she asked: "Are you gods?"

Cortés remained silent, ignoring her. Then, he stood up and gave new orders: "Double the watch and the patrols. Keep the dogs on alert. When you sleep, remain fully armed and leave the horses bridled and saddled."

In the early pre-dawn, the dogs began to bark and the army prepared to continue its march.

The scouts ran back to inform the leaders that a huge number of Indians dressed in beautifully adorned war regalia were approaching. When the sun cast streaks over the land, the Indian units began to blow their shellhorns, to beat drums, *teponaxtles*, and to howl. The Spanish elements formed their order of battle.

The war against Tlaxcala. The Spanish square is formed.

"Diego de Godoy, Royal Scribe!" shouted Cortés. "Ask Aguilar to make the Official Summons."

Which is what Godoy did in the midst of great whistling and a shower of arrows.

"*Santiago y a ellos*," shouted Cortés, who attacked them at half rein and with lance blows to the Indians' faces, while the Spanish foot soldiers advanced in formation to the sound of the fife and drums.

The Indians retreated slowly in good order toward the edge of the valley which was quickly sealed off. This slowed the horses' pace and the attack shifted to the foot soldiers.

"Another ambush! Horses to the rear!" Cortés shouted, dismounting to help reinforce the squadrons, which advanced with difficulty over rough ground.

"Assemble! Assemble! Close lines!" shouted the captains.

"Open fire at once! Close up in order to load." Slowly, the Spaniards advanced across the rocky field amidst a shower of arrows, tempered poles and hurled stones. The Spaniards repelled the attack. They opened ranks, fired the small cannon, then closed ranks while reloading and continuing to advance behind drawn swords.

As the day passed, many were wounded, some with head wounds. The Spaniards managed to reach the Tzompantzingo Valley, where they reorganized. Again, the horses advanced, then retreated when the artillery was deployed.

Late in the afternoon, more Indian troops appeared and again the Spanish soldiers closed ranks. The horsemen withdrew to rest and regroup before re-entering the fight.

An hour before sunset, at the sound of shellhorns, the Indians began an orderly retreat, leaving the outcome of the battle in doubt.

All the Spaniards were exhausted, thirsty and hungry.

"Halt! Halt!" Cortés yelled at the cavalrymen who were still eager to attack the retreating Indians. "Use the small cannon and spare yourselves. You are exhausted. We'll camp here in this little village next to these *cúes* [temples]. Put out scouts and patrols! All well armed! Put hot grease [they rendered the fat of a plump dead Indian] on the men's wounds as well as the horses'. Compress them well and rest as best you can. The Indians will return to continue the fight."

The little army found sufficient food and supped on turkey and small dogs bred for meat.*

The next morning, when the scouts informed Cortés the enemy had vanished, he decided to take the initiative.

"Captain Alvarado!" he called. "You are in command of the camp. With the horsemen and one hundred foot soldiers and Indian warriors, I will reconnoiter the neighboring village to learn what we can and forage for more food. Send the Cempoaltecan ambassadors again to Tlaxcala to ask for peace and friendship. Inquire from the prisoners if they know anything about Xicoténcatl's plans."

---

* Many women breast-fed the *Xoloitcuintli*, or common hairless dog. These dogs were used for foot warmers and were also bred for meat. (Smith, Bradley. *Mexico: A History in Art*. New York: Doubleday, 1968.)—Trans.

Cortés went about the valley burning huts in the little villages and returned later that afternoon with prisoners, food, and information.

"What news do you have, Alvarado? Have the ambassadors come back?"

"They returned with a somewhat haughty reply. The Indians said we should go to the village and there peace would be declared by their satiating themselves on our flesh and honoring their gods with our hearts and blood."

"Brave they are, no doubt. What did the prisoners have to say?"

"They said there is little love lost between Captain Xicoténcatl and a certain Maxixcatzin and another Chichicamecate and that they blame each other because no one has defeated us though we are such a small number."

"That's what I have heard, too. But we cannot be sure, because tomorrow they intend to attack us again with more warriors. It seems that Xicoténcatl has ten thousand men and Maxixcatzin another ten thousand; Huejotzingo has ten thousand and Chichicamecate ten thousand Chichimecas and Topeyanco and Guaxobcin another and I don't know how many more and each one with his own colors and flags. It will be as if it were a white bird with its wings extended, wanting to fly. All of us will have to fight, including the wounded, who should be placed in the center of the squadrons just to make the body of men complete. Now, let us rest and eat because tomorrow we will fight."

On hearing this, Bernal said to his companions: "I am a man and I fear death. Now I will go to confession with Father de la Merced, that God may help us and we will not be defeated."

All night Father de la Merced and the Priest Juan Díaz heard confessions.

The rising sun found the Spanish army organized as Cortés had ordered. Everyone, even the wounded men and horses, joined the ranks and marched out to the field of battle. Soon the Tlaxcaltecan armies appeared, filling the valley with plumed warriors displaying their diverse colors. The Indians arrived singing, shouting, playing musical instruments and blowing their shellhorns and trumpets, beating small drums as well as huge *teponaxtles*.

While the Spaniards were compiling the Summons of Command, the Tlaxcaltecans, under a flag of truce, came up to the Spanish lines and deposited more than three hundred turkeys and two hundred baskets of tamales. The ambassadors said:

"This is for you to eat. We want you to be energetic and strong when we kill you."

The Spaniards waited.

The battle commenced at close range with a barrage of Indian arrows so dense they blocked out the sun.

The white men replied with a cannon volley that decimated many Indians. The Spaniards soon found themselves surrounded, so they formed the square troop formation which parted to permit cannon fire. Immediately, the horsemen charged along the path of the barrage, turning at a certain point and returning to the square, which opened again so they could gallop back inside to regroup.

"Para que comáis, pues no queremos que aleguéis
falta de fuerza cuando seáis vencidos".

". . . we want you to eat so that no one lacks strength when we kill you."

The Spaniards repeated this maneuver while the foot soldiers, elbow-to-elbow, flung their missiles at the Indians. Noticing a weakness in the Chichimeca front, the cavalry and the troops advanced. As the Indians retreated noticeably, Xicoténcatl, enraged, ordered Chichicamecatl to hold his ground, declaring that he was a coward. Equally infuriated, Chichicamecatl shrieked that his men had fought more courageously and with better results than Xicoténcatl's. Furthermore, since Xicoténcatl did not agree with him on this point, Chichicamecatl was pulling his men out of the battle. As soon as he did, Huejotzingo's forces retreated also.

Instantly, the Spaniards charged the remaining Tlaxcaltecan forces with such determination the Indians were forced to retreat before sundown.

As the Indians departed, Cortés cried: "Halt! Halt! Do not pursue them. The horses are exhausted and some of you are wounded. The battle has turned in our favor because Our Lord wished it and because of His help."

He turned to his officers. "As the enemy withdrew early, it seems there must have been wrangling among them, especially the Chichimecas and those who wear Huejotzingo's insignia."

He pointed to one of the captains. "Alvarado, tomorrow morning, the cavalry and one hundred foot soldiers should reconnoiter the valley so our enemies will not think we are fatigued or that we lack strength. For the third time, send ambassadors to Tlaxcala to ask their permission for us to pass in peace and friendship through their territory on our way to Temistitan."

While Cortés' force pillaged the valley, burning houses, capturing prisoners, and gathering food and supplies, the Cempoaltecan ambassadors returned to Tlaxcala where they were received by the four chiefs.

They repeated their request for the Spaniards to go to Tenochtitlan in peace and friendship.

The chiefs said: "You may go in peace, ambassadors. Tomorrow we will send our reply to the *teules*."

The chiefs continued to deliberate. Xicoténcatl, the elder, was with his son, the warrior. The older Xicoténcatl opened the discussion. "These soldiers seem to be *teules*. They are invincible and we cannot kill them. We must consider whether we should seek their friendship because they are Moctezuma's enemies."

"They are not *teules*," insisted the young warrior. "They are human beings as we are and they become tired and must eat. We would have defeated them if the Chichimecas had not weakened and Huejotzingo's men had not bolted."

Maxixcatzin said: "My opinion is that we accept them as friends. To me, they seem to be *teules*."

The diplomatic Tlehuexolotzin proposed, "Let us investigate if they are gods by sending them five fattened Indians to see if they wish to eat their flesh and drink their blood. If they are gods, we will send them more food to eat and drink and make peace with them. If they are men, and as it is said 'sons of the Sun,' they can only achieve victory in the daylight. So we must attack at night."

Xicoténcatl, the elder, said: "It is not our custom to fight at night. Much ill-fortune will befall us."

"Let me try it," urged the young man. "I am sure we can defeat them in a night battle."

Eventually, after considerable haggling, the Council agreed.

The following day, the Cempoaltecan ambassadors returned from Tlaxcala and spoke to Cortés: "We come in peace from Tlaxcala. The four chieftains send this message: 'If you are a god, one who eats human flesh and drinks the blood, then eat these Indians and we will bring you more; if you are a true god, we offer you incense and feathers; if you are but a man, here are some turkeys, bread* and fruit.'"

Cortés thought for a moment before delivering his response. "I and my companions are men such as you are; and I would like very much for you not to lie to me because I will always speak the truth to you. Now, I say truthfully I very much hope that you will see reason and cease fighting us so you do not suffer further losses. We have not been defeated."

With Cortés' answer, the ambassadors returned to the Council.

After listening to it, the Tlaxcaltecans came to this conclusion, voiced by Xicoténcatl, the elder: "Our priests, magicians, and wizards have concluded that these beings are not gods but 'sons of the Sun,' who possibly are those it has been prophesied would come from the East to rule over this land. Their great strength comes from the Sun so we shall attack them at night. That is what I command you to do with our army, son," he said to the youth.

The warrior was delighted. "Although it is not a Tlaxcaltecan custom to wage war at night, we will do it so we can take advantage of the darkness against the horses and their mouths of fire," he declared.

He organized the night attack exclusively with Tlaxcaltecan warriors and ordered his captains to send groups of spies to plot the positions and movements in the Spanish camp.

---

* Probably tortillas (which is a Spanish word). The Náhuatl word is *tlaxcalli.*—Trans.

141

The spies were traders of turkeys and vegetables. One morning, more than fifty of them were roaming about the Spanish camp looking at everything. Teuch, the Cempoaltecan *cacique*, warned: "Look, Captain, these traders are really Xicoténcatl's spies. See how they sneak about and then whisper together."

"Lieutenant!" Cortés ordered. "Grab those Indians who appear to be spies and have Pedro de Alvarado interrogate them about their mission here. They are much too curious about the details of our camp."

After a short while, Alvarado reported to Cortés with some restraint. "Captain, you are correct. The Indians are spies and wished to learn the entrances and exits to the camp and our lodgings, because they plan to attack us at night. They believe we will become weakened by the lack of sunlight."

"Cut off their hands, Alvarado, and send those bastards back to Xicoténcatl. And you make certain the spies tell him that by day or by night, whoever attacks us will discover with their own blood who we really are."

When he saw the mutilated Indians, Xicoténcatl roared with fury, resolving to attack the Spaniards that very night. Secretly, after sunset, he began to assemble his troops behind some nearby hills close to the corn fields.

Alerted now, Cortés fortified the camp and stiffened its defenses, assigning extra scouts, lookouts and spies.

As night fell, the lookouts reported back. "Captain, Xicoténcatl's troops are advancing along the flanks of the camp."

Cortés issued his orders to the other officers. "We will not allow them to reach us. We will attack when they reach the plain so we can take advantage of the moonlight. Mount your horses! One hundred foot-soldiers follow me and the rest stay to defend the camp gates."

The Tlaxcatecans, inexperienced in night battles, were still sneaking toward the Spanish camp when the horses with the bells tinkling on their trappings charged upon them at half gallop, followed by the Spanish soldiers. The Tlaxcaltecans were quickly routed, withdrawing into the corn fields, where the Spaniards pursued them. Disconcerted, young Xicoténcatl broke off the fight and retreated to Tlaxcala.

Disheartened, he reported to the Council: "We couldn't defeat them at night, either. Those wizards tricked us, so they probably are the ones predicted by the prophecy."

Let Us No Longer Tempt God

fter the attacks ceased, the Spaniards, well-supplied with provisions, rested for a few days. With *Doña* Marina at his side, Cortés relaxed in his lodging next to the temple.

"Rest, my lord," she said, stroking his beard. "You must rest."

"The battle against the Tlaxcalans was cruel. And you knew they were coming to fight us."

She nodded. "Yes, they had to, in order to discover for themselves if you are *teules*. What happened to me, has happened to them. Even I, Malinalli—the moon destined to Quetzalcóatl, to whom I was delivered, to whom I am destined—even I do not know if you are a God or the son of a god."

"We are all sons of God, Marina," Cortés reminded her gently.

"But I do not understand that idea, my lord. I only know I accept my destiny to serve you forever, to be faithful to you, and to care for you." She embraced him warmly.

As they comforted each other, Cortés noticed far off lights and smoke, which suggested the presence of a large village. He decided to go there.

"There seems to be a great city about four leagues away, Marina. There are many lights over there." He pointed. "We will go and surprise them. Idleness is a sin!"

He moved away from her and issued orders: "Get the horses ready and assemble one hundred soldiers."

The march began in the chilly darkness. Marina accompanied him. Along the way, a horse fell and Cortés ordered it returned to camp. Soon after, another horse fell, then another.

"*Señor*," a soldier said to him, "the horses falling is a bad omen. Shouldn't we wait until daylight, when we can see where we are going?"

"Why do you believe in those superstitions? I will not suspend this march because we have much ground to cover before the sunrise. We must consider that God is more powerful than nature."

When his own horse stumbled and fell, Cortés, without flinching, ordered all the horses sent back to camp and he and the soldiers continued on foot. Before dawn, the Spaniards razed several villages with butchery and destruction. They arrived at Tzompantzingo, a large village, which they bested by surprise attack. Naked, the inhabitants burst from their huts, unable to oppose or resist the attackers.

Cortés stopped the raid when the Indian officials, through Marina's intercession, asked for peace.

"*Señor*, please do not do any more damage. We are a peaceful people," they cried.

"But we are at war with the Tlaxcalans," Cortés told them.

"That is entirely the fault of young Xicoténcatl. We are not a warlike people. We wish to have only peace with you."

Because they had offered no resistance, Cortés ordered no reprisals.

He walked up a hill to survey the area. In the distance, he could make out the city of Tlaxcala. "There is where we ought to go," he told his lieutenants, thrusting his arm toward the town.

"We won't accomplish anything by killing these people. So let's go back to camp reassured that these Indians are peaceful, grateful for the provisions we have been given as well as for the women they have sent back with us to prepare the food."

When Cortés and his men returned, they discovered their absence had caused great uneasiness. Some of the troops were afraid a disaster had befallen Cortés because he had left with all his captains, leaving only Gonzalo de Sandoval in charge.

"Thanks be to God!" Sandoval cried when he spotted Cortés. "You have finally returned! There are cliques in the camp and rumors about the dangers that each day threaten us. When you didn't return, I had to calm them as best I could because they believed something had happened to you and the men."

Cortés smiled calmly. "We had an interesting experience. We visited a large village and we have come back with food and women who will prepare it. Now, what is this nonsense about cliques and conspiracies?"

Sandoval was crestfallen. "I can tell you that some of the men are worried because we are so few in the midst of so many extreme dangers."

Cortés nodded. "All right. When I make rounds, I will speak with the men and listen to their complaints."

That night, with Sandoval at his side, Cortés moved about the camp among the torches and huts. Outside of one, he overheard one of the soldiers.

". . . stuck here in this land, among so many enemies, with so many battles and so many dangers that we cannot rest by day or night."

"We are crazy to be here," another put in.

"The person who dragged us to a point of no return is the crazy one," said another.

Sadly, Cortés listened, then whispered to Gonzalo. "Are these the ones you told me about?"

"Yes."

"Order them to come to my quarters tomorrow."

Early next morning, that squad reported to Cortés.

He welcomed them pleasantly. "They tell me you have certain fears. Let us deal with them now, so we can clear this up once and for all."

Hesitantly at first, one of the men spoke up: "Captain, we come before you very calmly, without guile or disrespect, merely to express our advice. Look at us, sir, we are emaciated and some are badly wounded. There is not one among us without at least a bruise or head wounds. We have even made a mighty effort to do battle at night against Indian scouts and spies, while making our sentinel rounds to guard the camp. By day and by night, we have been fighting without enough rest. If we were to make an accounting since we left Cuba, we have lost more than fifty-five men, and that is without having any news of those we left behind in Villa Rica. Until now, God has given us victories in our battles and encounters, and with His great mercy has sustained us. But surely, we should not tempt God so many times because what happened to Pedro Carbonero may happen to us."

He paused with head bowed, then continued. "Think about the past, of the Romans and Alexander. None of those other great captains would have dared to invade these lands with their huge populations and thousands of warriors. What we have already experienced makes it look like suicide for us to continue—especially with the misfortune of the ships sinking and having so few troops." He paused again.

"Because of all this tragedy, and because it has been three days since we last fought, before Xicoténcatl can attack us with even more warriors and the danger that they might kill us or capture us as human sacrifices for their idols, let us go back to Villa Rica and wage no more wars or tempt God again."

With a kind expression on his face, Cortés heard them out. Then he replied gently: "I know all too well what you have told me. But precisely because of what we have accomplished and will continue to accomplish, I believe that in this universe, there are neither Spaniards nor any other men stronger or with more spirit than you men. We have fought and have produced extraordinary results. We have had our weapons constantly on our shoulders and have known the fear and the anxiety of constant vigilance; on guard duty and in the bitter cold of this land. How then can we evaluate these brave efforts, which truly Our Lord has offered to us? In my mind, I see us besieged by opposing forces. And I see also how they wield their broadswords whenever they come close to us. Even I was frightened when the enemy decapitated that mare with a single stroke of his weapon. For a moment, I thought all was lost, but that was when I recognized your amazing valor. Think about this, too, in the midst of all these dangers, did you ever witness any negligence on my part? No! I was always right beside you."

He stared grimly into each soldier's eyes. "About tempting God: remember, in serving Him we are praising His holy doctrine. By destroying graven idols, we continue to serve Him, just as we *are* doing now."

More quietly, Cortés continued: "Xicoténcatl and his troops will not be back. We have defeated him three times and he no longer dares to try again. So listen to me closely. Now the war in this territory is over. Even the natives from Tzompantzingo are bringing us food and are peaceful. As to the scuttled ships, that was a very wise decision reached by your own leaders, the same ones who think it unwise for you to ask that we quit now. We joined one another as brave men—not to retreat."

He paused. "It is a fact that no Roman general ever undertook a great mission such as ours. Now and in the future, God willing, history will reveal that what we are accomplishing here is far greater than anything ever attempted. So when you speak about dying, wounds, cold, and hunger, remember that God will provide us with the strength of many. Unfortunately, it is in the very nature of war that good men and gallant horses must be sacrificed."

Finally, he said, "Therefore, men, it is never a wise strategy to retreat. If these natives and those we have made peace with see us go back—the very stones themselves would rise against us, because now they take us for gods. If we retreat, they would all judge us cowards. Everything would turn around and where we thought we had friends, there would be enemies. And what do you think the great Moctezuma would do if we retreated? What would he say? That it was all just a joke! Remember the old saying, men, 'it's bad enough over there, but a lot worse further on.' So you must be better off right here."

The men managed to display rueful smiles.

"Meanwhile, I would ask you men, as a favor, because you are strong, do not think about Cuba and what you left there. Instead, we will endeavor to do what we always have done as good soldiers. Besides God, our support and help, we must rely on our own courage."

When Cortés paused, one of the soldiers said, "But there are so many dangers and hardships, Captain. Take our advice, let us retreat and tempt God's kindness no further."

Losing his temper at last, Cortés boomed out: "It is better to 'die for a cause,' as the song goes, 'than to live dishonored.'"

Heads lowered, the grumblers left. From then on, although there were the usual soldier's complaints, everyone obeyed orders.

In Tenochtitlan

octezuma continued to receive reports about the Spaniards: "They arrived at Xocotla and Olintetl welcomed them and provided lodging. . . ."

"They have passed through the mighty wall at Tlaxcala. . . ."

"They arrived at Tecoac, in Tlaxcalan territory, where the Otomies live."

"They went out to receive them in the guise of war; with shields they welcomed them."

Others reported: "But they were totally victorious over the Otomies of Tecoac, they conquered them. The gods were divided into groups: a division of troops, a cannonade; they attacked with their swords and many more Otomies were wounded by arrows. 'Not just a few of them, but all perished.' The Otomies are very brave and good warriors, but were not successful. They did not know what to do."

Anguish tearing at his heart, Moctezuma listened to them all. When he heard about Tecoac, he said: "We will send more ambassadors. Let them go out in the guise of peace and make sure they carry enough gold. That seems to be the gods' food. Be certain you tell them we take great pleasure in their wondrous victory over the Tlaxcaltecans and that we welcome them."

Peace with Tlaxcala

Meeting with Moctezuma's latest emissaries, Cortés was deep in conversation with them when *Doña* Marina interrupted. Whispering confidentially, she said, "Lord, end these talks as quickly as you can. You are ill with fever and you need medicine and rest."

At once, Cortés stood up and asked the ambassadors to excuse him, promising to continue the meeting later. Marina followed him to his quarters and undressed him. Then she made sure he took his medicine. While she was tending to Cortés, an aide asked for permission to enter.

"Captain, a very tall Indian with big shoulders who says he is Xicoténcatl is here with fifty officials from Tlaxcala. His insignias are red and white and he comes with a sign of peace. He wishes to speak with Your Grace."

"I will come," Cortés groaned. "Assemble my captains as well. You see, Marina, there is no time for me to rest or to take the medicines you wish to give me. Dress me!"

Meekly, she complied.

With great pomp, Xicoténcatl arrived, making gestures of salutation and burning incense. Quite pleasantly, Cortés welcomed him. Victor and vanquished sat side by side.

"Lord," Xicoténcatl said, "I come in peace as a representative of the four chieftains of the Tlaxcalan Republic to ask you to accept us as your friends. We waged war against you because we did not know who you were, or from where you came, and we still are not sure if you were sent by Moctezuma. We used all our knowledge of war in daylight and at night so we would not be made subject to anyone. Never has this Republic been defeated or obeyed any alien ruler. We have always defended ourselves against Moctezuma's great power, as well as his father's and grandfather's.

"They have conquered this entire territory except for Tlaxcala. Yet they have never been able to subdue us even though we are completely surrounded by them and cannot leave our lands. We have no salt to eat with our food because there is none in our land, nor do they allow us to leave to obtain it. We have no clothes made of cotton because the climate is too cold to grow it. We are poor—we have no gold, no silver, or many other products. That is why we could not bring you any gifts. I hope you will pardon us.

"Moctezuma violated the *Guerra Florida* pacts and we have defended ourselves well against all of his allies. But you we could not defeat. Three times we gathered our warriors and we have found out that you are invincible. So, we wish to be your friends and loyal followers of the King you call Carlos. We are certain that allied with you and with your friendship our people and property will be defended so we will not be assaulted by the treacherous Mexicans. The four chieftains invite you to Tlaxcala to honor you."

Xicoténcatl, the Younger, proposes peace

Cortés listened impassively, then answered.

"We have had battles. That cannot be changed. We came to Tlaxcala believing it was a friendly country, because that is what the Cempoalan people told us. After we sent messengers of peace, good will and friendship, without warning you attacked us, killed our horses and tricked our ambassadors and waged war against us, for which we are not to blame. Three times you notified us that there would not be a battle and then you attacked anyway. It is you who are responsible for all the dead and the wounded. You can alter nothing that has already happened, but we can arrange a just peace.

"We came here in peace and peace is what we wish. Consider the peace of mind we offer you now. It is unswerving and firm, but if it is broken, we will show you no mercy. So, let there be peace! You are now subjects of his Majesty *Don* Carlos!"

Xicoténcatl nodded deliberately. "It will be steadfast, unswerving, and genuine. Because of it, we have become your hostages and subjects of your King. We await your arrival in Tlaxcala."

Cortés gave Xicoténcatl an *abrazo* and presented gifts to him and the other chiefs.

The entire episode was witnessed by the Mexican ambassadors, who were quick to express their displeasure. Atempanecatl, leader of Moctezuma's delegation, said to Cortés: "Great shameless phrases have the Tlaxcaltecans spoken. They only continue to deceive you. Have no confidence in them! We ask you please to wait here six days so we can send two of our ambassadors back to tell Moctezuma what has happened here. Then they will return with his reply."

"Very well," said Cortés. "I will wait here for six days as you ask."

"You must take advantage of this truce and attend to your fever," *Doña* Marina said once more.

Cortés waved a weary hand. "Yes, yes. And to write to Juan de Escalante in Villa Rica, who I am sure is most anxious about us. Tell Brother Bartolomé to take advantage of this calm to whitewash the altars, erect crosses and indoctrinate the people."

Eventually, the six days passed, while Cortés and his men rested and recovered from their wounds.

On the seventh day, the Mexican ambassadors arrived with gifts of gold, silver, fabrics and feathers. "Moctezuma sends you these gifts for your pleasure and in honor of your victories. But do not allow yourself to be fooled by these Tlaxcalans who only want you to enter their city so they may steal your gold and cloths because they are very poor and needy."

They were still speaking when the ensign approached Cortés.

"Captain! The arrival of four chieftains from the Republic of Tlaxcala has been announced. They wish to see you."

Cortés nodded at the report and turned back to the Mexicans. "I thank you very much. Please give these gifts to the great Moctezuma and tell him of my deep desire to visit him as soon as possible."

"We will tell him," the chief emissary replied. "We know of the many hardships you may encounter on the journey. He sends you these gifts and later on, other presents to encourage you to return to the sea from whence you came."

Cortés accepted the emissary's advice somewhat coldly. "Excuse me." He turned to an aide. "Please, present the Tlaxcalan chiefs who have come to greet us."

The Mexicans moved to one side and soon Xicoténcatl the elder appeared on a litter with the others—Maxixcatzin, Tlehuexolotzin and Citlalpopocatzin on foot paying him homage and waving smoldering aromatics and incense. A large retinue followed them. When he arrived, Xicoténcatl the elder spoke.

"Malinche, Malinche,* we have sent many messages begging you to forgive us because we waged war against you. Now we wish to unburden ourselves and admit that our real reason was to defend ourselves from Moctezuma's evil ways and from his great power. We thought you were one of his allies and if we had known what we know now, we would have received you on the road to our village with food and provisions and would have swept the paths clean for you. We would even have gone down to meet you at the sea, where you arrived in your ships. You have pardoned us, now we beg of you to come with us to our city where we will give you all that we have. Our people will be at your service. And listen, Malinche, when you accompany us,

---

* *Doña* Marina's prestige soared when the natives transferred her name to her *señor*, referring to Cortés himself as "Malinche." The name *Malintzin*, formed from Malinalli and the Aztec suffix *tzin*, denotes nobility.—Trans.

pay no attention to the lies these Mexicans tell about us. We believe that may be the reason you have not yet visited the City of Tlaxcala."

"Honorable chiefs," Cortés answered, "we always heard the Tlaxcaltecans were good people and because of that we were amazed when you declared war on us. However, before we go to Tlaxcala, we wish to dispose of some matters with the Mexican ambassadors. We would have come sooner if we had had enough help to move our cannon."

"Is that why you have remained here without replying to our invitation? We will dispatch at once five hundred *tamemes* to assist you."

"Then tomorrow, with their aid," said Cortés, "we will leave for Tlaxcala. The Mexican ambassadors will accompany us and we will continue our talks concerning peace. From Tlaxcala, they will return to Mexico."

"They will be welcome, as well. We await your arrival tomorrow."

On the 23rd of September, 1519, the Spanish army entered Tlaxcala peacefully.

Although not expecting treachery, Cortés' force set out in combat order, and remained alert. After arriving in the city, the Spaniards were received by the officials of the Republic amid flowers and garlands. The people came from the four corners of the city: the chiefs, the priests with their smoking braziers and decorations—everyone made an appearance.

Upon receiving the *abrazo*, Cortés greeted the chief by lifting the right hand of his host with his own left, a tactic that left Cortés' sword hand free.

They enter Tlaxcala in peace

A huge throng attended the reception for the Spaniards. The streets, the *azoteas* [flat limestone roofs] were filled with crowds of enthusiastic people whose curiosity about these strange men, horses, and dogs could hardly be satisfied.

Then the Spaniards were led to their lodgings, freshly cleaned and adorned with flowers and straw mats. All the embroidered decorations were on *henequén* for the Tlaxcalans had no cotton. Cortés insisted that the Mexican ambassadors be lodged next to him.

151

Once everyone was settled, a lieutenant who was responsible for placing lookouts and night guards reported to Cortés. "Sir, it seems quite peaceful here and there doesn't appear to be a need for so many guards or for us to be so cautious."

Cortés shook his head impatiently. "Look here, lieutenant, I appreciate what you are telling me. But we will follow our usual practice of being prepared for anything, even though these are good people. It is not as if we do not believe in their peace, but we must stay alert—just as if they were going to attack us and even as if they were actually advancing against us. Through over-confidence and carelessness, many captains have been defeated. Especially because we are so few—we must be careful!"

When Xicoténcatl noticed that the Spaniards were mounting night guards and lookouts, he was enraged.

"Malinche, either you think we are still your enemies or you doubt our good intentions. It is clear to me you have no confidence in our people or in the peace assurances we have given you. Obviously, you have been unduly influenced by the treacherous advice the Mexicans have whispered secretly to you. You must not believe them! You are our guests in our city and we will give you everything you wish, even our people and our children. You may even demand that we become your hostages, if that is your will."

"Xicoténcatl," Cortés said. "I do have confidence in your word. There is certainly no need whatsoever for hostages, which I know would deeply offend you. Please do not misunderstand why we keep our usual vigil. We simply cannot do otherwise. But know I am most grateful for all that you have offered and I will repay you in time."

At least somewhat mollified, Xicoténcatl left.

The Tlaxcaltecans supplied the Spaniards with whatever materials their austere community had to offer.

The wafers and wine had arrived from Juan de Escalante, so the following morning Cortés ordered an altar built to celebrate the Mass.

"Have Father Juan Díaz chant the Mass now that we have the wafers and wine from Villa Rica, where through God's mercy everything is going well," Cortés ordered.

After Mass, which the four chiefs attended, Xicoténcatl said to Cortés: "I wish to give you some gifts." He displayed on some *henequén* cloths a few insignificant pieces of gold. "Please excuse their poorness."

Cortés held up his hand and smiled. "It is more important to me that these are given by your own hand than if others had brought a house filled with gold. I accept them with gratitude and much respect."

Cortés gave the elder chieftain an *abrazo*.

Then Xicoténcatal ordered five beautiful Indian girls to come forward. "We know from our ancestors that their gods told them men would come from the part of the world where the Sun rises. They would come from distant lands to conquer and to rule over us. If you are these men, we are pleased because you are vigorous and good men. When we arranged the peace agreements, we remembered an important fact. Therefore, Malinche, we present to you our daughters so we may have offspring who will defend us against the Mexicans. Malinche, this is my own daughter, who has never married. She is a young girl, please take her for yourself."

He took her by the hand and presented her to Cortés, who replied, "Yes, we do come from where the Sun rises and our King and Lord has sent us here to accept you as brothers. I receive and take your daughters, but for the moment have their fathers keep them."

"Why do you not accept them now?"

"Because before we do, we must perform a ceremony that God, Our Lord, demands of us. He is the one we believe in and He orders that you destroy your idols and prohibits you from ever again making human sacrifices, or killing more men, or committing other disgraceful acts. You must believe in Who we believe in. There is only one true God."

Shaking his head sadly, the old man answered. "Malinche, we have understood, even before today, and we certainly do believe that your God and great *Señora* are very good. But you have been here such a short time. In time, we will understand more clearly your beliefs and then we will do what is right. How can you expect us to reject our own *teules*, who for many years our ancestors respected as gods, worshipping them and making sacrifices to them?

"If we who are old, just to please you, did as you suggest, what would our priests think? What about our neighbors and the young men and children of this province? Why, they would rise up against us, especially since the priests have spoken with the gods and these *teules* told them we should not forget to make sacrifices as soon as possible. If we do not, this entire province will be ravaged by hunger, pestilence and war."

Just as Cortés was about to reply, Padre de la Merced drew close beside him. "*Señor*, I beg Your Grace not to press this topic any further. It is not right to force them to become Christians as we did in Cempoala, where we destroyed their idols. I do not believe we should pursue this until they have more knowledge of our Holy Faith. What do we accomplish now if we take away these idols from one temple and the *teocalli* if they merely go to another? It is enough that they listen to our admonitions, which are holy and good."

Juan Velázquez de León and Francisco Lugo responded. "Very well said, Padre. What Your Grace has done already is sufficient. It would be wiser not to bring up this subject again to these *caciques*."

Before replying, Cortés glanced toward *Doña* Marina, who signalled her assent by a blink of her eyes. Cortés said to Xicoténcatl: "We will consider what you have asked of us, but we request that you make available a temple where we may honor our God and His Holy Mother in order to conduct our ceremonies and baptize your daughters with Christian names."

Xicoténcatl agreed and ordered an altar erected.

As soon as it was ready, the first Mass was sung at the new altar and the five Indian maidens were baptized. They named Xicoténcatl's daughter Luisa and Cortés gave her to Pedro de Alvarado, saying to Xicoténcatl: "He is my brother and captain."

Maxixcatzin's daughter they named Elvira and Cortés gave her to Juan Velázquez de León. Another was given the name Juana and she was led over to Gonzalo de Sandoval. María was given to Cristóbal de Olid and the last, Mercedes, was presented to Alonso de Ávila.

Cortés and his entourage stayed in Tlaxcala for almost a month, gathering their strength and preparing for the journey to Tenochtitlan. Cortés actively cultivated the friendship of the four principal *caciques*, inviting each to join him for a meal. As he went about the city, he commented to his captains: "This is a larger and more populated city than Granada [Spain]. Their market is amazing with the great variety of goods and food they have there. They have steam and hot water baths and even maintain order with a police force. One can see they are a practical people who keep their affairs in good order. They cultivate every available plot for their crops and they govern themselves almost like the Lordships of Venice, Genova or Pisa, republics which have no overlord. The city is divided into four quarters, which band together to wage war and to judge punishment for crimes, and each has an adequate jail."

The Popocatépetl

From Tlaxcala, the Spaniards could see Popocatépetl and Iztaccíhuatl with their eternal snowy peaks. Popocatépetl, with its great smoke-belching cavity, was so intriguing to the Spaniards that after a brief rest, Diego de Ordaz asked Cortés' permission to climb it.

"My Captain, I have an ardent desire to visit that great mountain that spews smoke. I ask your authorization to scale it with two soldiers whom I have spoken to about it and with any Indians who wish to accompany us."

"Of course," said Cortés. "Not only do I give you permission, I order you to do it. See if there is any sulfur that one usually finds in volcanoes, in case we need some to make gunpowder."

Two soldiers and some chiefs from Huejotzingo accompanied Ordaz; the Indians made the preparations.

"One cannot ascend higher than where we have certain temples because of the land slides that cause many stones and ashes to fall."

Diego de Ordaz ascends the Popocatépetl

"We will see," said Ordaz, beginning the ascent.

The Indians stayed behind in the temples they called *Teules de Popocatépetl*. When Ordaz reached the crater, he took time to examine the by-products of the periodic eruptions that had spewed out pumice and ashes. From the peak, Diego de Ordaz and his companions were the first Spaniards to admire the splendor of the Great Tenochtitlan. When they descended, they brought back trophies of snow and icicles.

"We went right up to the very rim itself, Captain, and walked around the mouth when it was not discharging flames. It is round and wide, about a quarter of a league, and from there we saw the great Valley of Mexico. In the center of the lake is the great city of Temistitan and a splendrous sight it is. With much effort and bravery, we can reach it. We can also avail ourselves of the sulfur, which smells strong yet appears to be the usual amber color."

Forward! When the Time is Right!

After the third week of rest and recuperation, Cortés ordered a general review of the army. When they were assembled, he announced, "Men and companions. During our rest here in Tlaxcala, we have heard about Moctezuma's great riches as well as the power of his vast army. He can assemble one hundred and fifty thousand. He controls the entrance to his city through the water upon which it is built. I wish to hear from all of you, captains and soldiers. Tell me if we should go ahead with our adventure."

"Forward! Yes!" shouted the captains.

"Advance! Now!" shouted most of the soldiers as they joined the captains.

"Captain," said a soldier, "we know you have decided to advance. I vote with the group that objects and wishes to return to the beach. As we are so few, it is foolhardy for us even to try to enter such a stronghold. And consider Moctezuma's huge army! There are many other men with the same opinion."

"Yes, yes!" a few cried out. "Let us retreat! We do not want to advance."

"Comrades, we have listened to your opinion. Even so," Cortés said, "I think we shall move on. We can do nothing less because we have insisted all along we must meet with Moctezuma. If we retreat now, we will only display our fear. The results of the glory that lies ahead may be the same in the end, or it may seem the same, but at least we will not have brought shame upon ourselves and our families."

"Forward! Well and good!" shouted most of the soldiers.

After consulting with one another in whispering groups, the rest eventually agreed, too. "So be it! Let's go on!"

"Yes! We shall go forward at once!" shouted Cortés. "As soon as we can, we depart!"

Opportunely, another of Moctezuma's ambassadors arrived with six other officials and a large entourage.

The ambassador declared, "Once more Moctezuma sends you greetings and expresses his pleasure that you have invaded and defeated the Tlaxcalan forces and now you have lodging in that city. Moctezuma wishes to be your friend and subject of your King. You ask for gold, silver, precious stones and slaves to be paid as tributes to you each year. Moctezuma agrees, but you must not advance from here or try to visit him or invade his lands, because you will find that road rugged and full of obstacles. Besides, in his city there is not enough food to supply your army. He sends these gifts for you."

He handed over some gold jewelry and cotton clothing.

"Please thank Moctezuma for his offer to be a subject, but tell him I have been mandated by my King and Monarch to visit with him and conclude a treaty. I am determined to fulfill that mission, so tell me which is the best route."

The ambassador frowned. "Malinche, no matter which road you take, it will be a great risk. But if you are so determined, our advice would be by way of Cholula, a large city with plenty of supplies. Their people are friends of Moctezuma and will treat you as you deserve."

When the Tlaxcaltecans found out that Cortés and his forces were heading for Tenochtitlan by way of Cholula, Maxixcatzin said: "Malinche, you absolutely must not go through Cholula. That is Moctezuma's territory and no doubt he has ordered some treachery against you when you are within the city. Have no faith in the Mexicans. There will be fifty thousand men in ambush and they can destroy you. That road is full of traps, pits and dugout holes with pointed stakes that can injure your horses. If you are truly determined to proceed, then go through Huejotzingo. At least they are our friends and will treat you well."

Xicoténcatl, the Elder, advises Cortés

"Many thanks for your advice, but I will deal with the Cholulans and teach them how to be subjects of my King. I am quite prepared for their treachery. Besides, if we did not go through Cholula, we would appear to be afraid of them and that would reveal weakness. It would also be most unwise to leave a fortified city to our rear. However, we shall see. . . ."

That night, in their lodging, *Doña* Marina said to Cortés: "My lord, the Tlaxcalans are right. We should not go through Cholula, there will be treachery."

"Then we shall confront it, woman. We must. We cannot afford to reveal fear. After all, we are *teules*." He smiled broadly and held his arms wide.

"As for myself, I do not know what you are, my lord, you seem to be everything! But now, my eager cavalier. . . ." She drew him close.

Cholula: The Massacre

On October 13, 1519, the Spanish army, assembled in their accustomed marching order, began to move toward Cholula.

As Cortés left his Tlaxcalan friends, Xicoténcatl, the Council spokesman, said, "Malinche, we are worried about your determination to march through Cholula because we know there will be great treachery and double-dealing. As we are now brothers and subjects of the same King, we have decided that our warriors should accompany you so they can help defend you against the Mexicans' duplicity in any way they can."

So it was that six thousand Tlaxcaltecan soldiers accompanied the Spanish force.

At the end of the first day, when the vanguard was only about a league from Cholula, Cortés called a halt, then set up camp with a tight ring of sentinels.

Early the next morning, the Cholulan officials presented themselves at the Spanish camp. As their retinue of priests, timbrels, shellhorn players and singers appeared before Cortés, the Cholulans said: "Malinche, please pardon us for not visiting you in Tlaxcala with gifts and food. We were willing, but the four Tlaxcaltecan chiefs are our enemies and have said many bad things about us and the great Moctezuma, our lord. And now, with your permission, they have the audacity to come armed to our city."

Cortés listened closely to *Doña* Marina's translation, then nodded grimly at the visitors. "About the Tlaxcaltecan army, you are right." He turned to his lieutenants, standing alertly behind him. "Olid and Alvarado, please ask our Tlaxcaltecan friends to set up their camp here in the field and to refrain from entering the city, except those who are helping with the artillery and our allies the Cempoaltecans. I don't know how this plan will be received by the Tlaxcaltecans, but reassure them that when we move on we will ask them to join us."

Turning back to the Cholulans, Cortés remarked: "We have decided the Tlaxcaltecans will remain here. We wish to go through your territory to Temistitan as commanded by our Emperor, who has great power to ask for your vassalage, and to inform you not to pray to idols or sacrifice human beings, or eat their flesh or commit other disgraceful acts, but to be our brothers."

"Malinche, you have not even entered our land yet, but you order us to ignore our *teules*. We cannot do that. As to giving obedience to your King, whom you tell us about, we are pleased to do that and give you our word."

"Then let it be as we arranged in Tlaxcala with their *teules*. Now we must move on," Cortés said, ordering his Spaniards to enter Cholula peacefully.

The ragged little force was received by thousands of people amid flowers, songs, and great curiosity. They were given lodgings in great halls and that first day they were fed very well. The following day less food appeared and on the third there was nothing, nor did the *caciques* visit them.

Moctezuma's ambassadors were still accompanying Cortés, and through Marina, he spoke to them: "I wonder at this reception, so meager, and now they do not even feed us. Please order the *caciques* to bring us food; otherwise they will anger us."

"We will tell them," said the Mexicans.

As a joke, the Cholulans appeared with water and fire wood.

Soon new Mexican emissaries hurried to see Cortés and said brusquely: "Malinche, our lord Moctezuma sends word to you that you should not continue on, sparing yourselves the dangers along the road. Neither in Tenochtitlan nor in Cholula is there food for you."

Calmly, Cortés replied: "I am astonished that Moctezuma, such a great lord, changes his mind so often. We must go to see him. And you will stay with us until we do."

He turned his back on the Mexican ambassadors. Cortés ordered his men to meet him on the patio outside their billet. "These people appear to be most confused; so please be extra alert."

He turned to his translator. "*Doña* Marina, please call the principal *cacique*."

A little later, she informed Cortés: "He is ill and cannot come."

"You see?" Cortés commented wryly. "Alvarado, bring before me those two priests from that temple. Right now. But treat them gently."

The soldiers soon came back with the priests.

"Tell me, my friends, what are your *caciques* so afraid of? I have invited them to visit me, but they refuse."

The chief priest puffed out his chest arrogantly. "We are not afraid of you. I will personally go to the officials and bring them here to meet with you."

When the Cholulan *caciques* appeared, their heads were lowered and they were sullen.

"Tell me, sirs, what you are so afraid of that you refuse to face us? Why have you stopped feeding us? If you are troubled because we are here, then rest easy because tomorrow we will leave for Temistitan to speak to Moctezuma. But you had better provide *tamemes* to carry our soldiers' baggage and to help with the cannon. And, of course, bring us some food soon or we will become very angry."

One *cacique*, almost speechless with fear, uncertain what to say, squeaked in a tremulous voice: "I will search for whatever small amount of food I can find, but I tell you that Moctezuma does not want you to go any further and you must go back." The priests left.

Almost at once, Teuch, the Cempoaltecan, with two of his tribe, came in. "Captain, we have discovered holes close to your quarters, covered with boards and dirt which hide sharpened sticks inside. The *azoteas** have many rocks stored there and adobe screens [breastworks] appear to have been recently made."

That night, eight Tlaxcaltecans appeared before Cortés: "Look, Malinche," they said, "these people are planning something devious. We learned that tonight they are going to sacrifice to their idol, the war god, seven people, of which five are children, just so that they may be victorious over you. We also saw them removing from the city all of the women's and children's effects."

"Go back to your Tlaxcaltecan captains and have everyone on the alert, if we should call upon them."

Then Cortés turned to Marina: "Go and get those two Indian priests who came down from the temple earlier. Use flattery and offer them presents so they are not frightened."

Marina soon returned with them.

Cortés conducted the interrogation himself: "I ask you to tell us what is happening in Cholula. Strange events seem to be taking place. Now, tell me, truthfully, how is it that you priests, as well as your officials who worship idols, all lie to us? If you will just tell me the truth, then I will give you many gifts. I promise no one else will know about it. We will leave tomorrow anyway. However, if you remain silent, then you will learn what I am capable of doing to you."

As Marina translated, she added a few more reasons for the priests to cooperate. Finally, they said, "The truth is that when Moctezuma found out you were coming to Cholula, every day he issued different orders and we did not know which to obey: some days he told us to honor you, another to withhold food, another he wished to invite you to come to Mexico, the next day he changed his mind. We believe you ought to go away."

That night, *Doña* Marina said to Cortés: "My lord, a lady, the wife of an official, came to see me, accompanied by her son. She said, 'Malintzin, come with me to my house if you wish to save your life. You can marry my older son and be saved from the slaughter of these *teules* that Moctezuma ordered. I have seen you and you are young and you should not die. Marry my son.'"

"Tell me more," said Cortés.

Marina shrugged. "I answered her. 'Oh, Mother! I am very grateful for what you have told me. I would go with you now, but I have no one I can trust to bring my clothes and jewels. Wait a little while and tonight we will go. As you can see, these *teules* are watching and they can hear us. What did you mean about killing the *teules*?' The woman said: 'Moctezuma's Mexicans are allied with these Indians from Cholula to ambush you from the ravines along the road.'

"'If this is such a secret,' I said, 'how did you find out about it?'

"'My husband is captain of a militia group and right now he and his warriors that he commands from this city will give the order that the Cholulans should join with

---

* *Azotea* is a flat roof of a house with a surface firm enough to walk on and to place supplies, (*Academia de la Lengua Española*)—Trans.

the Mexicans in the ravines and kill and capture the *teules*. Moctezuma himself sent my husband a beautiful drum adorned in gold to flatter him.'

"'Oh, how happy I am to learn that your son, with whom I will marry, is a chieftain. Wait for me here so I may bring my things and we will go together.'"

Upset by this news of Cholulan duplicity, Cortés said, "Marina, go and summon the head priests and the *caciques*, tell them I wish to bid them farewell as we are leaving tomorrow."

Soon, she was back with the Cholulan officials.

Cortés stood tall as he spoke to them. "I have asked you to come here because we wish to leave tomorrow. Although you have provided us with very inadequate subsistence, do not be afraid of retribution, as long as you do not break the promise you have offered us. So we can prepare for the march and take our leave of your good selves, please come early tomorrow morning to the patios of these temples." Cortés swept his hand wide to encompass the plaza in which he stood.

"All the nobles, lords and the *caciques*, their aides and two thousand soldiers should accompany you."

Cortés then assembled his captains. "*Señores, capitanes.* You already know about the ambush the Cholulans and Mexicans have prepared for us on the road. Well, we shall carry on as if we were ignorant of it. Tomorrow at dawn, pretend to bundle your clothes and weapons and when the horses are ready, we will attack the Indians who are waiting for us in the courtyards. Each captain will place a guard at the exit and at the first shot from a musket we will give them what they deserve. We dare not leave such a treacherous city in the rear guard without punishment."

He continued: "With Moctezuma's emissaries, we will explain that the evil Cholulans wished to commit a deceitful act against us and blame it all on their lord Moctezuma. They must be confined to quarters, with no chance to speak to the town officials. They may even accompany us to Mexico. From nightfall on, we must be prepared and armed, with look-outs and night patrols."

Very early the following morning, wreathed in smiles, the noble Cholulan warriors assembled in the courtyard. They were unarmed.

The alert Spaniards, well-armed themselves, placed guards with bucklers and swords at the exits. Cortés was mounted, surrounded by soldiers. Next to him was *Doña* Marina. He sneered: "With pleasure these traitors wait to see us among the ravines so they can satiate themselves on our flesh. The Lord will do things better."

Through Marina's voice, he spoke to the *caciques*: "Why did you want to kill us in ambush? We have done nothing to cause you to treat us so treacherously. You refused to feed us and even made a joke by bringing water and firewood and telling us there was no corn. It is sinful that the Mexican units are waiting in the ravines to kill us and capture us. It would have been better if you would have waged war as brave and good warriors, like the Tlaxcaltecans—instead of treasonously. What do you have to say?"

Stunned and stuttering, the *caciques* said: "We know nothing about any treason. Ask Moctezuma's emissaries about the orders of their lord."

"With treacherous orders like these, our royal laws mandate that you must be punished. And for this crime, you must die!"

Cortés flicked his hand and the musket was fired as a signal to attack.

The slaughter at Cholula

And so the slaughter at Cholula began. The killing lasted two hours, and then the Tlaxcaltecans who had stayed in the outskirts invaded the city, killing, stealing and capturing, easily defeating the Cholulan squadrons.*

As the sun set, they told Cortés that more Tlaxcaltecan warriors were on the way to finish the destruction. Cortés ordered Cristóbal de Olid to bring all the Tlaxcaltecan captains before him.

"Brother Tlaxcaltecans!" Cortés smiled. "You have fought bravely and helped us with a great victory. But we cannot leave this area until these people and our allies have become friends. So go back to your camp and await my orders."

Soon, some other chieftains and priests came to see Cortés. "We come from another area and were not involved in the treason. The traitors have paid with their lives and we wish to have peace and become subjects of your great King."

"Let there be peace; death to all traitors!" Cortés cried.

---

* The Cholulan *caciques* appeared, leading a body of levies, *tamemes*. Thousands were marched into the square. In an instant, every musket and crossbow was leveled at the unfortunate, unarmed Cholulans as they stood crowded together like a herd of deer. Then the Spaniards rushed at them with their swords. The half-naked bodies of the natives offered no protection. While this work of death was going on, their countrymen on the outside of the plaza commenced a furious assault on the Spaniards. But Cortés placed his battery of heavy guns in a position that commanded the avenues and swept them away as they rushed in. The horses charging in the middle confused the Cholulans, as did the flash of firearms and the deafening roar of the artillery. Some accounts say six thousand were slaughtered and others say the number was greater. (Prescott, William H., *The Conquest of Mexico*, New York: Modern Library, 1936.)—Trans.

"Malinche, our chief died in the battle, will you be kind enough to name a successor to lead us?"

"Who should be named?"

"The brother of the dead *cacique*!"

"Very well, he is your new *cacique*. Now order the people to return to their city and go back to work without any fear. Our anger ceases once the punishment has been inflicted."

"In a few days, everything will be normal within the city, Malinche," said the new *cacique*.

Cortés became very solemn. "Eventually, you will hear the good news of our Holy Faith, then you will learn to treat with contempt your idols and your human sacrifices. Remain peaceful subjects of His Majesty *Don* Carlos and you will again be friends with the Tlaxcaltecans as you were before Moctezuma divided you."

For fourteen days, the Spaniards stayed in Cholula, a religious center in a fertile valley with as many temples as days in the year.

The March Continues

Once again, the Spaniards pushed forward. Cortés rode at the head of his army, followed by the Cempoaltecans and Tlaxcaltecans. Teuch, the Cempoaltecan *cacique*, said, "Malinche, we are far from our own land and we miss it very much. If you won't take what I say personally, my warriors would like to return home, but the chiefs will remain with you."

"Very well. I am grateful for your companionship. Remind the fat *cacique* of our desire that he and his people continue in the Holy Faith."

Then Cortés turned to the Tlaxcaltecan captains.

"From now on we enter populated lands. We would regret another episode that we witnessed in Cholula. I know it looks peculiar to them for Tlaxcaltecan forces to be entering their territory. Therefore, I would like about one thousand of your best warriors to serve as baggage handlers. They must wait here until I decide if we need their support."

The army marched in its usual order: field scouts on horseback with the dogs in front of them and the foot soldiers at route step close to them. In the middle of the column were the cannon carried by the *tamemes*, then musketeers and crossbowmen and another body of horsemen in lines of three. The rear guard consisted of Tlaxcaltecan Indians carrying baggage, protected by other Indian warriors and a few more horsemen.

When they arrived at Huejotzingo, they were received peacefully and with gifts.

In Tenochtitlan

Moctezuma continued to vacillate as he received the new information from the emissaries who had met Cortés.

The ambassadors related their impressions of the Spaniards to the harassed Moctezuma. The first ambassador reported:

"The defeated Tlaxcalans said, 'Now we march beside him, we are his friends; we seek his friendship.' Quickly, the lords of Tlaxcala, went to meet the *teules*. They brought food: turkeys, eggs, thin white tortillas. Then these Tlaxcalan traitors said: 'You must be tired, our lords.'"

A second ambassador added: "They led the white men, guided them, and made them welcome in the royal castle. And then the *teules* asked: 'Where is Mexico? Is it very far?' The enemy Tlaxcalans said, 'No, it's not far. It may take three days to get there. It's a wonderful place. The Mexicans are very courageous, conquering warriors. All of their invasions are victorious.'"

The very soul of the Tlaxcalan Indian hated the Cholulans, which is why they spread that rumor to Malinche that he must kill the Cholulans.

"The Tlaxacans said to Malinche: 'Our enemy, the Cholulans, are wicked people and as brave as the Mexicans as well as friends of the Mexicans.'

"When the *teules* heard this, they went to Cholula and took the Tlaxcalans and the Cempoalans with them as allies, all in the guise of war. When they arrived, they shouted their challenge. There was also notification by crier. 'All the nobles must come; the lords; the captains; the guides and the men of the village,' was the order given. "Everyone came together in the plaza of the temple. When everyone was assembled there, the white men sealed the entrances to the atrium with warriors," continued another ambassador.

The first ambassador spoke again, "Suddenly, there were sword thrusts, death, blows to bodies! Those Cholulans had no spirit in their hearts! They did not even defend themselves, not with swords or shields against the Spaniards. Only by treachery were they slaughtered. They died like blind men without knowing why.

"After the slaughter at Cholula, the Spaniards have set out on their march and now they are coming toward Mexico. They are coming in a great throng, with the goal of conquest. Yes, they are truly coming, raising the dust of the roads into a whirlwind. They are coming with their lances raised; there are so many arrow shafts they resemble bats leaving a cave; they are coming in their brilliancy. They threaten us with their swords glittering in the sun as they brandish them like the swells of the waves.

"With their coats of mail, their helmets of iron, these people create a great clatter as they march along. Some are dressed all in iron; they are coming adorned in it. They shine so brightly! Their coming terrifies everyone. Oh, my Lord, they are truly dreadful and horrendous.

"They have 'dogs' leading the way, patrolling in front of the army. These creatures hold their heads high, pointing their noses. They dash about wildly and saliva drips from their jaws."

Moctezuma, astonished and horrified by the reports, almost prostrate with fear, issued his orders.

"As the head of the tax-collectors, Tzihuacpopocatzin should take gifts of gold for the *teules* to satisfy their greed.

"They should await them in the *Tajón del Águila* and inform the *teules* that I do not want to see them. They must go away. I will give them all the gold and tributes their King desires. But they must retreat. . . . There will be no food for them and my subjects are already armed to stop them from entering the city. After they receive the gold they should depart."

Cortés Pass

On November 1st, the Spanish army and their allies began to climb the sierra between the two volcanoes leading into the valley of Puebla and Mexico. From the place known now as Cortés Pass, they admired the splendor of Tenochtitlan, set in the middle of the great lake.

En el Paso de Cortés

At the Cortés Pass

It was in the pass that Moctezuma's ambassadors appeared with their gold presents. After the usual polite exchanges, Tzihuacpopocatzin spoke: "Malinche, these are new presents our great lord Moctezuma has sent to you. He says he is very sorry for all the hardships you have suffered, to come here from such distant lands in order to see him. Again, he sends you a message: He will give you much gold and silver and *chalchihuites* as tribute for your Emperor and also for you and the rest of the *teules* with you. But he does not want you to come to Mexico. He requests that you do not continue on, but that you return to where you came from. He promises to send to the port a large quantity of gold, silver and precious stones for your King and for you personally four loads of gold and one load for each one of your brothers. To go on to Mexico is useless; all of Moctezuma's subjects are armed and will prevent your entrance and besides, there is no safe route and no food."

Cortés embraced the ambassadors, received the gifts with great joy and said to them: "I am astonished that Moctezuma, having said he is our friend and being such a great lord, changes his mind so often. Sometimes he says one thing, then sends messages to the contrary. As to the gold for the Emperor and for us, I am grateful for it and will repay it with noble deeds in the future. However, since we are so near him, it seems most inconsiderate to expect us simply to turn back without accomplishing what our King has commanded us: To meet him. As for the scarcity of food, we are men who are able to get along with very little. We are proceeding along this road into your city and we will arrive there very soon."

In Tenochtitlan

By forced march, the ambassadors hurried back to Moctezuma. "Lord, great lord: We gave the *teules* the golden flags and the *quetzal* feathers. When we presented the gifts, broad smiles revealed their pleasure and they were all very happy. They were more than pleased. As if they were monkeys, they lifted up the gold, then settled down with expressions of great pleasure as the gold renewed and illuminated their hearts.

"What is certain is that they desire gold with an avid thirst. They assume an air of importance; they have a furious appetite for the metal. Like some hungry beasts, they crave the gold.

"Zealously, they grabbed the golden flags, turning them from side to side. They looked at one side and then another. They act like people who speak a savage language; everything they utter sounds savage. When they saw Tzihuacpopocatzin, they asked: 'Is he by chance Moctezuma?'

"Those who marched with the Spanish army, their fawning allies from Tlaxcala and Cempoala who so cunningly and cleverly accompany them responded, 'Oh, it is not he, our lords. That is Tzihuacpopocatzin, he merely represents Moctezuma.' Regardless, the *teules* said to him, 'Perhaps you are Moctezuma?'

"'Yes,' Tzihuacpopocatzin said, 'I am your humble servant. I am Moctezuma.' But they answered: 'Why do you try to fool us? Who do you think we are? You cannot play a trick on us. And do not try to make fun of us either. We know very well you are not he. . . . *There* is Moctezuma. You cannot hide him; you cannot conceal him from us. Where can he go? Is he a bird that will fly away? Or will he make his path on the earth? We must see him. It is absolutely imperative that we see his face. We must hear the words from his lips, we will hear him.'"

Again these official greeters said: "They are coming! They are coming down the unswerving road."

Moctezuma, with every exposure to news of the Spaniards' progress, became more transfixed. Now, he decided to meditate, shutting himself into a private room, alone with his gods.

When he came out, he announced: "One more time, I would like the wizards to go out to see them and this time take along the magicians and some priests from Chalco to meet them and bewitch them. These new emissaries must tell them that if they continue their advance, then they will soon be dead! Terrify them!"

In the Valley of Mexico

The Spanish army and its allies descended into the Valley of Mexico, wary of the obstacles placed on the road by the Mexicans: holes, tree trunks, stakes and sudden detours. The Tlaxcaltecans pointed out to Cortés the best route around the hazards and dangers. Cautiously, the army entered Amecameca, where they spent the night. Almost before they were settled in, delegations from nearby villages appeared before Cortés seeking to enlist his support against Moctezuma's abuses.

Doña Marina informed him, "*Señor*, delegates are here from Chalco, Chimalhuacán, Tlalmanalco and Ayotzingo, pleading for your protection against Moctezuma's tyranny as well as the excessive tributes he demands."

In Amecameca, the representatives of Chalco, Chimalhuacán, Tlalmanalco, and Ayotzingo complain about Moctezuma

"Tell them, *Doña* Marina, how happy I am to see them and I offer my help in every way I can. After all, that is why my King sent me here. It would please me greatly if they would listen to some words about our faith from Father de la Merced. A few from each village may come forward now."

Gonzalo de Sandoval and Pedro de Alvarado were standing near Cortés and he turned to them. "More and more I am convinced Moctezuma governs by oppression. The conflicts with his subjects must be serious if even villagers as close to his city as these ask for our protection. And it would be quite foolish of us not to take advantage of that situation. From now on, at each town through which we pass, we must invite a few representatives to accompany us to the city of Mexico. Their presence will send an unmistakable signal to Moctezuma."

The next day, Cortés was at the vanguard when he halted the march. "Sandoval! There appears to be a fork in the road ahead. One looks as if it has been swept clean—no doubt its ditches are filled with lurking Indians as well. The other seems less appealing, but passable."

"Captain, the Tlaxcaltecans said the swept road is indeed smooth and straight all the way to Mexico. They also said the god Huichilobos has advised Moctezuma to let us enter the city, then we will be killed later."

Cortés nodded. "That may all be so, Gonzalo, but we cannot afford to reveal the slightest tremor of fear before these people. Therefore, we will march along the swept road. You and Alvarado must take extra precautions with the lookouts and sentries, especially after dark, because we are moving into much more heavily populated territory. And we will not show fear! The good Lord is with us, as usual, but take care that the night guards are alert. Now, Gonzalo, go and fetch the Mexican ambassadors and bring them to me."

The Spanish Captain looked sternly at the Mexicans. "My soldiers and I will be marching along the road," he said, pointing toward the swept surface. "Because we will be encountering more inhabitants the closer we get to Mexico, there are likely to be some more accidents, especially at night. You must get word to the local people that they should remain calm and not approach our camps. My troops do not sleep, neither by day nor night—they are always armed and ready for trouble.

"Therefore, after sunset, no one is permitted to approach our camp or he will die. And tell them all that I always feel very bad when that happens."

That same night, Cortés himself made the rounds to test the camp's defenses. When he came upon one of the sentries, the man pointed his weapon at Cortés, who quickly yelped, "Ah, the guard!"

The man heard his shout just in time, and nervously cautioned Cortés, "Next time, *señor*, tell me who you are sooner. If you had come any closer, there might have been a most unfortunate accident."

Cortés could hardly contain his laughter as he thumped the guard good-naturedly on the shoulder. "Good for you, Martín López."

The next day as the sun rose and at many of the dawns that followed, Indian bodies were discovered just outside the camp, mortal proof of the marksmanship of Spanish crossbowmen.

On the 5th of November, 1519, the army advanced along the road toward Chalco, arriving at Ayotzingo, constructed on the shore of the lake, within sight of Ixtapalapa.

Chalco

The following day, without incident, the Spanish army entered Chalco. By another route, but in full view of the foreigners, the Aztec wizards and priests arrived simultaneously. Before the magicians could unpack their mystical wares to confront the Spaniards, a drunk leaped into their midst dressed in the Chalco costume, with eight strings of grass tied across his chest. He barged right in among Moctezuma's soothsayers, waving his arms and ranting.

"Why do you come here?" he cried. "What do you want? What is Moctezuma trying to do? Is he coming to his senses at last? Is he still a miserable, frightened devil? Oh, he has made so many mistakes. Destroyed so many people. . . ." Without finishing his tirade, the drunk vanished as suddenly as he'd appeared.

Flustered and disconcerted by his presence, the Aztecs whispered together. "That apparition posing as a drunk who just disappeared was no ordinary man. He is the young Tezcatlipoca. We had better prepare an altar to beg his indulgence."

As the Mexicans gathered some grass from the roadside to build the tiny altar, the Spaniards halted and watched.

Suddenly, everyone present heard a mighty voice. "What is the point of your coming here to stop us? There will no longer be a Mexico! Everything is finished forever! Away! Be gone! You cannot stay here! Return to where you came from! Direct your sight toward Mexico! What has happened has already happened."

Panicked, without having made contact with the Spaniards, the priests, wizards and magicians quickly gathered up their potions, powders, feathers and instruments and fled along the road to Mexico.

Cristóbal de Olid, standing with the vanguard, turned to Jerónimo de Aguilar. "What did you make of those Mexicans who were making that fuss up the road?"

De Aguilar shrugged. "Who knows? But they seemed to be Mexican priests who got into an argument with a drunk; but now they left."

In Tenochtitlan

When the wizards arrived to tell Moctezuma the results of their abbreviated efforts to bewitch the army of the Spaniards, they found Emperor Moctezuma

173

consulting with Cuitláhuac, lord of Ixtapalapa; Cacama, lord of Texcoco; Totoquihuatzin, lord of Tacuba, and Cuauhtémoc, the noble Captain.

"Oh, great lord," the priests cried, "there was nothing we could do. Actually, we never had a chance to invoke our spells. We couldn't get close to them. They ignored us and insisted on seeing only you, great Lord.

"There even appeared before us, disguised as a Chalco drunk, the young Tezcatlipoca, and he told us some terrible things. He showed us the temples and the communal houses and the sacred academies and all the houses in Mexico were ablaze. It all appeared to have been destroyed in a great battle. Then it disappeared from our sight."

Horrified by the priests' account, Moctezuma was scarcely able to control his anguish. He went to meditate before some idols and a few priests soon joined him.

"Well, what solution do you suggest, oh mighty ones?" Moctezuma asked. "Now we are lost. We have swallowed death itself. We can no longer climb a mountain, nor can we flee. We are Mexicans! But tell me truly, is there still a chance glory will come to the Mexican nation?"

"I am deeply saddened for the old men and old women and for the little children, for whom there is no possibility of rescue. Where will their fathers take them for safety? What can we do? We are as nothing—we can only let happen what will. Despite our fear, we will have to see it through. . . ."

He paused for a moment and stared at the idols. "Can there be any solution? Perhaps, if we pray to and consult with Huitzilopochtli. . . . There must be something we can do, even though we are overcome by terror. You must advise me, my nobles." Moctezuma stretched out his arms imploringly toward the priests.

After a brief meditation, the high priest spoke. "We have consulted Huitzilopochtli and he orders us to allow the *teules* to come here. But once they have entered the city, we must kill them."

"Let us kill them!" [Moctezuma consults with his chiefs.]

174

Both Cuitláhuac and Cuauhtémoc chimed in vigorously. "We will kill them as soon as possible!"

"Well, we will try," Moctezuma added. "Let Cacama lead a great committee which will welcome them at the entrance to Ixtapalapa, and invite them into our city."

Cacama

Just as the Spaniards were leaving Chalco, one of the scouts reported to Cortés. "Captain! A huge contingent of richly dressed Mexicans is approaching, bearing flags of peace."

"Very well. Lieutenants! Forward march, but maintain the formation." Cortés remained in front of the troops.

Four lavishly garbed *calpixques* led the Mexican delegation. One of them stepped forward when he reached Cortés. "Malinche, representing Moctezuma is his nephew, Cacama, King of Texcoco, who offers you his greeting."

The Spaniards were soon mingling with the Mexicans, who wore the most elaborate costumes and adornments the Europeans had ever seen.

When young Cacama appeared, he was being carried in a beautifully decorated litter borne by eight chiefs wearing elegant mantles. As the litter approached Cortés, the bearers lowered it and Cacama dismounted. With grandiloquently obeisant gestures, the king's minions swept the pathway as he walked toward the Spanish captain.

When Cacama was in front of Cortés, he said, "Malinche, I and these lords are here to serve you and otherwise to administer to your needs and those of your companions. We welcome you to your house, which is our city, as our lord, the great Moctezuma, has asked us to. He begs your indulgence, because he cannot be present today. We have appeared in his stead because he is indisposed, not because he did not wish to be here. Our city is quite close, and as you are determined to go there, you will see Moctezuma and become acquainted with his benevolence.

"Nevertheless, if it is at all possible, I must ask you not to go there because you will encounter many difficulties and shortages. Moctezuma is ashamed that as much as he wished to, he could not meet your requirements."

Cortés smiled warmly at the king. "Cacamatzin, kindly greet the great Moctezuma in my name and inform him that I rejoice at the opportunity to see him so soon. We are coming in peace, as friends, to make his acquaintance. Please assure him we will not harm him or his country. And take him these gifts. We have no others."

After a further exchange of formalities, Cacama departed with his grand retinue.

"How often Moctezuma changes his mind," Cortés remarked to his lieutenants. "He invites us to come, then insists we do not. The only missing element is a warning that they will defend the road if we persist in proceeding. Therefore, gentlemen, we shall proceed—but with great caution."

Cortés ordered the march to Ixtapalapa to begin. The troops passed through Mixquic, a village built on stilts right over the lake, entering it on the causeway that connected Mixquic with Ixtapalapa. The avenue itself, according to the Spaniards, "was as wide as a cavalryman's lance," and was constructed of mortared stone.

On both sides of the causeway, throngs of local inhabitants paddled canoes close enough to the shore to stare at the visitors, who returned the favor, gawking in amazement at the strange new sights.

Bernal said, "Truthfully, this place seems to be a work of enchantment like those described in the writings of Amadís of Gaul." He pointed to the side of the road. "Consider those towers and the temples and so many buildings which appear to grow right out of the water. And see how this causeway separates the fresh water from the salt."

The others agreed enthusiastically. "Indeed. The whole place seems like a dream."

Cuitláhuac

They reached Ixtapalapa near the hill of *La Estrella*, el Citlaltépetl, its ceremonial building displaying signs of recent fiery sacrifices. It was there they discovered the fresh water lake separated from the vast salt water lake.

Wearing his war regalia, Cuitláhuac, *cacique* of Ixtapalapa and Tláhuac, himself welcomed the visitors. "Malinche, I am Cuitláhuac, brother of Moctezuma and chief of Ixtapalapa. As Moctezuma has asked, I welcome you in peace and am honored to present the gifts he sends you, as well as these slaves. I will make quarters available to you as the great Moctezuma has ordered."

Soon, the Spaniards were housed in elegant buildings with shaded canopies that were built around ornamental garden plazas and along canals.

Bernal was ecstatic. "I do not believe," he told his companions, "that anywhere in the world has anyone ever discovered lands like these where every sight is such a marvel."

After spending a lavish night in Ixtapalapa, the next day, the 7th of November, 1519, the Spanish army began its march toward Tenochtitlan. They advanced along the causeway, one of the three extraordinary arteries that joined the city to the mainland.

The causeways were so broad, the width of two lances, the horses could easily march down eight abreast, which permitted the army to follow in its usual order: the horses went first, because the mounted men were reconnoitering; then the vanguard of soldiers with dogs, musketeers and crossbowmen. This time, the baggage was in the center of the column, carried and defended by Tlaxcaltecans.

Behind them were foot soldiers with shields and bucklers and swords, then the artillery transported by the *tamemes*. Finally, at the rear, came the Indian allies and village delegates who had been added along the way.

Flags unfurled and snapping in the breeze, the Spaniards marched to the thumping of drums and the shrill tweeting of flutes.

The causeway was jammed with curious Mexicans and the lake surface on either side was almost invisible there were so many canoes whose crews were staring at the invaders.

As they were advancing, the Spaniards marveled at the profusion of buildings and the bustling pedestrians. The roadway was interrupted in places by draw bridges guarded by attendants.

Once again, Bernal turned to his friends. "Just think, *amigos*, in history there have never been men with our daring. Here we are, scarcely four hundred, and we calmly enter a vast city with such a large population."

"You're right about that," said one of the men, "but we do so against the advice of our Tlaxcaltecan allies. Their god, Huichilobos, told them that once we entered this city, we would be killed."

"Have you forgotten our motto, comrade?" Bernal grinned wryly. "'Advance when the time is right!'"

Tenochtitlan

Under strict discipline, the Spaniards marched into Tenochtitlan, taking careful defensive precautions. At the head, four riders paced back and forth, scrutinizing the whole scene, particularly checking the *azoteas*. Also with them were the dogs, each kept in check by a handler. The dogs strutted nervously, too, sniffing everything. Behind them, the standard bearer held his banner with great elegance. Sometimes, he held the flag on his shoulder, but he also waved it vigorously and wagged it from side to side.

Then came the fife and drum contingent, playing their tunes with vigor and enthusiasm.

Behind them, the foot soldiers marched, their shiny swords sparkling in the sunlight, their shields and bucklers dangling from their shoulders.

Following the troops rode six officers in two ranks three abreast, their lances propped in their stirrups, their swords hanging sheathed by their sides. Caparisoned with tiny tinkling bells, which chimed gaily, the horses puffed and blew, nickered, pawed the hard earth, and dripped foamy lather. Whenever one of the steeds shied or sidestepped, the spectators reeled backward in consternation and confusion.

The corps of crossbowmen followed the horses, some of the men with their weapons held in their hands, others resting them on their shoulders. They marched three abreast wearing the padded cotton armor coats that reached to their knees. Their shiny helmets were ablaze with feathers.

Behind them were the arquebusiers, their muskets either shouldered or cradled, with the stubby muzzles angled across the riflemen's arms.

Following the muskets were the Indian *tamemes* hauling the artillery on its wooden rollers.

Finally, there was Cortés, mounted and riding along with his three captains, Alvarado, Velázquez de León and Sandoval. The group also included the rest of the officers and Cortés' own standard bearer.

After the Spaniards came the masses of Indian allies, doing their best to maintain some sort of line, some carrying bundles, others crude arms. They shrieked their war cries, adding to the considerable confusion and startling the Mexicans.

179

Ya van Entrando

Now they are entering [Tenochtitlan]

Thus, Cortés arrived at Xoloco, close to the grand plaza of Tenochtitlan, at a point outside the main fortifications where the three causeways converged.[1]

It was there that the city officials, arrayed with gold and jewels, waited to greet Cortés. They dipped their fingers toward the ground, then lifted their hands to their mouths, welcoming the strangers. They were adorned with and carried profusions of colorful flowers and garlands.

At Alvarado's command, the musketeers, as one, fired a sudden volley, which echoed thunderously among the buildings and sent thick acrid clouds of smoke coursing through the area. Dozens of Mexicans, terrified, screeched in fear, then doubled over gasping and choking from the effects of the gunsmoke.

Soon, the lords of Texcoco, Tacuba, Coyoacán, and Ixtapalapa arrived and greeted Cortés with immense pomp and dignity. They invited him to enter the fortified enclosure, which was protected by a removable bridge, beyond which was a broad boulevard lined with houses and temples.

In two long lines, single file along either side of the road and staying close to the buildings, two hundred Mexican nobles advanced toward the Spaniards. Barefoot, they wore showy, ornate costumes in brilliant colors. This honor guard preceded the Emperor himself, whose litter could be seen by the Spaniards in the distance, borne on the shoulders of other nobles. Its thick canopy was woven of brilliant green *quetzal* feathers.

---

[1] This description is based on Sahagún, a Mexican version. (Sahagún, Fray Bernardino de, "Historia General de las cosas de la Nueva España.," México: Archivo General de la Nacíon, 1982, 1989.)

Moctezuma

The Emperor's entire retinue gleamed with gems. His royal litter, hoisted on the shoulders of four noblemen, was met by the lords of the Alliance, who moved forward to greet him. Moctezuma was wearing a brilliant garment and golden sandals. As he stepped from his litter, some of the nobles swept the road and placed cloths for him to walk upon.

No one among the crowd looked directly at the Emperor, lowering their gaze as he passed. Cortés dismounted and stood waiting where the Mexican nobles indicated.

Moctezuma, preceded by three kings-at-arm with gold staffs, walked carefully and with great dignity. Over the necks of the Spanish captains, who formed a line, he hung garlands and floral chains. Around him were the lords of the Alliance. Moctezuma gave an order and men carrying rich presents placed them before Cortés and withdrew.

After Moctezuma had finished placing the garlands on the officers, he stepped forward and confronted Cortés, by whose side was *Doña* Marina.

The two men evaluated one another for a moment. The Mexican was almost solemn; Cortés was smiling warmly. Then the Spanish captain took out a necklace of *margaritas* [blue glass beads] and placed it gracefully around Moctezuma's neck. However, when Cortés attempted to give Moctezuma an *abrazo*, Cuitláhuac stopped him. Cortés nodded in understanding and demured.

Then, as she had so often when Cortés spoke, *Doña* Marina translated. "Are you truly Moctezuma?"

"Yes, I am."

After a pause, the Emperor began to speak, *Doña* Marina's voice like an echo behind his.

"Our lord, you must be fatigued. Very tired. Well, now you have arrived in your land. You have come to your city, Mexico. You have come here to sit under your canopy on your throne. Oh! For such a short time, very short, have the old ones reserved your seat, guarding it well, those who have passed away: your predecessors, the lord kings Itcoatzin, Moctecuhzomatzin the elder, Axayácatl, Tizoc, Ahuizotl. Ah! For such a short time they have watched over it for you, only for you! They once ruled this City of Mexico and under their protection, they shielded all the humble people. Will fate let them see now what is left of their posthumous generations?

"Would that one of them could see, with trepidation, what I can see approaching me, what I now see! I, the survivor of our Lords. Oh, no, I am not dreaming. I did not just awaken from a drowsy dream. I am not dreaming. In fact, I have already seen you. And at last, I have placed my eyes on your face.

"For the past five, ten days, I have been anguished, staring into the Region of Mystery. You have come here under clouds and mist. This was what the kings bequeathed to us, those who once governed here. 'You must install him in your chair,' they said, 'in your seat of honor. He must come here.' That prophecy is fulfilled. You have arrived here, despite your great fatigue and anxiety you came. In this land you arrived. Come and rest. Take possession of your royal houses and refresh your body. You have come to your land, our Lords!"

"And you have come here under clouds and mist."

A long silence ensued before Cortés replied.

"Kindly inform Moctezuma, *Doña* Marina, that I and those who came with me like him very much and that he should feel comforted by that and not fear that any harm will come to him from us. We are delighted to see him and to make his acquaintance, which we have deeply desired for many days. This was our wish and it has been fulfilled. We have indeed come to your house, Mexico. In time, we shall become better acquainted."

The ceremony was not prolonged and soon Moctezuma's retinue was filing away, paying homage to Cortés by kissing the earth in front of his position. After the ritual exchange, Moctezuma went back into his litter to return to the city.

Flanking him on one side was Cacama, on the other, Cuauhtémoc. Dancers and priests led the way with incense braziers and there were musicians who played flutes and shellhorns. There were also kettle drummers and an honor guard of *tigres* and *águilas* warriors, the highest echelon of elite Mexican soldiers.

Cuitláhuac remained to accompany Cortés, who was walking now. The Mexican took the Spaniard's hand and would let no one else come near.

A messenger arrived with a small packet, delivering it to Moctezuma. Stepping down from the litter and before Cortés again, he placed around the Spanish captain's neck two necklaces carved from red spiral shells. From each strand hung eight spirals, a symbol of the wind, which to the Spaniards resembled shrimp made from gold.

Moctezuma spoke. "This is the jewel of the Wind. Quetzalcóatl has that same symbol in his temple. The moment I saw you, I knew what gift would be most appropriate."

After he re-entered the litter, the grand march resumed.

Despite lowering their eyes at the Emperor's passage, the people were fascinated by the strangers. Marina translated one comment from some young people: "These are the gods who come from where the Sun is born."

Some elderly people said, "These are those who must rule and command our people and lands. Despite being few in number, they are powerful and have conquered many."

When the women saw Pedro de Alvarado, they giggled: "That one, by his coloring and handsome features, resembles *Tonatiuh*, the Sun."*

Moctezuma himself pointed out their lodging to the Spaniards: the palace of Axayácatl, which had been his own father's and was now the priests' residence and also held the secret sealed vault containing the Aztecs' golden treasure trove.

As he entered the grand plaza, Moctezuma took Cortés by the hand and led him to his quarters, luxuriously appointed, adorned and perfumed. Someone had lit a fire in the fireplace, which Cortés had missed during his mostly tropical service.

"Malinche," said the Emperor. "You and your brothers are in your own homes. Please rest."

Then he left for his palace.

---

* Pedro de Alvarado had a reddish blond beard and hair, features the women associated with *Tonatiuh*, "the Sun."

In the Axayácatl Palace

The Axayácatl Palace accommodated comfortably the four hundred Spaniards, the two thousand Indian allies, the native women who accompanied the army, the horses and the artillery, with everyone lodged under cover or a canopy. There were straw mats for beds, even for those who were looking after the group.

Cortés issued these orders: "Divide the lodgings by each captain's company; the horses must be well within reach and the artillery mounted at the entrances. The building is ideally situated for defense, but we must remain alert, armed and ready. At sunrise and sunset fire a booming cannon salute."

After they were settled, everyone was served a sumptuous meal, which was eaten with great relish.

In the lodgings, Bernal Díaz del Castillo commented to *Doña* Marina, "Moctezuma must be very rich to provide us with these spacious palaces for a barracks."

"This was the palace of his father, the Emperor Axayácatl. They are now temples. Because he considers you *teules*, these are your lodgings," Marina said.

"Why all the perfume?"

"In part to flatter you—as *teules*—but more practically, to make the place smell more pleasant. The stench from the odors from where the palace priests make their sacrifices and other holy acts emit a nauseous smell."

Moctezuma Acknowledges Cortés

Just as the banquet was concluding, a flurry of activities in the palace announced the arrival of the Emperor, who soon graced the hall with ceremonial pomp.

Two lavishly decorated *icpallis* [thrones] were set in place and Moctezuma and Cortés were seated opposite each other.

The Emperor spoke first. "Malinche, I am most pleased to have here such vigorous *teules*, whose visit was announced by two previous expeditions. I can actually see you; you are here! For a long time, we knew that we were foreigners in these lands; that we came from very strange places ruled by a lord. We were his vassals. This lord returned to his land, occupied the throne and declared that his brothers and descendants must be people just like you who would come from where the Sun rises. We believe that the lord, your King, is our natural lord and from him, through you, we acknowledge you. You may now command us from your natural setting, your own house."

"Actually, lord," said Cortés, "I and my men do come from where the Sun rises and our lord is indeed the most powerful in the world. He knows about you and ordered us to make your acquaintance so that the events predicted by your elders could be realized."

Conversation in the Axayácatl Palace

After they exchanged greetings and Moctezuma delivered presents for everyone, he left. He had ordered the splendid meal that was served to the Spaniards and all their companions.

Cortés and Marina

That night in his private quarters, with Marina—who never left his side—Cortés declared, "I am amazed by what has occurred so far, Marina. We are actually here! I longed to learn the secrets of this land and with you I am in the very heart of it; within the unbounded greatness of a land as great as our own boldness. Everything here is like a miracle, a dream, a mystery. It is as if it had been prearranged. Everything was merely awaiting our arrival. Even you. Through your eyes, I can see clearly the enormousness of this country. Through you I feel that your world looks toward me as its destiny. I must ask myself, who am I?"

"I perceive you as a *teule* my lord, a god who wishes to be a man to whom I surrendered, fully accepting and loving that destiny."

"Why, Marina?"

"Because I deeply appreciate the events that were decreed and because of me have come about. They are so important. I feel all of the ages of my ancestors have culminated in me. In me, my lord, is what was foretold in all its wisdom! Destiny is wisdom itself. Consider how Moctezuma recognizes who you are, better even than you yourself. He even offered you his throne. He accepts and at the same time fears what is taking place. I know you are my *teule* because you were selected so the prophesy would be fulfilled. I know all that and I love what is happening."

"I, on the other hand, Marina, do not even know what will happen tomorrow, except the continuation of my fate. What I like best is the uncertainty of my adventure which, perhaps, may be called the will of God."

"Maybe it is, my lord. But to me it was all foretold and you seem to ignore that. So I will tell you," she said, smiling, "what is going to happen tomorrow: You will visit Moctezuma in his palace, just as he came to see you in yours. That is the custom."

"We will see whether tomorrow brings what you say, wise, beautiful Marina, from this my strange land."

Visit to Moctezuma

"Pedro de Alvarado, Juan Velázquez de León, Diego de Ordaz and Gonzalo de Sandoval," Cortés ordered his lieutenants the next morning. "Please accompany me so we may repay Moctezuma's visit. Bring five soldiers with you, among them Bernal Díaz del Castillo and Juan Jaramillo and three others of your choice. Tell the officer in charge of the barracks about our visit to Moctezuma's palace and give him the names of the men going with me."

Presently, they crossed the great plaza, admiring the grandeur of Tenochtitlan. Moctezuma's palaces were more modern and luxurious than the Axayácatl.[1]

They were presented to the Emperor, who was with his nephews (among them Cuauhtémoc), the only Mexicans who had free access to the interior halls, which occupied a spacious and lavishly furnished section of the palace. Moctezuma stood up from his throne and moved to the center of the great hall to greet Cortés. He took him by the hand and led him to the seat next to his own. The Aztec prince asked the other Spaniards to come along. The nephews remained standing around their uncle.

Cortés addressed him through Marina: "Lord Moctezuma, heed the words from my King that I am relaying to you. He would like for you to become a Christian and to believe in the one God who is the Father God, the Son God and the Holy Spirit God in three distinct persons, the only true God, who created the heavens and the earth and Adam and Eve, who are our father and mother. As we are all brothers, and in order to save us from sin, He sent his Son, who died on the cross. My King regrets that you cannot go to heaven because you sacrifice human beings and eat their flesh and practice other infamous rites. You must renounce all worship to your idols. As time goes on, we will dispatch to you some pious men, priests, far better men than we are, to lead your people along the path of truth."

As soon as he finished this soliloquy, Cortés said to his companions: "I have done my duty by offering the first divine admonition."

With great dignity, Moctezuma replied: "Lord Malinche. Clearly have I understood your words and wisdom, because I learned about them from my servants even before you came here. You have been speaking about them along your route—all about your three gods and the cross. But we have not responded to your message

---

[1] This description from Salazar, Francisco Cervantes de, "Crónica de Nueva España," México: Talleres Gráficos del Museo Nacional, 1936.)

because from our beginning we have worshipped our own gods and we revere them the same way you venerate your three. Do not insist that we reject ours. We have said nothing against yours. As you do, we believe that the gods created the world and for that reason we are certain you are the person our ancestors told us would come from where the Sun rises. I will give to your great King what he wishes, because for two years I have known that two other captains came to our shores sent by that great King you spoke about. For that reason, I wish to know if all of you, with them, are brothers."

Cortés smiled and nodded. "Yes, all of us are brothers, subjects of the same great King. The first ones sailed the course and inspected the ports so we would be able to come."

"Well, now you are here in your houses at last," Moctezuma said. "Take pleasure and rest in them. If some time past I asked you not to enter our city, it was not my personal desire but because my subjects were so afraid of you. Among other childish stories, I heard that you can cause thunder and lightning and can kill us with your horses and that you are valiant *teules*."

"But now you see we are of flesh and blood," Cortés said.

"Yes," Moctezuma said, smiling. "I know well what the Tlaxcalans, with whom you have made friends, have told you—that the walls of my palaces are of gold, silver and precious stones and that I think I am a god. I know you do not believe that and you took those words as a joke. As you see, these walls are stone, wood and lime, and I am but flesh and bones," he said, glancing down his body and patting himself.

"If I am a great King and have riches, all that derives from my ancestors. So surrounded by the gold and *teules*, the thunder and lightning, we laugh about those stories."

Then Moctzuma, as was his habit, ordered gifts of gold, silver, jewels and beautiful clothes brought forward.

"Lord Moctezuma," Cortés said, "you always heap gifts upon gifts for us. . . . We will take our leave now, it must be the time for Your Grace to dine."

"Merely by visiting me," Moctezuma replied, "you have given me great pleasure."

With courteous gestures, they took leave of each other.

As they walked across the plaza on their way to their own palace, Bernal commented: "Truly, Moctezuma has wonderful manners and excellent breeding."

"Quite true," Cortés said, "and it would be a good idea for all of us to remember that whenever we greet the Emperor we should remove our headgear and our cotton mail."

Visit to the Teocalli

s they entered their quarters in the Axayácatl Palace, Cortés said, "Until we are certain about our situation, we must maintain order and stay in our lodgings. If we do, we can avoid trouble."

Four days went by as the Spaniards rested within the palace, enjoying the gardens, the fruit trees, the fountains and the perfumes. While inspecting the building, Cortés found a locked door and ordered it opened. Inside was a large room full of Aztec weapons.

"Obviously, this is an armory. Let us take what we can use and guard the rest so no one else can use them," Cortés said.

Early on the fifth day, Cortés met with his captains. "I think it is time we made our presence known. *Doña* Marina, you go with Aguilar and the page Orteguilla and tell the lord Moctezuma we would like to visit the great *teocalli* of Huichilobos."

When Moctezuma received the petition from Marina, he said, "I will personally await the *teules* in the *teocalli*."

When Moctezuma left his palace, he was preceded by three heralds and the usual entourage. As he passed through the city, the people paid him their habitual gestures of respect. At the *teocalli* of Tlatelolco, on the shoulders of six priests, he was carried up the one hundred and fourteen steps and began the propitiatory ceremonies.

Cortés left his palace with all of his officers and almost all the soldiers, except those who stayed behind as guards. In parade formation, they passed down Tepeyac Avenue to the north, passing in front of the *tianguis* [city market] in the great plaza of Tlatelolco. From there, they soon arrived at the plaza of the Great *Teocalli*.

When Moctezuma spotted Cortés, preceded and accompanied by his officers, he sent the six priests who had climbed the temple steps to aid Cortés.

Cortés dismounted, rejected the aid of the priests and with his captains, Marina, and a good number of soldiers, bounded up the steps at a light pace.

Moctezuma greeted them at the top.

"You are probably tired, *Señor* Malinche, after climbing the steps of this great temple."

"Neither I nor those who are here with me ever tire," Cortés said.

Taking him by the hand, Moctezuma pointed out the splendor of Tenochtitlan, built on the lake with its three causeways, its sacred buildings, the houses among the canals, sweeping his arm as he mentioned the details.

[A view] from the *teocalli*

Among themselves, the soldiers chatted. "This plaza seems bigger than the one in Salamanca. In Spain, we have nothing to compare to this," Bernal said. "In all of Italy, there is nothing like this," said another. "Nor in Constantinople," put in another.

Cortés turned to his men: "Well, what do you think of all this, *caballeros*, about the grace God has bestowed upon us? After experiencing so many dangers and so many victories, He has placed us here where we can witness this great city. Truly, my heart tells me that from here we can go on to conquer many great kingdoms, for this is the nucleus, where the devil himself has his throne. Once this city is subdued and conquered, it will be easy to master the entire country."

Cortés turned toward Padre Olmedo. "*Señor Padre*, I think we should suggest to Moctezuma that he allow us to build our church right here."

"*Señor Capitán*," said Olmedo, "that would be wonderful if it were possible, but I do not think it is appropriate to mention that just yet. I do not think Moctezuma would accede to that request."

Cortés accepted the priest's advice and turning to Moctezuma, he said, through Marina, "What a pleasure to view your city with the guidance and great insight of yourself, noble lord. Since we are here already, may I humbly request that Your Grace show us your gods and *teules*."

Slightly taken aback, Moctezuma said sternly, "First, I will speak with the priests."

After he did, he offered Cortés his hand. "You may enter the altars."

There were two. The first honored Huitzilopochtli, the god of war, with his broad countenance and frightful eyes. In the body of the idol were embedded precious stones, gold and pearls with snakes in bas-relief encrusted with the same brilliant jewels. In one hand the idol held a bow, in the other, arrows.

On the altar were some braziers with copal and three human hearts from recently sacrificed Indians. Everywhere, thick crusts of dried blood emitted a stench that was stomach-churning. Cortés almost gagged, leaving the temple after only a few seconds.

On the other side was Tezcatlipoca, with his eyes of shiny obsidian. On that altar were five human hearts and an odor almost as horrible as in the first.

Outside, between the two temples, was a great drum made of serpent's skins. When struck, its sad and gloomy tone could be heard two leagues away.

All around were instruments and articles appropriate to the Indian ceremonies.

The Spaniards, holding their noses and grimacing, hurried from the temples.

"Lord Moctezuma," Cortés said, "I don't know how such a great lord and wise man like Your Grace has not deduced that these idols of yours are not gods, but symbols of evil, which are called 'devils.' So that Your Grace becomes acquainted with it and your priests can consider it, grant me the favor of allowing us to place a cross at the top of this tower. And somewhere within these temples where you have your Huichilobos and Tezcatlipoca, we would like to place the image of *Our Lady*. Then, you will witness the fear your idols display and know how they have deceived you."

As Cortés continued, Moctezuma became angrier, frowning until his features revealed deep furrows. Listening also to the indignant voices of his priests, the Emperor responded: "Lord Malinche, if I thought you were going to suggest such a disgraceful plan, I would not have allowed you to see my gods. We believe they are good. They give us health and rain and good sowing periods and good weather and victories, as many as we wish. We worship them and make human sacrifices to them. I beg you not to insult them further."

Cortés accepted Moctezuma's fury with a broad smile, indicating through *Doña* Marina he would not carry the ideas forward.

Then he spoke to Moctezuma. "By Your Grace's leave, we shall depart."

"Go," said Moctezuma, "I will stay here to make amends to my gods for the insult you committed by saying they were evil. I will worship them and pray to them."

Cortés shrugged. "Do what you must, Lord. Please accept my apologies."

As they strolled back to their palace, Cortés cautioned his captains: "I'm afraid I made Moctezuma angry. From now on, we must be extremely careful because we are surrounded by thousands of his subjects."

"I suppose we will now experience what happened in Cholula: They will begin to withhold our provisions," said Juan Velázquez de León. "We must remain very alert."

"But without displaying fear," Cortés insisted. "I will ask Moctezuma to allow us to build an altar in our quarters as he refused to have it in his temple."

He turned to Marina. "Please inform Moctezuma's stewards that we shall construct an altar in the Axayácatl Palace."

Moctezuma's Treasure

Two days later, the altar was completed and, as an example for the Indians, Spaniards prayed devoutly to their God.

While Alonso Yáñez, the carpenter, was looking for the right location for the altar, he noticed marks on a wall that suggested a door had once been there. Now, the area was well covered with plaster.

After carefully inspecting the markings and tapping the wall gently, Yáñez went alone to see Juan Velázquez de León and Lugo. "*Señores*, I think there is a room behind a wall that has been carefully hidden. With your permission, I would like to inform the captain," said Velázquez de León.

Quickly, they went to Cortés and told him about Yáñez's suspicions. Accompanying his captains and the carpenter, Cortés watched as Yáñez tore down the wall.

In the closed-off room was Moctezuma's treasure.

Awestruck, the Spaniards could only stare; they were speechless until Cortés said quietly, "No one is to touch any of this. A few at a time, in absolute secrecy, allow our other captains and the troops to see this. You, Juan, will place guards here. No one may enter this room without my express permission."

In the Trap

Six days after they arrived in Tenochtitlan, after praying the first Mass at the altar, a few of the men asked to speak confidentially to Cortés.

In his quarters, Alvarado spoke first. "Captain, ever since we became aware of the immense size of this land and of the great multitude of people who surround us and now that we have witnessed Moctezuma's anger concerning his idols, we are very worried. It looks to us as if we are in a snare, a trap."

Juan Velázquez de León added, "We have seen the fortifications of the city and its few exits, those causeways cut by canals with their draw bridges." The others nodded agreement.

Bernal said, "Remember our Indian allies warned us we should be prepared for the Mexicans' treachery because they only allowed us to enter their city with Huichilobos' consent in order to kill us, once we were inside."

Ordaz added: "Now that we have seen another side of Moctezuma, I am no longer confident he means his pious words of 'love' and 'good will.'"

Gonzalo de Sandoval said: "The most crucial element of this trap is the one Alvarado spoke about. Whenever it suits Moctezuma to attack us or to withhold food or water or to isolate us by raising the bridges, we will be powerless, surrounded as we are by this huge multitude of Indians."

"We are alone, with only our Tlaxcalan friends, and how can they really help us?" Alvarado asked. "Remember how fickle Moctezuma is. No amount of gold or any treasure should stop us from thinking night and day about anything else but this great danger we find ourselves in.

"We have discussed these matters among ourselves," Alvarado continued, "and decided to come to you—without further delay—and suggest that we seize Moctezuma if we wish to save our lives. We must act immediately!"

"Don't think for a moment, *caballeros*," Cortés said, "that I am asleep or that I haven't had your same concerns. But how much strength do we have to attempt such a bold act: seizing this great lord in his own palaces, guarded closely by his own loyal warriors? What tactic can we use that would keep him from ordering his warriors to attack us?"

"Captain," said Sandoval, "Your Grace has the strength of will to lure him from his palace to our quarters. Once he is here, simply tell him he is our prisoner."

"And if he will not come, give us permission and we will force him," said Juan Velázquez de León.

"Of all the dangers we are exposed to, the least is to seize him now, instead of waiting for his warriors to attack," said Alvarado.

"It is obvious," Jaramillo added, "just like in Cholula, the servants who bring us food are impudent, not hospitable as they were in the first few days. I think we ought to act quickly."

"There is no doubt," said Bernal, "among the Tlaxcaltecans, our friends. They told Jerónimo de Aguilar that they never took seriously the Mexicans' so-called benevolence."

Cortés held up a hand to stop the discussion. "I understand what you are suggesting. I agree. Tomorrow I will let you know how and who will do what."

That night in his quarters, Cortés spoke with *Doña* Marina: "I have seen changes in Moctezuma since the incident in the temple."

"Yes, Lord. The people say he is angry and that Huitzilopochtli has asked him to atone for the insults. I overheard the Tlaxcaltecans say the Mexicans are preparing to attack us."

"Do you think if we seized him unexpectedly it would be advantageous?"

"Lord, I believe that everything you undertake goes well: To remain here in this palace is dangerous; but less so if you capture the chiefs, those who command."

"Let us see what tomorrow brings."

"It will go well, my lord. If you command, I will go with you and I will convince him."

Moctezuma Captive

Early the next morning, two Cempoaltecan emissaries visited Cortés. "Malinche, here are some messages from Villa Rica."

After Cortés read them, he assembled his captains and some of the troops. "Listen to this! These messages report that Juan de Escalante and six Spanish soldiers have been killed in skirmishes with Mexicans led by Cuauhpopoca, by order of Moctezuma. A horse died and so did many Totonacan Indians. All the people who live in the sierra and Cempoala are upset. They no longer consider the Spaniards *teules* and refuse to feed them or help defend the fort.

"This is our first defeat. We are no longer *teules*, but mortals who can be killed."

He looked up from the reports. "Your plan has merit. We will take Moctezuma prisoner and this is how we will do it: I was thinking all night about a plan that would not make a scene or cause any excitement.

"We will announce a visit as we have usually done. All the captains plus Marina and Aguilar and two hundred foot soldiers will go. Some will be stationed at the street crossings and the exits to the plazas, which will appear normal. At the entrance and outside the palace, others will be stationed who will permit no one to leave. Then we will enter Moctezuma's great hall with thirty soldiers and I will speak to him and convince him to come with us willingly."

"Or by force!" said Alvarado.

"Let us do it!"

As Cortés proposed they arrived at the palace; the four captains and the thirty soldiers entered.

Moctezuma, somewhat surprised, said, "Welcome, *señores*. Although I did not expect your visit so soon, I am prepared to give you some gifts as an expression of our generosity. Malinche, a young girl for you and other noble maidens for your captains, which will make us brothers."

"And good brothers we may be, Lord Moctezuma, but I marvel that you, being such a courageous prince and supposedly our friend, ordered your captain—who is at the coast near Tuzapán—to attack my Spaniards who guard and protect our King. The Mexican captain killed some of them, as well as a horse.

"This was done by Cuauhpopoca who denies responsibility, saying that he only carried out your orders as your captains did in Cholula. Until now I have not brought up this matter because of the deep respect I bear for you. But you must bring Cuauhpopoca here to tell you what has occurred so the guilty ones may be punished.

"While this investigation takes place, I will send an account to our Emperor *Don Carlos*, telling him about the Spaniards killed by Cuauhpopoca. But now, quietly and without any alarm, you must come with us to our quarters. There, you will be well attended and as well taken care of as in your own palace. But if you sound an alarm or call for help, my captains will kill you. That is why I brought them."

Frightened, Moctezuma stood up from his throne, then sat down again with his eyes closed. Some of the nobles present tried to leave the hall but were restrained by Spanish soldiers.

Recovering, Moctezuma removed from his arm the royal seal and handed it to his emissaries. "I agree to order Cuauhpopoca to come here and to punish the guilty ones. As for my becoming your prisoner and leaving my palace, I am not a person who can be ordered to do anything. I will not leave."

"You will come with us. Your captains and subjects have acted shamelessly and held secret discussions that you wish us killed."

"The Tlaxcaltecans are telling you those lies," said Moctezuma.

"Perhaps," Cortés said. "But we do not wish to start a war or to destroy this city."

"I do not want wars against the *teules* either, and I do not see why I have to leave my own house because of some insidious rumors," said Moctezuma.

"Because that serves our needs best," said Cortés.

At this point, a snarling Juan Velázquez de León interrupted the discussion. "Why is Your Grace using so many words? Either we take him prisoner or we kill him."

The other captains approached, hands on their swords and with their voices raised. "Yes! Yes! Enough words! Prisoner or death!"

Frightened, Moctezuma asked *Doña* Marina: "What are the captains shouting about?"

Cleverly, she said, "Lord Moctezuma, I suggest you go now with them to their quarters, without making any disturbance. I know that they will honor you as the great lord that you are. If you do not go with them, you will die."

Absorbed in thought, Moctezuma mused for a few more seconds. "Malinche, if this is what you want, so be it. I have a son and two daughters. Take them as hostages instead. I do not have to suffer this disgrace."

"Lord Moctezuma, you must do as I have asked and quickly. My captains are impatient. Your servants may come along to prepare your quarters in the Axayácatl Palace. Let them carry you in the royal litter."

Then various nobles of the Court, guarded by Spanish soldiers, took off their cloaks and shoes and ushered the Emperor to his litter. Silently, weeping, they left the palace. Immediately, Spanish soldiers and horsemen surrounded the retinue, which quickly made its way to the Axayácatl Palace.

There, on the 8th of November, Moctezuma was installed in all luxury with his servants and his customs respected.

The news of his capture spread throughout the city and began to upset the people. Moctezuma's relatives appeared: Cacama, Totoquihuatzin, Cuitláhuac, Cuauhtémoc and others. They were worried and angry.

"Lord, my lord, great lord. Why did you consent to this? Now is the time to wage war against these impudent *teules*."

"Do not even think such a thing, my nobles. I am happy to spend a few days with the *teules*. I came on my own will and not by force. When I want something, I will let you know. Do not create an uproar. Keep the city calm. According to Huitzilopochtli, all is well, or so the priests have assured me."

Murmuring among themselves and scowling, the relatives and chiefs left.

Moctezuma maintained his usual existence of luxury and personal comfort. He dispatched ambassadors and conducted important business. Indians and Spaniards alike continued to treat him with the deference he expected.

Death of Cuauhpopoca

Twenty days after Moctezuma became a prisoner in the Spanish quarters, Cuauhpopoca finally appeared as he had been ordered. Amid great pomp, he arrived in a litter with his son and fifteen chiefs from his region. After he stepped down, he changed his luxurious vestments for a plain cotton mantle and removed his sandals. He and Moctezuma conferred privately and after a few minutes, they summoned *Doña* Marina, who was waiting outside the room with Cortés, his captains, and some armed soldiers.

"Have *Doña* Marina come here," the Mexican emperor requested.

After speaking with Moctezuma, she said to Cortés: "Moctezuma will deliver Cuauhpopoca so you may administer justice according to your law."

"We will judge him under the code of warfare. Interrogate them, Alvarado."

He left with the accused men and after a short while reported back to Cortés. "We have found them guilty. They should all be put to death."

"This sentence must set an example," Cortés said, "one that will terrify them. They are much too accustomed to simple dying. The guilty ones will be burned alive in front of Moctezuma's palace and the fire will be made with the Indian arms from the arsenal of Axayácatl Palace."

While the sentence was being carried out, Cortés ordered Moctezuma placed in shackles, which frightened him and caused much deeper indignity.

With astonishment, the city witnessed the Spaniards' display of supreme power. They asked themselves: "Who rules here?"

Until the sentence had been completed, Moctezuma was kept chained. His servants wept and tried to relieve the pain caused by the fetters.

Once the guilty were dead, Cortés himself began to remove the chains. "These sentences of justice, my lord Moctezuma, whom I respect very much, I perform for your well being and so that my brothers will never harm you. You are a great lord of many lands and we will make them even greater. If you wish, you may now return to your own palaces."

When Cortés finally removed the chains, he added, "All is not in vain, lord Moctezuma. I honor you as I do myself."

Free of the chains, resigned, Moctezuma said: "It is a great blessing that you are willing to let me go, but it is more fitting that I remain here with you because that is the will of my gods. If I were to go, my nobles would wage war against you as they already have demanded. I do not want the city to suffer, so I will stay here with you.

Summon the page Orteguilla who can speak my language. It is time I learned about your land and your King and about other things I do not understand."

Cuauhpopoca and his companions are burned alive

After Cuauhpopoca's death, Cortés met with his captains. "*Señores y amigos*, with your advice and by our daring, we hold Moctezuma captive. But now is the time to be extremely careful, as we applied a royal warrant to execute these Indians."

"Because of the actions of these rebels," said Diego de Ordaz, "the whole territory is now aware that we are mortals and can be defeated, just as happened with Juan de Escalante."

"I feel as if we were in a swamp, surrounded, and sinking. What can the possible outcome be? How will it all end?" asked Gonzalo de Sandoval.

"My idea is to perform more acts of sovereignty and of religion. Gonzalo de Sandoval, you will go at once to Villa Rica as chief *Alguacil* in place of Escalante. You will look after the town and be respectful of the natives. Do not allow anyone to harm the Indians, or to take anything from them by force. Live peacefully with them. When you get to Villa Rica, send me the two blacksmiths with the iron parts that were salvaged, the sails, the rigging and cordage and a mariner's needle. I plan to make two brigantines to sail the lake."

"As your lordship commands," said Gonzalo de Sandoval.

Explorations

"I have asked Moctezuma to show me where the gold mines are located," announced Cortés to his lieutenants. "Tomorrow some of his men will go with several Spaniards I have assigned to explore the gold and silver mines. These mines are in Cozula, others are in Tamazulapa and Malinales. Still more are in Tuxtepec and Maramalco and there is one whose name I do not remember. In this way we may continue to serve better His Majesty and we do not become lazy. I think there are some maps that show the location of the rivers and small inlets that we should explore to be better acquainted with the territory."

"I ask myself," said Juan Velázquez de León, "how long can we live in peace without these multitudes rising up because their Emperor is our prisoner?"

"Until that happens, let's keep on going," said Cortés.

Again at the Teocalli

Moctezuma's life in captivity was normal: He delivered judgments on judicial matters, he received audiences. He was amused by organizing Indian games with Cortés and his captains and there were frequent jokes and laughter. Forever magnificent, always courtly, Moctezuma pampered his captors, lavishing the Spaniards with girls, jewels and fine clothes.

One day after a game of *tololoque* [an ancient Indian sport], the commentator, Alvarado, curried favor with Cortés by telling jokes, much to the amusement of Moctezuma. Confidentially, he said to Cortés, "Malinche, my people, especially Cacamatzin and certain nephews, are making a great fuss about my incarceration, against my will, and they would wage war against you to free me. So that the people are certain it is my will to stay with you and to understand I do so by order of Huitzilopochtli, I would like to go to his temple and offer sacrifices and make prayers to him."

"Go right ahead, lord Moctezuma, by all means, my soldiers will go along to make sure there is no foolishness. And remember, do not sacrifice any humans because the true God does not favor it."

With his usual retinue and all its pomp and ceremonies, Moctezuma proceeded to the Huitzilopochtli temple. One hundred fifty soldiers commanded by Alvarado,

Juan Velázquez de León, Alonso de Ávila, and Francisco de Lugo and the priest, Father de la Merced, accompanied them vigilantly.

Moctezuma, as a captive, visits the *Teocalli*

At the temple, the lords of Texcoco, Tacuba and Ixtapalapan were waiting for Moctezuma and although their ceremonies were terminated, they carried him on their arms to the temples, even though the Spaniards were ostensibly guarding him. Although the soldiers could not halt the human sacrifices which had been committed earlier, the Spaniards denounced and reproached the Aztec priests, which caught Moctezuma's attention.

"These are acts of the devil!" said Father de la Merced to the Mexican priests.

Alvarado reproached Moctezuma. "It is unbelievable to me that a great lord such as you, with so much compassion, tolerates these sacrifices."

Although Moctezuma kept silent as the religious ceremonies went on, Cacama said secretly to the lords who were with them, "Our lord Moctezuma is a prisoner even though he denies it. The *teules* guard him; they reprimand him and do not show him enough respect."

The lords of Tacuba and Texcoco agreed and Cuitláhuac from Ixtapalapa said: "Moctezuma is not the same person. He is no longer himself; he is not the master of his own will."

Cacama concluded: "Let us convene the Council; it is time to decide if we must fight the *teules* in order to free him. I am calling for a meeting."

They waited while Moctezuma was carried down from the *teocalli*, and frowning, they bid him farewell.

Cortés was waiting in the Axayácatl Palace when Moctezuma returned, still in the custody of the Spanish soldiers.

"I am pleased to see you, lord Moctezuma. I hope there were no incidents while you were performing your religious ceremonies," said Cortés, who had Marina with him.

Moctezuma, looking stern and worried, stepped from the litter, aided by his chiefs. "The road Huitzilopochtli has recommended that I follow is a difficult one," he said. "Only I understand it."

"What do you mean?" asked Cortés.

"What Cacama and the rest of my nephews are mumbling means they don't understand where the road leads. They are bitter and will soon conspire against you."

"Tell me about it."

Moctezuma merely shrugged, and accompanied by his retinue went to his quarters.

Cortés was thinking over this exchange when an officer entered. "The sails, tackle, rigging, cordage and iron parts you asked Sandoval to send from Villa Rica are here."

"Deliver them to maestros Martín López and Andrés Núñez. Combined with the wooden joints they have already made and with the help of the assistants Moctezuma has provided, they can build two brigantines to sail on the lake.

In a short time, the brigantines were completed and launched, to the amazement of the Indians. With the sails unfurled and aided by oars, the boats moved through the water much faster than Indian canoes.

Once, well-guarded by the Spaniards, Moctezuma and some of his chiefs boarded the brigantines to sail to the *Peñón*, where Moctezuma had a private hunting preserve.

The Counsel of the Culúa Alliance

In the Texcoco council house, the chiefs of the Culúa Alliance convened.

"I have summoned you," said Cacama to the lords of Tacuba, Ixtapalapa and Matlaltzingo, "so that we may decide what our plans should be. We have seen how our lord Moctezuma has been a captive for more than two months and has only the freedom the *teules* grant him. They are now lording over and ruling everyone. I have been told they have opened Teucalco, the door to the treasure house, and act as if they are the masters of its contents."

Cuitláhuac, lord of Ixtapalapa, and next to him, the young Cuauhtémoc, said: "Let us attack them, now! That has always been my desire. Let us invade their building and free Moctezuma. Make war, now!"

"What if they kill Moctezuma?" asked Totoquiahuatzin, lord of Tacuba.

There was a silence which Cacama broke. "All right, there is a risk. We must elect someone to succeed him."

"I am the one," said the lord of Matlaltzingo. "The honor belongs to me because I am Moctezuma's brother, his oldest and closest relative. If you all agree, I will come with all my warriors and we will get rid of those *teules*."

"The lordship belongs to me," said Cacama. "Not only am I Moctezuma's nephew, but I am also the lord of Texcoco. Truly, I have enough warriors, thus there is no need to accept lord Matlaltzingo's offer. I have put my troops and officers on notice to enter the *teules*' palace and kill them all."

"Lords," said Totoquiahuatzin, "Moctezuma is alive and you are making plans as if he were already dead. He is the great lord and he still rules. We must ask him first and obey his wishes. He is the great lord."

There followed another period of silence, which Cuitláhuac broke: "He is still the lord; he lives and rules."

"We must ask his advice," said Totoquihuatzin.

They all huddled, absorbed in thought. Then Cacama sat up and abruptly left the Council room, "For me, it is as if Moctezuma were already dead! I will be alone!"

Later, Cacama said to his officers, "Moctezuma is as weak as a bird. In four days I will have killed the *teules* as I would have in the Chalco sierra if Moctezuma had let me. We give them gold and they want to destroy our gods. Those others in the council do not understand. With your help, my captains, we will attack the *teules*."

Moctezuma's informants told him about Cacama's decision. He summoned Cortés.

Cacama Prisoner

"Malinche, my friends tell me Cacama, the lord of Texcoco, has gathered the lords of the Alliance to wage war against you and free me. You know I do not wish to see that come about. By Huitzilopochtli's desire and my own, I wish to remain with you. If you happen to know something. . . ."

Cortés interrupted him: "I have already been advised about the Council meeting, and about Cacama's cleverness: not only to declare war on us, but also to make himself Lord of Temistitan, as if you were already dead. If you wish, I would be willing to lead a contingent of Mexican warriors, seize him and bring him here."

"I do not think that is a very good idea. I do not want conflicts among the members of the Alliance so far as it pertains to an ambitious rebel. However, you do whatever you like."

"I will order an investigation," Cortés concluded.

He sent Mexican ambassadors to Texcoco, who said to Cacama, "Malinche ordered us to demand that you stop trying to foment wars. That will only be the cause of your downfall, because he will come and seize you. Even so, he wishes to be your friend and to live in peace with you and he wishes the best for you. But you must not dishonor your King."

"Tell that Malinche I am familiar with his lies and his flattery. I no longer wish to hear any more of it. Let him come here with all his men. I do not recognize the King and I wish I never heard of Malinche. With his slick words and untruths, he seized Moctezuma, who no longer has the will to rule over Tenochtitlan."

When Cortés found out about Cacama's reply, he went to see Moctezuma. "Lord Moctezuma, you know about the arrogant remarks Cacama used in answer to our demands for peace. I do not believe I can tolerate him. If you allow him to continue, soon he will be Lord of Temistitan. If you do not want me to go and capture him, then you, the great lord that you are, must have *caciques* and relatives who do not like Cacama because he is haughty. Order them to go quietly, seize him and bring him here into our custody."

"So Cacama wishes to be the lord of Tenochtitlan. I will order him brought here," said Moctezuma.

He instructed his people to go secretly at night to Texcoco, tucking their canoes beneath Cacama's house built on stakes in the lake. They were to wait until late at night when there were fewer guards, capture Cacama when he was asleep and bring him in the canoes to Tenochtitlan and in the predawn hours deliver him to the Axayácatl Palace.

Cacama was brought to Moctezuma, who then sent him to Cortés.

Cacama preso, por orden de Moctezuma

Cacama, a prisoner, by Moctezuma's orders

"Take this arrogant man to jail and place him in irons," said the Spanish captain. After they carried out their orders, Cortés reported to Moctezuma.

"Lord Moctezuma, I have placed Cacamatzin in irons. He has rebelled. His seat of government is empty and we ought to think about who should be the lord of Texcoco, preferably one of your own relatives who is loyal. From what I have learned, there have been internal struggles in Texcoco for a long time, even fighting between brothers for power."

"Cacama has a brother," said Moctezuma.

"Cucuzcacin?" interrupted Cortés. "That's perfect! With your approval, he will be named lord of Texcoco."

At a formal ceremony, over which Cortés and Moctezuma presided, seated in their respective thrones, Cucuzcacin was installed as Lord of Texcoco.

First, Marina translated for Cortés.

"In the name of the King of Spain, Cucuzcacin, who will be named by *Don Carlos*, will be the lord of Texcoco."

Then came the Indian rites.

The lords of Tacuba and Ixtapalapa, afraid that they would be captured, too, would not face Moctezuma. After twenty days, Cortés noticed their absence.

Prison for the Lords of Tacuba and Ixtapalapa

"Apparently, Lord Moctezuma, the lords, your chiefs, no longer come to show their respect as they should. They were present when Cacama planned his conspiracy to remove you from your throne. May I suggest you order them brought here to be under guard. . . ."

Moctezuma did not reply. He concentrated, closing his eyes for a moment. "Malinche, in eight days they will be here."

Exactly eight days later, the lords of Tacuba, Ixtapalapa and Matlaltzingo arrived. Once they had paid homage to Moctezuma, Cortés awaited them outside the great hall and seized them. They were placed in irons and taken to prison along with other members of the Culúa Alliance who had accompanied them, including the high priest.

Overwhelmed and confused by events, Moctezuma closed his eyes and sat back on his throne.

Moctezuma Pays Tribute

Eventually, the Spaniards returned. Led by their Indian guides, they had traveled everywhere in the Culúa Empire where they had been informed there was gold. With great joy, they displayed samples of the metal. They had actually seen many gold panning operations and mines. The last to arrive was Diego de Ordaz, who had gone to explore the Coatzacoalcos River.

With Ordaz's return in mind, Cortés ordered an assembly of the other captains as well as representatives of the troops.

Cortés spoke to them: "Comrades. Everyone we sent to explore this territory and to learn about the mines and panning operations for gold and silver has returned. They all report this land is rich. Gonzalo de Umbría, let's hear from you first."

Umbría's feet had been injured so some Indians helped him stand up.

"We went to Zacatecas and found. . . ."

"Pizarro, you speak." Cortés pointed to him.

"We went to Tuxtepeque and we found. . . ."

"You speak, Heredia '*el Viejo*' and you Escalona '*el Moro*' and you Cervantes '*el Chocarrero.*'"

"Last, Captain Ordaz, you speak."

"We went to where the Coatzacoalcos River meets the sea. . . ."

"As you have seen, this land is rich and we can accomplish more if we exploit it as well as we have the islands. I think this is the time to establish sovereignty."

"Some other officers and soldiers believe we should ask Moctezuma, as the ruler of this land, to pay a tribute in gold to His Majesty *Don* Carlos and all his provinces as well," Ordaz said.

"I agree, and I will ask the great Moctezuma to do it," Cortés said.

Cortés went to Moctezuma's quarters. "Lord Moctezuma, you know that our King needs gold for the many projects he has planned. As a sign of your vassalage, the time has come for you to order the *caciques* of all the provinces in the Culúa Empire to pay tribute in gold and silver to the Catholic Majesty of *Don* Carlos as well as your own share of tribute."

Moctezuma closed his eyes for a moment, and after a short silence, he spoke. "I want you to know, Lord Malinche, that our ancestors ordained that these lands and all their riches must be delivered to the children of Quetzalcóatl, whose throne we have borrowed. I have been chosen to fulfill that demand. However, I understand that your great King is now the one who will rule this land. The words of our ancestors and even our gods have made us understand this. Therefore, in twenty days, the tribute from the provinces will be ready. What I have set aside for the Emperor is the entire treasure I inherited from my father, which already is under your control in your section of this palace. I am aware that as soon as you came here you opened the treasury and saw the contents. Then, you tried to seal it closed the way you found it.

"When you write your letters, tell the King that his subject, Moctezuma, is sending this treasure to him. I will add to it some precious stones and other riches in the possession of my noble house. I will give you everything I have, even though it may be a small amount, because I have been giving you presents ever since you arrived."

He remained silent in the presence of the Spaniards' astonishment. As a sign of respect, they took off their head coverings and removed their weapons.

The Treasure

Some of Moctezuma's stewards went to the Axayácatl Palace, broke down the wall the Spaniards had sealed closed and delivered the gold. There were three piles of jewel-encrusted gold, precious stones, and beautifully woven feathers and silvered jewels, plus pure gold nuggets.

At the sight of the treasure, the Spaniards' greed erupted and their jubilation got out of hand.

"Let's divide it!" "Divide it!" [The treasure]

"Let's divide it! Let's divide it!" they began to shout.

"I will have order!" Cortés shouted. "Jewels cannot be divided. We will leave it as is until we have assembled even more."

"No! No! At once! Now! Gold disappears!" said one impudent soldier.

"Yes," cried another, "I remember when I first saw the treasure, there was more gold than I see now."

"The division! Let's divide it!" shouted the greed-possessed guards.

Moctezuma's stewards gaped with amazement at the disorder and all the shouting.

"Silence," said Cortés. "All right. We will do as you wish. But only in the presence of officials of His Majesty's finance minister. But remember, in order to divide it, we must weigh each piece, which is difficult because it is jewelry and made in many styles."

"Melt it down—take the gold and the silver!"

"Melt it! Melt it! Get rid of the feathers and jewels!"

"Very well, that is what we will do. We will melt the gold and silver and mold it into bars," Cortés said.

"Put it on the scale! Weigh it!" the soldiers demanded.

"Put the King's seal on the bars," said Gonzalo Mejía, the army's treasurer, "so we can facilitate the division, separate the Fifth belonging to the King."

Moctezuma's steward reported to him that they had completed the task of delivering the gold. "Lord, great lord, my lord, we have obeyed and carried out your order. The Aztec treasure has been delivered to the *teules* who immediately demonstrated shameful greediness. There was shouting and wild demonstrations. They all acted like ravenous predators growling hungrily for gold, which seems to be their real food."

Moctezuma closed his eyes and became silent. In a low voice, he said to himself:

"To conclude this episode, I must swallow this most distressing potion of *chile*. As commanded, I have delivered the treasure. Now, I will deliver the nation's honor and its glory."

His eyes became dewy, yet his voice was strong. He said to his stewards: "Ask Malinche to come here. I wish to speak to him."

The Subjugation

By the time Cortés appeared, Moctezuma was calm.

"Malinche, I have placed in your hands all of the Aztec treasure. As soon as possible, I would like to fulfill the wishes of the gods, as my grandparents and ancestors demanded of me. I will command all the principals of the Culúa Empire to swear obedience and subjugation to your Emperor."

Cortés, quite astonished, consented.

Ten days later, all the chiefs and officers of the Culúa Empire, except from Tula, arrived. They convened in the great hall of the Axayácatl Palace into which Moctezuma was carried in his luxurious litter. He alighted and took his place on the throne. Next to him was Cortés with his secretary; close to them were the captains. Around the room were more Spanish soldiers.

"Lord, our lord, great lord," they all greeted Moctezuma. For a few moments, there was silence.

"Brothers," Moctezuma said, "many years ago you and your fathers and grandfathers were subjects of my ancestors, and of mine for the past eighteen years. All this time, you have been loyal, and I have enriched you and extended our land and our power.

"From the earliest time, we learned from our books and from the legends of our ancestors that from where the Sun rises would come white, bearded men, sons of Quetzalcóatl, to rule over these lands, to claim the throne we have borrowed and to end the reign and lordship of the Mexicans. We have always known this and we have always awaited their arrival. Now it has happened! They have come! They are these men who are here before you! We give thanks to the gods because what we have waited for so long came in our time. It was our turn to witness the dread and fear. I have already delivered the treasure. Now we must relinquish the power of the Aztecs. Until now, you have respected me as your lord. But from this time forward, I ask you all to obey that great King, *Don* Carlos, as your lord. He is the natural lord of this land and representing him is his captain. I, myself, according to the mandate of my gods, must do the same and submit to him whatever he asks of me.

"In this way, besides doing what you must and what the ancient times demanded, you can join with me in this distressing act, just as it has been my duty to witness and appreciate what has come to pass."

Deeply moved in the presence of his peoples' emotional reaction—many were sobbing—Moctezuma became silent.

Then Hernán Cortés stood up from his throne and spoke while Marina translated. "Pedro Hernández, in your position as Scribe of the King, you draw up the official decree of this oath."

Then he spoke to everyone: "Lord Moctezuma, *señores*, Mexicans, do you swear and promise obedience and respect as subjects of *Don* Carlos, King of Spain?"

"I swear and I promise," said the weeping Moctezuma. "Everyone swear."

"We swear and we promise!" they all said, with tears streaming from their eyes. Many of the Spaniards witnessing the scene cried too.

The Division of the Treasure

The next day, Gonzalo Mejía, the King's Treasurer, reported to Cortés: "Captain, with the help of some instruments from Atzcapotzalco, for the past few days, we have been removing the jewels, feathers and precious stones from the gold and silver and have cast the ingots for the division of spoils. Many are in twenty-five pound chunks, others are half that and there are even some four-ounce weights to ensure a fair split."

"Excellent report, Treasurer. Call a general assembly with the Royal Scribe present so that we can make the division."

With great excitement, the Spaniards gathered in the same room where the precious metals and the bars had been melted down and were piled neatly.

"*Señores* and comrades," Cortés said, "in the presence of the King's Treasurer and the Royal Scribe, we will now proceed to divide these riches."

"We have cast," said the Treasurer, "not counting silver or the precious stones, gold ingots valued at more than six hundred thousand pesos [the value at that time] and we will now divide it. First, I will separate the Fifth that belongs to the King."

There was an immediate murmur of assent. "As for me," said Cortés, "I will draw the portion for the seventy comrades who stayed behind at the Villa Rica de la Vera Cruz and a double share for Gonzalo de Sandoval as a captain."

Again murmurs, most affirmative.

"That's fine! It is fair!"

There were others who complained. "They didn't fight against the Indians. They were on the coast."

"Does anyone object?" Cortés asked sternly.

No one dared speak.

"Now, I withdraw the fifth that you offered me when I was named Captain General in Villa Rica and to compensate for the losses of my horses and other expenses."

There was much louder grumbling, more overt expressions of complaint.

"Why does he get a fifth? As if he were King! There were no losses! It is not fair! What will be left for us?"

"Is there anyone who objects to this arrangement?" asked Cortés, somewhat annoyed.

Not one person dared speak up, even though the muttering went on.

"I have already set aside double shares for the captains and the horsemen," the Treasurer said.

More complaints.

"I also set aside a share and a half for the crossbowmen and musketeers."

Now the clamor increased.

"For those with the sword—there is nothing!" came the shouts. "As if we were the least! Did we not also risk our lives?"

"And," concluded the Treasurer, "this share is for the foot soldiers with sword and buckler."

The reaction was immediate and bitter.

"This is nothing! Hardly one hundred pesos! It is not just! So much effort for nothing!"

"I don't accept," said one soldier.

"Nor I, nor I," yelled others.

"We do not accept!" chorused most of the foot soldiers.

"This matter is closed!" bellowed the King's Treasurer, facing up to the troops.

In the midst of much tumult and shouting, the meeting was adjourned. Cortés and the captains stood up and left the room while the argument went on.

Juan Velázquez de León and Gonzalo Mejía stayed behind. "I learned," Mejía said, "that you ordered a special gold chain made which you named *la Fanfarrona*, and it was not counted with the gold melted down by the instruments from Atzcapotzalco."

"Liar! It was some gold that I found in a mine! I am not a thief!" Velázquez de León cried.

"Well, what do you call it when you cheat the King and your companions?"

"Shut up or I will not be responsible for my actions."

"Well, be responsible to the King! Return that gold!"

"All right! With the point of my sword! Come and get it," he grunted, drawing it from his scabbard.

Mejía followed suit and they began to duel.

Hearing the commotion, Cortés quickly returned and with his own sword separated those of the two antagonists. "For God's sake, and for the King! Stop!"

First one, then the other duelist began to justify himself.

Cortés interrupted, "I do not want to hear any of that! It was probably because of the gold! We have orders that no duels will be fought among ourselves, under penalty of prison! Ensign! Arrest these two officers and see that they are secured with strong chains."

Enraged, Cortés stalked out, leaving behind the astonished captains and soldiers who had witnessed the fracas.

The rest of that afternoon, the arguments, shouting and grumbling about the division went on unabated.

Vexation and Dissatisfaction

Cortés ordered Ordaz and Alonso de Ávila to come to his quarters. "*Señores*, what do you think caused so much discontent during the division of the gold? Why didn't the men accept what they were offered?"

"Ever since the division assembly," said Ordaz, "there has been great rancor among the troops. They criticized everything, especially when you took the same amount as the Royal Fifth for the King."

"But they offered me that in Villa Rica," Cortés said.

De Ávila nodded. "We are simply telling you what is going on."

"And I appreciate your frankness, gentlemen. Tomorrow we will carry on."

The next day, in the presence of Mejía and Velázquez de León, who were still in chains, they continued the division. Before beginning, Cortés ordered Mejía freed so he could act as the King's Treasurer.

Cortés said, "Men and comrades, you will remember that when you appointed me your Captain General in Villa Rica, I only accepted on the condition that I be given a fifth of all our riches. But yesterday, when I set aside that fifth, many of you seemed to consider that wrong of me.

"I am well aware that when it comes to gold, we are all quite greedy, but I do not wish to take advantage. All of you, and I, have shared and will continue to share the same dangers. So I tell you now that I do not wish to receive more gold than is allotted to each Captain and I hereby give back to the pool the share that was my right to receive.

"But I ask you to consider this: the gold we have accumulated up to now is little more than a puff of air when you consider the vast riches of this land which we now control. Just look at the cities and villages, the mines and the agricultural products. That is the real treasure, not what we have here, divided good or bad."

The soldiers cheered, even though one, still grumbling, said, "Lovely words, as usual, but why don't you tell us as well how much you laid aside?"

Cortés concluded:

"Under these rules, the King's Treasurer, the captains' and soldiers' representatives will now make the division. Do you agree?"

"We do," they all shouted.

More Idols Are Demolished

The mood in Tenochtitlan was hostile, but peaceful. As Cortés, accompanied by his captains and some soldiers, went about the city, he commented: "What a beautiful valley is this tableland of Temistitan. It resembles a saucer full of water."

"Yes, but the lake is salty up to this earthen barricade and on the other side is the pure water," said one of the men.

"Temistitan is almost two leagues in circumference," said another.

"It is as large as Seville or Córdoba," another remarked.

The comments went on.

"Half is water and half land and there are many plazas."

"Tlatelolco is a great market that often has as many as sixty thousand people including the buyers and sellers."

"There is. . . ."

One particular day, when Cortés returned from visiting the temples where human sacrifices were still continuing, Moctezuma asked to see him. *Doña* Marina translated, her face revealing her concern.

"Look here, Malinche," said the Aztec Emperor. "I care for you very deeply and I wish to present you with one of my beautiful daughters to marry and consider your true wife."

Cortés stared into *Doña* Marina's eyes as he said to her: "Translate this very carefully: Lord Moctezuma, you honor me greatly, but I am already married and the Spanish custom is to have only one wife. I would accept her were I not married because she is your daughter. But, I must ask that she become a Christian and be baptized."

"Very well," said Moctezuma.

"I do not understand you, Lord Moctezuma," said Cortés. "You agree that your daughter shall become a Christian, yet you, whom I have begged to pray to our true God, continue to make human sacrifices to your idols, which are devils."

"We have already discussed that, Malinche. My gods are very good to me as your three gods, the Father, Son, and Holy Spirit, which you say are one and the other goddess, his mother, are good for you. Let us drop that subject."

"We cannot ignore it if we are to baptize your daughter. That must take place in a Christian temple and for that occasion I ask your permission to use your Great

Temple, where we will erect an altar for the Cross of Christ and to Our *Señora*, the Virgin."

Moctezuma made a gesture of annoyance. "Oh, Malinche! You wish to destroy this city. Our gods and our people are very angry with you, and I do not know how safe your lives are. Yet you continue to pursue this point. I will summon the priests and listen to their advice."

"While you are speaking with them, I will go to see where and how to erect the altar."

He left Moctezuma, who was plainly worried.

Along the way, Cortés came upon ten soldiers, among whom was Andrés de Tapia. "Tapia, you and your comrades come with me up to the top of the *teocalli*. And bring an iron bar."

They climbed the steps to the enclosed temples of Huitzilopochtli and Tezcatlipoca, represented by figures shaped from ground up seeds and blood molded in the form of human beings, superimposed on stone idols. Everywhere inside the temples there was dried or fresh blood and even a few hearts recently torn from the bodies.

With Cortés came Jerónimo de Aguilar who had learned to speak Náhuatl. With his sword, Cortés tore away the hangings at the doorways. He noticed the remains of the humans who were sacrificed and in a voice that all could hear, he said: "God, in whom we all believe, wishes us to be moral and not sacrifice human beings. Here in this place, we pray to His only Son, who died on the cross for our sins, as later we will explain to you. I demand that this image of God and his Blessed Mother be placed here where you have these idols. You must bring water to wash these walls and get rid of all this."

The priests smiled. "Not only in this city, but in the entire land, we have these gods. Here is Huitzilopochtli, which we worship. All the people venerate these gods even more than their fathers, mothers and children, and would die for them. Look, just seeing you ascend the temple's steps, the people are taking up arms, because they are ready to die for their gods."

Cortés grabbed a soldier. "Go and bring back all the men you can find as quickly as possible. Hurry!"

He turned to the Indian priests. "I order you to bring water to clean this place."

They smiled again.

Then brusquely, Cortés shouted: "I will be delighted to fight for my God against your gods, which are worthless."

Furious, Cortés, with the iron bar the soldiers had brought him, began to batter the idols, whose veneer of flour paste and blood crumbled. Cortés leaped, smashing the stone and destroying the idols while the soldiers held back the priests at sword point.

Tapia later described the scene. ". . . and I promise, by my faith, as a gentleman and I swear by God that this is true. I believe that the marquis sprang with supernatural force, thrusting forward as he grabbed the iron bar in the middle and struck the eyes of the highest idol and shattered the golden masks, as he shouted: 'We have something else to erect here, for our God.'"

To one side of the *teocalli*, at double time, forty or fifty Spanish soldiers ran up the steps. To the other side were many armed Indians. On the top, the ten Spanish soldiers pushed the priests down the steps. Cortés shouted:

"Help me knock down these devils!"

Together, using the iron bar as a lever, they toppled the idols down the steps onto the Indians who were climbing up. The stone figures broke into pieces and smashed into some of the Indians who were trying to reach the temple. The armed Spaniards kept others from trying to mount the steps.

Cortés ordered the temple washed and soon they erected a cross. With their swords drawn, they remained on top until the cross was finished, then they descended.

A great muttering of angry astonishment spread through the city.

"They will be angry," said Andrés de Tapia.

"But they don't have any chiefs," grunted Cortés. "All their kings and chieftains are our prisoners."

"¡Mucho me holgaré yo de pelear por Dios"

"I take great pleasure to fight for God."

The City Wants War

It was late afternoon by the time they washed the blood, cleaned up the debris and the remains of the idols in the temple. Cortés descended the *teocalli* steps and headed toward Moctezuma's quarters. Disturbed and frightened, Orteguilla was leaving the monarch's room and he approached Cortés. "Moctezuma has many priests with him and they are speaking so quietly I cannot hear what they are saying, nor can I understand them. But they seem very serious. They are very angry and upset."

"When they have finished their meeting, let me know."

At nightfall, Orteguilla came to Cortés' quarters and with him, *Doña* Marina, and some captains, went to visit Moctezuma, who received them in a very sober manner but with his anger in check.

"Oh, Malinche!" Moctezuma declared. "You have committed a very serious violation by destroying our gods. You have offended them and now the whole city is aroused and up in arms."

"That action was accomplished for the greater glory of God," answered Cortés righteously.

"And at the risk of your lives, Malinche. The priests came to tell me that Huitzilopochtli and Tezcatlipoca spoke with them and said that they wish to leave here and that the priests will take their remains to a place where they will be honored. If not, they will kill you. They have spoken to the captains of the warriors, who will soon declare war, enter the city, and kill you. The people are furious because the gods' jewels have been turned into bricks. And now you have sovereignty over all our land. Oh, Malinche! Oh, captains! How it grieves me, what you have done to our gods, and said to our priests. All my people wish to fight and kill you. Before they begin the slaughter, I suggest you return to the sea. Leave this city and you save your lives."

"I appreciate your suggestions, but two matters worry me. First, we have no ships, because the ones we had were burned. Second, either voluntarily or under guard, you and the other lords who are prisoners will have to come with us so that you may be presented to our Emperor. Therefore, I must ask you to restrain your priests until we can build three new ships in Villa Rica. We believe that will be best, because if there is war, all the chieftains, all the priests, will die along with all your warriors."

After meditating, Mocteuma conceded. "I will try to pacify my priests and warriors and will order my stewards to provide men to build your ships."

Divinities

When they returned to their quarters, Marina said to him: "My lord, never, not even in battles, have I seen you as angry as you were today. Jealous is the God in whom I believe. Because of you, I believe in Him as well as you, but you risk all to serve Him. And that explains to me how the three [Father, Son and Holy Spirit] are one. You will not allow another to join Him and because there can be no other, you risk everything."

"It is all very mysterious, Marina. But really, this is not the time to discuss theology, but to serve the God of the Armies."

"As Huitzilopochtli is the god of the Mexican armies."

"Nevermind the subtleties, Marina, I am in no mood for them."

"I do not mean to offend you, lord, I only wish to understand you in order to serve you better. Today you are not fighting men, but gods, in order to raise up another God."

"We must do something for Him."

"Well, the deed is done, my lord, and you know why. Only I warn you of the great danger that we are now facing. If before huge numbers surrounded us, now we are in the heart of fierce enemies. And the Mexicans are furious: You have made their chieftains prisoners and you have destroyed their gods."

"I know that, Marina. We have defied them." He left his room and shouted an order: "From now on, night and day, behave as if we were in a battle campaign: clothes, footwear and arms; horses saddled and the cannon charged and in place. Double the watches and night patrols."

So began days of great tension for everyone. But as time passed and the city was still without chiefs and afraid to lose their *caciques*, there was no uprising. Cortés continued his expeditions.

Spring, 1520

In mid-April, 1520, Cortés announced to his captains: "Lords and friends: the spring of this year is advancing and the city is, if not calm, at least in peace, no doubt because they are afraid we will injure their chieftains. It is not virtuous to be idle, so it is appropriate that we continue to find out more about the secrets of this land.

"Juan Velázquez de León, with one hundred and fifty men, you will go to the Coatzacoalcos region to explore the river and to see if the port can be fitted out where Ordaz indicated. You, Rodrigo de Rangel, will go to the Chinantla region with one hundred ten men and establish control and explore the pearl fishing and mines. . . . The rest will remain here to keep peace in the city and watch over its chieftains."

Once Again, Diego Velázquez

Early in March, 1520, in Guaniguanico [Guantánamo], the western point of Cuba, Governor Diego Velázquez chose Captain Pánfilo de Narváez to command an expedition to capture or to kill the rebel, Hernán Cortés. More than one thousand men and eighty horses boarded twenty ships. In spite of Velázquez's zeal, organizing the expedition had taken more than a year, partly because of a smallpox epidemic that ravaged the place. Afterward, the sheer size of the enterprise was daunting, because Velázquez was afraid to risk failure.

Under a canopy, Velázquez was speaking with Narváez. In front of the bay where the ships were anchored, they observed the process of provisioning the expedition.

". . . and do not let that traitor, Cortés, escape. I neither listen to nor read his letters, which are wordy and full of snares. Bring him back to me by his ears to receive justice and chastisement. Ever since he left, I have not had one day's peace."

"I know your *compadre*, Cortés, very well. Have no fear; because of your insistence in capturing him, I have more than one thousand soldiers, eighty horses and sufficient ammunition. With considerably less force, I could defeat him."

"What is important to me is that you bring him here by the ears. There is the *licenciado* Lucas Vázquez de Ayllón whom the *Audiencia de Santo Domingo** sent to me in order to speed up the dispatching of this armada. He says we should avoid any disputes among Christians with Indians looking on, because we would only be teaching them disrespect. As if Cortés' disobedience and disrespect were not bad enough, by his acts he has reduced my authority."

"Good morning, Your Excellency," said Ayllón. "I see the fleet is ready to sail, Governor, and still I do not have your reply to the *Audiencia, Señor* Velázquez. You seem more disposed to dissemble rather than to execute the instructions not to fight *Señor* Cortés, but instead to negotiate a peace treaty and other accords so he will return the commission of Captain he signed."

"Oh, all right, *Señor licenciado* Ayllón. You must realize we cannot pretend to have justice if I do not punish Cortés for his arrogance and insolence."

"But no fighting, Governor. The *Audiencia de Santo Domingo* does not wish to have any conflicts among Christians, especially not in front of Indians."

"There will be no fighting, *Señor licenciado*. As soon as Cortés finds out I am sending someone for him, he will surrender and become submissive," blustered the presumptuous Narváez.

Ayllón spoke next. "I have been authorized to make certain these instructions are carried out. If you do not give me a reply with your signature and promise that you will not attack Cortés, I will have to accompany *Señor* Narváez so as to certify that he carried out the instructions of the *Audiencia*."

"Do as you wish, *Señor licenciado*; there is a ship at your disposal."

---

* *Audiencia de Santo Domingo*. This body was entrusted not only with the highest judicial authority, but with civil jurisdiction.

Once Ayllón had left, Velázquez said to Narváez: "With the *licenciado* or without him, you bring me Cortés, dead or alive. You know what I mean. If the *licenciado* interferes, then you found a Villa, just like that traitor Cortés did. Send the *Ayuntamiento* to me in Santo Domingo. To assist you with these details, take as your secretary Andrés de Duero. He knows Cortés and his tricks very well."

"Have no fear, *Señor*, for I am man enough to handle Cortés and a legion of *licenciados*. With your permission, we will set sail in two days."

"Why not tomorrow?"

"Because we do not wish to take anyone who is sick with smallpox. The naval surgeon is checking the whole crew."

"Oh! The smallpox! How horrible it has been," agreed Velázquez.

Narváez

Two days later, the flotilla set sail from Guaniguanico and about the first of April, arrived at San Juan de Ulúa. There was bad weather, so the fleet became separated and the first ship to arrive in Yucatán was Ayllón's. The Indians who worked at Villa Rica were serving as look-outs. They ran to inform Sandoval.

The interpreter said to him: "Captain! Captain! In San Juan de Ulúa a ship has dropped anchor and just sits there looking peaceful. They say there are also many others coming to port."

"You, Pedro de Solís, the most able of my men, go and evaluate the situation. If on the way you meet Cervantes, "el Chocarrero," and Escalona and Alonso Hernández Carretero, whom Cortés sent to search for mines, inform them about the arrival and tell them I said they should go with you!"

Solís left at once and halfway down the road he met Cortés' men, who were returning to the Villa.

"Where are you going so out of breath, Solís?" one man asked.

"To San Juan de Ulúa. It seems there is a ship anchored in the port and I'm on my way to investigate this great surprise by order of Sandoval. He asked you all to come along."

"Fine, but not at your pace," said Cervantes. "We will get there at our speed."

Solís jogged down the path and soon arrived at San Juan. From the beach, he made a signal with his shirt and the ship sent a skiff ashore to fetch him.

Somewhat abruptly, *licenciado* Ayllón greeted Solís at the rail. "Who are you and where do you come from?"

"I am Pedro de Solís from the garrison of the Villa Rica de la Vera Cruz, founded by Cortés and the men who came with him. At this time, Captain Gonzalo de Sandoval bears the emblem of authority. Who are you?"

"I am *Licenciado* Lucas Vásquez de Ayllón," he puffed self-importantly. "I come as a Judge of the *Audiencia de Santo Domingo* to examine Cortés' discoveries and to mitigate any armed conflicts between Christians now that Pánfilo de Narváez and his men are coming here to demand that Cortés relinquish his office of Captaincy."

"Did you say more Spaniards are coming?"

"Yes, many more . . . so many I am afraid they may not respect the order of the *Audiencia* which demands that any differences between Velázquez and Cortés be resolved peacefully. Please place your trust in me and tell me more about the situation here." They left for Ayllón's quarters.

During that afternoon and evening, the rest of the ships arrived. By early morning, they were all anchored in the bay.

On the beach at dawn were Cervantes, "el Chocarrero," who now spoke some Náhuatl, his friends and some of Moctezuma's scouts, who were sketching all the events on their papers and cloths. The Spaniards on the beach signalled and a skiff from Narváez's ship soon arrived to take them aboard. On the way to the flag ship, they passed the small boat returning Solís to shore.

Pánfilo de Narváez himself greeted the men, recognizing them as neighbors who had lived in Cuba.

"Ah, Narváez! I'm delighted to welcome you here. Notice how punctual I am in accepting your invitation to drink a glass of fine wine," Cervantes said from the skiff.

"Chocarrero! Come ahead, good Cervantes, climb aboard. I am most anxious to chat with you."

"I can imagine what it is you wish to discuss. What was Velázquez's reaction to our arrival here?"

"You can just imagine! Furious! He sent me to collect that rebel, Cortés."

"Congratulations!" grunted Cervantes as he stepped on deck. He looked about, taking in the whole fleet. "A great force!"

"Come to my cabin and tell me everything."

Cervantes raised his arms to the sky. "Thank God that you have freed us from Cortés' tyranny and from being trapped like rats in Temistitan! How many times we begged to return and then he burned the ships!"

His companions nodded agreement.

In Narváez's cabin they were served glasses of wine. As Cervantes tasted the liquid, he said to his friends: "Look, isn't it better to be drinking good wine here than to be captives of Cortés' authority? He subjected us night and day to such servitude that we dared not speak out and we expected death from one day to the next. Oh, Narváez, Narváez, how fortunate that you are here and especially now! That traitor Cortés has collected six hundred thousand pesos worth of gold and all the men are dissatisfied with his division of shares."

"That's enough, Cervantes. I fear you are speaking too hastily. What is all that about Temistitan and gold? Tell me all about it, because my mission here is to seize Cortés."

"Well, friend Narváez, you know that. . . ." And he proceeded to tell all.

When Cervantes finally stopped, Narváez said, "These Indians who came here with you, who are they?"

"They are Moctezuma's observers. It would be a good idea for you to send a message with them that you have come to seize that thief and traitor Cortés, so he can be delivered to the court of justice. Say that all those loyal to Cortés are thieves and that you are here to free Moctezuma.

"Can you explain to these Indians what you are telling me?"

"I understand their language well enough."

"Good. Do it!"

Cervantes, Escalona and Hernández spoke to the Indians, Moctezuma's pictographers and agents went right on sketching everything.

When the conversation ended, the three Spaniards stayed on board and the Indians were taken back to the beach. They left immediately for Tenochtitlan.

El Licenciado Vázquez de Ayllón

While this was going on, *licenciado* Ayllón boarded Narváez's ship. With Cervantes and his companions present, Ayllón said: "Captain! I have been told by a soldier from the Spanish Villa founded here how Cortés has taken over this land and has pacified a great part of it. He said the Indians work and obey everything that Cortés asks. Now that we have arrived in this territory, I demand in the name of the *Audiencia de Santo Domingo* that you do not take up arms against Cortés but settle your affairs peacefully before me, as Judge. It would be most unfortunate if the Indians witnessed a dispute between you."

"Look, *licenciado* Ayllón, I am tired of hearing what I must do with that traitor Cortés, who has refused to give Diego Velázquez, Governor and *Adelantado*, his share of the gold. He has sent me here and I will obey his orders," said Narváez.

"As *Adelantado* of Yucatán, he is subject to the jurisdiction of the *Audiencia de Santo Domingo*," said Ayllón.

"Let's see if we are subjects!" Narváez turned to his lieutenant: "Detain this *licenciado*. He is not allowed to return to his ship."

Cervantes, "el Chocarrero," commented to Narváez: "It's always the same with these pettifogging, mean-spirited Dominican fellows from the *Audiencia*! Why don't you do what Cortés did to Velázquez when he founded the Villa Rica de la Vera Cruz in order to ignore his orders?"

"Just what I was planning, good Cervantes, and that is what we will do," Narváez agreed.

Some days later, Ayllón, humiliated, left for Santo Domingo aboard a ship.

"Greetings to the priests of the *Audiencia* from the *Ayuntamiento de San Juan*," shouted Cervantes, "el Chocarrero."

Moctezuma and Narváez

In the meantime, the Aztec agents and pictographers had force marched to deliver their information for Moctezuma. At first, he received them fearfully, but that quickly turned to joy.

". . . And the tall captain with a squeaky voice says he comes here to take Malinche prisoner, as a traitor and thief. Along with this captain are three of his friends from Malinche's *teules*."

225

"Give me the sketches and do not speak about this to anyone." Then Moctezuma called his stewards. "I want Quetzalaztatzin, who resembles Malinche, to head a group of ambassadors to take gold and cloths to the new *teule* who comes to fight with these other *teules* and tell him I will send Malinche as a prisoner to him if he promises to leave this land with everyone."

The stewards left to organize the trip.

Sandoval and Narváez's Men

Sandoval received similar information from Solís and wrote a letter to Cortés.

"Solís, take this letter to Captain Cortés. Go with two companions and as many Indians as you wish. I cannot give you a horse, because no doubt I will need it as I can well foresee what may happen here."

Sandoval went down to the beach and, ringing the bell, assembled his men.

"*Señores* and friends. You know me as a man of few words. There has come to San Juan a certain Narváez with orders to capture Cortés and his soldiers. I want to know whose side you are on?"

"With Cortés," they shouted in a single voice.

"Swear it!"

"We swear!"

"Fine. We cannot all fight, so those who are disabled will go to the Indian villages nearby and the rest will stay with me. Don't show your faces until I give the order."

Soon the Villa was like an empty wasteland.

Sandoval Seizes Three of Narváez's Forces

Prudently, Narváez began to unload his horses and equipment in San Juan de Ulúa.

He was on the beach resting in the shade of a canopy, chasing mosquitos and drinking wine with Cervantes, while he observed the handling of the equipment.

"Friend Cervantes, how far are we from that place, Villa Rica, where they have the old and crippled men?"

"Less than a day's march."

"I think now is the time to order an investigation. Captain! Tell the priest Juan Ruiz de Guevara and the scribe Alonso de Vergara and Pedro de Amaya, Velazquez' nephew, to notify the Alcalde, or whatever he is, that Velazquez' written instructions be surrendered and that he come immediately before me, with the Municipal Council, or whatever they are, to receive further orders."

Escalona, who was nearby with Hernández, commented: "The truth of the matter is he thinks Cortés will be there in person. Narváez is over-confident."

The three men left for the Villa Rica and found it apparently deserted. "Let us go to that house over there, which seems the best one here."

Gonzalo de Sandoval came out and stared at them.

"Fortunately, you are here," said the priest.

"Lucky you arrived at the right time. How may I help you?" Sandoval asked.

"I come here to demand . . . ," said the scribe, "by order of Pánfilo de Narváez, Captain. . . ."

"Don't demand anything of me without showing some authority," Sandoval said, agitatedly.

"I have plenty of evidence for you," said the scribe, dropping the papers he was shuffling.

"If that's an indication of your powers, they have fallen to the ground and the wind is carrying them away!"

"Why are you bothering with these traitors?" shouted the priest. "Pick up those decrees and inform them!"

"You are the traitor, you lying priest," Sandoval shouted, turning to the Indians who were with him. "Seize them!" he ordered in Náhuatl.

Quickly, the Indians grabbed the three Spaniards and wrapped each one in a large net. They were hoisted onto the shoulders of four *tamemes*.

"You will go along as the constable Pedro de Solís! And don't stop until you reach Temistitan and deliver these three to Captain Cortés so he may examine their Summons," instructed Sandoval.

". . . deliver them to Captain Cortés. . . ."

Once Again, Moctezuma and Narváez

After leaving Moctezuma's quarters in the Axayácatl Palace, Cortés commented to *Doña* Marina: "Something doesn't smell quite right, Marina. Moctezuma seems a bit too smug. Either something is about to happen or it already has."

Marina answered: "Yesterday, Moctezuma's spies returned from the coast and revealed some secret to him. They were smiling after they left him and did not say a word. So you may be right. This afternoon, why don't we return to pay our respects to Moctezuma and learn why he is so happy."

"Excellent."

That afternoon, Cortés returned to Moctezuma's apartment to find the Mexican monarch in high spirits, as his expression revealed.

"Malinche, how nice that you have come to visit me twice on the same day," said the Mexican.

"It's a pleasure to see you as contented as you were earlier. I'm also delighted that my presence pleases you. But I think there may be other reasons for your cheerful state of mind."

Silently, Moctezuma stared at Cortés for a moment. "*Señor* Malinche, a little while ago some messengers arrived from the port where you disembarked, advising me that eighteen ships and many horses have arrived there." He showed Cortés their sketches.

"Since you have come to visit again, I thought you might wish to tell me about them. Now, I do not think you will have to build any ships. Because you yourself did not tell me this news, I should be upset with you for keeping me in the dark. On the other hand, I am pleased because your brothers have come so that all of you may return to Castilla. I have nothing more to say."

Cortés studied the pictographs. He exclaimed: "Thank God, who provides for us when the time is right."

Some soldiers who were close by overheard and shouted cries of jubilation. When Cortés came out of Moctezuma's rooms, they came up to him, bombarding him with questions.

Thoughtful, Cortés said to them: "Don't be so exuberant. It would all be very well if there were one or two ships, but so many—I smell the devious odor of Diego Velázquez."

That night, Pedro de Solís finally arrived with Gonzalo de Sandoval's letter.

As usual, Cortés summoned the captains and soldiers in whom he had the most confidence.

"*Señores*, friends. The news is that Pánfilo de Narváez has arrived at San Juan de Ulúa, sent by Diego Velázquez to seize me and all of you who have been loyal to me. They came with many men and horses and a large force. I will not try to stop those of you who wish to join him. But if you remain here, then you must resist him when he comes to subdue us. Let us remind you that we control the territory and we have much treasure, which may become greater or which can be lost entirely."

"I do not doubt," said Alvarado, "that ever since we left Cuba we all recognized the risks. I believe my companions hold the same opinion."

They all voiced agreement. "You can count on us!" they cried.

"Juan Velázquez de León and Rodrigo de Rangel are not present and they have power," said Cortés.

"Do not worry," said Diego de Ordaz. "At Villa Rica, Juan and I gave our word of honor to remain at your side forever."

Cortés nodded. "The second important point I wish to propose is that Pedro de Alvarado should stay in Temistitan in charge of eighty men, five horses and all of the artillery. The rest of you, totaling sixty, will come with me to confront Narváez. Along the way, as soon as possible, we will join with Velázquez de León and Rangel, who are closer to them than we are. All of the supplies we have requested from Tlaxcala—corn, as well as turkeys—are provisions for those who stay behind and should be sufficient until we return. Pedro, it could be that Moctezuma, seeing how few men we have left behind here, may feel encouraged to try something. He seems to be in touch with Narváez and I think they may have some sort of understanding already. You must be very alert."

"You know me, Captain," said Alvarado.

Cortés smiled. "I will write at once to Juan Velázquez de León, giving him a chance to choose sides. I will send another letter to Narváez by Father Olmedo so that the Padre can talk to our acquaintances and try to win them over to our cause."

"When do you expect to leave?" asked Alvarado.

"In just a few days, or until I can find out what Moctezuma is up to. We will take advantage of this time to shore up the palace defenses and stockpile provisions. Alvarado, you are in charge of that. We should reinforce the walls at certain points and fortify the positions."

From that time, the activity was frantic: the delivery of provisions from Tlaxcala was expedited, and the Spaniards began to build walls and earth fences and to reinforce the ramparts.

In the midst of this activity, Cortés took Padre Olmedo aside: "Once you have delivered my letter to Narváez, you must try to speak in secret with any of those in his group who are our friends. Share this gold with them and suggest to them that instead of returning to Cuba, they stay here to colonize this land. Tell them there is plenty for everyone. In this way, they can better serve His Majesty."

Soon after Padre Olmedo departed, the priest Guevara, Vergara and Amaya arrived in panniers and still entangled in the nets, as Gonzalo de Sandoval had dispatched them.

Solís, anticipating their arrival, met with Cortés, who said, "It is not right that the Indians should see other Spaniards held prisoners. I will go to greet them personally. They can enter the city on three horses that I will send. They should make their entrance as is fitting."

Which is the way it happened. Cortés greeted them warmly and pointed out the splendors of the great city, its treasures and potentials and even presented them with exquisite golden gifts.

When the trio arrived at the Axayácatl Palace, they began to speak, "We are astonished," said Guevara, "at the splendor of this city and by the many populated villages we passed through."

"This is a great country," said Cortés. "There is enough here for everyone and great riches. It is a pity that some Spaniards are moved to contend with Spaniards over its sovereignty."

"We were ordered to come, Captain, we. . . ."

"Please, do not get the wrong idea! Look, in order to appease your treatment and these inconveniences, accept these gifts. There are more gifts for any who wish to colonize here instead of returning to the crude way of life in Cuba."

Padre Olmedo

"I have agreed to see you only if the matter concerns you, Padre. I do not wish to hear anything about Cortés—unless it is to acknowledge Diego Velázquez's orders. It would be best if the renegade came before me humbly before I bring him back by his ears," shouted Narváez.

"You certainly have the force to back up that threat, Narváez, but it would set a poor example for the Indians, who are presently at peace."

"You sound like *licenciado* Ayllón, Padre. Let us get this over with. Give me the letter!"

Olmedo handed it to him. Narváez read it aloud and made snide comments to his men: "'Fear does not journey on a burro.' Listen to what the valiant Cortés writes: 'I ask Your Honor not to give Moctezuma a reason to rebel. He is my prisoner; if he is freed and this city rises up in arms, we will lose everything we have accomplished and we would die. Moctezuma is upset and the city is disquieted by what you have said.'"

Narváez stopped reading and exclaimed: "What does this traitor want? That we go march up there to applaud his treacherous actions?"

"Captain Narváez," said Captain Salvatierra, "why are you so concerned about a letter from a traitor like Cortés? Let us attack him and his men and eliminate them. I swear I will personally roast Cortés' ears and dine on them."

Everyone laughed.

"You are right, Salvatierra, let us dispense with the reading."

"Do you not wish to reply to it?" asked Olmedo.

"There can be no answer. This letter means no more to me than a castanet." He snapped his fingers.

Everyone laughed again.

That evening, Padre Olmedo began to speak with the men who were Cortés' friends and gave them jewels.

". . . and this is only a small token of the great riches in this land, plenty for everyone if you stay here to populate and do not return to Cuba."

Days later, smiling, the cleric Guevara and his two friends were received by Narváez.

"Welcome, Father Guevara. I congratulate you! I heard you were captured by Cortés. What happened?"

"Captain, we went to Temistitan and there Cortés received us royally. We witnessed the grandeur of this land and saw many cities, much abundance and even riches. I believe this land should be colonized. And it would be a good idea if you and Cortés could reach an understanding in a peaceful way and without differences. There are many places where one can find lodging and you may choose the location and Cortés will accept it."

"What are you saying, Father? Has that fast-talking Cortés convinced you, too? Are you asking me to commit treason like Cortés? You and your companions get out of my sight before I punish you for attempting to mislead me, because I came here to punish traitors!"

Frightened, Guevara and his men left. That night, under the torchlights, he was chattering and showing off the jewels Cortés had given him.

". . . and this is nothing compared to the other treasures. This country is huge and it would be wise to colonize it now that so many Indians have been pacified. There is plenty for everyone. . . ."

Father Olmedo, who was privy to most incidents, commented to his companions: "Our Captain is most wise. Narváez's men are more anxious to explore and colonize the land than they are to capture Cortés and go back to Cuba."

Cortés Leaves Tenochtitlan

In the Axayácatl Palace, Cortés was chatting with his captains: "I received a letter from Juan Velázquez de León declaring his loyalty. He will meet me in Cholula so we can confront Narváez, who is doing his worst to disorganize this country. Now I shall go and bid farewell to the optimistic Moctezuma."

When Cortés reached Moctezuma's quarters, he was welcomed with a mocking smirk. "*Señor* Malinche, I have noticed that your captains and soldiers seem quite agitated. I also noticed that you do not visit me as often as you used to, only now and then. Orteguilla, the page, tells me you wish to confront your brothers who came in the ships and that you will leave behind *Tonatiuh* [Alvarado] to guard me. Please tell me how I may be of assistance, which I would do willingly. One other point, *Señor* Malinche, I do not wish to have anything happen to you because you have few *teules* and those who have recently arrived have five times more. They say they are Christians as you are and servants of that Emperor and have the same holy images and they place crosses and pray the Mass as you do. They charge that your men fled from your King, so they came here to seize and kill you. I do not understand that, so be careful what you do."

Cortés, no less mocking, replied. "Lord Moctezuma, I did not come here to describe the situation so that it would make you unhappy. I know you feel friendship toward us and you must be saddened by our leaving. Those others, like us, are subjects of the same King, just as the Otomies and Totonacans were subjects of Culúa. But we did not flee. We were sent by our King and if we are too few, then our Lord Jesus Christ will give us enough strength and we will soon return victorious. So, do not worry about us. Alvarado will be in charge and I ask you not to encourage disturbances by your priests or captains."

"Do not worry, *Señor* Malinche. Quite the contrary. I promise to send five thousand soldiers to help you."

"Thank you, but there is no need. We have enough men for this campaign. We will return soon. I recommend to you the image of Our Lady and the Cross, because there you will understand better the depth of our friendships, not by supplying warriors."

Before Cortés left, they exchanged *abrazos*.

For a few moments, Moctezuma was pensive, in a musing tone, he muttered: "I do not understand any of this. What has befallen us? *Teules! Teules!* Strange *teules* who quarrel among themselves. Malinche! Malinche! Now I am sure you are not who I thought you were! The very heavens are tumbling down! And I delivered all the power to you—the riches and the glory of Quetzalcóatl! What a blunder! What a horrendous mistake!" Almost crying, he added:

"Men; they are only greedy men, like wild beasts, as vicious as their dogs and as lewd as monkeys. What a blunder! Death. All I want is to die. To die!" He slumped in his throne, patting his sweaty face with a cloth.

Cortés leaves Tenochtitlan

Cortés Once Again in Cholula

Those Spaniards who were leaving bid the others farewell, exchanging *abrazos* with those staying behind. They took no Indians or necessities and left at once for Cholula. On the road, Cortés sent a Tlaxcaltecan emissary to ask their Senate for five thousand warriors.

The reply from Xicoténcatl brought by the same messenger was decisive:

"The elder Xicoténcatl, in accord with the four chieftains, says that if you want warriors for fighting against Mexicans, that is fine, but not against other *teules*. However, he will send food."

When Cortés' force reached Cholula, Juan Velázquez de León and Rangel, their troops and four horses were waiting. The combined forces numbered three-hundred-twenty soldiers and eight cavalry.

In front of all the captains, Cortés and Juan Velázquez de León embraced each other.

"Juan, I am grateful for your decision. I knew you were a gentleman of your word."

"And I have only one, Captain. I am with you and your mission, until we succeed or die."

"No doubt we will succeed and we will triumph. Narváez is the sort who naps."

"According to my information," said Velázquez de León, "he is now in Cempoala and on his arrival he confiscated the gold, jewelry and clothes that you gave the fat *cacique*, as well as the daughters of the chieftains that they had presented us."

Cortés shrugged. "That's the way Narváez is, arrogant and rebellious. If he is there, then Sandoval and all his soldiers will be waiting in Tampanquita and Mitlanguita, twelve leagues from Cempoala. We will send our scouts one day ahead into those areas to observe the Indians.

"I don't see Alvarado," observed Velázquez de León. "Did he stay in Temistitan as your surrogate?"

"Yes," said Cortés, "but I have been thinking that I left too small a force there."

"I think so, too," said Velázquez.

"Captain Rangel," Cortés ordered, "take a hundred men and return to Temistitan to reinforce Alvarado's garrison. The rest—march on!" The troops continued down the road.

Another Summons

When the force reached Quecholac, the scouts told Cortés that certain of Narváez's Spaniards under the command of Alonso de Mata, the scribe, had arrived to serve a summons.

They met on the road. Both Cortés and Mata dismounted.

"I came to find you, Captain Hernán Cortés."

"How may I help you?"

"I came in my capacity as a scribe to serve a formal summons upon you in the name of Pánfilo de Narváez," said Mata, shuffling his papers.

"As you may know, my friend, in my position as Captain General de la Villa Rica de la Vera Cruz, only a King's Scribe is able to serve me a summons. Do you have such a commission? Are you the Royal Scribe? If so, prove it!"

"Well. . . . I am Narváez's . . ."

"Then you can keep your papers. But, why don't we have something to eat?" After they had eaten, Cortés took the scribe aside.

". . . and I give you and your companions these jewels so that you will become familiar with the riches of these lands which we wish to colonize, instead of returning to Cuba. Give that message to your men and to Narváez. Tell him I will see him soon, so that we can resolve fully these matters." Mata and his comrades returned to Cempoala.

Cortés continued on, but in Atailicapan a storm delayed the march.

"I will write to Narváez," Cortés said to his scribe, "allowing him to select a location to meet with us where he may present his credentials. If he chooses not to do so, he should return to Cuba and not continue to go about agitating the people in this country. The captains and the soldiers' representatives will co-sign my letter. Father Olmedo, together with Usagre, will deliver it. They tell me that Usagre's brother is in charge of Narváez's artillery. Speak with him and present to him our warmest regards."

As Cortés finished the letter, he handed it to Father Olmedo. ". . . and make sure you persuade Narváez that this letter is a trick by my soldiers to set an ambush for me. This is what he is relying on."

Then he gave Usagre some gold chains. "Give these as mementos to your brother and to his closest friends, and tell him about the abundance of riches in this land. Tell him there is no reason to go back to Cuba."

As the storm continued, Cortés continued to explain his strategy: "Have Tovilla, the one who came with Rangel from Chinantla, come forward." When he appeared, Cortés told him, "Go at once to the Chinantecas, the Indians who use the long lances. Tell them they must make, very quickly, three hundred lances, even longer than their usual ones. Instead of flint, tell them to use copper on the point, with a barb, like this one." He gave Tovilla the lance. "Then rejoin us with the lances wherever you can."

He turned to the captains. "With these long lances, we will attack Narváez's horses, his chief advantage over us."

On the Road to Cempoala

Cortés' army continued its march toward Cempoala. At Huatusco, another of Narváez's emissaries arrived, along with the clerics Vergara, Juan de Léon and also Andrés de Duero, Narváez's secretary, who had been Diego Velázquez's secretary and Cortés' accomplice at his commissioning.

"Welcome, friend Duero, and you, too, Guevara. I suppose you have another charge of some sort. Come into my tent."

They dismounted and Guevara said: "Captain, Narváez sends you this letter."

"Save me the bother of reading it and just tell me what it says."

"Briefly, Narváez proposes that you deliver to him all the land conquered. In exchange for that, he will provide two ships and all the necessary provisions for you and your associates to go wherever you wish."

"Is that all my friend Narváez suggests?"

"He also proposes that you and he meet in some convenient place, each with a retinue of ten men, after exchanging safe conducts."

"Fine. I agree to meet with Narváez. On my part I will increase the number of safe conducts."

Narváez's men left and Cortés began to compile the list.

After a short while, Duero returned. "Captain, I see that fate has rewarded you and you have made an advantageous arrangement. I hope you will not forget our friendship, but I must remind you I am serving as Narváez's secretary."

"I shall bear that in mind, friend Duero. Tell me, whatever became of Amador de Lares?"

"He died lamenting that he would never see you again."

"Life is too fleeting, Duero. How would you feel about accepting Amador de Lares's share?"

"What can I say, Captain, other than to offer, as always, my friendship, intelligence reports and timely advice."

By those same representatives, Cortés dispatched his safe-conduct list to Narváez.

"Here is my safe-conduct list with the names left blank so Narváez may fill them in to his satisfaction. I shall expect his list in return and will not advance until I receive his decision."

Two days later, Father Olmedo returned from his assignment and asked urgently to speak with Cortés. "Captain, Andrés de Duero sent word by me that your meeting with Narváez will be an ambush. Do not depend on his word. Narváez is arrogant, and if not for Duero's intervention, I would be a prisoner, accused, if you can imagine it Captain, of corrupting the troops and officers with gold."

Cortés Signs the Summons

"Duero is a loyal friend. And his message is timely. This means war, Father, but I do not wish to bear the responsibility for it. Therefore, in my position as Captain General of the Villa Rica de la Vera Cruz, I will notify Narváez, in His Majesty's name, that he must not attempt to exert his authority in these lands we have already colonized. His followers must abstain from obeying Narváez's illegitimate authority and if they disobey this order, the responsibility for any deaths or injuries will be on the heads of the violators."

Cortés signed the indictment and sent it off with Rodrigo Álvaro Chico and Pedro Hernández, his adjutant and his scribe.

When they got to Cempoala and delivered the indictment, Narváez became enraged after reading it. He roared: "He must be crazy, this Cortés who has such impudence! Place those traitors in irons!"

"Place these traitors in shackles."

Sandoval Rejoins Cortés

After an inspection of his troops, Cortés resumed the march. Diego de Ordaz presented the report. "Captain, we are two hundred forty counting the drummer and fifer; five cavalry, including you; ten crossbowmen, seven musketeers and two smaller pieces of ordnance."

The small army continued its advance until it reached the village of Mictlanmautla, where they encountered Sandoval with the sixty available soldiers, who were recuperating at the Villa.

"Captain Cortés," Sandoval saluted him. "I present you with sixty loyal troops. I have left the others in Indian villages, those who are too old or wounded or unfit to come with us. I also command five soldiers, followers of Magistrate Ayllón. They escaped when they were sentenced by Narváez to imprisonment. We also brought a horse which we took from Salvatierra and two other soldiers who can pass for Indians."

"Now we will be more of a menace, since we have been so few," Cortés said. "What other news do you have of Narváez?"

"While you were on your journey here, he made the move from San Juan to Cempoala, where he is enjoying the climate. He infuriates the fat *cacique* and is always boasting how he is going to grab you by your ears, and other such insults. His soldiers are not used to hard work or inconveniences and the gold that you sent is breaking down their resistance. More of them wish to remain here to colonize than to fight against us and return to Cuba. Usagre is here with me. Let him tell you about his brother, the artilleryman."

Juan Velázquez de León

"Everything is fine," said Cortés. "We will advance until we set up camp at the Canoas river. I must ask a favor of you, Velázquez de León."

"I am at your command, Captain," he answered.

"Look, Juan, it will be a good idea for you to go to Narváez's camp wearing your gold chains, especially that 'Fanfarrona' that you wear on your shoulder. Speak to them about peace and show off your riches so your friends can see how prosperous you are. Then they may feel like staying here. Check with Duero and ask if he has any messages for us."

"I understand what you expect of me. I will carry it out to the letter."

On the 28th of May, Juan left the camp on the back of his grey mare and soon arrived at Cempoala. The Indians recognized him and ran to tell the Spaniards.

At a slow walk, Velázquez entered the village, flaunting his horse and his gold chains. Narváez had been notified, but he left his quarters still straightening his clothes. It was not his habit to rise very early.

With a pleasant expression, Narváez greeted Velázquez.

"Welcome, Juan Velázquez de León, I'm pleased to see you. I blame you for not coming sooner. Surely, you must know how anxious I was to see you and speak with you. Now, come to my quarters and share some breakfast and some hot chocolate, which they prepare here very nicely."

"My dear Narváez, I do not wish to upset you, but I must leave soon. I have come here to greet you and to try and negotiate peace and friendship between you and Cortés, who are both my friends and who should be able to live together."

"Peace, friendship and understanding with a traitor?" sneered Narváez.

"Cortés is no traitor, but a good servant to His Majesty. I beg Your Grace not to use such words in my presence."

"Very well, in consideration of you, I will keep my opinions to myself. Even so, come and refresh yourself in my quarters."

While this was going on, officers and soldiers of the camp recognized and made sure it was Juan Velázquez de León. They came to greet him, pat him on the back and to admire his rich gold jewelry, especially the "Fanfarrona" chain wound around his arm four times.

The display of riches had its effect.

While they were breakfasting, Narváez said to Velázquez de León: "I have a special order from your relative, Diego Velázquez, to relieve you from Cortés' force and to offer you the post of the second in command of this camp as the highest ranking officer."

"For God's sake, Narváez, I am a gentleman and man of honor. I have given my word to Cortés."

"You have no duty to keep your promise to someone who did not respect his own word with your uncle."

"My word is mine and I will uphold it. There is no point in beseeching me."

Narváez was called aside by Hernández de Mata, who said, "*Señor capitán*, it would be a good idea to seize Velázquez de León and the other representatives of Cortés, especially since Velázquez is a high-ranking officer and his loss would weaken Cortés' ranks. Besides, he is reluctant to help us."

"Your suggestion is enticing, but before we follow it, let me consult with Duero and the priests, Guevara and Bermúdez."

Duero's reaction was decisive: "We think it would be a serious error if Your Grace would treat Cortés' men disrespectfully when he received us with such ceremony. Moreover, *Don* Juan is a famous nobleman. If he were not treated honorably, it could cause serious repercussions. On the other hand, in order to discourage the impetuous Cortés, we suggest you display the force of your troops and artillery. He only has a few men to confront us."

"That's an excellent suggestion," Narváez declared.

He went back to his breakfast and when they had finished, he invited Juan Velázquez de León to observe the review of his troops: more than one thousand soldiers with eighty cavalry, eighty musketeers and one hundred twenty crossbowmen and about forty cannon of various types, twenty-three of them large caliber.

Velázquez commented: "What great power Your Grace displays. May the good Lord continue to increase it."

Narváez commented pompously, "So, you see, Your Grace, if I had wished to fight against Cortés, I could have easily made him my prisoner along with all the others with him."

"Your Grace can be sure that the soldiers who are with him know how to defend themselves quite well!"

After the parade, Velázquez de León had a brief word with Duero, then took leave of his friends and Narváez himself and began his return journey. He found Cortés' troops camped by the Canoas river. And Tovilla had delivered the Chinantecans' lances.

That afternoon, the 28th of May, was sultry and rainy.

"Welcome, Juan, we were waiting for you before we continued the march."

"Captain, I carried out your orders. Narváez's men know about the riches and splendor of this land and they have an ardent wish to experience it firsthand. He has a strong force, but Narváez is over-confident and lazy."

"Yes, he does love his siestas and a good night's sleep."

"I did not see much esprit de corps among the soldiers, either. According to what Duero told me, they will camp on the outskirts of Cempoala to await us, placing the artillery in front and the foot soldiers and horses to the rear."

"What an idiot! That is a cadet's strategy! So, let us proceed quickly, keeping as much as possible under cover until we come to the Chachalacas river. We must stay alert until we find the right moment to surprise them."

They halted about one league from Cempoala, well hidden in the heavy brush.

In the meantime, Narváez left Cempoala with his army in a heavy downpour. He was mounted on his horse. To his captains, he said, "It's a joke to come out here in this torrent with this mighty force just waiting for Cortés to attack. Even though the Cempoaltecans and their *cacique* say he is close, why should we believe them?"

"That *Cortesillo* and his puny force would never dare to confront us. It is also ridiculous to endure this rain," said Salvatierra. "We do not need to go any farther through all this mud."

Nevertheless, they went on, struggling, until the army bivouacked a quarter of a league from Cempoala. There they stopped to wait out the storm. Everyone was grouchy and blasphemous. Still, the rain went on. So did the daylight, and soon late afternoon darkness began to frustrate the officers, soldiers and even Narváez.

"It is pointless to wait," Salvatierra said. "*Cortesillo* is not coming. We have already eaten one wet meal, Captain Narváez, are we going to have a wet supper, too?"

A little later, Salvatierra resumed his tirade, "Sir, how can Cortés dare to confront us with the small force he has? Would he dare to invade our camp, just because the fat Indian said so?"

"You are right!" Narváez said. "This is an insult."

"It is ridiculous to stay here in this downpour, waiting for that tiny bunch of *Cortesillos*. Leave forty cavalry here and we will place sentinels on the perimeter."

Cortés Prepares the Attack

Everyone gathered to hear the report from Cortés' spies, who quickly related their information. Night had fallen; Cortés' men were also being soaked by rain. Hidden in the brush, they waited anxiously. Secretively, Cortés summoned his officers to a clearing.

Mounted, he spoke to them: *"Señores* and *compadres.* Now we are faced with the unpleasant task of fighting our own brothers, through no fault of ours, but because of the stubbornness of Diego Velázquez and his toady, Narváez. Remember, the Governor only wanted to extract riches and I insisted we must colonize. Thanks to my persistence, we have occupied this country. Narváez's arrival threw everything into chaos even before he disembarked. They are calling us traitors and sent word to Moctezuma—not words from a wise captain—but from the agitator himself. He even arrested His Majesty's magistrate and Narváez declares war against us without giving us quarter or allowing surrender, as if we were Moors.

"So we must fight—for our honor and for our lives, because if we fall into Narváez's hands, all our efforts on His Majesty's behalf would become gross violations of law. They would initiate lawsuits against us, charging that we have robbed and killed, then they would strip us of everything we have gained here. So, as loyal *caballeros*, we are obliged to restore His Majesty's honor and our own and to defend our houses and *haciendas* in Cuba.

"However, *amigos,* I am only one man and I can only do what one man can do. Some of you have been in favor of exploring this country and others wish only to return to Cuba. I have not accepted that choice. Each of you has the right to fight or to demand peace. Each may express his wish and I will not stand in his way. Informants have told me that in our adversary's camp, there has been talk that you are deceiving me and wish to put me in their hands. Finally, each one say what he thinks. Now is the time to find out—since there are so few of us—if we fight or surrender."

"We are with you!" they shouted. "Long live Cortés!"

Then Velázquez de León spoke up: "Captain, we are all with you and will obey your orders. Just tell us what do to."

Thrilled by the response, Cortés said to his troops: "I will recite a verse that comes from Castile: 'Whoever goads the ass dies with him.' My opinion is: 'Long live the Conquest.'"

"Yes, yes," they shouted. "Long live Cortés and death to that ass Narváez and Diego Velázquez who goads him on."

They lifted Cortés onto their shoulders in the middle of the jubilation as the rain poured down.

After setting him down, the men began to build fires so they could roast some deer, but Cortés stopped them.

"No fires; they will reveal our location. I know I am asking you to expose yourselves to great perils, but only with prudence and boldness can we overcome such a great number. Remember, it is customary among warriors to say: 'At dawn, fight the enemy,' which is fine, but if we had been discovered, they would merely wait until dawn and attack us. Since they have not noticed us yet and in this terrible weather, we would not be able to sleep anyway, so why not attack them tonight, rather than wasting time standing here in the rain? Do you agree?"

"Yes, yes. Order the advance!" they shouted.

"All right, then that's what we will do. You, Pizarro, take sixty men at a fast pace, and without letting them detect you, capture Narváez's twenty-three heavy cannon and aim them toward the plaza. Use your new lances against the cavalry as I have shown you by knocking down the rider between two of you. They thrust their spears singlehanded. Protected by the darkness, smash through their line of fire and thrust your spears at the artilleryman. Our spies tell us most of the soldiers are in the three temples surrounded by their officers. Narváez is in the main temple."

Then Cortés added: "You, Sandoval, with eighty men take the temple where Narváez has his quarters and seize him or kill him. The other two temples are not important and I know why. You, Juan Velázquez de León, command fifty men to prevent any reinforcements from reaching the temple where Narváez is housed. The rest of you come with me to help whomever needs it. As we will be moving through dense underbrush to capture the forty cavalry Narváez has stationed there, it's useless to take our own horses because they have so many. For our password, use *'Espíritu Santo.'*

"Forward! Remember, it is better to die valiantly than to live in shame. Let us go!"

The Attack

Stealthily, they left for Cempoala, arriving about midnight. In the meantime, discouraged, Narváez's army returned to Cempoala. They were all drenched and griping.

When the fat *cacique* saw them returning in so disorderly a fashion, he said to Narváez: "What can you do with such a slipshod army? Do you think Malinche and his *teules* are like you? Whether you realize it or not, he will come here and kill all of you!"

"Shut up, you fat buffoon! You do not know what you are talking about!" barked Salvatierra.

Pánfilo de Narváez laughed at the *cacique*.

"Calm down. *'Cortesillo'* and his ragged band are probably huddling together out there," he waved his hand toward the wilderness. He turned to his men: "I will give two thousand pesos to any man who kills Cortés, if he dares to come here," Narváez said, grinning. "To pacify the *cacique*, we will leave twenty cavalry on guard and sentries at the temple where the officers sleep. The artillerymen will sleep next to their cannon and post sentries and lookouts on the road. Our password is *'Santa María.'*"

Narváez went up the temple steps into his own quarters. He took off his armor, dried himself, changed into his night shirt and went to bed.

Out on the road, Cortés' men surprised two lookouts, capturing one. The other escaped, dashing back and shouting, "To arms! To arms! Cortés is coming!"

"Charge!" shouted Cortés. "Sandoval's and Pizarro's foot soldiers go first. We will follow."

All of them took off after the sentry. The river was rising because of the heavy rains, so their armor prevented them from catching him and he got away.

The rain continued. The downpour and the cry "to arms!" took by surprise Narváez's over-confident and unenthusiastic army, which replied with the password *"Santa María!"*

Out of the darkness, running at full speed and shouting *"Espíritu Santo,"* Cortés' men arrived. Narváez's artillerymen tried to fire their large cannon, but only four ignited, killing three of Cortés' men. With their long spears, the rest knocked over the artillerymen, who failed to hit their targets (or perhaps did not wish to). Soon, the contingent led by Pizarro captured the cannon and defended themselves against

Narváez's foot soldiers. The twenty cavalrymen, the outpost guards, confused by the rain and darkness and unable to organize a counterattack, were coming and going—pell-mell. They hurled their lances at Cortés' soldiers. The aggressors, using the barbs on their longer lances, snagged and hooked Narváez's riders and brought them to the ground. The riderless horses added to the confusion. Many lancers could not remount because their cinches were loose.

Up in his temple, Narváez dressed, awakened by the shout of "to arms," and as he donned his armor, shouted: "*Santa María*! Captains! Come to me!"

Sandoval, with his men and their long lances, advanced as fast as they could among the horses. At the base of Narváez's temple, they encountered only the enemy sentinels. The rest of Narváez's troops were elsewhere or at the encampment. The guards fired arrows and gunshots at anyone running in the darkness, wounding some, including their own men.*

Leading his soldiers, Sandoval scrambled quickly up the temple steps. The great length of the enemy lances surprised Narváez's men, many of whom were pulled down with the barb and hurled down the steps. Even so, they regrouped themselves and succeeded in forcing Sandoval's men to retreat two flights of steps.

Attack at night during a rain

---

* Cortés received support from an unexpected source. The air was filled with *cocuyos*—a large beetle which emits intense phosphorescent light from its body, strong enough to read by it. These wandering fires, seen in the dark, were perceived by the besieged as an army firing muskets! (Prescott, William H., *The History of the Conquest of Mexico*, New York: Modern Library, 1936, 203)

Meantime, Cortés and his army reached the artillery, shouting: "*Espíritu Santo*! The artillery has fallen to Cortés!" Cortés shouted to Pizarro's men. "Hurry to help Sandoval at the temple. We will take charge of the cannon."

Juan Velázquez de León's men confronted those in the encampment and kept them from reinforcing Narváez while Pizarro's foot soldiers hurried to help Sandoval, who had rallied his forces and already had begun to ascend the temple steps.

Narváez, who was distinguished by his great bulk and squeaky voice, shouted: "*Santa María*." He had not managed to put on his helmet and was fighting without it which gave Sandoval, who reached the top of the temple, the opportunity to strike Narváez with his lance, hitting him in the eye.

"*Santa María*, save me! They have killed me and plucked out my eye!" screamed Narváez.

Then Cortés' soldiers, who were already fighting in the temple, shouted, "Victory! Victory for all in the name of *Espíritu Santo*. Narváez is dead. Victory, victory for Cortés! Narváez is dead."

Narváez and his men sought shelter in the temple and defended themselves there until the carpenter, Martín López, who was tall, took a firebrand from the torch and set fire to the straw roof. Narváez's men burst from the temple, choking and reeling down the steps. Among them was the fat *cacique*, who had been wounded. Farfán shackled Narváez.

With twenty men at his side, Cortés maneuvered rapidly, helping anyone who needed it. To some he ordered: "Attack that group with lances! Help the others!" He was everywhere.

"Scribe: Tell those men in Salvatierra's camp to submit themselves to the authority of the King and in his name, to the Chief Justice, Hernán Cortés."

When he descended the steps of the main temple, breathless and sweating, Cortés asked: "What happened to Narváez? What happened to Narváez?"

"Right here, and well guarded," said Sandoval.

"Listen closely, Sandoval, my son, don't leave him alone; you and your companions must not let him loose."

"Is it all right for the surgeon to tend to Narváez's wound?" asked Sandoval.

"Absolutely!"

Finally, the rain stopped, the moon appeared and little by little, all of Narváez's men surrendered.

Stealthily, Cortés approached the site where they were dressing Narváez's wound. Everyone cried in a chorus, "Here is Cortés."

Narváez, in his high-pitched whine, exclaimed: "*Señor Capitán* Cortés, you have won a great victory over me and you have me, personally, as your prisoner."

Cortés replied: "Many thanks to God Almighty that he gave it to me and to those valiant gentlemen and friends of mine who played such a vital part in it. We have overcome one of the lesser episodes in this land we call New Spain, by seizing you and destroying your forces. Do you still think it was wise to have the audacity to seize His Majesty's magistrate?"

Cortés turned his back and strode away.

As he left, a soldier said to him: "The fat *cacique* is wounded."

"Be sure his wounds are tended and treat him well."

Cortés turned to his aides. "Cristóbal de Olid and Diego de Ordaz, go where the forty cavalrymen are waiting and win them over to our cause. Then bring them here and we will accept them as our comrades."

In the morning, Olid and Ordaz returned with the cavalrymen, who came before Cortés and knelt down to kiss his hand. Among them, grinning broadly, was Andrés de Duero.

The date was May 29, 1520.

One of the Negroes who had arrived with Narváez shouted: "Just imagine, not even the Romans could achieve such a feat! Long live Cortés! Long live Cortés!"

Meanwhile, the kettle drummer was beating the drums with such enthusiasm that Cortés ordered him to stop.

By mid-morning, all the resistance had ceased and Sandoval came to ask the Captain-General: "Captain, what are we going to do with Narváez?"

"Keep him prisoner in Villa Rica!" one soldier cried.

"He should be hanged!" said Cristóbal de Olid.

"I am the Chief Magistrate of His Majesty," Cortés said.

"What shall we do with his officers?" asked Sandoval.

"Those who swear allegiance to our cause are to be freed with arms. Any weapons we captured must be returned, too. They are not war booty. Whatever happened to Salvatierra?"

"His men say that in all their lives, they never saw a man less prepared to fight or so afraid of death. When he heard we were victorious, he became sick to his stomach."

"Imprison Salvatierra with Narváez. You, Francisco de Lugo, take two hundred men to Villa Rica for the garrison. There, order them to remove from the ships the sails, rudders and compasses, and the ship captains should come ashore to swear allegiance. You, Pedro Caballero, will be Admiral of the Sea."

The next day, Cortés assembled his officers and said to them: "*Señores compañeros*. This victory, God's work, has been ours. We returned to establish sovereignty over this land and how wonderful that now we may continue to explore. . . ."

News Arrives from Tenochtitlan

They were still celebrating their victory when two Tlaxcaltecan runners arrived at Cempoala, asking for Cortés.

"Malinche! Malinche! *El Tonatiuh* [Pedro de Alvarado] sends urgent word that there is insurrection in Tenochtitlan. He is blockaded with all of his soldiers and in danger of being annihilated. He needs your help!"

"When? Why?" asked Cortés incredulously.

"At the fiesta of Toxcatl, the *Tonatiuh* killed many nobles and chieftains and the city is revolting. . . ."

This was the setting: In the middle of May in Tenochtitlan, they celebrate their most important religious festival, the Toxcatl, in honor of Tezcatlipoca and Huitzilopochtli. During the complicated ceremonies, two young men, chosen for their perfect bodies, are sacrificed. Moctezuma had asked Alvarado's permission to celebrate the fiesta and it was granted, but without human sacrifices.

Slaughter at Toxcatl

It all began on the 19th of May with the formation of an idol composed of a herbal paste mixed with human blood. The main event began very early the next day with the dance of the serpent, which featured four or five hundred unarmed noble warriors, who held hands as they moved to the drum beats. The ceremony would end with the sacrifices of these exquisite young men amid singing, the burning of incense and the clamor of musical instruments.

They begin the slaughter of Toxcatl

The ceremony began in the central plaza, while Alvarado and his armed soldiers watched. Also present were three- or four- thousand spectators, eventual participants in the festivities. While the dance progressed, Alvarado's soldiers closed off the entrances to the plaza: the Águila, the Acatliyacapan and the Tezcoacoc, so no one could leave.

Suddenly, the Spaniards charged at the drummer and cut off both his arms with one stroke and with another decapitated him. As the slaughter continued, the Spaniards killed the naked Indians and exposed their entrails with deep slashes.

Those who tried to escape, they ran through with spears; those who tried to scale the walls, they jabbed with lances. Every corpse was stripped of jewels and gold ornaments.

The blood flowed like water. Everywhere, the Spaniards searched for survivors among the communal houses and among the dead.

When the citizens found out what had happened, there was an uproar.

"Mexican captains . . . assemble! To me! Everyone bring arms and insignias, shields, darts. Come quickly! Hurry! All the officers are dead! They have killed our warriors! They have been annihilated! Oh, the Mexican captains!"

Rebellion after the Slaughter

Then throughout the city there was an uproar as the people shrieked, beating at their lips with their palms. All of the Mexican officers who had survived assembled. Soon the battle began as everyone revolted against the Spaniards. They hurled darts, lances, and light spears with which they hunted birds, so many it seemed "as if it were a yellow cape of reed unfolding against the Spaniards."

As the attack commenced, the Spaniards quickly crowded together and retreated to the Axayácatl Palace.

Juan Álvarez, who was supervising the recovery of his soldier's weapons, noticed the crowd of Indians and immediately ordered the Spaniards to withdraw to their garrison. The last one to leave was Alvarado, who suffered a blow to his head. As blood streamed down his face, he shouted:

"Retreat and give the devil his due!"

"What is happening, sir?" a soldier asked.

Annoyed, Alvarado said: "I swear to God that we have defeated these sly Indians! They were planning to attack us, so we struck first. 'One mean trick will bring another; the first one to strike, wins.' We killed thousands! Now, withdraw!"

The Spaniards confined their troops to the barracks. A throng of furious Aztec warriors rushed toward the palace, from which the Spaniards defended themselves with cannon fire, muskets and crossbows.

Meantime, the dead Indians were removed from the temple patios. As families identified their relatives, a great wailing arose. After the bodies were taken to their homes, everyone gathered at the Sacred Patio for cremation of the corpses and religious rites.

The bloody massacre lasted an entire day and all night the dead were cremated.

After the sunset, at Alvarado's suggestion, Moctezuma appeared on the roof of the Axayácatl Palace and through Itzcóatl, his spokesman, said: "Mexicans, tenochcatlatilolcas: I speak in the name of Your King Moctezuma. All Mexicans hear me. I do not want you to continue fighting. Put down your shields and arrows in peace. The old people who deserve our respect will only suffer, as will the children. So stop fighting. Moctezuma is in shackles."

A Mexican officer shouted:

"If you wish to have peace, free Moctezuma."

"Yes! Yes! Yes!" they all shouted.

Alvarado placed his dagger against Moctezuma's breast and said: "If you don't stop the war, I will kill you on this very spot!"

A flurry of arrows and rocks forced the Spaniards to leave the roof.

"Kill that weakling and free him from his duty."

Thus began the methodical siege of the Axayácatl Palace.

The Mexicans no longer brought food for the Spaniards; and guarded closely the palace entrances. They raised the bridges over the canals, and continued daily attacks. To get drinking water, the Spaniards dug a well.

Cortés Returns

At last, the news of Cortés' victory over Narváez reached Tenochtitlan. When Moctezuma heard it, he ordered his officers to moderate the war against Alvarado and sent messengers to Cortés complaining about Alvarado's actions.

The messengers reached him as Cortés was preparing to leave for Tenochtitlan.

"Captain," said the assistant. "Moctezuma's messengers are here complaining about Alvarado."

"Tell them I will not listen to messengers from anyone who plotted with Narváez. When I return to Temistitan, I will look after things. Have our couriers take this letter to Alvarado, informing him of our victory and that he must be patient until I get back."

From horseback, Cortés called together Narváez's defeated soldiers. "Men, although yesterday we were enemies, we are all Spaniards and vassals of the same King. As you know, our companions in Temistitan were attacked by the Indians whom Narváez incited. Let us forget our differences. Join me to free our people and to save the riches we have accumulated. If with four hundred men and thirteen horses, we conquered this land, now it will be even easier as we have many more men, ninety horses, plenty of ammunition and many arquebusiers."

"You can count on us! On to Temistitan!" shouted Narváez's men.

"We will prepare to march at once. You, Rangel, will remain in command of the Villa Rica with three hundred men, one hundred of which will stay here in Cempoala."

During the first days of June, the return was organized and with all possible speed the army set out for Tenochtitlan.

When they reached Tlaxcala, the four chieftains offered them one thousand warriors whom Cortés accepted gratefully.

"We will enter through Texcoco," Cortés decided, "and the thousand Tlaxcaltecans will make up the rear guard." When they got to Texcoco, they found the city deserted. Only two Spaniards were guarding the place—one was Cortés' secretary, Pedro Hernández.

"What happened?" asked Cortés. "Are we still fighting them?"

"Yes, Captain, some of us have been killed and almost all are injured and we have no more provisions. But since they found out about your victory thirteen days ago, and that you were returning, the attacks have diminished."

252

"Apparently, our return was enough to pacify the rebels," said Cortés, proud and vain.

When they entered Tenochtitlan from the north on the road from Tepeyac, one of the horsemen fell in the water because the leg of his horse slipped between two girders of the bridge.

Botello, the astrologer, mused: "A bad omen. This entry into Temistitan begins with a misstep. It would be better if we did not enter the city and if all our men came out."

¡Mal agüero ... Más valdría no entráramos y ellos salieran...

"A bad sign. It would be better if we did not enter and all our men came out."

The throngs who usually milled about in the city were nowhere to be seen.

"Another bad omen. It's a bad sign to see the city deserted," said Botello.

Cortés was aware of the effect of Botello's observations. "Yes, my friends, our work is done and if the Indians have not recognized it, it is from fear and the shame of having dared to rise against us. With compensation, we will reconcile them and they will be our friends and all our efforts will bear fruit."

Thus, on the 24th of June, 1520, Cortés returned to enter the Great Tenochtitlan. From the temples, the Indian officers saw him make the entry into their city and smiled.

"Now they have entered the trap. . . ."

Cortés knocked on the closed door of the Axayácatl Palace.

From behind the wall, Pedro de Alvarado called out : "Who is there?"

"Hernán Cortés."

Alvarado asked, "Are you as free and powerful as when you left?"

"Yes and also with victories and reinforcements!" answered Cortés.

The palace doors were thrown open and a long line of military men and equipment entered—eight hundred soldiers, ninety horses with twenty-three large cannon and many smaller ones. Bringing up the rearguard were one thousand Tlaxcaltecans. Among them, and almost the last, was the Negro agitator from

Narváez's forces, who could not manage the last few steps—he fell to the ground, suffering from smallpox, and there he remained until some Indians came to see what happened and removed him.

Alvarado, standing, handed over the keys to the garrison.

Cortés jumped down from his horse, greeted Alvarado with an *abrazo*, quite formally, and said dryly: "We are here!"

Later, when the two were alone, Cortés said: "By my conscience, Pedro! What have you done? You saw they were disarmed."

With his head down, Alvarado answered.

"Captain! The Indians conspired to kill us, using their fiestas as a pretext and they had their arms hidden in the temple. . . ."

"But I have been told that they asked your permission to have that particular dance and the other dances and that you granted the permission."

"That's true, but we had to attack them when they least expected it and not let them attack us as Moctezuma had announced they would."

"You have committed an unpardonable act and it has been a great madness on your part."

"Captain, it was similar to what happened in Cholula."

"It was a madness. But now is not the time to discuss it. Now is the time to get out of this place."

Doña Marina waited until Alvarado left, then she went in to speak to Cortés: "The lord Moctezuma wishes to greet you."

"Tell him I do not greet or speak with a wretch who conspired secretly with Narváez. Besides, now he does not even give us food."

"My lord," *Doña* Marina said, "temper your ire and consider how good and honorable this King has been to you. He even gave you his daughter."

"That bastard can go to hell!" grunted Cortés.

Cuitláhuac

eñor Malinche, we are pleased you have returned and that *Tonatiuh* is no longer in command," said a Mexican emissary to a disgruntled Cortés.

"Well, I do not understand your 'pleasure' when you not only do not feed us, but have closed the market to us," said Cortés snidely.

"Malinche, it was only done to placate the people who were very upset. But now everything is settled, thanks to the grace of Moctezuma, who, when we spoke to him, said now was the time to seek peace."

Cortés meditated a moment and replied: "So be it! You speak to Moctezuma. I do not wish to speak to him."

When the emissaries returned from Moctezuma's quarters, through *Doña Marina* they said to Cortés:

"The lord Moctezuma sends word that he agrees with you and the market will reopen. So that the people will believe it, Cuitláhuac should speak out and through him there will be a better understanding of the situation."

After vaccilating for a moment, Cortés answered: "All right! Alvarado! Free Cuitláhuac. And you listen! If this city does not quiet down and if they do not reopen the market, I will punish your impudence," he said to the emissaries.

Cuitláhuac immediately gathered the noble Aztec warriors, among whom was the bellicose presence of Cuauhtémoc.

"What do you decree, Cuitláhuac?" asked the young Cuauhtémoc.

"That the war should continue, from this very day!"

He immediately summoned Tlatocan to designate who would lead the warriors, saying, "as Moctezuma is incommunicado and besides no one pays any attention to him. Even Malinche insults him and he himself says he wishes to die."

That day, Cuitláhuac was elected chief pending the formal ceremonies to elect *Uei Tlatoani.** Once he was designated, he sat on his throne and shouted the war cry, beating his lips:

"War and death for the *teules*."

"War and death!"

"War and death," the whole city responded.

---

* *Uei Tlatoani*, Supreme Chief of Mexico, was the Great Lord or literally "the great one who speaks" and as such enjoyed universal respect.

"War and death to the teules."

From the palace, Cortés and his men heard the shouting and looked out to see what had happened. Coming toward them across the plaza, running very fast, they saw a wounded Spaniard being pursued by Indians. They opened the gate and a few soldiers went out to him.

"It is Juárez, our man who stayed in Tacuba with our Indian allies and Moctezuma's daughter," commented a soldier.

"Captain Cortés, the entire road from Tacuba and all the streets are crowded with people who shout 'Death to the *teules*,'" said a runner. "They captured our Indian servants and Moctezuma's daughter and I escaped from the canoe in which they were taking me to be sacrificed. They are coming to attack us!"

"Diego de Ordaz," shouted Cortés. "Go with four hundred men and twenty horsemen to see what is happening."

Ordaz left. He had hardly entered the city when he was attacked by a great many warriors. From the house tops, the streets, the canals, they fired arrows and darts.

When more than ten Spaniards were killed and many had been wounded, including Ordaz, the Spaniards retreated to the fortification, which they found besieged. Totally surrounded, they had to open a path to enter the palace whose patios were so full of rocks and arrows that they were hardly able to walk.

The Aztecs set fire to the building. To avoid the flames, Cortés knocked down a wall, at great risk, so the artillerymen, crossbowmen and musketeers could try to hold back the assailants. There were so many of them that when the cannon shot opened lanes in the Indian ranks, these were immediately filled with more warriors. This battle raged all day until nightfall, when the attacks finally stopped.

Many Spaniards were wounded, including Cortés, who was hit by a stone and broke two fingers on his left hand. The Spaniards spent the night tending to their wounds.

The following day, the 26th of June, the slaughter resumed. Again, cannon shot made breaches that the Aztec multitudes soon closed, shooting arrows and darts. That day, twelve Spaniards were killed and many were wounded.

The Wooden Machines*

While the fight continued, Cortés decided to build three wooden "machines" to be placed on rollers, which could advance toward the houses and demolish them. The rubble would be used to fill in the canals so the horses could pass more easily. Twenty Spaniards manned each machine. That day, the 27th of June, the conquerors stayed in their quarters and spent their time building these machines, while the Mexicans shouted insults and the rock slingers and archers assaulted the walls. Every Indian who fell was immediately replaced.

Considering the great force of the Indian attacks, Father Olmedo suggested to Cortés: "It is a good idea if Moctezuma, himself, would go up to the terrace to calm the warriors. Why don't you ask him to do this?"

"I will never speak to him again. You and Cristóbal de Olid do it."

In response to that request, the unfortunate Moctezuma, now the deposed, *Uei Tlatoani*, answered Father Olmedo through Marina: "I had already made up my mind it would be useless to use my influence to end this war. They have already named another lord, Cuitláhuac, as the ruler and they have resolved that none of you should leave this city alive. So I believe you all have to die . . . as I will die . . . and nothing matters to me any more."

"For everyone's sake, go out and speak!" Cristóbal de Olid cried impatiently, unsheathing his sword and threatening him with it.

Moctezuma shrugged skeptically, but went up to the roof accompanied by Itzcóatl. A great barrage of arrows greeted him.

---

* A military machine of Cortés' own invention, called a *manta*, based on the mantelets used in wars of the Middle Ages. It consisted of a tower made of light beams and planks, having two chambers, one over the other, filled with musketeers. The sides had loop holes from which to fire on the enemy. They protected the troops against missiles hurled from the terraces. Three were built, which rested on rollers and had strong ropes attached, by which they were to be drawn along the streets by Tlaxcalan Indians.

Moctezuma Stoned

All he could manage to say was "Tenochcas. . . ." when the young Cuauhtémoc, who was leading the warriors assaulting the walls, in an angry voice, shouted: "What can that weakling, Moctezuma, do, whom the Spaniards have turned into a weak woman?" He fired an arrow that struck a Spanish shield.

A rain of arrows and darts fell on the group and three stones struck the ex-*Tlatoani*; a large one hit him on the head. Semi-conscious, Moctezuma was carried to his quarters. Three days later he died, but no one really knew the cause of his death.*

On the fifth day of the siege, the 28th of June, Cortés ordered: "Let us prepare with the wooden engines our retreat from here to Tacuba, which is the closest mainland town. The machines will go out first and from them we will destroy the houses and use the rubble to fill in the canals so we can leave."

He ordered early departure and the engines began the march. To the amazement of the Tenochcas [Mexicans] they approached the first houses, but there was such a heavy barrage of stones hurled at them that the Indians halted the engines' advance. The Spaniards became frightened and at noon, after much fierce fighting, were forced to return to the garrison very discouraged.

That afternoon, the Indians sealed their success in one audacious move by taking over the *teocalli* in front of the Spaniards' quarters. Five hundred nobles with arms, rocks, provisions and water climbed to the top of the temple and from there attacked the Spaniards very successfully.

When Cortés realized the advantage of their position, he ordered his steward: "Escobar, with one hundred soldiers, musketeers, crossbowmen and soldiers with lances and swords, go up to capture the *teocalli*. Not only can they attack us from there, but they are overly proud of their position."

Three times Escobar tried to ascend the temple and was driven back, in the presence of the Indian armies and the whole city. The Spaniards shot their bows and muskets; from the top, the enemy hurled arrows, rocks and wooden logs.

Realizing that not only the position but his prestige was at stake, Cortés, whose left hand was still injured, resolved personally to participate in the fracas. He directed

---

* Some say the wounds were superficial and that Moctezuma could have recovered, but he pulled off the bandages and said he wanted to die.

them to tie his shield to his left hand. "Ordaz, with the horses and soldiers, circle the temple to keep reinforcements away from those on top. Come with me, anyone who dares to capture this temple where they have removed the cross and now jeer at Our Lady."

By courageous effort, at a cost of forty-six Spanish lives and many wounded, Cortés took the *teocalli*. The Aztecs began to drop down from terrace to terrace "like ants." At the base, the Spaniards and Tlaxcaltecans who were protecting that area attacked them and a great butchery ensued. The struggle lasted three hours. Cortés ordered the temples set ablaze.

After the *teocalli* was captured, hostilities ceased for a bit. Cortés took advantage of this to ask for a parley with the Mexican captains, among whom was Cuauhtémoc, who approached him.

Through *Doña* Marina, Cortés said: "Look, you cannot defeat us. We have caused you great losses. Moreover, we could destroy this city, but we don't wish to. Let there be peace."

Young Cuauhtémoc answered: "We know all too well the damage you have caused, but we are resolved that all of us should die so that we may destroy you and your forces. There are thousands of us to every one of your men, so you will be defeated first and will never leave here. All of the bridges have been removed and you do not have any food and soon will have no water.

"Until your death or mine!" he shouted.

The fighting went on.

"Tenochcas!" [the natives of Tenochtitlan]

259

The Death of Moctezuma

That night, Father Olmedo spoke with *Doña* Marina: "Moctezuma and Itzcóatl just died."

"As a result of the blows from the stones?"

"I have never seen stones as lethal as if they were knives. It's better to assume that than to try to find out the exact reason. I will ask Cortés what we should do with the bodies," he said.

After speaking to Cortés, he said: "He says we should lay them at the edge of the water and see if this will distract the Indians."

That night, they removed the bodies. They were left near a large stone shaped like a turtle in a place named Teoyac.

The next day, the Aztecs discovered the dead and there was a great sound of shouting and wailing. The bodies were cremated. As the body of Moctezuma was consumed by the fire, an old Indian meditated: "That miserable man inspired fear in everybody. . . . He was venerated in the whole world. And now his scorched flesh stinks."

They take away the cadaver of Moctezuma

260

On learning of Moctezuma's death, Cuitláhuac immediately convoked the Council. "Nobles," he said, "the lord Moctezuma has died at the hands of the *teules*, who threw his body in Teoyac along with Itzcóatl's, as if they were garbage."

"Immediately, we ought to elect an *Uei Tlatoani* according to our laws."

"Only Cuitláhuac can lead us!" cried out Cuauhtémoc.

"Only Cuitláhuac," agreed the Council.

So, in a very brief ceremony, by acclamation Cuitláhuac was elected *Uei Tlatoani*.

"To sanctify the ceremony, we need our High Priest whom the *teules* have as prisoner," observed the oldest member of the Council.

"I suggest a commission ask Malinche to free him in exchange for a truce and peace talks," suggested Cuauhtémoc.

"Do it," ordered Cuitláhuac.

Sixth and Seventh Day of the Siege

On the sixth day of the siege the Spaniards, finding little resistance, with the aid of the Tlaxcaltecans, left the garrison, determined to fill in four water openings with debris from the barricades and houses, which they destroyed and burned. Cortés left forces to defend them. The Aztecs' attacks were not very vigorous, as they were preoccupied by the election of Cuitláhuac.

On the seventh day, the 30th of June, Cortés and the cavalry were able to reach Tacuba on the mainland. A group of Indians approached him stating they wanted a parley. He returned with two of the horsemen.

"Malinche," they said to him, "we will agree to a truce if you will free the High Priest who is your prisoner and then we all will discuss a peace treaty."

After consulting with his captains, Cortés said: "Yesterday and today those crazy people's attacks have lessened and are not as furious. It seems they wish to have peace. I believe we can free the priest whom they request. It costs us nothing. Are you not of the same opinion?"

The captains agreed.

"All right," Cortés said to the Indian delegation. "Free him!"

Entirely satisfied, he entered his quarters. He was eating when his steward, very upset, interrupted him.

"The Indians are again attacking and have taken over the bridges. Those on the mainland are cut off from us."

"They tricked us and have separated us from our men who remained in Tlacopan," shouted Cortés.

"My lord," said *Doña* Marina. "They wished to have the priest to sanctify the ceremonies which named Cuitláhuac *Uei Tlatoani.*"

"To hell with their ceremonies."

Quickly, Cortés left with ten horsemen and one hundred soldiers. With the cavalry, they opened the road to Tacuba. The exhausted soldiers could not follow as fast and an enormous force of Indians in canoes were attacking them with long poles (with copper or flint points) and missiles from both sides of the causeway. The Spaniards joined their companions in Tacuba and began the retreat in the face of great resistance. But they overcame the Indians, many of whom fell or were thrown into the water. They opened the road.

The Indians' great desire was to seize Cortés when he chanced to become separated from his men for a few minutes. The other riders had passed him or fallen in the water and were swimming. He struggled to open a path through the horde with blows from his sword and at a half gallop advanced along the causeway. At the last canal, which the Indians had again opened by removing the fill the Spaniards had placed there, Cortés and his horse made a great leap. Finally, exhausted, he arrived at his quarters to greet the soldiers, who were worried about his safety.

"Thank God that He saved you. We thought you were dead!"

Preparations for the Departure

"We will all die if we don't leave this trap at once! They are on the verge of destroying the road. We cannot keep filling in the places where the bridges were. We must leave! Have the carpenters make a big wooden platform that is transportable so we can cross the canals!"

"Sir, we do not have enough wood."

"Take some from the roofs and walls of the houses," answered Cortés.

So the carpenters went to work. That night, the heavy portable bridge was finished. Forty *tamemes* would haul it.

Then Cortés called for a general assembly. "Everybody gather here except the lookouts and scouts!"

Cortés said: *"Señores y amigos.* Because we have suffered so many deaths and there are so many wounded who cannot fight, your officers believe we must leave this trap tonight. Each day we have fewer able bodied men and the enemy force increases. We now have a portable bridge to cross the canals, but we must proceed stealthily without attracting attention."

"What about the gold treasure?" some asked.

"Before the King's treasurers, Alonso Dávila and Gonzalo Mejía, we will open the room containing the gold, and the one-fifth which belongs to the King which has already been separated will be loaded on the wounded horses and guarded by eighty Tlaxcaltecans. From the rest, although it was divided, each one may take what he wishes. But think about the weight of an excessive load, when we have to fight, march and run."

Great jubilation broke out among the soldiers.

"Wait until we separate the King's Fifth!" Once they had, Cortés said: "Take what you can! In one hour we leave and it will be in this order: The four hundred Tlaxcaltecans will carry and be in charge of the portable bridge, with one hundred fifty Spanish soldiers to guard its passage. Two hundred Tlaxcaltecans will carry the artillery and the fifty artillerymen.

"Gonzalo de Sandoval, Diego de Ordaz, Francisco de Lugo and Francisco Saucedo will lead the vanguard with one hundred young, fast soldiers who will reinforce anyone who needs it.

"Alonso de Ávila, Cristóbal de Olid and I will accompany the main body of troops with the gold treasure and a special guard of three hundred Tlaxcaltecans and thirty soldiers to protect *Doña* Marina and *Doña* Luisa as well as Cacamatzin and the other captives.

"Pedro de Alvarado and his brothers with Juan Velázquez de León are the rearguard.

"In between the army, Narváez's officers and soldiers.

"It would be a good idea for the horses to have cloths wrapped around their hoofs so they do not make noise. On second thought, that will not be necessary. The rains and the mud will muffle the sound."

Greediness overtook many of the men, who dashed for the ingots and jewels. They filled their shirts, armor, helmets and knapsacks. Cortés' more experienced veterans, like Bernal Díaz del Castillo, Jaramillo and Tapia took only a few jewels and put them in their knapsacks and watched, very concerned, those who were overloading themselves.

In his quarters, Cortés finished arranging his baggage for the departure. Marina was helping him.

"*Señora*, I have arranged that you and *Doña* Luisa will be protected by a special garrison of Tlaxcaltecans and Spaniards determined to die before they abandon you."

"I want to go with you, my lord! Give me a shield and sword!"

"That is not possible, *Doña* Marina. I must be in so many places. You have said that we will be in great danger and we will be. . . . But take this light shield and this sword. It will give you some protection. If it is in God's plans that we do not see each other again, I want you to know that you are my most precious possession. If my soldier's words and phrases are not full of tenderness, that is not because I do not love you, but because it is not natural for me to say them. Be careful and I will take care of you. Goodbye, *Doña* Marina. God willing, we will see each other in Tacuba."

"Goodbye, my lord. I know nothing will happen to you. You came as it was prophesied. Many times I have told you and now I repeat it, I was born to be yours. All of my light, all of Malinalli, is yours, my lord. All my love; all my being, forever, happen what may. . . . We will see each other in Tacuba, my lord. . . ."

Desperately, *Doña* Marina embraced Cortés.

At Last, We Are Going!

 "At last, we are leaving," was heard and the chamber that housed the gold began to empty out, but more than eighty soldiers stayed behind, maddened by gold fever as they struggled to carry away the riches.

Rain fell and a light fog shrouded the silhouettes of the men.

As silently as they could, they opened the garrison gates. In a long line, the army began their exit. First went the bridge, which they placed over the first water opening.

It was the 30th of June, 1520.

They crossed the Tecpantzingo, Tzapotlan and Etenchicalco canals, but when they came to the fourth, the Mixcoatechaltitlan, a woman who was drawing water shouted in alarm: "Mexicans! Come over here! They are leaving. Now our enemies are crossing the canals! They are leaving, secretly."

Although distracted by the ceremonies to enthrone Cuitláhuac, the [Mexican] garrisons were alerted.

In the Huitzilopochtli temple, the great drum sounded and a spokesman shouted: "Warriors, Mexican captains! Our enemies are leaving! Let us pursue them with barges defended by shields. Everybody! On the road!"

The news spread rapidly across the city. From every direction, the Aztec warriors appeared, on the roofs, in the streets, in canoes on the water and the attack began.

Back in the Axayácatl Palace, the eighty Spaniards grappling with the gold fought desperately in the treasure chamber where many died and the rest were captured.

In the Canal of the Toltecas

Despite the casualties on both sides, the Spaniards crossed the fourth bridge, but when they arrived at the Toltec canal the fighting became furious. The horses were slipping on the muddy ground.

A struggle ensued in which many died, others fell in the water and still others would swim to the other shore to place the bridge after overcoming savage resistance. The bridge was made secure and the vanguard was able to cross—while there were only a few enemies on the other side. The attackers redoubled their efforts when the main body of the army began to cross. From the other side, Cortés urged them to hurry.

"Hurry! Hurry! Faster! The gold treasure through here! *Doña* Marina! *Doña* Luisa! Run now! God save them, soldiers! Quickly! This way! Hurry!"

The horses passed that were hauling the treasure and with them *Doña* Marina and *Doña* Luisa, surrounded by Tlaxcatecans with their shields raised up to protect them, amidst great pushing, slipping, rocks and arrows. With the vanguard, Cortés went ahead trying to clear the street.

When the main body of the army tried to advance, the Indian attack intensified and the Aztecs were successful in tilting the bridge causing one part to fall in the water. The main body of the army was bottled up and when the rearguard reached them there was horrible confusion. Cacama, Totocauhtzin and the other Indian captives died when they fell in the water. Many were wounded.

The throng pushed against those who were already there "as if they were thrown down a hill."

In the horrible disorder—the shouting, the screams, the complaints, the cursing, and the beating of the drums, the *teponaxtles*, fifers, shellhorns—slowly the canal was filled with the bodies of Spanish soldiers unable to swim because of the weight of their gold, and with Indians, horses, treasures, cannon. Over the bodies and refuse passed those coming from the rear.

The Aztecs were fighting on one side and the other, from the canals and from the roofs. They shouted: "*Cuilones, Cuilones!*"

The Alvarado brothers with Velázquez de León, from the edge of the canal, struggled to lift up the portable bridge and successfully disengaged it so that from the other side it could be pulled into place, and the survivors carried it to place over the last canal. A group of Mexicans dashed at Juan Velázquez de León, who struggled desperately but helplessly. With his horse, he fell into the canal and many soldiers stepped on his dead body. He lay there, still wearing his famous gold chain, "la Fanfarrona."

The Sad Night: The Night of the Victory

They placed the damaged bridge over the last canal, the Petlacalco, and the vanguard and the surviving troops crossed over and arrived at Popotla. There, in the plaza, far from the attacking canoes, they regrouped, safely on the mainland where it was much easier to combat the enemy. They killed all the Indians in the plaza. The vanguard passed, as well as *Doña* Marina and *Doña* Luisa, the treasure and a large part of the army. Back on the causeway, the fighting was brutal.

At a gallop, Cristóbal de Olid and other horsemen arrived at Cortés' side. *"Señor Capitán,* wait for us. Our friends say we are fleeing and we left them on the bridges to die. We want to turn back to see if we can help them, if any are still alive."

The rain, lighter now, continued to fall.

"It was a miracle that any of us came out alive. We are going to help them!"

The remaining thirty horsemen rode along the causeway, opening a path through the Indian warriors. Just ahead, they spotted Pedro de Alvarado afoot, wounded, a lance in one hand, accompanied by his four brothers and some Tlaxcaltecans, also wounded, who were defending themselves against the attacks of the multitudes chasing them.

"There come the Alvarado brothers! All together!" shouted Sandoval, and the riders hurried to help them.

"With them is Botello, the astrologer!"

"No one else is coming. We are the last!" Alvarado said, haltingly.

As the rain came down, the fog lifted. Just then, the Indians reached Botello and killed him, scattering all his magic symbols in the mud.

The riders continued along the causeway, but found no more Tlaxcaltecans or Spaniards.

Later, some Aztec warriors and Aztec captains appeared shouting: "Tlacopan! Atzcapotzalco! México!" Cortés and his horsemen attacked them at the canal and returned at a half gallop, trampling the Indians.

"No one else is coming!"

Cortés and his men returned to Popotla. The rain stopped, and a late-rising moon illuminated the ground weakly through scattered, ragged clouds.

Under a great *ahuehuete* tree, Pedro de Alvarado was resting, dressing his wounds.

Cortés jumped off of his horse and asked anxiously, "And the rest?"

"They stayed at the bridges, many . . . many. Juan Velázquez de León, who wore his famous gold chain 'la Fanfarrona,' died. I saw him fall, horse and all. Many trampled on his body as they passed. Saucedo and De Morla and even Lares, a good rider, fell and so many others . . . so many. . . . Almost the entire rearguard died, Captain, our men as well as Narváez'. Many died because they were weighted down with gold. With my brothers, we were able to escape, swimming, lancing and assaulting the warriors. I don't know how we made it!"

Cortés sat down on the roots of the tree and said:

"What a sad night." He wept.

As warriors from Tacuba and Atzcapotzalco arrived to reinforce the Indian attack, Cortés regrouped his men and led them through some cornfields to the *teocalli* of Cuauhximalpan [now Los Remedios], which was on top of a hill and whose patio was defended by stone and wooden fences. They arrived in the early morning hours of the first of July. There the surviving Spaniards and Tlaxcaltecans would rest. They dressed their wounds, but did not eat, even though they lit fires to dry their clothes and weapons.

The *teocalli* was surrounded by Indian warriors who shot slings, never ceasing their aggressive yells.

The Survivors

A cloudy morning allowed the Spaniards to assess the magnitude of the tragedy. Gonzalo de Sandoval gave a report to Cortés: "We have about four hundred men left. . . . Most of the eight hundred who died were Narváez's men, many of whom were so weighted down with the gold they could hardly move. About eighty others barricaded themselves in the palace and we do not know what happened to them. There are only twenty-four horses, all wounded, some very seriously. All the artillery was lost. Even though we saved some arquebusiers, we have no powder. We saved a few crossbows and almost all the Indian servants were killed or taken prisoners. Cacama and the Lord of Tacuba and the chiefs who were captives and Moctezuma's relatives also died."

"A sad review of troops! Let us rest here," said Cortés. "We need it very badly. We'll take advantage while the attacks have lessened. Tonight we will leave for Tlaxcala . . . to learn the disposition of our *Tlatoanis*! [The four chiefs in Tlaxcala.] I would like some Tlaxcaltecan guides to go ahead to scout the best and safest road."

The Victory. The Smallpox

The Aztec camp was overjoyed. The eighty Spaniards who stayed behind in Tenochtitlan had either died or were taken captive. They were prepared for sacrifice along with those captured on the causeway. From the canals, and alongside the causeway, the Indians removed the dead bodies. The naked Spanish dead were piled up and looked like "the white blossom of the cane." The bodies of the women, Tlaxcaltecans and Cempoaltecans, were thrown into canoes and deposited in the reeds of the salt lake.

Out of the canals they salvaged armor, swords, lances, arquebuses, crossbows, cannon and gold in bars, in grains and gold jewelry. Those who searched for the treasure with their hands and feet, or by diving, apportioned the precious metal among themselves. Someone found "the Fanfarrona."

In the huge city, the Aztecs celebrated the Spaniards' rout, once again enthroning and adorning their gods in the temples. But now, the victims sacrificed were Spanish captives, some from the Axayácatl Palace, others from the Tacuba causeway. Their heads were displayed on the points of their own pikes, alternating with the heads of the horses. But soon smallpox began to ravage the land. One of the officiating priests was already covered by the sores of the disease.

Route to Tlaxcala

The Spaniards rested during the day and left quietly that night in squadrons, the guides leading with the reconnoitering horsemen. The wounded, Spaniards and Tlaxcaltecans, were in the center—those most serious were on wounded horses. Those who could no longer fight or ride were carried by *tamemes*. Others limped with the aid of wooden staffs. Anyone still able to fight went ahead, along the flanks and in the rearguard. In this order, they arrived the 2nd of July at Calacuaya and at Atizapán entered the houses to search for food. They killed whoever opposed them. They found some food, but not very much.

By that time, the Aztecs reached them and attacked. The rearguard was engaged in skirmishes as the army advanced slowly toward Cuautitlán.

The attack was furious and a horse was killed. The Spaniards fortified the *Teocalli* of Cuautitlán and ate the dead horse, even its bones and hide.

The third day of the withdrawal, the 3rd of July, they passed through Tepotzotlán close to Zumpango and Xaltocan, which they found deserted although there was some food. When the Mexican attacks diminished on the 4th and 5th of July, they rested in Aychucualco.

In Tenochtitlan the rejoicing and jubilation over their victory had diminished. The first cases of an unknown sickness had appeared: Smallpox!

Otumba

he Spaniards left the valley the 6th of July and arrived at Xoloc, where they fought the entire day. Cortés himself suffered two blows to his head. They built fortifications and spent the night there.

The following morning, the camp scouts and the Tlaxcaltecan guides said to him: "From here on ahead in the Ápam plains, close to Otumba, is the Mexican army. They seem to keep pushing us forward to have the final battle here. They are spread over the plain and are dressed luxuriously in their cloaks and feather headdresses."

"If it is a plain with a slope," said Cortés, "for the horses it will be an ideal place to fight. However, the wounded should not assemble with the rest. When we reach the plain, we will form a squadron placing the wounded in the center. Then, the horsemen will exit from one side, circle around and enter the other side to regroup. Form lines of three. Remember, lances to their faces and the foot soldiers should aim blows with their spear points to the stomach. Now, we shall place ourselves in the hands of Our Lord and those of Our Lady as we enter battle. *Santiago y cierra España*!"

The Spaniards advanced toward the Ápam plain to the timorous sound of the fifes and three drums.

On the other side, the Aztec army was commanded by Cihuacóatl, or the "Woman Serpent," Captain General of the Aztecs, a command belonging to Matlitzcatzin, Cuitláhuac's brother. Cihuacóatl, carried in a litter, was luxuriously dressed and adorned with jewels. Surrounded by his captains who were also wearing their multi-colored feather headpieces, Cihuacóatl carried on his shoulder the war standard, the Quetzaltonatiuh—a Sun of Gold symbol encircled by *quetzal* feathers. The command group stood out from the mass of warriors.

As the Spaniards advanced, Cortés remarked: "There are many warriors and they will try to stop us. But this is our war, on a terrain where we fight best, not like the causeways, where they came at us from all sides and we could not organize a proper defense. This time, it will be different."

"That's right, Captain!" said Sandoval excitedly. "This is our day for victory! That's right, friends. Have faith in God that we will leave here alive to fight for another good cause!"

All the people from around the lake and the valley concentrated on the last great battle. The Mexicans came, the Acolhauns, those from Texcoco, Tlalnepantla,

Cuautitlán, Tula, Tenayuca and Otumba, each with their individual war regalia beautifully decorated with jewelry, with the great multicolored feather headdresses and the *teponaxtles*, the shellhorns and small drums, flutes and a kind of clarinet.

The noncombatants were watching from the heights. In the early morning, when the Spaniards reached the plain to begin the battle, a great outcry erupted.

"Death to the *teules*! Death to the *teules*! Not one *teule* will be left alive!"

The Mexicans who were spread across the lower slopes of the Tonán mountain shouted as they rushed precipitately toward the Spanish and Tlaxcaltecan army, which quickly formed a square and was immediately surrounded "like a schooner in a stormy sea, struck by waves from all sides."

Far off, on top of a small hillock on the plain, one could distinguish the flags and banners of the Aztec Captain surrounded by nobles and chiefs directing the battle with their shining colorful war regalia amid drums, *teponaxtles* and shellhorns.

Inside the square, the twenty-four horsemen were prepared for battle. There were two lines of twelve horses, one, commanded by Cortés, the other by Alvarado. Cortés shouted the final orders.

"Alvarado! You and your men go out the small opening on this side and I and my men will do the same on the other. Be sure of your point of return and circle around to the right, then we will enter by opposite openings. Remember: horsemen, lances to their faces and soldiers—a blow with the point to the enemies' stomachs!"

"Now! *Santiago y cierra España!*"

Among the Indian forces, the outcry was horrendous.

"Mexico! Death to the *teules*!"

On opposite sides, the square opened to make way for the cavalry to charge out and begin turns in opposite directions, disorganizing many of the Indian warriors.

The exhausting battle lasted four hours, when Cortés noticed—at the insistence of Ixtlixóchitl [Tlaxcalan chief]—the group of ornately dressed warriors surrounding their Chief Cihuacóatl, who directed the battle amid the blare of shellhorns and drums.

The Battle of Otumba

272

"Let us finish off Cihuacóatl! Kill every chief," shouted Ixtlixóchitl.

Then Cortés, leading his horsemen, ordered them, "Go after them! Kill all the chiefs!"

Crashing through the Indians who opposed them with the strength of the iron-hoofed horses, they reached Cihuacóatl, causing the Indians to become disorganized when their chief was knocked to the ground. Juan de Salamanca, after thrusting his lance into the Indian's body, removed the feathered helmet and standard and presented them to Cortés, who waved it over the heads of his soldiers, to the jubilation of some and the astonishment of others. The fighting ceased. Then from the Spanish square, the Tlaxcaltecans dashed out to fight the Mexicans, now discouraged, who began to disband their ranks. The Spanish cavalry and the Tlaxcaltecans pursued the Mexicans for some time, causing many casualties.

Thus the battle of Otumba concluded.

"We were victorious!" announced the delighted Sandoval.

Cortés nodded without joy.

"But almost all our Tlaxcaltecan friends died and I even saw how bravely Calmecahua fought and died, the brother of Maxixcatzin."

On the way back to Tenochtitlan, many of the Mexican warriors collapsed, weakened, along the side of the road.

Smallpox!

The Return to Tlaxcala

As the Spanish and Tlaxcaltecan forces regrouped, their guides pointed out the Matlalcueye sierra in the distance. Behind this mountain range was Tlaxcala, which pleased them all. When the march resumed, a small band of Mexican warriors continued to shout insults and shoot arrows from time to time at the rearguard. Many of the enemy were overcome by smallpox.

With a head wound and with his left hand injured, Cortés exhorted his men: "Comrades, we do not know in what frame of mind we will find our Tlaxcaltecan friends; therefore, I suggest and order that you do not anger them by taking anything. I hope we find them kind and loyal to us. But if all is not as I expect, we must be prepared, as always."

On the eighth of July, they entered Xaltelolco in Tlaxcalan territory, after passing through a fence and screens marking the frontier with Mexico. Soon they arrived at Hueyotlipan, where the four *tlatoanis* of the Tlaxcaltecan senate greeted them.

Xicoténcatl, the elder, speaking for all, said: "Oh, Malinche! How badly we feel about your losses and the many of ours who died. We warned you not to trust the Mexicans and that sooner or later they would attack you. But there is no use lamenting. Now you must heal your wounds. We will give you food. You are welcome here. Please rest. We know you made a valiant effort. Many of our women have cried at the loss of their sons. You owe much to your three gods [The Lord, Mother Mary, and Jesus Christ] for having saved you from the multitude that awaited you in Otumba."

All the chiefs embraced Cortés and demonstrated their relief when they saw that *Doña* Marina and *Doña* Luisa, the daughter of Xicoténcatl [Alvarado's wife], were safe.

Then Cortés, with great deference to the Tlaxcalan Republic, thanked them for their friendship and handed over the Mexican standard, the Quetzaltonatiuh, to Xicoténcatl. "No one but the Lordship of Tlaxcala deserves to have this Mexican standard, which we would not have been able to achieve without the courageous efforts and the deaths of so many Tlaxcaltecans."

The Spaniards were housed in the chief's houses and there they regained their strength and tended to their wounds and convalesced. Cortés became ill because his wounds were neglected. He became furious upon learning that Captain Juan Páez, whom he had left in Tlaxcala in charge of eighty Spanish soldiers, had refused Maxixcatzin's offers to send thousands of Tlaxcaltecan soldiers if Páez would go to the Spaniards' rescue.

Cortés reached his quarters with his head bandaged and his left arm in a sling displaying signs of great anger.

Marina, very concerned, received him.

"Coward, a weak-spirited captain of rabbits, not men! He is like a weak woman! A coward!"

"What is wrong, my lord?" asked *Doña* Marina. "I have never seen you so angry. Calm yourself. You should not lose your temper. It will make you ill."

"To hell with all cowards! That coward of a Páez would not come to our aid even with a generous offer of support from the Tlaxcaltecans! Coward! Coward! We could have avoided so many deaths!"

"Calm yourself, lord, calm down!"

Doña Marina took him in her arms and led him to his bed. She removed the bandages from his head. "These wounds look bad and are swollen. The doctor must see you."

"I do not want anyone fussing over me!" Cortés said, still upset.

"You lie down. I will not let you leave until you are better! You have a high fever," cautioned *Doña* Marina.

Cortés tried to protest further, but he fell back into the bed.

Doña Marina called the doctor, who cleaned Cortés' wounds. "You must rest, Captain," the doctor said. "Your fever is high and although I cleaned the wounds and placed Indian herb poultices on them that *Doña* Marina recommended, it will take time for you to heal."

"What about the fingers of his left hand?" asked *Doña* Marina.

"He will lose some movement and they will become stiff."

"Maimed or not maimed, get me Sandoval," Cortés insisted.

When he appeared, Cortés said to him: "Sandoval, my son! Send three Tlaxcaltecan runners to Villa Rica to find out how things are. Tell them what happened to us and that they must watch Narváez and Salvatierra carefully, especially that they don't sail off in Narváez's ships. Tell them to send us arms and gunpowder; all they have."

For twenty days, the Spanish army rested.

Alliance Refused

In Tlaxcala, Xicoténcatl, the son, received secretly Cuitláhuac's ambassador.

"The *Uei Tlatoani* of Tenochtitlan, Cuitláhuac, sends a proposal to you—since you have fought against the *teules*—and we have defeated them—that we should kill them and evict them from our lands which they should never have entered. In Tlaxcala they have their force and their sanctuary. If the Tlaxcaltecan wills it, the *teule* dies."

"I agree," said young Xicoténcatl, "but in Tlaxcala, every matter is discussed and decided by the four *tlatoanis*, one of whom is my father, Xicoténcatl, the elder. I must consult them."

The Tlaxcala Senate was convened and Xicoténcatl, the son, reported. ". . . and this alliance is what the *Uei Tlatoani* Cuitláhuac proposes: Evict forever from the country these false *teules*."

The four *tlatoanis* listened closely. Maxixcatzin, who was presiding, said, "Now we will deliberate. Everyone else leave."

After a discussion, they ordered: "Have Xicoténcatl, the son, come in with the rest of the audience."

"Young man," said Maxixcatzin, "we have deliberated and tell you this. Never, from time immemorial, have the Tlaxcaltecans had such prosperity or been so rich since the *teules* arrived here. We refer to food, jewels, salt and cotton for clothes. Nor have we ever enjoyed such high esteem as we do now. Everywhere in the territory we are honored. And remember what has been told to us by our forefathers, that from the East will come those who will rule the land."

Xicoténcatl, the son, replied: "In spite of that, Moctezuma allowed the false *teules* to enter his city and he delivered the gold and the honor of Tenochtitlan to them. Then, other white *teules* came who said Malinche was a thief and a traitor and they fought among themselves. Then the Tenochcans and Tlatelolcans waged war against them and they were defeated. Since there are so few, we can defeat them. They are like hawks who wish to rule over the land."

"But son! Now that they are wounded, you wish to attack them? We Tlaxcaltecans are not traitors. We welcomed them as our brothers and with them we can defeat the Mexicans."

"Don't you understand that an alliance with the Mexicans will be advantageous and will free us from the foreign lords? Can't you understand this?"

"Watch your insolence, young man!" said Maxixcatzin.

"You are all blind. Not only my father! You will regret your decision! They will be the lords, we will be the slaves! Blind! Blind!"

The *tlatoanis* would not tolerate the young man's arrogance and pulling at him they tore off his garments and pushed him down several steps.

"You arrogant and presumptuous young man! You deserve to die as a rebel."

"No, death! No! He is my son and has served Tlaxcala," cried the young man's father.

The Tlaxcala Council denies the alliance

Assistance from Villa Rica. Triumph in Tepeaca

After resting and convalescing in Tlaxcala for twenty-two days, Cortés received news from Villa Rica de la Vera Cruz.

"Señores y amigos," he addressed his men, "we have word from Vera Cruz: Cempoala is peaceful and loyal; there is no fighting. They will send us reinforcements under the command of Lencero, also cords for the crossbows. In Tepeaca the Indians killed the Spaniards who were bringing gold to those in Vera Cruz who had never received any."

"Where are Lencero's reinforcements?" asked Bernal.

"Here," said Cortés, pointing to seven soldiers, thin and sickly.

Everyone smiled and Bernal commented: "So this is Lencero's 'help'—seven soldiers, five of whom are marked by pus-filled pimples and two with swollen stomachs."

"These are all we have," said Cortés. "We are no longer the invincibles; the Mexicans defeated us and we lost our prestige as the *teules*. The Tlaxcaltecans are loyal, but they pity us and wish only to protect us. So we must win back our prestige and our sovereignty. First, I propose an advance on Tepeaca, where they killed the Spaniards who were carrying the gold to the men in Villa Rica. We must destroy that garrison of Mexican soldiers before we can begin our return to Temistitan. Remember—fate is a woman who favors the brave.

"We must isolate Anáhuac and ensure our communication with the East coast. According to some information from the Tlaxcaltecans in the West, it seems that Michuacán is Mexico's enemy and will not aid them. To the North, Huaxtecapan is also not a friend of the Mexicans. Knowing that, we ought to maintain our own control of the land in the East and the route to the coast, thus isolating Temistitan from the Mixtec and Zapotec lordships, and to the South from the Cuauhnahuac and Malinalco and the neighboring valleys. Only by doing this can we enter Temistitan again."

When they heard about Cortés' plans, Narváez's survivors, headed by Andrés de Duero, requested before the Royal Scribe that Cortés should arrange their return to Cuba.

"Captain Cortés," said Duero, in the presence of all the troops, "before the Royal Scribe, we, the soldiers who came with Narváez have had only misfortunes— even the accursed gold was lost along the retreat and in the canals—we demand that you order our return to Cuba as we do not wish to go on to Tepeaca or to any other war. What we have experienced up to now is enough. We want to return to our homes. We have lost quite enough since we left Cuba."

"Duero," said Cortés, "the Royal Scribe certified that I order you to serve God and his Catholic Majesty, by not abandoning this country or leaving it, until we have punished those guilty of killing so many Spaniards. Brave men do not abandon the King's interest because of a bump on the head."

"Do you call a 'bump' losing more than two-thirds of the army? And still you wish to fight on against thousands with only four hundred and forty wounded soldiers and a few horses, without artillery, without gunpowder and without cord for the crossbows. That is lunacy, Captain! Let us return to Villa Rica while the road is clear before the enemy has captured the ports. And from there, on to Cuba before ships are destroyed or burned as they seem to be so often in these waters."

"I have already given my opinion, Duero. I wish to serve God and His Majesty to the best of my ability by conquering and colonizing these lands which will be a New Spain. You are only one of the soldiers. But let us hear what the others say. What do you think, friends?"

"Onward, Captain! To serve God and the King. That is the right thing to do and not return to Cuba," shouted the soldiers, Cortés' supporters, who were in the majority. "Do not give them permission to return! On to Tepeaca! On to Temistitan!"

"Do you hear the opinion of the others, Duero? Have the King's Scribe make a notation that the majority wishes to serve God and His Majesty."

Thus with his army in shambles and with four thousand Tlaxcaltecan allies, Cortés initiated the return to Tenochtitlan.

Reinforced by the Tlaxcaltecan warriors, the Spanish army triumphed in Zacatepec, Quecholalc and Acatzingo and advanced toward the important city of Tepeaca, the center of the region at the crossroads of the routes to the coast. To consolidate further his strategy, Cortés founded on the 4th of September, 1520, the Villa Segura de la Frontera. He took possession of the territory and sent a second Letter and Account to the King informing him the Spaniards would brand the captives with the letter "G," *guerra* [war].

Outside the burnt out ruins of Tepeaca, Cortés, mounted, turned to Alvarado, also on his horse, "Pedro! Let the captives who will be our slaves be branded with the letter 'G.'"

Father Olmedo asked Cortés: "Why are you doing this, Captain? This is the first time you are making slaves of the captives and branding them!"

"We use the letter 'G,' which means war, because they rebelled against His Majesty to whom they had sworn allegiance and they killed the Spaniards in ambush and ate their flesh, and also to frighten the other Culúas. Without punishment, they will never change their ways."

Father Olmedo lowered his head. From that time on, they began to brand the captives and slaves with the letter "G" on their cheeks.

Turning to his officers, Cortés said, "The fighting in Zacatepec, Quecholalc, Acatzingo and even in Tepeaca was fierce. With the help of God and our patron saint, we have won, but more important is we are now masters of these plains where the roads cross from the coast to Temistitan. We must found a Villa here and make Alvarado the *Alcalde*. The soldiers will vote for magistrates and scribes. You, Cristóbal de Olid, send out expeditions to take control of the whole territory. Set fire to any place that resists!"

More Aid

rom Cuba, Diego Velázquez continued to send ships in order to discover what had happened to Narváez, assuming he had triumphed over Cortés.

First came Pedro Barba [who had tried fruitlessly to arrest Cortés in Cuba]. He brought a letter from Velázquez for Narváez. Barba invited Caballero, the "Admiral of the Sea," whom Cortés had left in Vera Cruz, to join him on ship. When Caballero boarded, he was welcomed cheerfully with this question from Barba: "How is the *Señor* Captain Pánfilo de Narváez and how is he managing with Cortés?"

Caballero, wanting to lure Barba off the ship, said: "Very well. Cortés is fleeing with twenty of his men and Narváez is thriving and is very rich. I invite you to come to rest and I will tell you more news."

Confident, Barba went ashore, where he was apprehended. He and his companions were sent to Cortés, who received them warmly. "Welcome to Segura de la Frontera, my friend Barba. You and your thirteen companions have come at a good time. We need you desperately and the horse and mare you brought for our expedition."

Placing his arm on his shoulder, Cortés took him aside. After they returned, Cortés introduced him to his captains. "May I present the Captain of the crossbowmen—without any crossbows, but which he will be providing."

"I have the honor of joining you. As for the crossbows, I know some are on their way in another ship sent by Velázquez along with ammunition and cords."

In fact, a few days later, another ship landed at Villa Rica commanded by Rodrigo Morejón de Lobera, who brought eight soldiers, six crossbows, a mare and plenty of cord for the bows and iron for points. The *conquistadors* used the same ruse and this crew was captured, sent to Cortés and convinced by him to remain.

Cortés commented: "Providence is helping us. The fame of these lands and what we are accomplishing will encourage other reinforcements to come here."

"Yes, they [the reinforcements] are like a birote [roll] to a starving man," said Bernal.

A few days later, Caballero sent a messenger to Cortés, announcing he was in Segura de la Frontera [Tepeaca]. "Captain, Admiral Caballero wishes to advise you that a ship with Garay's men arrived from Pánuco. They were defeated by the Indians who did the same to Pineda and his soldiers. Garay's men are ill and wish to join your ranks."

"They will be welcome."

Fifty sick soldiers came, their stomachs swollen, with a green pallor in their faces.

"So this is Garay's bread; green, swollen stomachs," commented Bernal Díaz del Castillo wryly.

Reinforcements: De Garay's humbled men

Later, Caballero sent more word to Cortés: "More people have arrived, sent by Garay to Pánuco and when they found no one there, they have come to join us, very anxious to explore the territory, if you are willing to have them."

"Of course," said Cortés.

Soon, fifty strong soldiers with strong backs arrived with seven horses. Bernal commented:

"Another crust from Garay. The kind with 'strong backs.'"

Later, forty soldiers sent by Garay arrived in Tepeaca well armed with shot, gunpowder, crossbows, and arquebusiers, to reinforce his destroyed expedition. They brought cotton quilted jackets of such thickness and weight that no arrow could penetrate, but which made the wearer perspire heavily. Pending further orders, they placed themselves under Cortés' command.

Bernal commented: "Another crust of bread from Garay. But this is like the armor on horses, which protect them, but makes them sweat."

After the triumph in Tepeaca and the founding of Segura de la Frontera, Cortés' forces soon pacified the land and had total control of the road to Villa Rica de la Vera Cruz. Once the region was peaceful, the Indian villages made him the arbiter of the complex problems that came up because of the many deaths from smallpox.

"*Señor*," said *Doña* Marina to Cortés, "representatives from four villages from the volcano region have come to see you. They are from Ocupatuyo and they want you to designate successors for the *caciques* who have died from the smallpox."

The representatives appeared and presented their requests.

Other Representatives to Spain

oon after this meeting ended, Pedro de Alvarado appeared. Cortés greeted him, smiling. "Welcome, Mayor of the recently founded Villa Segura de la Frontera, formerly Tepeaca."

"How may I be of service?" asked Alvarado.

"Quite a while ago, Portocarrero and Montejo went to Spain to speak to His Majesty. According to Narváez's men, we know they arrived at La Española in Cuba and then left. But we do not know what happened after that. I believe another delegation from Segura de la Frontera should go to Spain to legalize our petitions and to present a report on the importance of this country."

"What about Diego de Ordaz and Alonso de Mendoza as magistrates?"

"Excellent! We will send some documents with them, too. A Second Letter to His Majesty will apprise him of everything that has taken place since the First Letter, wherein we asked him to send examiners to clear up the matter of Velázquez and to give the details of the confusion in the territory caused by Narváez's clumsiness. Another letter will go to the Dominicans of the *Audiencia de La Española* to explain our gratitude for Ayllón's appearance and what happened with Narváez."

"That sounds very good and I will confirm the details as *Alcalde* as well as the other authorities."

"And those of the soldiers," concluded Cortés.

From Segura de la Frontera, Cortés returned to Tlaxcala. It was there he learned that Maxixcatzin had died of smallpox.

"Malinche," the Tlatoanis said to him, "Maxixcatzin died from that terrible disease which causes blisters and his firstborn died fighting with you in Tepeaca. The father wished for his younger son be a knight and even to become a Christian."

Father Olmedo performed the ceremony. "I baptize you with the name of *Don Lorenzo Magiscacin*."

The elder Xicoténcatl, very emotional, approached Cortés: "Malinche, I, too, wish to become a Christian."

"I will baptize you, " said Father Olmedo, "with the name of Lorenzo de Vargas."

After that ceremony, Xicoténcatl the younger left, completely disgusted.

The Return. Brigantines

"Soon the year 1520 will end with the pacification of Huejotzingo and Cholula and just look how much has occurred," commented Gonzalo de Sandoval. "If anyone would have told me. . . ."

"Even more took place, son," replied Cortés. "We have subdued the lands from the volcanos to the coast and secured the road to Villa Rica. Now is the time to think about returning to Temistitan. But not until we have rested from these furiously fought battles that the Mexicans from Guacachula and Huejotzingo waged against us."

"In Izúcar and Cholula, everywhere there were garrisons," added Alvarado. "I do wish to see Temistitan again."

"We must organize ourselves well to be worthy of our allies, the Tlaxcaltecans, who are most courageous and each time more anxious to conquer their Mexican enemies. Now there will be no problem for them to invade the lake area [Mexico] with us. Do you not agree, Captain?" Sandoval reflected.

"Absolutely. I have been thinking about our plans. . . . We should enter by all three causeways and attack from the lake at the same time. To do that, we must construct some boats. We have the iron, the rigging and the sails. I have already ordered horses, cannon, arquebusiers, gunpowder and stores of everything available in the islands, where surely men will join us."

"I, too, wish to go to Temistitan again," concluded Alvarado, with satisfaction.

At Tlaxcala, Cortés sent for Martín López, the shore-captain.

"Martín," he said, "with the help of the Tlaxcaltecan carpenters you have taught, I want you to build thirteen brigantines that can sail in the lake waters."

"But we are so far from the lake. Where will I construct them?"

"You will cut the wood here and in the Atempan district make the frames and the keels according to the large model of a brigantine which I ordered from Villa Rica. I will give you everything you need. Then the *tamemes* will haul the sections to Texcoco, which we shall subdue, and where you will assemble the boats. Then we will launch them."

"It will be an enterprise fit for Romans," commented Martín.

"It is better that we do it," smiled Cortés.

In November of 1520, they began to cut the lumber.

Smallpox in Tenochtitlan

Tenochtitlan was badly affected and totally disrupted by the smallpox epidemic that extended throughout the valley, especially during the summer of 1520. Many died from the festering sores. Many more died of starvation. No one cared about anything or anyone else.

The smallpox wages havoc

Cuitláhuac, the King who succeeded Moctezuma, died of smallpox in October that year.

His direct descendants either had no capacity to reign or were not the proper age. After a selection process that lasted all of November, at the end of December, 1520, the Aztecs enthroned Cuauhtémoc, who, in spite of his youth, was the High Priest. Immediately, he married Tecuichpoch, daughter of Moctezuma and widow of Cuitláhuac. As soon as Cuauhtémoc began to rule, he prepared to attack and to resist the Spaniards.

"My nobles," he said to the Council of Imperial Culúa, "this horrible disease has prevented us from defeating the *teules*, who are building up their forces in Tlaxcala. The Council of the *Tlatoanis* did not accept the alliance that Cuitláhuac proposed to Xicoténcatl, the son. Neither did the *teules* leave. Now, they want to return here and more are joining them from the coast. We must prepare ourselves, organizing our warriors once more. Unfortunately, many of them died from the disease. We must strengthen our city with canals and walls, make our lances longer, and form new and stronger alliances. From the villages in the volcano area to the sea, the *teules* control the land and plan to attack us again. The Tlaxcaltecans are their allies. They will be coming through Texcoco. So let us seal off the roads. It is either we or they."

The Return. Route to Texcoco

The year 1520 was ending. The 26th of December, after the Christmas fiestas, before the assembled Spanish troops, Gonzalo de Sandoval gave a report to Cortés: "Captain, the review of soldiers you ordered is complete. We are 550 foot soldiers; of which eighty are crossbowmen and musketeers and the rest with swords, shield and lance; forty on horseback and nine pieces of artillery with some gunpowder, but not too much ammunition. That is without counting the Tlaxcaltecans, which Ojeda and Márquez organized, who are perhaps more than ten thousand.

"Add thirteen soldiers and the three horses which we are buying in Villa Rica from ships recently arrived from Castile and from the Canary Islands carrying merchandise, gunpowder, crossbows, muskets and some ammunition. We will divide the foot soldiers into nine companies of sixty men each and four squads of horsemen."

"To Temistitan! To Temistitan," shouted the soldiers joyfully.

"To Temistitan we will go, by the road to Texcoco, within two days, on the 28th of December. We will conduct ourselves as valiant men. Either we return to regain what we lost or we will die for our faith in service to His Majesty!"

28 December, 1520. Tlaxcaltecas and Spaniards set out for Tenochtitlan

"Let's go back! Go back!" shouted the army.

On the 28th of December, 1520, the Spanish army left Tlaxcala. Ten thousand Tlaxcaltecan warriors accompanied them, captained by Chichicamecatl and Xicoténcatl.

Mounted with his captains, Cortés announced: "We will advance through Texcoco, where we will set up our fortifications. It will be our base for assembling the thirteen brigantines; in one more month all the lumber will be ready. We will move to Texcoco along the mountain road of the sierra where we will have less resistance. We will spend tonight in Texmoluca."

The following day, they left Texmoluca en route to Texcoco, crossing the sierra, overcoming obstacles such as tree trunks and stones set out to impede their march. After engaging in minor skirmishes, they arrived at Coatepec and on the next day, Texcoco. Along the road, they again observed the great Valley of Mexico, the grand splendor of Tenochtitlan. From the high mountains, they noticed the smoke signals—the Aztecs were announcing the advance of the Spanish army.

In the rocky and narrow passes where the horses could not easily progress, the Tlaxcaltecans fought the skirmishes and collected spoils of war from occupied villages.

Before they reached Texcoco on the 31st of December, seven residents came out to meet them in peace, under a golden flag. To Cortés, they said: "Malinche: Coanacochtzin, Lord of Texcoco, begs to receive your friendship. He is awaiting you in peace in Texcoco and as a sign, please accept this flag. He asks as a favor that you order the Tlaxcaltecans and your brothers not to destroy the land and that you come to make your quarters in Texcoco. There you will have everything you need."

Cortés received them happily. "We never do any harm to anyone who receives us peacefully. Tell our ally leader, Chichicamecatl, that his people must enter this town with civility and not destroy property or take any spoils as we will be provided with everything we need."

Then Cortés turned to the Texcocans: "I am well aware that your people killed forty Spaniards here when we left Mexico and that they took loads of gold. Tell your *cacique* to return the plunder."

"Malinche, it was not we Texcocans, but the Mexicans from Tenochtitlan; they sacrificed the *teules* and they have the gold. Please come to our houses; we have food for everyone."

The Spanish army encamped in the outskirts of Texcoco.

The following day, the 1st of January, 1521, the ambassadors were gone. The Spanish army entered a deserted town. All the inhabitants had fled to Tenochtitlan over the causeway and in canoes.

"The emissaries lied, Captain," Alvarado said. "They only wanted to gain time so they could all leave."

"You and Olid go up to the top of the temple with twenty soldiers and observe the area."

At the highest point on the temple they found the severed heads of Spanish soldiers and horses. They could see the spread of the entire lake.

"Captain, I saw a great many canoes loaded with people rowing toward Tenochtitlan. The women and children are overburdened with their possessions."

"No doubt they want their city vacant so they can wage war more effectively," said Cortés. "Set up the camp by companies and assign the places and posts where each should be positioned if there should be a surprise attack by the Mexicans. Put the cavalry and the foot soldiers in front of the causeway in case they come in canoes."

"I will do it," said Alvarado.

Cortés continued, "Sandoval, old son, come with me and bring Chichicamecatl. We are going to find the best spot for the shipyard to assemble the brigantines."

They located what they wanted in a protected area, close to a plaza. "The Tlaxcaltecan friends and the local Indians must make this canal deeper," said Cortés, "because we are going to assemble and launch the brigantines from right here."

Immediately, they began work in the Texcoco shipyards. During the following days, delegations from the neighboring villages began to arrive.

"My lord, the representatives of Cuatlinchan, Huexotla, Atenco, Chalco and Tlalmanalco have come," *Doña* Marina informed Cortés, "to offer peace and to say that the Tenochcas [people from Tenochtitlan] made them fight the *teules* and then disappear. They wish to offer themselves as subjects of His Majesty if you will defend them against Mexicans."

Cortés received them courteously. "I don't like wars, so tell your neighbors that we come in peace, they should be calm, and we promise to defend them from the Mexicans."

Soon, a commission of Texcocanos arrived. *Doña* Marina explained their request: "My lord, these people are from Texcoco and wish to return to their land, which they left when Cuauhtémoc, who now rules in Tenochtitlan, forced them to do so. They say that Coanacochtzin killed the person you call Cucuzca who was King of Texcoco. They do not want alliances with the Culúas and if you agree they would like Tecocoltzin to be the *tlatoani*. He would like to be baptized if you will act as the godfather, and to be named 'Fernando.' His brother Ixlixóchitl can organize an army with people from Texcoco to fight against Cuauhtémoc."

"That will be fine," said Cortés. "We continue to advance by the grace of God."

For twelve days, the army prepared their baseline.

Sandoval said to Cortés: "Captain, in the past twelve days, which have been so peaceful in Texcoco, provisions are becoming scarce, because there are many thousands of Tlaxcaltecans and other villagers to feed who are anxious for vengeance and the spoils of war."

"Then it is time we waged war. Call the Council," Cortés said with a glare.

Battle Plan

When the Council was convened, Cortés displayed a crude map to explain his strategy. "While they are building the brigantines in these first months of 1521, we will take advantage of the time to pacify the villages all around the lake and in the Valley of Mexico. Now, we control Tlaxcala and Tepeaca in the East, all the way to the coast. We also control Texcoco and we are going to reign over every area from here, the West and the North. We do not control the Valley to the South, where there is a village called Oaxtepeque and another between the ravines called Cuernavaca. Before skirting that area, let us make a trial run into the village around the lake to keep the Culúas busy and our Tlaxcaltecan friends, who are anxious to wage war against their enemies to avenge the deaths caused by the devastating *noche triste*. We must do this for a greater reason: There are no longer any provisions left in Texcoco and the Tlaxcaltecans have nothing to eat.

"Let us attack Ixtapalapa, which is about four leagues from here. Leading will be captains Pedro de Alvarado and Cristóbal de Olid, with thirteen mounted men and twenty crossbowmen and six musketeers, along with two hundred twenty soldiers and our Tlaxcaltecan friends. Gonzalo de Sandoval, you remain in charge in Texcoco, overseeing and protecting the shipyard."

In Tenochtitlan and Ixtapalapa

The Aztec spies reported to Cuauhtémoc that the Spaniards and Tlaxcaltecans were on the way to Ixtapalapa. The Mexican chief replied:

"The smoke signals confirm that the *teules* are going to Ixtapalapa. Our plan is this: Allow the Spaniards and Tlaxcaltecans to enter the city, displaying very little resistance. Once they are inside, open the dike of the salt water lake and drown them. Outside the town, we will be waiting with our warriors for those who did not drown."

Without suspecting such treachery, Cortés and his troops easily entered Ixtapalapa. The Tlaxcaltecans slaughtered many and captured a lot of booty before the Aztecs destroyed the dike and the salt water began to pour into the city. At midnight, Cortés became aware of the trick and ordered a retreat, but the Tlaxcaltecans did not obey. Many lost their lives and their booty. With the water up to their waists, the Spaniards left for the edge of the lake, where the Mexican warriors were waiting. The combat began. With difficulty, the Spanish horsemen opened a passage and the army retreated to Texcoco with many wounded Spaniards and many dead Tlaxcaltecans.

In Tenochtitlan, Cuauhtémoc ordered his captains: "The *teules* in Tlaxcala are plotting something. They are working with a lot of wood. Let us block their way with the aid of Chalco and Tlalmanalco. We will breach the road between Tlaxcala and the sea."

The Mexican army left for battle.

Sandoval Attacks

Two days after Cortés returned from the expedition to Ixtapalapa, Gonzalo de Sandoval, heading fifteen horsemen, two hundred soldiers and a squadron of one thousand Tlaxcaltecans, said to Cortés: "We are ready to go to Chalco and Tlalmanalco to fight the Mexicans who attacked us and blocked our pass to Tlaxcala."

"Good idea, son Sandoval. That will guarantee our passage to bring the wood for the brigantines from Tlaxcala, where it is being cut. The Mexicans control that road now."

"Be sure, Captain, that we will give a good account of ourselves."

Well organized, the young Sandoval had some problems at first, but finally gained success, defeating the Mexican units after several bloody battles. The connection with Tlaxcala was assured.

Transportation of the Brigantines

In Chalco, Sandoval received Cortés' messenger: "Captain Sandoval, Hernán Cortés received news of your victory here in Chalco and orders you to continue on the road to Tlaxcala. Organize the transportation to bring the wooden frames for the brigantines. In Zultepec, punish their rebelliousness and avenge the deaths of the Spaniards."

In Zultepec, Sandoval entered the *teocalli* and found the dried skins of the faces of two Spaniards "with their beards intact," given as an offering together with their clothes and the hides of the horses, hooves and all, and their tack. On the rock wall, Sandoval found lettering which read: "Here Juan de Yuste was a prisoner without hope with many others who were in my company."

Although the Spaniards became irate and asked that the Zultepecans be punished, Sandoval said: "I have instructions to pacify this territory without causing further damage. What use would vengeance serve the unfortunate Yuste, except to arouse pity for the people of this village?"

Sandoval called together the chiefs, who asked his pardon; he told them they could return to live in the town.

While still in the outskirts of Tlaxcala, Sandoval came upon the force who was transporting the frameworks for the thirteen brigantines. That mission was headed by Martín López, Ojeda and Márquez, who gave orders for transporting the lumber. Chichicamecatl, Teutepil and Ayotecatl led the Tlaxcaltecan warriors. The troop movement was impressive: Ten thousand Tlaxcaltecan warriors were the vanguard protecting eight thousand *tamemes* who carried the frameworks, and ten thousand more Tlaxcaltecan warriors composed the rear guard. The line of march twisted along the route for more than ten kilometers.

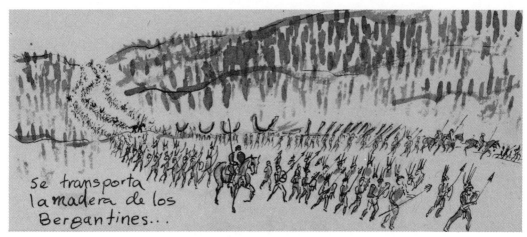

se transporta la madera de los Bergantines...

They transport the wood for the brigantines

Upon entering Mexican territory, the force was assaulted by Aztecs, who began to attack the cargo, causing Sandoval to reorganize his troops: First he divided the horses between the rearguard and the flanks of the shipment, joined with musketeers and crossbowmen. Then he ordered Chichicamecatl, who was leading the entourage, to join him in the rear.

After a few more days on the road, despite minor skirmishes with the Mexicans, Sandoval's men entered Texcoco triumphantly in February, 1521. The Tlaxcaltecans had adorned themselves with their finest headdresses. The parade lasted for six hours and the *tamemes* placed the frames in the shipyard under the close watch of Martín López.

Eight horsemen and a hundred Spanish foot soldiers led the march, followed by thousands of Tlaxcaltecan warriors dressed luxuriously in their war regalia, shouting: "Tlaxcala! Castile!"

Cortés and his captains received them with great pleasure.

"Welcome, friends Chichicamecatl, Teutepil and Ayotecatl! You have accomplished a feat that will be recorded for centuries to come!"

"We are very anxious to wage war against the Mexicans," Chichicamecatl answered.

"Soon we will," said Cortés. "But now, we have to put these frames in place and assemble the brigantines to achieve that victory."

Immediately, the carpenters began to assemble the boats. Martín López was the master; Andrés Núñez, Ramírez and Hernández were master cutters and smiths, along with many Indian carpenters who had learned the use of Spanish tools.

In Tenochtitlan

Cuauhtémoc's spies reported to him. "Lord Cuauhtémoc: The serpent of wood arrived at Texcoco and will be used to make houses that navigate on the lake. The wood is placed in piles and many are working to widen and deepen the canals and others are forming things like the ribs of a skeleton."

"My nobles," Cuauhtémoc ordered, "have some capable warriors set fire to the wood to hamper their work. The great war has begun; their deaths or ours. I want more work done to widen and deepen the breaks along the causeways and to fortify the walls and the barricades. We must begin to store the longer lances and place on them the *teules'* swords to fight the horses. Also, be sure more arrows and stones and all our arms are added to the arsenals. We will have a running battle on the land and on the water. Especially on the water, where their horses are useless. We must inundate everything we can and wage war from canoes protected by bulwarks of wood. The people in the villages on the mainland should come to the reed thickets or go to the hills. Let the *teules* enter the water and fight them there. I also order that we punish the villages that have betrayed us, like Chalco, so that it will confuse the *teules'* forces.

The Valley of Mexico is Encircled

At the beginning of April, 1521, Cortés left with twenty horsemen and three hundred Spanish soldiers and the Tlaxcaltecan allies to circle the Valley of Mexico from the South. Among the men was Alderete.*

Conferring with his captains, Cortés said: "Our requests for peace to Guatemocin** have been in vain; he even mistreated our messengers and sneered that he will kill us or he will die in the attempt and that we must leave. As we have already determined, we shall surround Temistitan. We already control the North and the East and defend it as ours. Now we will invade the Northwest.

"We must control the South. With twenty cavalry and three hundred soldiers plus the valiant and avid Tlaxcaltecan warriors, we will surround the valley through the South. We will go to Chalco," and he continued to point at the map, "Tlalmanalco, Chimalhuacán, Oaxtepec, Xiutepec, Yautepec, Cuernavaca, then down to Xochimilco, Coyoacán and back to Texcoco just in time to launch our brigantines."

The expedition departed on the 5th of April, 1521, and was joined by a huge gathering of Indian allies anxious for booty. Battles took place all along the route, which were but an omen of the ferocity with which the two armies would finally meet.

Outside Chimalhuacán, the Spanish army found the people frightened, hiding among sharp boulders from where they challenged the Spaniards. The enemy played their war instruments furiously.

The Spaniards and Tlaxcaltecans crossed the Cuernavaca valley, then came to the beautiful Oaxtepec gardens, taking Xiutepec, Yautepec. On the 13th of April, they attacked Cuauhnahuac, surrounded by deep ravines, which had been isolated by destroying or removing bridges. The Spaniards resolved to cross the ravine by taking advantage of the giant trees whose interlaced branches became fragile bridges. They surprised the Indian garrison and reestablished the bridge crossings. The cavalry took the city, where the Tlaxcaltecans obtained great booty.

During the day, Cortés and his army rested in a beautiful orchard where the local

---

* Julian de Alderete, the King's Treasurer

** Cortés could not pronounce the Náhuatl name Cuauhtémoc (Letter from Lic. José López Portillo to translator, July 20, 1988.)

294

Cuernavaca is conquered

chieftains came to ask for peace. Cortés pardoned Yoatzin, prohibiting him from giving corn or reinforcements to Cuauhtémoc.

From Cuernavaca, the Spanish army again crossed the sierra, descending to the Valley of Mexico. On the 15th of April, in the morning, suffering from thirst, they were again at Xochimilco.

From this point, both armies would assault each other with great cruelty and fury.

In Tenochtitlan and Xochimilco

Cuauhtémoc sent an order to the people in Xochimilco: "Oppose the *teules*, but let them enter the causeway by the lake. After they pass, we will destroy the bridges behind them and attack them by land and water. From Tenochtitlan I will send fresh troops to keep the attack going day and night."

That was the scenario for three days, beginning the morning of the 15th of April, 1521. The Spaniards and Tlaxcaltecans advanced along the causeways and bridges defended by the Xochimilcans who fell back gradually, allowing time for Mexican warriors in canoes to arrive. Then they cut away the bridges and opened the canals.

One afternoon, Cortés' horse collapsed from fatigue.

One Indian's joyous cry could be heard: "Oh, chiefs! Oh, Mexicans! Do not kill him! We must take him to Tenochtitlan alive!"

Thus began a great struggle to save Cortés. The Indians fell upon him. But Cristóbal de Olea, Cortés' bodyguard, supported by a group of Tlaxcaltecans, was able to reach him. Risking his own life, Olea brandished his sword, slashing many Aztec hands and heads. Finally, he was wounded. Fighting on the narrow causeway, the Tlaxcaltecans snatched Cortés away from the Aztecs. The Spanish general suffered a head injury and his horse was also wounded. They took him back to Xochimilco, where they were all reunited with the Spanish army.

Panting with fatigue, Cortés went to see Olea to express his appreciation for saving him. "Cristóbal de Olea, I am indebted to you for my life, which already was lost, had the Indians not wished to carry me away alive to be sacrificed."

Olea, gravely injured, made a friendly gesture to Cortés, but was unable to speak because of his wounds and exhaustion.

There was more fighting all night. From the *teocalli*, the Spaniards saw a huge number of canoes coming from Tenochtitlan.

The Spaniards took advantage of the night hours to make darts for the arquebusers, adding metal tips and feathers. They dressed their wounds with hot oil and repulsed many night attacks.

The houses and palaces of Xochimilco were sacked by both sides. While collecting booty, four Spaniards were seized and taken alive to Tenochtitlan.

On the third day, after setting fires and laying waste to Xochimilco, the Spaniards and Tlaxcaltecans, after many trials and great misery, again crossed the causeway by improvised bridges and went toward Coyoacán.

In Tenochtitlan

The four Spanish captives were taken before Cuauhtémoc.

"They should confess what they know and then be sacrificed to the gods. Cut off their heads, legs and hands and display these throughout the lands of the traitors to frighten them."

In Coyoacán and Tacuba

ortés and his men, under the constant harassment of the enemies in the canoes, arrived at Coyoacán, which he found deserted. Along the road, he saw that the soldiers were weighed down by booty.

"It will be a good idea, comrades, to leave most of your spoils, which hinders you in fighting."

Bernal and his companions answered: "We are men enough to defend ourselves and our possessions, which are few, indeed."

"I commend you to God's help."

So they arrived at Coyoacán, spending the night there. Cortés himself explored the causeway.

The following day, after the troops had rested, they made more darts and dressed their wounds. The Spanish commander ordered: "On to Tacuba! From Coyoacán onward, we must have a strong garrison."

On the Tacuba road, the Spanish army was harassed constantly by the Mexicans from the canoes. In one place, while the cavalry was attacking some warriors who blocked the causeway, they fell into a trap. From a thick growth of reeds, a large band of Indians sprang out and wounded the horses, capturing two of Cortés' young cavalrymen despite his vigorous efforts to save them.

Very distressed, Cortés arrived at Tacuba in the rain. The priest Melgarejo and the King's new treasurer, Julián de Alderete, accompanied him. With them and his captains, Cortés ascended to the top of the Tacuba *Teocalli* and saw again the unbounded greatness of the land and the immense fleet of Aztec canoes in the lake.

Cortés said: "Julián de Alderete, King's Treasurer, you have only recently arrived and are not acquainted with the immensity of this land. I invite you to go up to the temple so you may admire it."

Once he was there, Alderete said, "Truly, Captain Cortés, arriving in these lands and occupying them is not mere accomplishment of the human spirit, but an example of the mercifulness of God. I do not remember having read in any history that any subject has ever done such a great service for his King."

"But at a great cost, Treasurer. You see how I just lost those two young horsemen."

[The view] from Tacuba

A garrulous soldier, Alonso Pérez, said to him: "Your Grace should not be so sad. In wars, these things happen and it will not be said for Your Grace:

Nero watched from Tarpeia Rock
Rome at his feet was afire
Children and the old screaming,
But he suffered no grief.

Cortés smiled. "Imagine how many times I have sent messages to Mexico begging them for peace. I am so sad for only one reason: the great efforts it will cost us just to restore our domination, with God's help. Soon, we will be able to do so by our efforts. But now we have no gunpowder and only a few darts. Many are wounded, men and horses, so we must return to Texcoco."

On the following days, in heavy rains, the army passed through Atzcapotzalco, Cuautitlán and Tenayuca, finding each deserted.

Another Conspiracy

At the end of their circuitous route, they arrived at Acolman on the 22nd of April, to find Gonzalo de Sandoval and the new *Tlatoani* of Texcoco, *Don* Fernando, awaiting them. The following day, Cortés decided to go on to Texcoco, where his men were building the brigantines.

On the road there, a soldier came up to Cortés. "Captain Cortés, with all respect, I ought to speak to you in private about a serious matter."

"It must be very important when you approach me with such an expression on your face."

"Yes, it is," answered the soldier.

After Cortés jumped down from his horse, the soldier said: "My conscience forces me to inform you about the conspiracy and pact that Antonio de Villafaña, the great friend of the Cuban governor, is plotting with Narváez's men. They propose to kill you and your captains and those loyal to you. This is their plan: When you reach Texcoco and are eating with your captains, they will deliver a letter to you saying it is from your father that just arrived by ship. Then they will stab you and your men. A Captain General, *alcaldes*, peace officers and magistrates have already been designated."

"I thank you, friend. Keep silent about this matter."

Back on the road, Cortés rode beside his captains and told them confidentially about the plot. He ended with these instructions: "We will proceed directly to Villafaña's quarters, capture him and investigate the truth of the matter."

They entered Texcoco and without dismounting, the captains stopped in front of Villafaña's quarters, where he and some of Narváez's men were housed.

Cortés and his captains went inside and forced out everyone except Villafaña, who remained alone. Cortés reproached him brusquely: "Come on, *Don* Traitor, give me the letters from my father as well as the daggers to kill us."

Villafaña, terrified, raised his hand to his chest and tried to stuff some papers in his mouth. Gonzalo de Sandoval snatched away the evidence and gave it to Cortés, who began to read the list of names.

"There are so many important people in this conspiracy that we ought to pretend we do not know who they are, but be vigilant and only judge, summarily, Villafaña, letting the others think he swallowed the list with the conspirators' names."

Villafaña was judged immediately. He confessed to having received instructions from his brother-in-law, Diego Velázquez, who offered him the Captain-General's post. Cortés, the Chief Justice, sentenced him to death and he was hanged from the window outside his quarters.

The Brigantines are Finished

"Gonzalo de Sandoval, give us the report of the camp," said Cortés that very afternoon, after eating.

"Captain, the brigantines are finished, Martín López has informed us. They can be launched on the 28th of April, as the canal is now wide and deep and half a league long. The sails, rudders and oars are ready for sailing."

"Then we will launch them the 28th. Any other instructions, Sandoval?"

"The copper arrowheads that we ordered from the neighboring villages according to samples from Castile, about eight thousand per village, are finished, too. We will have fifty thousand copper arrowheads and darts."

"Have Pedro Barba distribute them among the crossbowmen. See that they paste feathers on the ends and give them two cords and guns, swords, lances and iron ornaments. We will have the review of soldiers on the 28th, also. Captains, please see to it that all the horses are shod and that your lances are in perfect condition. You, Gonzalo, send a message to the *tlatoanis* of Tlaxcala, keeping them apprised that following the day of Corpus Christi we will leave for Temistitan and begin the blockade. Have them send us twenty thousand warriors as well as Chalco and Tlalmanalco."

As planned, the thirteen brigantines were launched into the canal with the rudders, sails and oars in place. The whole Spanish army was present along with a great many Indian allies. A review of soldiers was ordered that same day.

"Gonzalo de Sandoval! Give an account of the review of troops!"

"Captain! Eighty-six on horseback, one hundred eighteen crossbowmen and musketeers, six hundred fifty soldiers with swords, lances and shields; three large cannon, recently arrived from Jamaica, fifteen small bronze guns, ten *quintales* (hundred-weight) of gunpowder and stores for all the arms."

"So informed, Sandoval! Now men and friends, the crier will read the Ordinances that you all must observe."

The crier read:

"No one may swear.

"No one abuse or take anything from our Indian friends.

"No one leave the camp, day or night, not even for food.

"Everyone protect his arms as well as the collar of his doublet, winter cap and his leg coverings and shield.

302

"No person may make bets, or games on horse or at arms.

"No one is to sleep without his arms, clothes and shoes, except those seriously injured.

"If anyone sleeps during this watch or leaves his post and goes from one camp to another without permission and if anyone deserts his captain in battle and flees, he will receive the death penalty."

More Warriors Join the Troops

In four days, just before Easter, the warriors from Tlaxcala, Cholula and Huejotzingo arrived. Cortés, accompanied by Sandoval, went out to greet them.

When they passed Chichicamecatl and Xicoténcatl, leading the Tlaxcaltecans, Cortés commented to Sandoval, "We must keep an eye on Xicoténcatl, the young man. I do not like the way he looks at us."

After the march, which lasted three hours, Cortés commented: "It's unbelievable that we are almost fifty thousand warriors. Now we are ready to begin the siege of Temistitan. Order a general assembly for tomorrow."

The Siege of Tenochtitlan

The following day in the main plaza of Texcoco, the Spanish army assembled, surrounded by its Indian warrior allies.

Cortés, mounted on his horse, shouted: "With God's help and in service of His Majesty, the 10th of this May, we will set out to lay siege to Temistitan. This is the plan."

On a simple map of adequate size, he pointed with his sword: "Captain Pedro de Alvarado with thirty cavalry, eighteen crossbowmen and musketeers and one hundred and fifty soldiers with sword and shield and the twenty-five thousand warriors from Tlaxcala, commanded by Chichicamecatl and Xicoténcatl, will set up camp in Tacuba. The first thing you must do is to cut off the drinking water from Chapultepec.

"Captain Cristóbal de Olid, with thirty-two cavalry, eighteen crossbowmen and musketeers, one hundred sixty soldiers with sword and shield and twenty-thousand warriors from Cholula, you will set up camp in Coyoacán, after checking with Alvarado in Tacuba.

"Captain Gonzalo de Sandoval, with twenty-four cavalry, four musketeers and thirteen crossbowmen and one hundred and fifty soldiers with sword and shield and all the people from Guajucingo and Cholula, you will take possession of Ixtapalapa and destroy it, then join the garrison in Coyoacán and set up camp where you think best and most convenient. We will leave the causeway open to Tepeyac if they wish to leave Temistitan when they feel the force of our assault.

"I will send all thirteen brigantines.

"Each boat will be manned by a captain, twelve crossbowmen and musketeers with twelve men to row. I know that few of you wish to row, so we will put our sailors there and those who came from port cities.

"The fleet will depart as soon as we finish the soundings and we balance them in the fresh water as well as the salt water by destroying this earthen dam called the Nezahuacoyo. We will go by way of Ixtapalapa to take control of the causeway."

On the 20th of May, 1521, Alvarado and Olid's forces left by way of the northwest, taking the road to Tacuba and Coyoacán, while Gonzalo de Sandoval left toward the east, to Ixtapalapa in the south. Cortés stayed behind with the brigantines.

The first day's journey of Alvarado and Olid's forces was to Acolman. There each wrangled because Olid's men had arrived first and occupied the best buildings. Tree branches announced their claim. They were at a point of crossing swords when one of Alvarado's soldiers intervened.

Strategy . . .

"Captain Alvarado, put away your sword. I wish to tell you that Xicoténcatl the younger, has run away to Tlaxcala."

"Let us settle the matter and forget about it. Soldier, you go tell Captain Cortés about this desertion, which pains me, because he is my wife *Doña* Luisa's brother," said Alvarado.

When Cortés heard about the dispute between the captains as well as the desertion of Xicoténcatl, he sent a message to the captains.

"Captain Cortés sends word that if the quarrel in the camp is serious, between captains it is shameful and such a bad example that he admonishes you to amend your ways or you will be dismissed from the ranks, which will be a great loss to the army."

Another message was to Captain Ojeda, at Tlaxcala, to inform the *tlatoanis*.

"Xicoténcatl the younger, deserted in Acolman and they say he is coming with his warriors to take possession of the dominion. In Spain, such a crime is punishable by death."

"We are aware of the crime the young man committed and know it causes his father great pain. We agree that he must be punished for the crime as Malinche orders."

When Cortés heard about that opinion from the Tlaxcala Council, he commented to Ojeda: "This *cacique* will never mend his ways. He will always be a traitor toward us. So we must order an exemplary punishment. Have the constable from Segura de la Frontera with four cavalry and some men from Texcoco seize him wherever he is and hang him."

Xicoténcatl was captured in Tlaxcala and there they hanged him.

In Tacuba, the Water from Chapultepec is Cut Off

I n the late afternoon, Alvarado and Olid came to Tacuba, which they found abandoned. When they settled in that night, there arose fierce challenging screams by the Indians from the lake.

On the morning of the 26th of May, Pedro de Alvarado and Cristóbal de Olid with their soldiers had set out on the Chapultepec road to cut the aqueduct. They encountered great resistance from the Aztecs, who were awaiting that tactic. The arrows that fell on the Spaniards looked like "yellow serpents."

With the aid of the artillery and the horses, the Spaniards broke through the Indian lines amidst loud war-whoops, war-commands and the loud noise of the Aztec war instruments. With dead and wounded on all sides, the cavalry succeeded in reaching the area where the clay pipes conveyed the water. They destroyed them, leaving the great city without drinking water.

The Chapultepec aqueduct is destroyed

"We left the Tlaxcaltecan garrison there to guard these pipes so the Aztecs could not repair them," said Alvarado, mounted on his horse, to Cristóbal de Olid who was riding next to him. He added, "Before going on to Coyoacán, I suggest we make a trial run along the Tacuba causeway." Olid consented.

The following day, the 27th of May, at dawn, the Spanish soldiers got ready.

"I invite you to Temistitan, Cristóbal de Olid!" said Alvarado solemnly.

At the vanguard, the cavalry lined up, followed by the soldiers and the Tlaxcaltecans. They advanced along the relatively narrow causeway.

From both sides the canoes began attacking with arrows, slings, staffs and lances. Before the Spaniards reached the first bridge, lines of Indian warriors closed the pass, flinging missiles. To blunt the attack of the horsemen, the Aztecs employed long Indian lances. When the Spanish army counterattacked, the Indians threw themselves into the lake, where they were taken into the canoes.

The narrowness of the causeway caused confusion among the aggressive Spaniards when they noticed a large number of canoes headed for the rear guard.

Olid shouted: "Alvarado, pull back! They are cutting off the rear guard!"

"You go on ahead, Olid, let us see who takes the bridge!" answered Alvarado.

"That's stupid! I'm going back," shouted Olid, who turned his horse around and with his men, added to the confusion.

That battle lasted more than an hour. The Spanish army and the Tlaxcaltecans were almost immobilized by attacks from land and the lake, amid hilarious shouting by the Aztecs.

Finally, Alvarado gave the order to return to Tacuba along the causeway, which cost eight Spanish dead and thirty wounded.

Once they were off the causeway, Alvarado found Olid.

"They attacked us with powerful, ferocious forces. We suffered great damage and we are so few. Slow down your advance to Coyoacán so we may join forces and advance through here."

"No, Alvarado. Two cannot command. This march was ill-planned. I am leaving right now for Coyoacán as Cortés has ordered me to."

"As you wish," said Alvarado, irritated.

In Coyoacán and Ixtapalapa

Thus Olid and his men left for Coyoacán, where they arrived the same day. Finding it deserted, they set up camp.

In Texcoco, Cortés received Olid and Alvarado's messengers. "Captain, Pedro de Alvarado set up camp in Tacuba and destroyed the Chapultepec aqueduct. Then, Captain Olid arrived in Coyoacán after making the first assault on the causeway. There, the very valiant Indian enemies and their canoes did a great deal of damage."

"Go back and tell Alvarado that Sandoval is already in Ixtapalapa. After a victory against heavy resistance and burning many houses, he has set up camp. I am leaving for Ixtapalapa now with the brigantines. Remember the command: No advance along the causeways without filling in the water openings to assure the return."

On the 31st of May, 1521, the brigantines were launched. Sails were hoisted and with all streamers flying and twelve men to row each one, the boats sailed to the astonishment of some and the great enthusiasm of others. Each had a cannon in its bow. On board the flagship, Cortés ordered: "Head toward Ixtapalapa!"

From the surrounding *teocallis* and hills of the lake the smoke signs announced the departure and route of the fleet.

Cuauhtémoc, from the Chief Temple where he commanded his Council, observed in the distance the spectacle of the thirteen vessels with their sails going toward Ixtapalapa. Toward the west he saw the Tacuba causeway, and with the smoke signals and drum beats issued orders.

"The floating houses are heading toward Ixtapalapa. We actually see them and how they fight. Have one thousand canoes protected with bulwarks go out to combat them and alert our forces at *Peñón de Tepepulco* and the Xoloc Fort. The *teules'* houses are going there; attack them by water and land. Tell those in Tlacopan to follow our signals and allow the cavalry to enter and attack them by land and water, but cut off their return by not letting them fill in the water openings. Keep the water flowing through them."

Cuauhtémoc orders the attack on the brigantines

The Brigantines Sail

ortés had previously ordered the opening of the earthen dam of Netzahualcóyotl, which separated the salt water of Texcoco from the fresh water of Tenochtitlan, in order to level the lake and allow the brigantines to pass. Commanding the fleet, he sailed toward Ixtapalapa. As the fleet approached the area, noticing smoke signals from the *Peñón de Tepepulco* where Mexican warriors shouted and challenged them, Cortés ordered: "Do not allow these forces in our path! Let them enter so we can destroy their canoes!"

When the brigantines closed on the *Peñón*, they fired their cannon at the canoes. One hundred fifty troops disembarked and battled their way up the *Peñón* and destroyed the Indian garrison.

From the top, Cortés observed hundreds of Indian canoes approaching. He ordered: "Let's hurry down and get back into the brigantines. Indians in canoes are coming to attack us. Let them come. We won't move, so they will think we are afraid to fight them. Then, at one shot from a musket, we will crash against them and be victorious. Since this will be our first encounter using the brigantines, we must frighten them."

The canoes came on as fast as the Aztecs could paddle. Four hundred meters away, twice as far as a crossbow could reach, they stopped, waiting to see what would happen. For a few moments—nothing—then a strong wind blew up that favored the Spaniards. Cortés ordered the sails trimmed and fired the single warning shot from a musket. With the help of sailors pulling hard on their oars, the brigantines dashed forward against the canoes, first firing the cannon. As the Spanish boats passed across the bows of the canoes, the Christians hurled lances and shot arquebusiers and crossbows. The great speed of the brigantines accelerated the damage and destruction of many Indian canoes.

From the land, those Spaniards in the Coyoacán camp and Tacuba watched the battle on the water and celebrated the victory.

Cuauhtémoc, from the *teocalli*, ordered, "Send signals that the canoes should disperse and head for shallow water!"

They Take the Xoloc Fort

Aboard the brigantines, Cortés was always accompanied by *Doña* Marina, who generally used a Spanish shield for protection.

"This victory has been marvelous and a model for the future," Cortés said to her. "Now, we will head for the point where the causeways from Coyoacán and Ixtapalapa meet at the site of the fort they call Xoloc, which we passed when we first came to Temistitan. We will capture it, as it is an excellent location to shelter the brigantines."

These sailed toward Coyoacán, going past the Xoloc Fort. Cortés disembarked his men on the causeway. They also unloaded two cannon, which they fired against the defenses of the fort, then captured it with the help of Olid's forces, which attacked from the other side.

It was almost dark when Cortés issued an order. "We will set up camp here. Keep the brigantines near these towers. Reverse the defenses and point the cannon toward the causeway so we are ready for battle. Tomorrow, they will attack us furiously."

Amphibious Battles

The following day from the *teocalli*, Cuauhtémoc ordered: "Let us attack along the causeway while the canoes assault the enemy from the shallow water where the *teules'* houses cannot navigate."

When Cortés learned of the concentrated canoe attack on the side where the brigantines could not pass, he ordered the Tlaxcaltecans to break through the causeway above the camp so the brigantines could pass from one side to the other, then on to Tacuba.

Four brigantines passed through to the other side, striking and pursuing the Aztec canoes.

Four brigantines en route to Tacuba

Throughout early June, the battle raged. The Spaniards fired the cannon along the causeway; they advanced behind it; they took the bridges; the Indian counterattacks came from land and from the water.

On one of those days, while Cortés and his men, Spaniards and Tlaxcaltecans, were fighting, Gonzalo de Sandoval arrived from Ixtapalapan.

"Captain Cortés, we captured and burned all the villages from Ixtapalapa to Coyoacán. I need instructions as to where to set up camp for my men."

"I have been waiting for you, Gonzalo. Because we have this camp in Coyoacán, there is no need for you to stay in Ixtapalapa. Alvarado informs me that from Tepeyac and the causeway to the north, many Indians and provisions are arriving. Take your troops and Tlaxcalans and set up camp there. Then Temistitan will be completely surrounded. When you pass through Tacuba, tell Alvarado that at dawn on the 9th of June, right after Mass, we will launch a coordinated attack: Alvarado from Tacuba, we from Coyoacán and you from Tepeyac. I will send two brigantines to you and four to Alvarado to protect you against the treacherous Indian canoes."

The Circle is Closed

At the beginning of June, 1521, the encirclement of Tenochtitlan was completed. The second stage of the siege began with some triumphs and some defeats for one side and the other, but it was the Aztec forces that continued to be worn down.

The first major attack of the Spaniards and their allies began on the 9th of June, 1521. Besides the Tlaxcaltecan allies, there were Huejotzincas and Cholultecas. Cortés was also assisted by thirty thousand Texcocanos commanded by Ixtlixóchitl, the brother of *Don* Fernando, who had been elevated to *Tlatoani* of Texcoco by Cortés. Previously, the Texcocans had been part of the Culúa Alliance. But now, the Aztecs, Tenochcas and Tlatelolcas were alone. Not only were they fighting against their traditional enemies, the Tlaxcaltecans, but against some of their own people, friends and relatives.

From that time on, Ixtlixóchitl was constantly at Cortés' side. His brother, Coanacoch, was with Cuauhtémoc as a member of the Council and a powerful and loyal warrior.

The first attack was generated simultaneously from all three causeways. The Spaniards and their allies penetrated all the way into Tenochtitlan, then were driven back to their camps. The troops commanded by Cortés actually reached the Main Plaza, but could not sustain their advance. The ferocious Aztec counterattacks forced them to retreat.

The battles provided tactical advantages for both sides. The assault planned by Cortés sent four brigantines to Pedro de Alvarado, two to Gonzalo de Sandoval and left seven for him, including the smallest.

The actions on all three causeways were similar. After Mass, Cortés' men took the initiative. They brought the cannon forward into range of the enemy. They fired as much to overwhelm the defense as to open a passage for the cavalry, who could not advance very easily on the narrow causeway. The horsemen were attacked in front by the Aztec warriors who now used long lances and hurled darts and stones; along the flanks, from the canoes and from the roofs of the houses, every type of missile came hurtling at the Spaniards.

Behind the horsemen and often mingling with them came the Spanish foot soldiers and the Indian units in great numbers, all subject to the same assaults.

Because the skirmishes were fought along the causeways, the Spaniards could not form a square. To cross the water openings, they placed their transportable bridges or filled them with all kinds of debris, including rubble from nearby damaged houses.

These events defined the tactics that typified the campaign: The Spaniards reached a water break and ousted the Aztec defenders, then crossed the break as well as they could, even by swimming or wading. At each break, they left a small force to guard the area against the Indians' constant counterattacks, which usually occurred as flanking movements supported by the canoes, some of whose crews had only their paddles as weapons.

These actions were repeated along many kilometers of the causeways that turned into a linear struggle. While the Aztecs were trying to halt the retreat, the Spaniards and their allies held the passes over the breaks in the causeway so that the "front" was unique: along both sides of the causeways, along every canal, there was fighting everywhere.

Cuauhtémoc Repels Cortés' Attack

"Lord Cuauhtémoc, the warriors from Texcoco have joined the fight with Malinche and his *teules*: The traitor, Ixtlixóchitl, commands many thousands of warriors who once were our brothers, sent by that evil man whom they now call Fernando and who rules instead of Cacama. He is the official Coanacoch King."

Cuauhtémoc, in his quarters on top of the Tlatelolco pyramid, replied in a deep voice: "So the warriors from Texcoco are with the *teules*. . . . We will have to fight against those who had been united with us—brothers, relatives, fathers, sons. We will be against ourselves. That prospect is horrible; it is evil. But so be it! We have sufficient resources to fight against all of them. Sound the alert signal."

The beating of the great serpents' skins drum could be heard throughout the entire city and much further.

At its call, the Aztec warriors arrived by land and water. Their shouts and war cries began.

Cuauhtémoc exhorted them. "Let me remind you, battle leaders who oppose the enemy: Let the *teules* advance until they have over-extended their forces, then attack them from both sides of the causeway, from canoes and rooftops. When most of the enemy has passed, go back and re-open the breaks on the causeway. Then be alert for our signals to counterattack."

At dawn, to the sound of cornets, fifes and drums, with banners unfurled, the Spaniards initiated their offensive and began the attack on the city. From Xoloc, Tacuba, Tepeyac, they advanced simultaneously.

Atop the *teocalli*, Cuauhtémoc, watching their movements, ordered smoke signals and the beating of the great drum.

Cortés, mounted and leading the cavalry, placed his cannon and fired on the enemies to make an opening on the causeway, many of whom, as soon as they heard the shot, jumped into the water and crouched as if to hide themselves.

The attackers advanced at half gallop and the soldiers at a fast pace. The Texcocanos were under Ixtlixóchitl's command.

When the Spanish force reached the first break in the causeway, they called for the artillery to advance to destroy the mud fences and walls. With their Indian allies, the soldiers put down wooden beams and began filling the break with debris from damaged houses.

After the Spaniards passed the first water opening, a signal from the *teocalli* brought into action armored canoes, which began to attack from both flanks. Cortés employed three brigantines on each side assaulting the canoes, in turn, with broadsides of cannon fire and shots from the arquebusiers and crossbows from the men stationed on the bows of the ships.

The next water opening at the entrance of the city itself was protected by the Xoloc Fort. Cortés also took it, with the aid of land artillery and the brigantines.

The Aztecs fell back, and these operations were repeated at each break. As the Spaniards advanced, their vanguards drew farther away, making the rearguard more vulnerable to the attacks from the canoes. Consequently, the brigantines found it difficult to defend such a long front. The Spaniards took the fourth water break and with great difficulties were in the city.

Cortés and his captains shouted orders and watchwords. The bellowing was constant. Some of the artillery fire wounded soldiers on both sides.

At every pass, Cortés screamed:

"Close the gap! Put fill in there!"

After they crossed the fourth break, Cortés ordered: "Protect this shallow part. It must not be abandoned. Onward! *Santiago!*"

"*Santiago!*" His men responded.

Careful to heed Cuauhtémoc's orders, the Aztecs continued an orderly retreat. Suddenly, at a signal, they concentrated their attack on the Spanish rear guard. They charged onto the causeway and their reinforcements opened the filled-in breaks, destroying the Spanish bridges and even making new breaches in the causeway.

As soon as Cortés was informed, he ordered his horsemen: "Ten cavalry return and clean the enemies off the causeway. Do not abandon the passes."

These scenes were repeated time and again until the Spaniards brought a cannon up to the entrance to the Tenochtitlan plaza. They fired repeated volleys until the defenses were breached.

Cuauhtémoc's warriors cut off the retreat [of Cortés' men]

Because the attacks on the rear guard had imperiled their retreat, at one moment there were no horsemen in the vanguard. Without cavalry, the foot soldiers, amidst victorious shouts and slogans, entered the half-empty plaza. Almost at once, at a signal from the *teocalli*, from all sides surged Aztec warriors, who attacked ferociously. In total confusion, the Spaniards began to pull back.

When Cortés heard about the difficulty involving his men, he ordered three horsemen: "At a fast gallop, hurry to save the soldiers who are pulling back! Tell them to keep orderly! They should sound the retreat bugle call. We cannot hold this position with our forces dispersed all along the causeway!"

In the face of the Aztec onslaught, but aided by the cavalry, the Spaniards began to draw back. Meanwhile, the jubilant Aztecs captured a cannon, which they threw into the water while screaming for joy.

Cuauhtémoc pressed the counterattack with constant smoke signals from the *teocalli*. Then the drums, shellhorns, *tepoanxtles* were sounded to signal the joyous victory.

By late afternoon, Cortés' troops had managed to return to Coyoacán, tired, wounded and confused.

Almost the same scenario had occurred with the assaults against Alvarado and Sandoval.

Cortés dismounted and assembled his captains:

"Today's battle was fierce. But from it we have learned that Guatemocin [Cuauhtémoc] knows what he is doing and that his warriors fight bravely.

"They made it easy for us to advance, so we overextended our forces. Then they could attack the rear guard. I am sure it will not be advantageous for us to advance farther unless we can ensure the advance by filling in the breaks and securing the passes. We must destroy the houses from which they attack us. What we cannot destroy we will burn."

He turned to one of his stewards: "Tell Sandoval and Alvarado not to attempt to reach the plazas with one charge; they should only attack to control the water areas to make them firm and well defended. They should never advance until the shallows have been filled in."

During the night, the Aztecs secretly returned to open all the breaches that had been filled in by the Spaniards during the previous day.

At dawn, the guards told Cortés the army was ready to continue the attack.

"But Captain, the Indians have re-opened the causeway water breaks that we closed yesterday."

"That was to be expected! We will strike back without going too far. We will gain ground step by step, destroying any adjacent houses to gather rubble with which to fill the breaks. In that way, we will also eliminate attacks from the rooftops. To leave garrisons at each break is impossible, because we are already over-committed. But let us proceed little by little as we tighten the blockade."

The same strategy was employed in the other Spanish camps.

The Defeat of Alvarado

"Go ahead and let *Tonatiuah's* men who attacked us from Tacuba come a little farther. Then we will cut off retreat at the Tenchicalco break where we have camouflaged the pass so that we can easily enlarge it," Cuauhtémoc ordered. He was observing the battle that Alvarado's men and their allies from Tacuba were fighting, threatening to reach the Tlatelolco plaza which had been the goal of all the Spaniard's advances.

At dawn in his Tacuba camp, Alvarado rode slowly before his troops. "This refreshing morning air inspires me to fight and to be victorious. With the help of our Saint Santiago, we will conquer more bridges."

His men shouted: "*Tonatiuh!* Let us have the honor to be the first to reach the market before Cortés."

"Advance," Alvarado cried. "First, the cavalry—and do not forget to fill in the breaks as we advance. Make sure they are defended as Cortés ordered."

"*Santiago! Santiago!*" the troops roared in reply.

The cavalry left at half gallop and the Spanish foot soldiers and Indian allies at quick march.

With apparent ease, they went from one bridge to another. The Aztecs seemed to be withdrawing in apparent disorder. However, all along the causeway, from behind the walls and the mud fence placed before and after the breaks, the Aztecs challenged and fought on both sides of the causeway from the canoes and the housetops. Each day there were fewer houses because of the destructive force of the Spaniards, who destroyed them to obtain debris to fill the breaks and to avoid being molested from above.

From their canoes, the Aztecs shouted and sang the usual sneers.

"*Cuilones! Cuilones! Cuilones!*"

"*Ai, Santa Malía manda Capitán daca zapato!*"

Fired with passion, the horsemen crossed a fairly narrow ditch, followed by the soldiers coming at a fast pace. Once the troops were well into the city, at a signal from the *teocalli*, the Aztecs removed the temporary supports that held the fill of the great span of the shallows. Instantly, it became a wide, deep canal. Then, at another signal from the drum, a great force of Aztec warriors charged to halt Alvarado's advance. As the Christian captain ordered the retreat, he discovered the breach wide open. Soon the Spaniards were surrounded. Across the water-break, other Spaniards and their allies tried to protect the retreat and defend themselves from attacks coming from Aztec canoes. Totally confused, the trapped Spaniards, shouting pitifully, threw themselves into the canal trying to swim across. Many were wounded or died, but many escaped, among them Alvarado. Many Spaniards were captured alive and the Aztecs dragged them toward the *teocalli*.

After a great effort, Alvarado was able to regroup his men. Exhaustedly, he said, "I swear to a thousand devils. How was our retreat foiled? Damn!"

"Captain, we fell into a trap."

"Not only could we not fill in the opening, but those damned Indians—I do not know how they did it—made the break even wider," said a standard-bearer, who with great effort had saved the flag.

"Cortés warned us to fill in the breaks. That is what I regret most," said Alvarado. "That and those unfortunate brothers who were captured alive. Damnation!"

Alvarado's defeat

Crestfallen, he returned to camp.

That night they heard the gloomy sound of the great drum. Amid flickering torches and a flambeaux, the Aztecs were leading ten to twleve captive Spaniards in a line. They were naked. On top of the *teocalli*, the Indians forced them to dance before the idols, punching the white men with spears. Then, one by one, the invaders were sacrificed in front of Cuauhtémoc.

At the end of the ceremony, he said, "On the tips of your pikes exhibit the *teules*' heads as well as their horses'! Then take some other heads and adorn them to send around so the people will know about the death of the *teules* and our victory over them. Tell our followers the gods have favored us and that we will destroy the *teules* and punish any traitors."

From Alvarado's camp, the Spaniards contemplated the spectacle with horror and great distress.

"That one looks like Yáñez! How ghastly!"

"Look, the one they are beating because he refuses to dance is González!"

"You can't distinguish one from another this far away! It may be any one of those we lost. I prefer to die in battle than listen to that mournful sound of their musical instruments," said Bernal. He added, "When you are in the battle, you feel a revulsion when you think about that kind of death."

When Cortés learned about the utter route of Alvarado's force, he was furious and went to their camp to rebuke Alvarado.

"Cristóbal de Olid, take charge of this camp. I am going to see Alvarado to reprimand him. He suffered a very grave defeat because he did not obey the orders I gave, both verbally and written: 'No one should advance unless they are sure the cavalry can return along that same route. . . .'"

"I regret this failure because it may give our enemies greater confidence. Now they will think they can stop us from entering the city. And all because our men did not carry out their orders in their greediness to gain the honor of reaching the market first."

Aboard his brigantine, Cortés sailed to Tacuba, where he arrived that afternoon. Alvarado was still at the front, so Cortés spoke to one of his brothers, Jorge, whom he also rebuked.

"By my conscience, Jorge! How stupid could your brother be to cause such a defeat? Where is he?"

"Captain, Pedro is fighting. He should be back soon. Then Your Grace can see how we made inroads into the city and how many passes we have taken."

"There is no way to justify his failure to heed the orders."

"Look, Captain, that happened because of a trick and we fell into it, although it was our own fault because we were not cautious enough."

Cortés went forward to assess the penetration of Alvarado's forces. He was quite surprised.

"I must confess I am surprised how far you have entered the city," he said. "The defeat will not have such serious consequences if you can hold what you have taken."

"I am sure we can, *señor*. Here comes my brother, Pedro."

When he arrived, Pedro de Alvarado jumped down from his horse, greeting Cortés respectfully: "I would have been more pleased to greet Your Grace in Temistitan itself."

"We will accomplish that, Alvarado. I was most disappointed when I heard about your defeat, which has satisfied our enemies and may make them very bold. But upon my honor as a *caballero*, I confess it surprises me how far you reached into the city."

"That's the way it goes, Captain, war is like that. I could not punish those who deserted the break. Many of them died defending it, or were captured."

"It has been explained to me and I do not wish to reproach you, but never neglect again to fill in the breaks on the causeway."

"I understand that very well. They tell me the opening was widened when the Indians removed certain supports. Our enemies were too clever for us."

"We cannot predict their plans. We must think ahead. What is important now is that they not become too encouraged. No doubt our enemies are saying we cannot invade the city."

"We will invade them, Captain! I will be very careful in the future."

"Then this is how we must proceed. Ahead of time, tell me your plans. It is important for my troops to know that you will not be advancing more rapidly than we. Even so, no matter how hard they may try to disguise their zeal, the soldiers want to reach the market before you."

"The same thing occurred to me," said Alvarado, as they strolled toward a secure and well-filled point on the causeway, halfway between Tacuba and Tenochtitlan.

"Here is where I plan to move my camp, Captain," said Alvarado. "It is too dangerous to be so far away, when we must march to the city every day to continue the fight."

"You have my permission. I will think about doing the same for my camp, as Coyoacán is quite far from the city. Although it is more secure, it requires more effort."

Battle in Tenochtitlan

The night of June 16, Cortés returned to his camp; once mounted, he ordered the army: "Let us make an entrance into the city and deflate their pride at their triumph over Alvarado."

During that advance, the fighting was as ferocious as the previous battles, but they reached the central plaza of Tenochtitlan. Cortés even had a chance to set fire to the Axayácatl Palace where they had had their garrison and the immense aviary. But again, they had to retreat to the camp because of harassing counterattacks ordered by Cuauhtémoc from his command post on the *Teocalli* of Tlatelolco.

"Lord Cuauhtémoc," an aide said to him, "the *teules* are coming with great force. They want revenge for *Tonatiuh*'s devastating defeat."

"Let them come; let them enter confidently; let them become arrogant. But they must pass no further than the Axayácatl Palace. At that point, we will counterattack."

Later, when Cortés again reached the plaza and began to set fire to the palaces, Cuauhtémoc, without a flinch, said: "It is a pity they destroyed so many fine birds, which my forefathers had collected over such a long period." Although his officers were terrified, Cuauhtémoc continued, "Even so, let them have their pleasure. Wait for my signal to mount an attack."

When he gave the order, the Spaniards were assaulted on land and water and were forced to retreat until they reached their camp.

The Battle of Tenochtitlan

322

On arriving there, Cortés said: "This is like the tale that never ends, like Penelope's cloth—she weaves it by day and rips it apart at night. Today we were victorious. Yesterday, Alvarado was defeated. We must tighten the blockade."

Doña Marina, who was next to him, said: "Lord, in your absence, the representatives from the *Chinampa* villages, Xochimilco, Mixquic, Churubusco, Tláhuac and Ixtapalapa, have come to declare their support. They regret the battles they waged against you and wish for peace. They are waiting in your quarters."

Cortés and Marina went there to receive the subjects from the *Chinampería*.

After that ceremony, Cortés met with Lugo, Cristóbal de Olid and Andrés de Tapia. "Now the Mexicans are alone; each day more Indian friends support us. Have Pedro de Alvarado and Gonzalo de Sandoval meet me tomorrow night so we can discuss how we should enter the city. At our present rate, we will never get there. Invite to the meeting ten soldiers from each camp and our friends, the Indian leaders."

The following night, joined by those who had been invited, Cortés spoke: "Brothers and friends. The great efforts and sacrifices that we make every day are apparent in the hard fighting. We fill ditches and build bridges and close breaks and at night the Mexicans open them. Then they build even stronger barricades than before. It takes a great deal of effort to fight and fill in ditches so we can cross. At the same time, we must defend ourselves vigilantly. It is a story without an ending. Therefore, I want your opinions on a plan Ixtlixóchitl suggests: At a given signal, we will attack simultaneously from all three causeways with the support of the brigantines, until we reach the Tlatelolco plaza. There, we will set up the three camps and stage our battles through the streets of Mexico itself, without having to retreat and to fill up the water breaks or guard the bridges. What do you think, Alvarado?"

"I am most anxious to join you in the Tlatelolco market. Even though there are risks, it is a good suggestion. We already moved our camp closer to the city after our unfortunate defeat and it is much easier to fight from there."

"What do you think, Olid?"

"I agree. It is a prudent plan, Captain," said Sandoval. "And you, Gonzalo, what do you think? If we move our camps into Tlatelolco itself, we can become the besiegers in the besieged area even though the Mexican fighters are numerous and have great strength. They can cut us off from the exits to the causeways and place stakes in the lake to restrict the brigantines from helping us."

The discussions continued and after a while, Cortés concluded: "You are correct, Sandoval, in that we will become the besiegers in the besieged area. However, it is clear to me that we can not continue as we have been. Next Sunday at dawn, we will attack simultaneously from all three camps to invade the market. In the meantime, we will all move our camps closer to Temistitan to tighten the blockade. Since we do not have a better plan, after this attack our goal will be to destroy all the houses and temples alongside the causeway and use the fill for the ditches and canals to ensure a clear passageway. To accomplish this, our Indian friends must come with their *coas*.* *Señores*, until Sunday! When we will count our blessings from *Señor Santiago*!"

"*Santiago*," everyone shouted as the meeting ended.

---

* Sharp stick used by the Indians for tilling.—Trans.

Cortés' Defeat

In the early morning of Sunday, the 30th of June, 1521, which coincidentally was the anniversary of the *Noche Triste*, the attack from the three camps was prepared. All three armies would converge on Tenochtitlan at the same time. Cuauhtémoc, already informed by his spies, was waiting.

"Men," Cortés shouted to his army, "on a day like today just a year ago we fled from Temistitan. Today, we will have a great victory. Onward! *Santiago*!"

"*Santiago*," shouted the Spanish army while the Indian friends roared their own battle cries.

In order, they advanced easily along the causeway and did not encounter any resistance until reaching the water crossings close to the city. There, a sea battle erupted. Cortés advanced confidently, inspiring his troops to begin taking bridges and passes with relative ease.

He spoke to Olid: "These Indians, assaulted by Alvarado and Sandoval's forces, are weakening. Let us take advantage of their weakness and make a strong assault."

In Alvarado and Sandoval's groups, the scene was the same except the Mexican resistance was fiercer. Noticing the resistance, Alvarado said: "These devils are fighting violently today. They do not yield at the passes and resist us as never before. At them! *Santiago*!" and he began fighting alongside his companions.

The same occurred with Sandoval. As he attacked, he said: "Today the resistance is like it never was before, as if they are inspired by our defeat a year ago! Onward! *Santiago*!"

From the *teocalli*, Cuauhtémoc directed the operations.

At dawn, smoke signals announced that the Spaniards and their allies began to advance.

"Lord Cuauhtémoc: The *teules* and the traitors are advancing along the three causeways as they had planned."

"That is fine, my nobles. Remember, a year ago we ousted the *teules* on the victorious night. Today we will have another, only greater. This we will do: At the first bridge, we will assault *Tonatiuh* and Gonzalo. As for Malinche, who set fire to our royal palaces and has become overly confident, we will allow him to enter just past the Tlacopan street. When he reaches the Lagunilla, we will widen the water break—just as we did with Alvarado, then counterattack. Be sure the officers are alert to our signals."

While Alvarado and Sandoval advanced slowly, making great efforts against a tenacious resistance, Cortés moved ahead with relative ease. Beside him was Alderete, the Royal Treasurer, who had begged to accompany Cortés. The Spanish leader reminded his men: "After passing each water break, be sure you fill in the ditch to assure our retreat."

Which is how they reached, with little resistance, the main plaza of Tenochtitlan. There, Cortés regrouped his forces and ordered: "These three streets lead to the Tlatelolco market. You, Treasurer Alderete, take ten cavalry as a vanguard with seventy soldiers and twenty thousand Indian allies from Tlaxcala. With eight cavalry as a rear guard, enter through the main street. Remember, while you cross the bridges and trenches, fill them with the aid of your twelve men with pick-axes and the help of the Indians. Don't forget it!

"You, Cristóbal de Olid, with Andrés de Tapia, take your horsemen and eighty soldiers and ten thousand of our Indian friends, advance along the middle street. You know what to do—cross breaks and then fill them. I, with eight horsemen, one hundred soldiers and the rest of the Indians will enter along this narrow street. In the Tacuba street we have two large cannon defended by eight horses and the artillerymen to cover the rear guard. Onward! *Santiago*!"

At the shout of *Santiago*, they launched the attack with great vigor along the three streets. In multiple onslaughts, they took two bridges and barricades and the Indian allies breached nearby houses. Alderete and Olid's charges moved ahead. With twenty Spaniards, Cortés stayed on a small islet helping the Tlaxcaltecans, who were fighting in the street with great difficulty, advancing and retreating. Their scouts had noticed many Aztec warriors in the nearby streets, waiting expectantly.

"Captain, there are many Mexicans lying in ambush behind those houses."

"Then we will stay here to forestall a blow to the rear guard. Alderete is advancing at his pleasure with great enthusiasm."

"Captain, Alderete sends a message. He is close to the Tlatelolco plaza and can hear the shuffle of Alvarado's men."

"Go back and tell him not to go one step farther without filling in the water breaks."

"That is what he is doing, Captain."

"Fine. Francisco de Lugo, sustain the attack along this street and be careful of the enemy. I am going to help Alderete. Something tells me the taste of victory may be too much for him."

Actually, Alderete's men, moving along the wide street after taking two bridges and barricades, reached the seemingly narrow Lagunilla canal, filled in the ditch with wood and cane and passed over slowly without Indian resistance.

From his post on the Tlatelolco *Teocalli*, Cuauhtémoc directed operations. When he saw that Alderete with his sixty men had passed with thousands of Tlaxcaltecans, he sounded a signal on the big drum.

Suddenly, from the neighboring streets, from the lake, canoes and roof tops, a great multitude of warriors appeared and assailed Alderete and his men.

At the same time, Aztec soldiers hidden in the cane reeds of the Lagunilla, pulled out temporary supports and barriers which had buttressed the dangerous water pass and the canal reopened to its great depth.

"Damnation! They did not fill in the pass. Not even one reed!" shouted Cortés, arriving at the break and seeing Alderete's men retreating in a stampede. He wanted them to stop before the open ditch. So he shouted: "Stop! Hold! Hold fast! Do not turn your backs! Stop!"

But no one heard him, or if they did, paid no attention. The Spaniards and Tlaxcaltecans, even the cavalry, dashed forward into the canal trying to swim across it. On the opposite bank, Cortés continued shouting orders.

From the Lagunilla and neighboring canals appeared a fleet of Indian canoes attacking the fugitives, who were also accosted from the land by many Aztec warriors.

Soon the whole area where they were fighting became a slippery mud hole. On his horse, Alderete was able to reach the bank and he continued to flee. Eight or ten horses died in the canal and the Mexicans captured almost all of Alderete's troops, about seventy, who were trapped on the other side of the canal. Amid the confusion, Cortés and twenty Spaniards became surrounded by Aztecs. Cortés went on shouting: "Reassemble! Retreat to Tacuba street. I will stay here and die fighting." Then Cortés' horse fell. A triumphant shout arose from the Mexican army.

"Malinche is down!"

From the *teocalli*, Cuauhtémoc, observing the development of the battle, ordered, "Do not kill a single Spaniard. Capture them all alive! I want Malinche alive!"

Seven Aztec warriors threw themselves on Cortés, who was half submerged in the mud bravely defending himself.

They tried to snatch him, but they all slipped in the mud. Then Cristóbal de Olea, captain of Cortés' personal guard, arrived. Ignoring the danger, he wielded tremendous blows with his sword, cutting off arms and slashing blows while he shouted to his friends: "Lerma, come here! They are trying to take away Cortés!"

"Kill them or die! Everyone! They are capturing the Captain! *Santiago*! *Santiago*!"

But soon other Mexicans came, who held their grip on Cortés, while Cristóbal de Olea continued fighting fiercely along with Lerma until they freed their captain. More Spaniards appeared to help and Cortés was finally able to stand up. Another group of Aztec warriors came through the mud toward Cortés, who was now standing with his sword in his hand. To his defense came Olea, who died killing the Indians. Lerma fell and was wounded. Now on foot, Cortés kept on issuing orders:

"Help Olea, he is down!"

"Captain, he is dead!"

"He gave his life for mine! How brave! Here I will die fighting! See how they are capturing the unfortunate Christians," he said. Cortés and his men repelled the attack of the ferocious Aztec warriors who were shouting victoriously.

From the *teocalli*, the drum sent the signal:

"Alive! Alive! Alive!" shouted the Aztec attackers. "Alive! Alive!"

Then Antonio de Quiñones, Cortés' personal guard, said to him: "Let us get out of here to protect you. Without you, none of us will escape."

"I shall die right here, Quiñones! It is a great dishonor to have fallen into this very trap I criticized Alvarado about! See how many Christians have been captured."

Then Quiñones grasped Cortés' arms, turning him around. Other soldiers did the same and, with Cortés in the center and protecting him, they began to retreat, slipping through the mud. He suffered almost as much from the efforts of the men trying to save themselves as he did from the attacks by the Aztecs. Just then, a young soldier arrived on a horse, shouting: "Captain! Here, I brought you a horse!"

Lances and rocks hurled from the nearby roofs killed both the young soldier and the horse.

Soon another soldier, Cristóbal de Guzmán, arrived with a horse for Cortés. An Indian killed the young soldier.

With great sorrow and ignoring everyone's warnings, Cortés mounted the horse, who was slipping awkwardly in the mud. Quiñones, holding onto the reins, guided it very slowly toward Tacuba, where Spanish reinforcements arrived to help. Cortés joined up with the seven other horsemen. There, he was able to reorganize the resistance by firing the cannon, which helped somewhat in the counteroffensive.

Cortés ordered two horsemen: "Go to Cristóbal de Olid and order him to retreat. He might be cornered like Francisco de Lugo."

From the *teocalli*, Cuauhtémoc, unperturbed, saw the development of his victory and ordered: "Attack! Attack!"

Then he told three captains: "Cut off the heads of the Spanish captives and after they are disfigured throw them at *Tonatiuh*, saying they are Malinche's and Sandoval's; throw some others at Sandoval, saying they are *Tonatiuh*'s and to Malinche if he is still alive, throw two at him and say they are *Tonatiuh* and Sandoval."

When they did that, it caused great shock and alarm among each of the Spanish companies.

The brigantines were unable to help Cortés' men very much because the Aztecs had placed stakes in the strategic points, preventing the boats to come close enough to help them. When they witnessed the rout of Alderete's men, the brigantines commanded by Barba and Portillo tried to close in, but ran aground and were attacked by Indian canoes. One of the brigantines, Portillo's, could not escape the trap and was set afire by the Indians. Portillo was killed, but some of his men escaped by swimming to Barba's boat. He, as captain of the crossbowmen, although wounded, was able to free his boat and by sheer effort of the oars ordered a retreat. Eight days later he died.

At another signal, Cuauhtémoc ordered his armies to attack fiercely in the Tacuba area. They routed Alvarado's men, but he was able to retreat in good order because all of the passes along the return route had been filled in.

When the Aztecs reached Alvarado's camp, he had arrived already with his men and guarded the passage with two cannon which they began to fire against those

Indians on the causeway. One man loaded, the other fired. Between shots, the cavalry charged the enemy and retreated. Then more cannon fire and more sorties by the cavalry.

All at once, some Mexican warriors dashed toward the camp and threw down four heads of dead Spanish soldiers.

"Here is Malinche's head!"

"Here is Sandoval's head!"

"Here is Olid's head!"

"Here is Tapia's head!"

"Yours will be next!"

All of this took place amid great shouts to the beat of the *teocalli* drums. The survivors could see a long line of nude, white bodies walking up to be sacrificed. The faces of the Spaniards revealed horror and terror.

The battle ended at dusk. Worried, Alvarado ordered: "Send a soldier to Cortés' camp and tell him about the defeat."

Sandoval's attack had had better success because it advanced steadily and cautiously. It stopped at a wide canal which they were forced to fill before passing.

They were busily doing that, when from the other side, protected by mud walls, the Aztecs threw four heads of Spanish soldiers and shouted:

"There goes Malinche!"

"And *Tonatiuh!*"

"And Lugo!"

"And Tapia!"

The heads splashed into the water.

Like all the others, Sandoval was wounded. He ordered: "Continue to fight and fill in the breaks. But do not retreat until you are finished, even though you must reach the garrison tonight. I am going by horse to Cortés' camp because the shouting indicates the enemy is victorious."

At nightfall, Sandoval arrived at Cortés' camp and found the leader in his tent where *Doña* Marina was taking care of him. She put a compress on his leg to ease bruises from the Indians' long poles. Exhausted, Cortés received Sandoval with pleasure. "Gonzalo, my son, how good it is to see you alive. The enemy threw some heads at us, and one, they shouted, was yours."

"The same thing happened when we reached Temistitan. Because of all their victory songs and glee, I am happy to see you alive. But Captain, what is going on? What happened? Is this the result of your strategies of war you have always described to us? How could this misfortune occur?"

With tears in his eyes, choked by his emotions, Cortés said, "Oh, my son, Sandoval! It must be because of my sins. But it is not my fault as many of our officers and soldiers claim. But the Treasurer, Julián de Alderete, whom I ordered to fill in that pass where they defeated us, failed to obey; perhaps he is not accustomed to war or to being ordered about by captains."

Alderete, who was close by, said: "Captain Cortés, that is not how it happened. You were moving ambitiously, shouting 'Onward, *caballeros*!' If you had ordered me to fill in that break, I would have done it."

"The damage is done, Alderete!" said Cortés. "Why are we wrangling? So many Christians captured alive. A punishment, no doubt, for my pride, which for much less I rebuked Pedro de Alvarado."

At one point, one of Cortés' aides said, "Captain, one of the brigantines arrived that we thought was lost. Pedro Barba, who is gravely wounded, would like to speak with you."

They brought Barba in a large basket into Cortés' tent.

"Cortés, seriously wounded, I come here. They attacked two brigantines with stakes and nets. Fighting ferociously, they wounded everyone and killed many, among them Portillo, who was in command of the other brigantine. By the sheer power of our oars, we got away. It was a miracle."

"My friend Barba, today I paid for my sins. It hurts me deeply to see you in this condition. But much worse are our brothers who were taken alive. It seems like yesterday that you wanted to capture me in La Española by Velázquez's orders and look where we are now. But do not exert yourself; the doctor will treat and dress your wounds, which are many."

"And mortal," gasped Barba. "But there is one thing I would like to suggest: The brigantines must not go close to the stakes. However, with a favorable wind coming from a distance with a fast pace and by rowing vigorously, they can destroy those stakes."

"Thank you, Barba. Rest now."

In Tenochtitlan

All night long, the Aztecs beat their drums, blew shellhorns and flutes and pounded *teponaxtles*, singing and shouting to celebrate, among lively torch flames, the sacrifice of the Spaniards and Indian allies who in an interminable line marched up the steps of the *teocalli*.

Cuauhtémoc, presiding over the butchery, ordered: "Send the heads of the *teules* and horses throughout the Culúa territory so they may learn about our victories. Tell them our gods have promised us victory over the *teules* and traitors. Tomorrow we will celebrate, sacrificing the *teules*, with celebrations to our goddess Vixtocioatl so that we may have enough salt."

The next day, the 1st of July, they beat the big drum constantly. A long line of victims went up the steps of the Tlatelolco pyramid. About eighty Spaniards were sacrificed, to the horror of Alvarado's people, who could see them from their camp.

The way to the sacrificial altar

330

Sandoval

Early that day, Sandoval came to see Cortés. "Captain, what are your orders? I am going back to my company."

"My son, I am wounded and cannot ride. Everyone else is wounded, some more seriously than others, and we are all exhausted. Please go to Alvarado's camp for me and see how they are. Until I issue new orders, they should not fight, not even a skirmish. They should not capture any bridges, but must defend their camp until we can agree how we should proceed with the fighting. Our swords are too short for fighting in the canals; we need the longer lances, which I have ordered, and soon we will distribute them. Recently, we received crossbows, gunpowder and some arms from a ship that arrived in Villa Rica captained by Ponce de León. You remember, he bragged that he had found the Fountain of Youth. While that may have been a catastrophe, we have benefited anyway, because gunpowder has become very scarce. What we have left we will use only to defend the camps until the new powder gets here. You are my right hand, so I must ask another favor. After you see Alvarado, go to Cuernavaca with ten cavalry and eighty soldiers to assist you. Those Malinalco people attacked us and now is not the time to reveal weakness, so the enemies do not become proud and haughty."

"I will do it, Captain Cortés. I hope you recover quickly."

Sandoval arrived at Alvarado's camp just in time to help him defeat an Aztec attack against two brigantines they were determined to capture. Six soldiers, Bernal Díaz del Castillo among them, were involved and very glad to receive help from Sandoval and his men.

When the attack was over, Sandoval delivered Cortés' orders.

"Alvarado, Cortés orders you not to take any more bridges or canals. Just defend your camp. It is all right to use the gunpowder because a shipment is coming from Vera Cruz. Cortés will send battle orders in the next few days."

"We can use the rest. We have many wounded and powder is scarce."

Chichimecatecuhtli, the *Tlatoani* of Tlaxcala, who overheard the order, said to Alvarado: "The Tlaxcaltecans want to fight alone against the Aztecs and match forces. What do you think about that?"

"Do it," said Sandoval.

For the next few days, only Indian fought against Indian.

331

Once More the Offensive

Eventually, a cargo of arms and gunpowder reached Cortés' camp from Villa Rica along with the long lances he had ordered made in the nearby villages. The spears had sharp copper points and he ordered them distributed among the camps.

"Andrés de Tapia, take a strong garrison and go throughout our area distributing these crossbows, powder and long lances to Alvarado's and Sandoval's men. Tell them this is how we will proceed:

"We will not attack the city and invade it as we have before. We will continue to destroy the houses and temples, fill in the water breaks and holes with debris. And not only the passes in the causeways, but also all the canals. Our Indian friends with their *coas* and we with our pickaxes will do this every day as if we were in battle. The long lances are preferable to swords at keeping the enemy under control. Horses and cannon will respond to attacks. We will do nothing more until a new order is issued. This way, the brigantines can harass the canoes bringing in provisions to Temistitan."

July

For the next few days of July, a month of heavy rains, the war changed: The Spaniards no longer took the initiative. They defended counterattacks with short pursuits, and defended their camps. Meanwhile, everyone, even Cortés, continued destroying houses and temples to fill in the canals, not just the breaks in the causeways.

Carrying a large beam, Cortés was firm, "We will not take one step forward without making everything level. Where there is water, we will make solid ground even though there may be delays."

Every camp followed the same pattern, leaving only the cavalry and the artillerymen with a few soldiers to defend the barracks. Now the water became a line of defense for the Spaniards, who used their long lances that stopped the Indian attacks. The brigantines had learned to overcome the obstruction of the stakes with speed from favorable winds and powerful rowing.

Cuauhtémoc, commanding in Tlatelolco, met with his captains. They said to him: "Lord Cuauhtémoc, the *teules* are afraid and do not attack us as before."

He shook his head. "No, we cannot hope the *teules* have changed their tactics. Now they are destroying the whole city and leveling off the land so it will be difficult to open the canals and passes. We must attack them day and night without stopping."

When the night attacks against the camps began, time and again the cannon, arquebusiers, crossbows and long lances and often the cavalry protected the camps from harassment.

Meanwhile, the filling in and leveling off of the city continued systematically despite the Aztec effort to stop it. The defensive war continued to favor the Spaniards. Now, the Aztecs were forced to return to their camps, retreating past their sentries, leaving themselves vulnerable to forays from the Spanish cavalry.

Offers of Peace

"W hy not make an offer of peace to the Mexican chief? He no longer has any allies or help, neither here nor in the other valleys."

"Good advice, Gonzalo. The longer this war lasts, the more time they will have to hide their treasure."

Accompanied by noblemen, Aztec prisoners, the Spaniards sent a peace mission to Cuauhtémoc.

"Tell the Lord Guatémoc that we offer peace. We recognize him as a relative of Moctezuma and if the war ends now, we will recognize him as an equal, in name, of the King *Don* Carlos. We forgive the death of Spaniards and our allies. Surely he is aware the blockade is closing and knows they need provisions and water. All the surrounding villages and the other valleys are subjects of His Majesty and are opposing the Mexicans. We do not wish to destroy the city; and we pity the children, women and old people. He should surrender."

"Malinche, we are afraid Cuauhtémoc will kill us if we speak to him about peace. Give us a letter of authorization."

On receiving the proposition, Cuauhtémoc convoked the Council of the Aztecs before whom the three Aztec emissaries, crying and sobbing, repeated what Cortés had told them. When they finished, Cuauhtémoc said: "You have been heard. Peace is good; but the Council must deliberate."

During the deliberation, the oldest member of the Council spoke: "Lord, great lord Cuauhtémoc. Now we have you as our King and Lord and your reign is good in every way. You have been a man of respectability and you have the right to reign. The peace offers they speak about are good, but think about it and consider them: When these *teules* invaded our lands and our city, everything went from bad to worse. And consider the benefits and gifts that the great Moctezuma gave them. And consider how it all ended. Look what your cousin, Cacama, Lord of Texcoco, did. And your relatives, the lords of Ixtapalapa and Coyoacán, Tlacopan and Matlatzingo, what did they do? All the children of the great Moctezuma died. Just consider what happened to your subjects in Tepeaca and Chalco and even from Texcoco and all your cities and villages. They have made slaves of them and even branded their faces. First, consider what our gods have promised you. Take good counsel from them and do not have confidence in Malinche or in his words. It is better that we all die fighting in this city rather than to be under the power of a man who will enslave and torture us."

Patiently, Cuauhtémoc listened to the deliberations of the Council. "If these are your wishes, safely protect the corn and provisions we have and we will all die fighting. From now on and in the future, no one dare seek peace. If he does, I will kill him."

"No one should dare to ask for peace. If anyone does, I will kill him."

For two days, Cortés waited for a reply. On the third at dawn, the Aztecs' instruments of war sounded. From the three causeways, Aztec heralds said: "Malinche should not speak to us about peace. Our gods have promised us victory and we have food and water. We will not spare any of your lives. So do not speak about peace; words are for women, weapons are for men."

With the fury of wild beasts, for the next seven days according to Cuauhtémoc's signals, the Aztecs assailed all three causeways, often reaching close to the camps defended by the Spaniards and their allies.

Suicidally, wave after wave of warriors attacked. If threatened by a sword, they hurled themselves against it, piercing their bodies, so eager were they to grab the riders.

More and more cannon, horses, long lances, and swords from many more allies contributed to the attack during those seven days in the middle of July, 1521.

From early morning to nightfall, amid the downpours of the Mexican summer rain, they fought those seven days. The brigantines cruised about the lake demolishing enemy boats. Many people who lived on the banks of the lake thrust their canoes against the brigantines to help in the war of persecution.

The Aztecs fought on alone. Their war cry was: "Until your death or mine!"

The desperate suicidal force with which they fought opened the Aztecs to frequent ambushes, which were now put in place by the Spaniards and Tlaxcaltecans.

There were seven days of great butchery. At the end of the period, the Indian aggression stopped and Cortés ordered his troops to wait. Only brief skirmishes occurred for five days. During that time from Villa Rica, arms and gunpowder arrived from a failed expedition that Vásquez de Ayllón had planned.

"Let us make Guatémoc another peace offer," Cortés said. So they sent another captive Indian chief as emissary. That same afternoon, the emissary's body was sent back with a message: "Cuauhtémoc says he will kill anyone who mentions peace. He will fight on until everyone is killed or everyone is dead. There will be no peace."

Coanacoch

The following day and for three days thereafter, the Aztecs launched another desperate offensive with the same ferocious characteristics they had exhibited before. After the threat abated, Cortés ordered his troops to continue filling in and leveling breaks.

From all three camps, the Spaniards continued destroying houses and temples. Their military efforts were employed only to defend the workers.

At the end of July, Cortés commanded: "Advise all three camps that we shall begin a simultaneous attack tomorrow at dawn."

The next day, from Tepeyac, Tacuba and Xoloc, the Spaniards and their allies, even more numerous than before, launched out against Tenochtitlan.

Cortés entered the city plaza after overcoming the Aztec resistance. In the rear guard, his men went on destroying the buildings and using the debris for fill. A huge section of the southern part of the city had been leveled and now the horses could follow the troops without the fear of traps or flooded ditches.

As the Aztec attacks ceased, they retreated beyond the plaza. Cortés ascended a *teocalli* and from there saw how Alvarado had advanced to Tacuba and Tlatelolco and how far he had penetrated the enemy territory, knocking down buildings and filling in the water breaks.

The *Teocalli* of Tlatelolco was close enough to observe the Aztec command post with Cuauhtémoc and his captains ordering the actions.

Cuauhtémoc in turn, was well aware of the bold presence of Cortés and his men, with their banners waving. "If Malinche ascends the *teocalli* again, we will assault it to capture him. Beginning tomorrow, assemble our warriors in the neighborhoods ready to attack at my signal. Coanacoch, Lord of Texcoco, will lie in ambush and will lead the offense."

Cortés told his officers: "Tomorrow we will return and mount an ambush. I think they are most anxious to capture me."

The next day, Cortés encountered no resistance along the causeway, but upon entering the main plaza, he found it full of large stones placed there to impede the free run of the horses. Earlier, hidden behind buildings that were still standing, he had placed in ambush thirty cavalry, many soldiers and a large force of Texcocans under the command of Ixtlixóchitl, the captain of the Texcocans who was allied to Cortés and brother of Coanacoch.

As soon as Cortés ascended the *teocalli*, from Tlatelolco the Aztec order was given and Coanacoch pressed an attack, commanding his men, who were loyal Texcocans and Tenochcas.

In the plaza, nine horsemen and many Spanish soldiers and Indian allies under the command of Ixtlixóchitl repelled the assault. The cavalry regrouped and attacked. While the Indian allies shouted their war cries, Cortés quickly descended the *teocalli* steps.

"Wait! Wait until Malinche comes down," cried the Indian allies. "Don't let the Aztecs capture him."

When Cortés came down and mounted his horse, all of his men retreated quickly, pretending to flee in disorder. With a great outcry, Coanacoch's men chased the Spaniards and their allies, almost catching up with the cavalry troop.

When those who were involved in the ambush saw the others pass who had pretended to flee, they charged the Aztec flank and rear guard and killed more than five hundred elite warriors.

Coanacoch, who had fought ferociously, was wounded and in that condition was confronted by his brother, Ixtlixóchitl, who was armed with a sword Cortés had given him. Both shouted: "Texcoco! Texcoco!" but one added, "Traitor!"

The Spaniards formed a circle around the two chiefs. Ixtlixóchitl, who was much younger, taller and stronger, easily overcame his wounded brother, capturing him. When he took him to Cortés, Ixtlixóchitl said: "Malinche, I deliver to you Coanacoch, my brother, the *Tlatoani* of Texcoco, who thought he had the strength to defeat me. He is crazy!"

"Traitor!" muttered Coanacoch.

"Put him in chains," Cortés ordered.

Duel between brothers: Coanacoch and Ixtlixóchitl

"Lord Cuauhtémoc," they came to advise him, "we fell into an ambush; Coanacoch was captured by his brother Ixtlixóchitl and more than five hundred of our best warriors were killed."

Cuauhtémoc's features froze into a mask. He said: "Coanacoch! How brave he is! A great warrior! And now we have lost his support! Five hundred of our best men! Let the war go on! Let us all die!"

During late July and early August, the war continued with daily skirmishes on land and water, which tightened the blockade around the city. The Spaniards had blocked almost every place where provisions could enter. The besieged had no food, so they ate birds, lizards, insects, roots, tree bark, salted grasses and even slime from the lake which burned their withered tongues. Many became ill with dysentery and others began to die from hunger and disease.

During a foray, in one drive before dawn in the Tenochtitlan plaza, the Spaniards encountered a large force of Aztecs, whom Cortés and his men attacked in the semi-darkness. The Indians hardly resisted, they were so weak.

"Captain, these are women and children searching for food!"

"Stop," Cortés ordered. "Leave them alone! They are dying of hunger!"

Even so, many were killed, especially by the Tlaxcaltecans.

At the same time, the brigantines began to find canoes with Indians fishing. They were easily destroyed. The brigantine captains reported: "They are dying of hunger!"

On the 24th of July, there was great excitement and joy when Cortés' men made contact with Alvarado's in the Tacuba street. Now they were able to enter the city from either camp.

Both mounted, Alvarado and Cortés greeted one another. Alvarado commented: "Congratulations, Captain, it is good to see you. Now we can also join up with Sandoval. The victory is ours, but the enemy has sworn to die. Even as they are dying of hunger and thirst, they still fight on like rabid dogs."

"It is that young Guatémoc who is so determined. He slaughters everyone who asks for peace."

"Over there, behind those canals, is Guatémoc's fortified house. Let us burn it, then break up the pieces and use the fill along the road to Tlatelolco!"

That very day they set fire to Cuauhtémoc's house and used the rubble to fill in the ditches around it.

The next day, the Day of *Señor* Santiago, the 25th of July, 1521, the three forces were reunited and the work to fill in the trenches went on. Now the Spaniards controlled the great canal that led to the Tlatelolco market.

The ferocious Aztec aggression continued. While they were filling in the great canal, the Spaniards did not have the support of the cavalry. When a large force of Indians attacked them, the Spaniards from the banks of the canals shot arrows and fired guns until the Indians withdrew behind the bulkheads.

By the end of July, the blockade had closed still tighter. According to plan, the Spaniards advanced. In the temples, they found the remains of those who were sacrificed. The severed heads of the *caballeros* whose beards and hair had grown longer made a profound impression on their comrades.

August

eginning in August, all the trench work and the attack on Tlatelolco plaza made it possible for Alvarado's men to capture the market. Without warning, four Spanish horsemen charged into the plaza at full gallop, surprising the Aztec defenders. Trampling everything under foot as they went, the riders made several turns around the market, returning to their starting point after setting fire to a temple and to the cotton hangings in the market stalls, which generated thick clouds of smoke. On top of the *teocalli*, Cuauhtémoc watched impassively as the drive went on. He ordered a counterattack, quickly ousting the horsemen who retreated with their wounded horses.

Some distance away, Cortés' unit was fighting and filling breaks. One of his men shouted at him: "Captain, look at that thick cloud of smoke over the Tlatelolco market. Maybe Alvarado has already taken it and won that honor from us. It looks like all we have left to do is fill in the canal!"

"Congratulations, men, that means this cruel war is coming to an end."

The following day, Cortés' men finished filling in the canal and with the cavalry crossed to the other side. When they did, Alvarado arrived with four horsemen, saying joyously to Cortés: "Captain, I invite you to the Tlatelolco market which is free of enemies. They have withdrawn into the fortified houses down near the wharf."

"Well done, Pedro! Lead on!"

As they rode toward the market, they noticed where the ground had been overturned and saw trees whose bark had been stripped away.

"See, Captain, food is so scarce and their hunger so great, they are eating roots and bark." When they reached the market, they rode around it.

From nearby rooftops, the Aztecs, anticipating them, watched the Spaniards and cursed them, but did not otherwise attack. They were clearly weak, but nonetheless determined. Cuauhtémoc had left the *teocalli* and was concentrating his defense on the northern part of Tlatelolco.

"Alvarado," said Cortés, "let us go up to the temple from where Guatémoc directed the war."

Leaving a strong garrison on guard, with Cristóbal de Olid and Alvarado, Cortés walked up the one hundred fourteen steps of the Great *Teocalli*. From the top, they could observe the parts of the city they had subdued.

"Take a look, Alvarado," Cortés said. "Of the eight sections of the city we have taken seven. It is hard to believe that so many enemies were in those narrow passages, between the tiny houses and those narrow streets and the other houses constructed on stilts over the water."

"There are so many dead that have not been buried that the foul odor has reached here," commented Alvarado. "I don't know how they can stand to walk among them."

"They are more resolved to die and not surrender," Cortés replied. "Remember how many times we sought peace. Then they killed the emissary and said they would fight against us until the last Indian is alive and that one will die fighting us."

After they descended the *teocalli*, Cortés ordered: "It is time to bring our camps forward and set them up in Tlatelolco plaza. Let us have a truce for a few days and again we shall propose peace." To accomplish that mission, they again chose some important Aztec prisoners.

"Take this letter and these gifts to Guatémoc, some cloths, some provisions and sweets. Ask him to surrender, because we have won. He need have no fear; we will respect him and honor him. Tell him that if it is a great loss to have torn down the buildings, it will be much worse to demolish the city. The populace of the surrounding territory opposes him as well."

Terrified, these emissaries presented the gifts and the message to Cuauhtémoc, who ordered his Council to convene. He said to them: "We told them we will not accept peace; that we would rather die and we would fight to the last man. Even the women and children are fighting now. So we will go on. Regardless, we gained time to build fortifications, to make arrows, to resupply weapons and even to rest. I will tell Malinche that in three days I will go to the plaza but no Tlaxcaltecans or other traitors may be there. Also, do not kill the emissaries so when they return with the answer the Spaniards will believe my message even more."

The Council approved the plan, which they sent on to Cortés with the same messengers, to whom Cuauhtémoc also delivered precious cloths as a gift for Cortés.

"Malinche, Cuauhtémoc presents these cloths to you," the chief emissary said. "In three days, he will come to the Tlatelolco plaza to speak with you; but no Tlaxcaltecans or other traitors may be there."

For three days, Cortés waited in the plaza. On the fourth, while he was waiting, from the canals and streets a huge force of Mexican warriors rushed out shouting. "There is no peace; only death!"

It was the last valiant Aztec attack, and although it took the Spaniards and their allies by surprise, at day's end it had been overcome. The Aztecs retreated, diving into the water.

Now, all Cortés could do was wait. Starving women, children and the old people came from behind the barricades defenseless, into the Spanish camp.

Cortés and his captains went up the Tlatelolco *Teocalli* and saw with horror and admiration how in the narrow streets of the blockaded section, among the houses constructed over the water, in the canoes and on the lake, thousands of Aztecs, even the warriors at their posts with shield and weapons, were waiting to die with sublime dignity while they walked or swam among unburied corpses.

The Catapult

Solís, an Andalusian soldier, came up to Cortés. "Captain, I know we have only a little gunpowder left and we should not waste it by destroying the houses on the other side of the canals. If you will find me a carpenter, I will build a catapult, the kind I learned to make in the Italian wars when I was there with the Great Captain."

"If you know how to make it, then do it. Tapia and his carpenters will help."

And they began to gather the parts for the catapult. Once it was finished, Cortés ordered that from the banks of the canal peace should be offered once more to the Aztecs.

"Listen," Jerónimo de Aguilar shouted in Náhuatl, "our war machine is finished and now we can destroy your buildings. Before we do that, Malinche wishes you come in peace so there will be no more damage and destruction."

An Aztec captain yelled back, "I will go to tell Cuauhtémoc. Wait until tomorrow." After the day passed, the Aztec captain shouted: "If you are sons of the Sun, kill us all now. Do not speak any further of peace!"

The Spaniards loaded the catapult with huge rocks and to the jubilation of some and the suspense of others, it was fired. The stones flew up into the air then fell back onto the catapult, whose operators just managed to escape their own barrage. Laughter and whistling, accompanied by flights of arrows hurtled across from the Aztec side. They kept on hollering mocking slurs.

"*Ai, Santa Malía manda Capitán daca zapato.*"

Cortés was furious. Solís, the Andalusian, who was watching the shot, was knocked to the ground. Cortés joined Alvarado.

"Alvarado, there is no end to this and now it has become laughable to the enemy. So let us get on with the fighting and invade this part of the city they hold. Even though the horses cannot be used, we will move on foot. Right now."

They organized the attack at once. From two directions, they assaulted the last Aztec-controlled section. Tlatelolco was still in communication with the mainland. The Spaniards and their allies invaded this part of the city, destroying the protective walls and barricades with cannon barrages. The accumulation of corpses was horrible. The soldiers were forced to wade through cadavers, many of them decayed, as they pursued unarmed women, children and old people, who fell back toward the barricades. The heroic Aztec warriors tightened their defenses and fought for every last scrap of territory. A few Aztecs retreated in canoes toward a large group of houses constructed over the water.

The Tlaxcaltecans were merciless with the Aztec prisoners. Cortés had to use all of his authority to make them stop killing. "Stop! Cease the slaughter of these prisoners and unarmed people. Stop! There are already more than twelve thousand dead!"

They had no place to stand except on the dead bodies of their people

Now August was upon them; it was the tenth of the month. Cortés and his officers once again went to the top of the *teocalli*. The spectacle was hideous. The primitive houses built over the lake waters were crammed with thousands of Indians "who had no place to go except on top of their dead." Countless Aztec canoes held thousands of wretched and starving human beings. But the warriors held their position: on the rooftops of the closest houses and in a line of canoes which faced Tlatelolco.

The Last Demand for Peace

"We cannot believe what we see," muttered Cortés. "They seem more anxious to die than to give up. I still feel I must ask for peace." So he came down from the *teocalli* and went to the bank of the canal with his hands held high toward the Aztecs, who were whistling and mocking him. "*Ai Santa Malía, mando Capitán daca zapato.*"

Through Jerónimo de Aguilar's intercession, Cortés shouted his last demand for peace.

"Malinche says he wishes to speak about peace with Cuauhtémoc. He waits here for him."

The Aztec captain answered: "I will go to tell him, although I know if I speak of peace, he will kill me."

After a few hours, another Aztec captain hollered across the water: "Cuauhtémoc will not come to speak about peace, Malinche! Kill us now, then we will not have to surrender. Cuauhtémoc says you will not find any gold. He has thrown it in the lake. You will only find death."

As Cortés left, a large force of Aztec soldiers in canoes, shooting arrows and hurling rocks, attacked the shores of Tlatelolco and were repelled after a bloody battle.

Cortés met with his captains in his quarters, now set up in the Tlatelolco market.

"Captain," said Alvarado, "I believe one last attack will finish off these Indians, who are half dead from hunger and thirst anyway. I do not think they have any more arrows or even rocks, at least very few. Then we will be done with them once and for all!"

"Look here, Alvarado, I know we can kill them all because they are determined to die rather than surrender. I have never seen such resistance. It is unnatural. I made the efforts for peace because if we take them by force, they will throw what they have into the lake. What they don't throw away, our Indian allies will take away from them. Our allies number more than one hundred thousand and we nine hundred. We will not be able to stop the slaughter or the robbery, but we have come to a point where we must take them by force of arms. Already, the pestilence from the corpses is unbearable."

August 13, 1521

"Because there is no land for us to cross, only water," said Cortés, "the day after tomorrow, the Day of San Hipólito, you, Gonzalo de Sandoval, commanding the brigantines, will attack from Tepeyac. There are many enemies there, but we will attack the rest from the banks of the canals. Do not launch your attack until we are in position."

At dawn of the 13th of August, 1521, the final assault began against the last bastion of the besieged city.

Since nightfall, twelve brigantines had been poised outside the main canals awaiting the attack signal.

The cannon were positioned before that area of the canal that bordered the few streets of the last Aztec refuge, which were defended with barricades and walls. Many canoes with Indian allies were in the vicinity. That night, a soft rain fell. The Aztec guards noticed a fire coming from the sky, whirling and scattering sparks. It disappeared behind a wall near the water and came to rest in Coyanacozco.

Not one of them cried out in fear. They only looked at one another, but one said in a low voice: "Tomorrow is the day of Miquixtli—death."

Kill Us Now, Malinche! We Will Not Surrender!

In the early morning hours, Cuauhtémoc was in a large canoe surrounded by many others.

His officers said to him: "Great Lord: We think the *teules* will attack today; their floating houses are surrounding us and there is a lot of commotion on land. We no longer have any arrows, or lances, or rocks with which to defend ourselves. We suggest you flee. For as long as there is a Cuauhtémoc there will be hope for the Aztecs."

"No, my lords. We shall fight with everything we have left. We will return their arrows and when we have no more, then we will fight with our fingernails and our teeth. Even the women must fight! Bring me my weapons!"

Dressed in his green suit—his war regalia—Cuauhtémoc took his shield and *macana* and led his warriors. He walked among the canoes to the roof of a main group of houses. As he passed by, everyone paid him reverence.

At dawn, the Spanish cannon blasted the walls and barricades and the defenses of the stilt houses. Then arquebuses, arrows from crossbows and darts were fired at the Aztecs, who held their ground with shields, *macanas* and lances as they stood on the corpses of their brothers and awaited the attack. Beside them, the women of Tlatelolco, their skirts hoisted to free their legs, fought ruthlessly as they had many times before.

From the banks of the canal and over the canoes the Spaniards placed a bridge which enabled them, the Tlaxcaltecans, and the other Indian allies to pass. They advanced against ferocious resistance along a few streets, attacking house by house and taking them one by one.

Tomorrow is the Day of Miquixtli—death

Aboard the brigantines, some Spaniards were rowing and others sailing. They invaded the broad canals with cannonfire, musketeers and crossbowmen, and fired at the Indian canoes, which were overcrowded and could not be maneuvered. The invaders attacked and pulled back after defeating the defenders and destroying many houses.

Here is how Cortés described the battle: "The crying and screaming of the women and children was so loud it became heart-rending for all of us. . . . The people were standing on the dead bodies; many Indians were in the water—some swimming, others drowning, in that large lake where the canoes were. There was so much suffering none of us could understand how the Aztecs withstood it. Many men, women, and children advanced towards us. Because they were running, some pushed others into the water where they drowned, among that multitude of dead bodies. The numbers were horrendous; more than fifty thousand souls died from drinking salt water and from hunger. The stench was unbearable. The Indians did not throw the dead bodies into the lake so that we should not be aware of their great catastrophe and the brigantines not hit the cadavers and the other Indians struggling in the water.

When the Spanish soldiers and Tlaxcaltecans penetrated the last Aztec stronghold, the streets were paved with the dead. There was no place to put one's feet except on a body."

The Aztecs who were not fighting thronged the streets. Many leaped into the water trying to reach the shore.

The rout caused Cortés to order: "Do not kill anyone who is without weapons or who flees!" Even when cornered on the rooftops and houses, in canoes and in the water, the remaining Aztec warriors—without arrows or other projectiles to throw— in their war clothes, with their shields, lances, *macanas*, steadfastly maintained a dignified and belligerent attitude.

The huge besieging army was face to face with, at the most, the last three or four thousand Aztec warriors. Among them was Cuauhtémoc. All the rest had been captured or killed. The two forces stared at one another.

Speaking through Jerónimo de Aguilar from behind a barricade, Cortés pleaded: "It is useless to resist further. Everything is over! Give up, you are defeated! Strike your colors."·

A loud whistle followed Cortés' words, then shouts of desperate courage.

"Kill us now, Malinche! We will not give up! Kill us now! Kill us now!"

Then came the mocking jeer.

"*Ai Santa Malía, manda Capitán daca zapato.*"

Then another pause, as each side stared at the other. When the afternoon was almost over, Cortés said: "It is late afternoon and these crazy people do not wish to surrender. Fire two warning shots from here. After one more warning, we will fire a barrage."

Again Jerónimo de Aguilar shouted: "Call Cuauhtémoc! Tell him he may come without fear because it is almost over. Do not let him cause you to lose everything. If he does not come, we will attack."

The 13th of August at three o'clock in the afternoon

348

Soon Tlacutzin spoke, the Cihuacóatl. "My lord will not come; he chooses to die. Do what you must!"

"Then go back to your men!" yelled Aguilar for Cortés. "And prepare to die!"

At three in the afternoon, Cortés gave the order to fire.

Without flinching, showing no emotion, without trying to hide, the Aztecs stood firm. They resisted the cannonfire that blasted the solid lines of the surviving warriors and closed ranks after each shot.

The Plan to Save Cuauhtémoc

"Lord, great lord Cuauhtémoc," his nobles said, "We have nothing left with which to defend ourselves."

"There is no peace, only death. We are a few. Let us all die," he responded.

"Lord Cuauhtémoc, if you die, everything will end. If you are saved with your family, the Culúa Empire will be revived."

"I must die with all of you!"

"No, lord, we beg you, do not do it for yourself, do it for us. You must live on," they begged, with tears in their eyes. "We have prepared the royal canoe. Your family is there and will accompany you along with Tetlepanquétzal, the Lord of Tacuba and the other nobles."

"I must not go! I will die here! And here I will hurl the *Quetzalteopámitl** into the water so the *teule* cannot capture it."

"Lord, you must live for the good of us all."

Then, at a signal, they took Cuauhtémoc by force to the canoe where his wife and children were waiting with Tetlepanquétzal.

"Pardon us, oh lord, great lord, please pardon us."

The canoe left at once, accompanied by many others trying to hide their flight by slipping through the thickets and the heavy growths of reeds.

The Spaniards kept on firing their cannon and still the Aztecs would not surrender.

"This is useless," Cortés said. "They will not give up. Tell our Tlaxcaltecan friends to attack and capture their houses. Let the brigantines destroy their canoes."

With Alvarado, Verdugo, Olid and Tapia and other captains, the Spanish officers ascended the *teocalli* to observe the final charge.

At the crack of a musket, the huge Tlaxcaltecan force attacked the remaining Aztec rampart. Although the resistance was ferocious, little by little those warriors left in the houses and on rooftops either died or were taken prisoner.

---

* The beautiful Aztec gold royal standard, encrusted with jewels.

The Capture of Cuauhtémoc

While the land attack was taking place, a line of brigantines, helped by a favorable breeze and with vigorous rowing, sailed swiftly toward the Aztec canoes firing at them from the cannon in their bows. The Aztecs tried to grab the Spaniards' oars; the Spanish sailors wounded many Aztecs with their long lances. The Indians no longer had any way to defend themselves.

Many canoes fled from Tlatelolco; the lake was full of them.

Next to the command boat of Gonzalo de Sandoval came a brigantine under the command of García Holguín, who shouted to him: "Captain Sandoval, in another part of the lake I saw a large group of big canoes, one with a canopy. They are paddling vigorously. I think Guatémoc is there."

"Whether he is here or there does not matter. He has no safe place and no doubt he is fleeing. If he is not in that group, he is with another. Order all the brigantines to stop attacking canoes and houses and go at once to the canoes that are fleeing. If they capture Guatémoc, they are not to harm him, but to treat him with dignity. You, García Holguín, leave at once. Go where you think Guatémoc is. Do not harm him, but bring him to me."

The brigantines left their piers and through the canals went out into the lake, pursuing the fleeing Aztec canoes.

García Holguín's fast brigantine with all its sails flying and with its capable oarsmen, was in pursuit of the group of canoes among which was Cuauhtémoc, his family and many Aztec chiefs. The distance between them closed slowly, although the Indian oarsmen were paddling desperately.

Finally, after a shot from a crossbow, García Holguín shouted, threatening with more crossbows and muskets: "Stop or I will shoot!"

No one in the canoe paid attention to his order, so he fired a warning cannon shot which landed close to them. They stopped rowing and the brigantine came alongside with its crossbows and muskets threatening.

Cuauhtémoc stood up. "Do not shoot. There are children and women here. I am Cuauhtémoc. Do not touch or harm anyone. Take me to Malinche."

Shouts of joy rose up from the sailors when the last Aztec emperor boarded the brigantine with his family and retainers, their personal belongings and treasure. The Spaniards made a comfortable place for the emperor in the stern of the brigantine.

The Aztecs were seated on straw mats and cloths and were given food and drink. Cuauhtémoc drank only water and remained in a squatting position, absorbed in thought. He displayed profound sadness and resignation. He was wearing a green cloth, made from the thread of the maguey embroidered with red and flecks of *colibrí* [hummingbird] feathers, but the garment was splattered with mud.

"I am Cuauhtémoc! Do not touch or harm anyone!"

By the time the brigantines got back to the Tlatelolco pier, all Aztec resistance had ended. Not one Aztec warrior was left; all were dead or in hiding, or swimming in the cadaver-filled lake which was blood red. Debris from canoes and houses floated in the water. An ominous silence replaced the sounds of war. No more orders, shouts, gunfire, swearing, musical signals, or the thunder from falling buildings. Only a grave silence.

Gonzalo de Sandoval was waiting for García Holguín. When he was alongside, Holguín shouted happily: "I have Guatémoc here. We captured him when he was running away, just as I told you."

"Congratulations, García Holguín. Deliver the Aztec king to me so I can take him to Cortés."

"Not on your life, Captain Sandoval! He is my prisoner and it will be I who takes him to Cortés for an *albricias* [a reward for good news]."

"That is true, but I am Captain-General of the fleet and it is my place to take the prisoner."

"No, I apprehended him and the honor belongs to me."

"And you have it. No doubt. Do not forget that you are under my command and I ordered you to go after Guatémoc."

"It is not right that you take him away from me. I captured him."

"Do not insist. If I sent you to capture him, it is because you are my friend and you should not have taken him from his canoe if you were not going to deliver him to me."

A soldier overheard the argument and dashed to the *teocalli*. Thrilled, he told Cortés what had happened. "*Albricias*, Captain, *Albricias*! Guatémoc is captured and there is a dispute between Sandoval and García Holguín about who should bring him to you."

"Francisco Verdugo and you, Marin, go and tell Gonzalo and García Holguín that they should stop arguing and come here with Guatémoc and his wife and family. They must treat him with great respect. I will decide who captured the prisoner and who will bear that honor."

After the men left, Cortés ordered: "As best you can, prepare a fine dais. We must honor someone who fought valiantly for his city."

Quickly, they brought together straw mats, cloths, an easy chair and thrones, as well as food and drink. The wait was not prolonged.

The historic afternoon of August 13, 1521, was coming to an end. The sky was darkening and a storm threatened as Cuauhtémoc ascended the corner of the Tlatelolco *Teocalli*, flanked by Gonzalo de Sandoval and García Holguín. Cortés stood up from his easy chair and walked toward Cuauhtémoc, who stopped a few paces before Cortés, at whose side was *Doña* Marina. The two men regarded one another and Cuauhtémoc made a dignified and profound gesture of reverence. Cortés came closer and gently patted his head.

[Cortés and Cuauhtémoc] look at each other

Then with a majestic gesture the young Aztec emperor said, as *Doña* Marina translated: "*Señor* Malinche, I have done what I was obliged to do in defense of my city and subjects. I can do no more. I come here before you by force as a prisoner and in your power. I wish you would draw that dagger and kill me with it," he said, his eyes full of tears.

At that moment, lightning crackled and thunder pealed through the valley. The storm was approaching from the Tepeyac.

Cortés invited Cuauhtémoc to sit on the dais under a colorful canopy.

"Lord Guatémoc, you have valiantly defended your city, like nothing or no one I have encountered in all the histories I am acquainted with. Now I respect you more as a man. Do not be afraid for yourself or for your family. You have done what you had to do and there can be no guilt. I accept the events in good spirit. If I asked you for peace, it was because I did not want to see your beautiful city destroyed or so many Mexicans die. But that is all past and there is nothing we can do about it. May your spirit rest easy. You will continue to rule these provinces as you did before."

"I am grateful to you, Malinche."

"Your women and children and the other older ladies who came with you, where are they?"

"Ask Captain Sandoval; he kept them in the canoes until he was told what Malinche ordered."

"Go and get them. We will join them in the plaza. Prepare food and comfortable lodgings for them."

Bernal Díaz del Castillo wrote in his diary: "It rained and lightning was rampant from that afternoon until midnight. The rain was heavier than usual."

That night, before Cortés retired to his room, Cuauhtémoc asked to see him. When he came before him, through *Doña* Marina, he said: "*Señor* Malinche, may I ask you to allow our people in the city to leave for the neighboring villages. They have nothing here and there is such a horrible stench."

"Of course, Lord Guatémoc. However, may I ask your people to repair the aqueduct of Chapultepec, to bury their dead and to clean the streets." Cuauhtémoc's officers issued those orders.

"Any who wish to leave the city may do so, but our garrisons will not allow them to take out any valuables, or any arms."

When the Royal Crest was lowered and the Aztecs were defeated, it was the year 3-Casa. The day on the magic calendar: 1-Serpent. On the Christian calendar: the Day of San Hipólito.

The Treasure of Moctezuma

The following day, Cuauhtémoc, Tetlepanquétzal, Tlacutzin, Ahuelitoc, surrounded by a long line of Spanish soldiers, were led to one of the few houses left standing, belonging to the *cacique* Coyehuetzin. On the roof, under a canopy of colors, were Cortés and *Doña* Marina, Alderete the Royal Treasurer, and the captains. Surrounding the house were Spanish soldiers.

Standing before Cortés, the Aztecs were interrogated through *Doña* Marina: "Where is the gold that was stored in Mexico?"

"As I have told you," Cuauhtémoc responded, "in that boat, guarded by *teules*."

By an order of Cortés, a group of Spaniards unloaded from the boat, which was at the wharf close by, a pile of gold; some ingots cast in Tenochtitlan for the Spanish division, diadems, bracelets, bands, helmets, all of gold. The men brought these to Cortés.

With his brows furrowed, Alderete asked: "Is this all the gold that was stored in Mexico? You must give everything to us, right now. Go and look for it!"

Then Tlacutzin spoke: "Listen, please Captain. When the Spaniards came to our palace, we sealed it behind a wall. Did not the *teules* carry it away?"

Translating for Cortés, *Doña* Marina said: "Yes, that is true, we took it all. It was all assembled and marked with the seal. But you took it away from us at the Toltecan canal. Everything fell in the water there. You must give it to us."

Tlacutzin answered: "The people of Tenochtitlan do not fight in boats. The people of Tlatelolco fight in boats. Could it not be they who have taken everything?"

Cuauhtémoc, frowning, said: "What is Cihuacóatl saying? That they did not deliver it all and collected it in Texopan? All that is here, isn't this what the *teules* took?" He pointed to the pile of gold.

"Only this?" Cortés asked Tlacutzin.

"It is possible that people from the village took some. Why not interrogate them?"

"You must deliver another two hundred bars of gold of this size," Cortés said, holding one hand apart from the other.

"It could be," insisted Tlacutzin, "that some woman carried it away hidden in her petticoats. Why not investigate?"

Cuauhtémoc insisted: "What you see is all that we have. The rest is where the *teules* lost it in the water. Either that or the Tlaxcaltecans took it."

"That is pitiful," shouted some soldiers, pointing at the pile.

"It is too little! They are fooling us! They have hidden it!"

"We will investigate," said Cortés.

"They must tell us where Moctezuma's treasure is," said Alderete.

"For the moment, Treasurer, make an inventory of this so we can divide what is here."

"It is very little, Captain. We could not agree on such an amount. We must look into this and if that does not work, we will have to extract the information with torture."

"Let us investigate and look for Moctezuma's treasure," Cortés concluded. "We have allowed the people to leave Temistitan and Tlatelolco, but the guards must be careful that they are not smuggling gold in their clothes. I guarantee there will be enough for all."

Then he added: "One more point: Yesterday was the Day of San Hipólito. By the grace of God, we achieved a great victory, which we should celebrate with a banquet as is our custom. I will invite you all when we have it in Coyoacán where we are housed, while this city is cleaned up and rebuilt. We must wait for some barrels of La Mancha wine and a herd of pigs from Villa Rica. You will be happy to know that some courageous and pretty women from the islands and Castile have arrived. More are coming."

Cortés could not finish. A roaring ovation drowned his words.

Exodus

That very day, the exodus began. For the next three days along the causeways, there was a continuous line of bedraggled men, women and emaciated children. At the gates, Spanish soldiers inspected everything looking for gold. Whenever they found some, they branded the face of that person, doing the same to any warrior leaving with weapons. The guards took aside the prettier women, many of whom covered their faces and bodies with mud to disguise themselves.

Half destroyed, the great city was empty. Only the immense monuments and a few houses were left standing. When Cortés and his captains went about, they covered their faces with handkerchiefs. A few sick Aztecs, unable to walk, crawled, half dead, among the debris of the houses and streets, which were still filled with bodies.

"Look," Sandoval said to Cortés, "all the ground looks as if it were ploughed because they were eating roots and the bark of the trees to satisfy their hunger. There is no drinking water. Even though their hunger was extreme, they never ate their own dead, only the bodies of their enemies."

"Yes, it appears their religion ordered them to eat only enemies. Quite mysterious, really, almost mystical," said Father Olmedo.

"This stench is unbearable! Let us leave for Coyoacán," Cortés announced. "My head aches."

Victory Banquet

In September, 1521, they celebrated the victory banquet in Coyoacán. Cortés arranged for it to be held in a wooded area, close to his own palace, which was under construction. They prepared lavish dishes and in huge copper kettles cooked the pork or roasted meat over open fires. There was constant music.

Besides those who were guarding the three camps, all the soldiers and captains attended, many with their Indian *barraganas*. Cortés was with *Doña* Marina; Alvarado with Luisa, and so on.

Soon the effects of the alcohol, which the Spaniards had not experienced for a long time, overwhelmed them and they became unruly, which spoiled the banquet.

The victory banquet

The Spanish ladies, even those advanced in years, danced on the tables with their gentlemen. Those with Indian women were even more boisterous. Everyone was giddy with laughter.

Some shouted out their plans for their gold—one wanted a gold chair—another would make gold darts for his crossbow.

The festivities ended in a drunken melee. The next day, Father Olmedo made everyone attend a Mass of apology.

"It would have been much better if you had not had this banquet—for many reasons. Some very unpleasant events took place at the banquet. You must make amends to God for your excesses and sins!" he said.

Still suffering the effects of their drunken party, contrite and ashamed, the conquerors joined the procession at the altar of the Virgin. After hearing the Mass and beating their breasts, they recanted their sins alongside their Indian and Spanish women.

The Torture of Cuauhtémoc

The year 1522 ran its course. Cortés' palace in Coyoacán had been finished and he was sharing it with *Doña* Marina and the royal prisoners: Cuauhtémoc, Tetlepanquétzal, and Cihuacóatl.

Alderete, the Royal Treasurer, came before Cortés and *Doña* Marina, who would soon give birth to a child. "Captain," he said, "you are aware that we have concluded all our attempts to locate Moctezuma's treasure. So far, we have found only small amounts, and of very little value."

"That is so," said Cortés.

"Therefore, Captain, in my position as King's Treasurer, I hereby ask you to allow me to torture Guatémoc and the other Mexicans so they will tell us where they hid the treasure."

Doña Marina shuddered.

"That would be contemptible of us," said Cortés.

"If that is how you feel, some will say you are protecting Guatémoc because you and he are hiding the treasure."

"Do not test my patience, Treasurer."

"Do not get upset, Captain. I am not of that opinion but the soldiers are. I wish only to avoid problems. Deliver the prisoners to me."

"Not on your life! Continue to investigate as you have been."

"All right, but do not expect any better results. Those are only bits and pieces they are finding in the lake. The people are most uncooperative. I will have to inform the King that you are impeding the work of the Treasurer."

"That is obviously not so! We have done everything possible to try to find the gold."

Alderete almost sneered as he squinted at Cortés.

"You know some even say they have seen *Doña* Marina putting loads of gold right here in your house."

"Do not bring *Doña* Marina into this dispute. If you do, you will reckon with me! She is about to deliver her child."

With obvious gestures of disgust, *Doña* Marina stood up and began to leave without speaking to the Treasurer.

"Pardon me, *señora*," Alderete said, "but I am merely repeating what I have heard. Even the very walls of this house are saying it. I am trying only to carry out the interest of the King and maintain the peace of mind of our Captain."

Doña Marina did not respond as she left the room.

"That is quite enough, Alderete. It is on your conscience, but take the prisoners and do with them what you consider to be in the service of His Majesty!"

With his aides, Alderete went to the quarters of Cuauhtémoc, Tetlepanquétzal and the Cihuacóatl, Tlacutzin.

Arrogantly and threatening, he said to them through an interpreter: "Now you will tell me where you threw Moctezuma's treasure. I have been told for certain you did it four days before you surrendered."

"We have told you what we did and what we know."

"Fine! If you insist, I will have to torture you! Think about it carefully!"

"Do what you wish. We cannot possibly know more than we do right now, even if you torture us," said Cuauhtémoc.

"Perhaps this will freshen your memory! Tie them up!"

Roughly, the aides chained the hands and feet of the prisoners.

"Sit on these benches." They did.

"Think about it and tell me the truth."

"It is useless; we know nothing."

"Smear oil on their feet." They did.

"Tell me!" Silence.

"Put their feet to the fire." They did.

A piercing howl of pain came from Tlacutzin, which was heard in Cortés' room. *Doña* Marina commented: "It is an outrage to treat such a valiant king this way!"

Tetlepanquétzal twisted with pain.

Cuauhtémoc tightened his jaws, hiding his pain.

"Where is Moctezuma's treasure?" shouted Alderete.

Silence. Tetlepanquétzal and Tlacutzin squirmed and bit their lips.

Tlacutzin managed to gasp: "Everything was given to the Captain. There is no more."

"Do you think I am in a delightful bed of roses?"

"No? More oil and move the flames closer. Where is Moctezuma's treasure?"

The skin on their feet crackled and the reek of burning flesh filled the room and spread outside. Their feet looked like burst blisters, from which charred bones were visible.

Tlacutzin, exhausted, sweating like his tortured companions, looked with distress at Cuauhtémoc, who could control his pain. He said to the Lord: "Lord. . . ."

Cuauhtémoc whispered, "Do you think I am in a delightful bed of roses?"

With a last shriek of pain, Tlacutzin lowered his head and his hair flared with fire and he died.

"This one is dead," said one of the torturers.

"Tell us now, before you die, too, where is the treasure?"

Just then, one of Cortés' officers came in and shouted: "By order of Captain Hernán Cortés, you will stop this inhuman torture and control your zeal for glory. This is no way to treat a King."

Shocked, Alderete said to his aides, "Stop! It is useless!"

The flames were moved away from the victims, who were dripping sweat. Tetlepanquétzal fainted. Cuauhtémoc, his eyes half closed, locked his jaws tight.

The doctor, Ojeda, came and took care of the men. He said: "They will never walk again. Their feet are destroyed."

In *Doña* Marina's room, Cortés held her as she sobbed: "Calm yourself, *señora*. Remember your condition. Be quiet now. The torture is over! Do not let it upset you!"

Racked with a sudden fierce pain, *Doña* Marina placed both hands over her stomach.

"Now?" Cortés asked.

"It is beginning!"

Martín Cortés [the son of Marina and Cortés is born]

Martín Cortés

In the pre-dawn hours, a boy was born, with the help of Indian midwives, the oldest of whom let out a war whoop, slapping her open mouth with her hand. "You are very welcome, my very dear son!"

When Cortés heard the cry, he came at once to the room where *Doña* Marina was recovering from the delivery.

The oldest midwife said to Cortés: "Your God has given you a son, a precious stone, a rich feather, an emerald, a sapphire. Take him!" She handed the child, wrapped in cloths, to Cortés.

Smiling at *Doña* Marina, Cortés said: "He will be named Martín, the same as my father." Marina answered: "That may be what he will be called; but with so many bloodlines in conflict, what will he be? He is my son, Captain Malinche. He is your son. I ask myself, who and what will Martín Cortés be?"

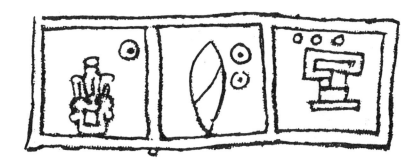

The three calendar glyphs taken from the Aztec Codex Mendoza are:

One Reed (1519, the year Corté's arrival in Mexico)
Two Flint Knife (July 13, 1520, the date of Moctezuma's death)
Three House (the Conquest of New Spain)

Bibliography

Codices

Anales de Tlatelolco. *Historia general.* México: Editorial Porrúa, 1956, t. IV.

Florentine. México: Editorial Porrúa, 1975.

Lienzo de Tlaxcala (linen cloth). México: Archivo General de la Nación, 1972.

Ramírez. México: Editorial Porrúa, 1975.

Books and documents

Aguilar, Fray Francisco de. *Relación Breve de la Conquista de la Nueva España.* México: José Porrúa e Hijos, 1954.

Alamán, Lucas. "Disertaciones Sobre la Historia de la República Mexicana." Biblioteca de Autores Mexicanos, de Agüeros, México, 1899–1901. México: Editorial Jus, 1969.

Alva Ixlixóchitl, Fernando de. *Obras Históricos.* México: UNAM, 1975.

Alvardo Tezozómoc, Fernando. *Crónica Mexicana.* México: Editorial Porrúa, 1975.

Argensola, Bartolomé Leonardo de. *Conquista de México.* México: Pedro Robredo, 1940.

Casas, Fray Bartolomé de las. *Brevísima Relación de la Destrucción de las Indias.* México: Fondo de Cultura Económica, 1951, 3 vols.

Cervantes de Salazar, Francisco. *Crónica de Nueva España.* México: Talleres Gráficos del Museo Nacional, 1936, 3 vols.

Chavero, Alfredo. "México a Través de los Siglos," Barcelona, España: (Resumen) Espasa y Compañía, 1884.

Chilam Balam. The book of *Chilam Balam de Chumayel.* México: UNAM, 1941; chapter 11.

Chimalpain Cuauhtlehuanitzin, Domingo de. *Relaciones Originales de Chalco Amecameca*. México: Fondo de Cultura Económica, 1965.

Clavijero, Francisco Javier. *Historia Antigua de México y de su Conquista*. México: Editorial Porrúa, 1945, 4 vols.

Cortés, Hernán. *Cartas de Relación.*" México: Editorial Porrúa, 1986.

Diaz del Castillo, Bernal. *Historia Verdadera de la Conquista de la Nueva España*. México: Manuel Porrúa, S. A. Librería, 1977.

Documentos Inéditos relativos a Hernán Cortés y su Familia. n.d.

Durán, Fray Diego. *Historia de las Indias de Nueva España e Islas de Tierra Firme*. México: Editorial Porrúa, 1967.

Fuentes Mares, José. *Hernán Cortés. El Hombre*. México: Editorial Grijalbo, 1981.

García Icazbalceta, Joaquín. *Colección de Documentos para la Historia de México*. México: Editorial Porrúa, 1947, 4 vols.

Gómez de Orozco, Federico. *Doña Marina, la Dama de la Conquista*. México: Ediciones Xóchitl, 1942.

Herrera, Antonio de. *Historia General de los Hechos de los Castellanos en Islas y Tierra Firme del Mar Océano*. (1601–1615) Madrid: Academia Real de la Historia, 1934–1937, 17 vols.

León-Portilla, Miguel. *Visión de los Vencidos*. México: Editorial Ambos Mundos, 1985.

López de Gómara, Francisco. *Historia de la Conquista de México*. México: Editorial Pedro Robredo, 1943, 2 vols.

López Portilla y Weber, José: *Dinámica Histórica de México*. México: Talleras Gráficos de la Nación, 1935.

Lorenzana, Francisco Antonio. "Historia de la Nueva España de Cortés, Aumentada con Otros Documentos y Notas." Imprenta del Superior Gobierno, del Br. Joseph Antonio de Hogal, 1770.

Madariaga, Salvador de. *Hernán Cortés*. Buenos Aires: Editorial Sudamericana, 1941.

Mendieta, Fray Jerónimo. *Historia Eclesiástica Indiana*. Biblioteca Porrúa, 46, México: Editorial Porrúa, 1971.

Orozco y Berra, Manuel. *Historia Antigua de la Conquista de México*. México: Editorial Porrúa, 1960, 4 vols., t. IV.

Payno, Manuel. *Moctezuma*. México: Imprenta de F. Díaz León y S. White, 1870.

Pereyra, Carlos. *Hernán Cortés*. (Biografía.) Colección "Sepan cuantos . . . ," México: Editorial Porrúa, 1971.

Pérez Martínez, Héctor. *Cuauhtémoc*. México: Editorial Leyenda, 1944.

Prescott, William. *History of the Conquest of Mexico*.

Residencia Instruída a Pedro de Alvarado y Nuño Beltrán de Guzmán. México: (Proceso) Impreso por Valdés y Redondas, 1847.

Residencia Instruída contra Fernando Cortés. México: (Proceso) Impreso por Valdes y Redondas, 1847.

Roldán, Dolores. *Códice de Cuauhtémoc*. México: Editorial Orión Biografía, 1980.

Romero Giordano, Carlos. *Moctezuma II. El Misterio de su Muerte*. México: Editorial Porrúa, 1960.

Romero Vargas Iturbide, Ignacio. *Moctezuma el Magnífico y la Invasión de Anáhuac*. México, 1963–1964, 3 vols.

Sahagún, Fray Bernardino de. *Historia General de las Cosas de la Nueva España*. México: Archivo General de la Nación, 1982, 1989.

Tapia, Andrés de. "Relación hecha por el *señor* Andrés de Tapia sobre la Conquista de México." (Colleción de Documentos para la Historia de México, publicada por Joaquín García Icazbalceta.) México: Ediciones de la UNAM, 1939, 41–96.

Torquemada, Fray Juan de. *Monarquía Indiana*. México: UNAM, 1975–1983, 7 vols.

Torruca Saravia, Genet. *Merodeando a Malinche, Doña Marina Malintzin*. México: Editorial Jus, 1939.

Uchmany, Eva Alejandra. *Moctezuma II Xocoyotzin y la Conquista de México.* México: Editorial Porrúa, 1964.

Vásquez de Tapia, Bernardino. *Relación de Méritos y Servicios.* México: Antigua Librería Robredo, 1953.

Veytia, Mariano. *Historia Antigua de México.* México: Fondo de Cultura Económica, 1966. 3 vols.

Index

Xocotla

Ixtacmaxtitlan

Atalaya

Tacuba

MEXICO

Texcoco

Tlaxcala

Tzompantzi

Iztapalapa

Guitlahuac

Huexotzingo

Xochimilco

Chalco

Flamanalco

Amecameca

Cholula

Mixquic

Ayotzingo

Puebla
(2,200 m